East plays West

In the forty-year long "Cold War" that followed World War II, international sport at the Olympic Games and elsewhere became symbolic of the new global struggle for supremacy. A high-profile sporting victory or a sporting boycott was seen as a powerful diplomatic weapon, as the world watched capitalism race against communism, and totalitarianism seek to outplay democracy. *East Plays West* examines the development, the reality and the legacy of Cold War sport, looking at experiences in the USA, UK, USSR, Canada, Cuba, Korea and China, and covering themes including:

- sport as an expression of allegiance, resistance and conflict
- media stories, legends of triumph, and the construction of Cold War sport
- drugs, and the quest for medal success
- identities and the stereotype of "other" – national identities, superhumans and freaks of nature
- post-Cold War sport in the former communist states.

Addressing major themes in the study of sport and society, and presenting original research on both Eastern and Western experiences, this book provides a fascinating insight into the political and sporting culture of this key period in modern history.

Stephen Wagg is Reader in Sport and Society at Leeds Metropolitan University, UK.

David L. Andrews is Associate Professor in Sport, Commerce and Culture at the University of Maryland, USA.

East plays West

Sport and the Cold War

Edited by Stephen Wagg
and David L. Andrews

 Routledge
Taylor & Francis Group

LONDON AND NEW YORK

First published 2007
by Routledge
2 Park Square, Milton Park, Abingdon, Oxon OX14 4RN

Simultaneously published in the USA and Canada
by Routledge
270 Madison Avenue, New York, NY 10016

Routledge is an imprint of the Taylor & Francis Group, an informa business

Typeset in Goudy and Gills Sans by
GreenGate Publishing Services, Tonbridge, Kent
Printed and bound in Great Britain by
Antony Rowe Ltd, Chippenham, Wiltshire

British Library Cataloguing in Publication Data
A catalogue record for this book is available from the British Library

Library of Congress Cataloging-in-Publication Data
East plays West : sport and the Cold War / edited by Stephen Wagg and
David Andrews.
        p. cm.
   Includes bibliographical references and index.
   ISBN-13: 978-0-415-35926-9 (hardback)
   ISBN-13: 978-0-415-35927-6 (pbk.)
   ISBN-10: 0-415-35926-0 (hardback)
   ISBN-10: 0-415-35927-9 (pbk.)
        1. Nationalism and sports. 2. Olympics—Political aspects. 3. Cold
War. I. Wagg, Stephen. II. Andrews, David L., 1962–

GV706.34.E37 2006
306.4'83–dc22

                                                    2006019800

ISBN10: 0-415-35926-0 (hbk)   ISBN13: 978-0-415-35926-9 (hbk)
ISBN10: 0-415-35927-9 (pbk)   ISBN13: 978-0-415-35927-6 (pbk)
ISBN10: 0-203-00711-5 (ebk)   ISBN13: 978-0-203-00711-2 (ebk)

For my Cassie and her Massy, wishing them *amore e pace*, and for Ron Greenall, with whom it's always good to talk.

SEW

To Peter Andrews

whose memories of the irrepressible Tiger Khomich are as vivid now as they were in 1945.

DLA

Contents

Contributors

Stephen Wagg is a Reader in Sport and Society at Leeds Metropolitan University, UK.

David L. Andrews is an Associate Professor in the Physical Cultural Studies Program in the Department of Kinesiology at the University of Maryland, USA.

Rob Beamish is Associate Professor and Head of the Department of Sociology at Queens University at Kingston, Canada.

Ian Ritchie is Associate Professor in the Department of Physical Education and Kinesiology at Brock University, Ontario, Canada.

Jenifer Parks is a doctoral student in the Department of History at the University of North Carolina, Chapel Hill, USA.

Robert Rinehart is an Associate Professor at Washington State University, USA.

Ronnie Kowalski is a Senior Lecturer in History at the University of Worcester, UK.

Dilwyn Porter is a Senior Research Fellow at the International Centre for Sport History and Culture, De Montfort University, Leicester, and a Visiting Research Fellow at the Business History Unit at the London School of Economics, UK.

John Bale is Visiting Professor of Sports Studies at the University of Aarhus in Denmark and Professor of Sports Geography at Keele University, UK.

Jeffrey Montez de Oca is a lecturer in the Department of Sociology at California State University, Long Beach, USA.

Paul Dimeo lectures in sports policy and sports sociology at Stirling University, UK.

Jay Scherer is an Assistant Professor in Faculty of Physical Education and Recreation at the University of Alberta, Canada.

Gregory H. Duquette is a doctoral student in the Faculty of Physical Education and Recreation at the University of Alberta, Canada.

Daniel S. Mason is an Associate Professor in the Faculty of Physical Education and Recreation at the University of Alberta, Canada.

Milton Jamail lectures in the Department of Government at the University of Texas at Austin, USA.

Damion Thomas is Assistant Professor in the Department of Kinesiology and the Department of African American Studies at the University of Illinois, Urbana-Champaign, USA.

Mary G. McDonald is Associate Professor in the Department of Physical Education, Health and Sport Studies at Miami University, Ohio, USA.

Evelyn Mertin teaches at the German Sport University in Cologne, Germany.

Susan Brownell is Chair of the Department of Anthropology at the University of Missouri, St. Louis, USA.

James Riordan is a former Professor of Russian at Bradford University and is widely seen as the leading writer on sport in communist societies. He is also a novelist and lives in Portsmouth, UK.

Michael Silk is an Associate Professor in the Physical Cultural Studies Program in the Department of Kinesiology at the University of Maryland, USA.

Bryan Bracey is a doctoral student in the Department of Kinesiology at the University of Maryland, USA.

Mark Falcous teaches in the Department of Physical Education at the University of Otago, New Zealand.

Eunha Koh works in the Department of Policy Development and Research at the Korea Institute of Sport Science in Seoul, South Korea.

Ryan White is a doctoral student in the Department of Kinesiology at the University of Maryland, USA.

Foreword

Robert Edelman

Disturbing as it may be for those of us who lived through it, the Cold War is now part of history. The confrontation between capitalism and communism is over, and scholars such as those in this volume can now turn their attention to the period 1945 to 1991 with hindsight and distance. Archives have opened on both sides of the divide. The great framing device of an ideologically driven, political, military and cultural confrontation that threatened the instantaneous incineration of humanity has been replaced by conflicts between globalizers who embrace modernity and their multiple opponents who oppose the modern world through a range of tactics from slow food to terror. Today, as John Hoberman has noted, sport is a "global monoculture." Soviet Communism turns out to have been the "shortest historical route from capitalism to capitalism," but are we any safer now that it is gone?

As I read this collection, I was struck by how significant and considerable an element of the cultural Cold War sport turns out to have been. The resources and attention devoted to it were indeed enormous. Yet, among academic experts on Soviet Communism, my own specialty, the subject was almost entirely ignored. During the second half of the twentieth century, there were just two works by scholars devoted to the historical examination of this subject. I can remember once telling a friend of Jim Riordan, the great pioneer in this field, "I'm the guy who wrote the other book on Soviet sport." The Russian intelligentsia had been historically anti-somatic, and Western students of the USSR took their cues from their Soviet counterparts. Those of us who had written on sport longed for the day when a generation of younger scholars would take up the study of this subject. That day has come. The appearance of *East Plays West* is a sign of the growing maturation of sport studies. Using a broad range of methodologies and examining far more than Russia, the scholars in this volume have opened up a new field of study.

Most of these essays deal in one way or another with the relationship between Communism and Olympism, two of the most important movements of the twentieth century, both of which, as Richard Gruneau has reminded us, believed in the possibility of social improvement. It was shrewd and clever of the Soviets to center on the Olympics as the centerpiece of their struggle with capitalism. Focusing on the Games, the USSR was able to pit its professionals against capitalism's amateurs, limiting the talent pool available to the West. Today, we know that Soviet professionals were not as professional as Western pros, and that capitalism's amateurs were less than pure. Nevertheless, this arrangement allowed the Soviet Union to dominate the Games and use them for diplomatic and domestic political purposes. The powerful sport system, as we all know, was supposed to reflect the larger strength of the Communist system. In the wake of the collapse of Communism in Eastern Europe and the USSR, we now understand the sport "machine" was actually designed to mask the system's many weaknesses. When Soviet athletes came to compete with Western professionals in football, hockey and basketball, it turned out they were roughly as good as their capitalist counterparts, but they did not dominate.

The multi-sport festival, of which the Olympics were the most visible example, allowed the Soviet regime to ascribe an array of changing symbols, slogans and meanings to sport, broadly understood. This approach proved harder to accomplish in a single sport competition like football's World Cups (men's and women's). There, the discourse has been about the game, its tactics, players and styles. Football was an arena in which the USSR had little success. It proved to be something different and difficult for the party state, what Simon Kuper has called "a slippery tool." This may explain why Americans, as opposed to the rest of the world, were always more impressed by Soviet Olympic success. The ideologies of Olympism, with its many events, lent themselves more easily to politicization than did single-sport competitions. The authors of these essays have taken as their task the analysis and explanation of the meanings generated by the interaction between sport and politics in an era when both were thoroughly foregrounded. This group of scholars has looked at the Communist sporting experience well beyond the Soviet Union, and they have employed significant theoretical approaches in making sense of the material they have uncovered. I commend their work to your attention.

Robert Edelman
Professor of Russian History and the History of Sport
University of California, San Diego

Acknowledgements

In addition to the book's writers, we would like to thank Barbara Keys and Steven Pope; at Roehampton, Helen Lynott; and, at Routledge, Kate Manson and Samantha Grant for particular help in bringing this book into being.

We are indebted to the people and archives below for permission to reproduce images. Every effort has been made to trace copyright holders, but in a few cases this has not been possible. Any omissions brought to our attention will be remedied in future editions.

Introduction

War minus the shooting?

David L. Andrews and Stephen Wagg

It is tempting to begin any discussion of the relationship between sport and the Cold War with reference to George Orwell's oft cited words: "Serious sport has nothing to do with fair play. It is bound up with hatred, jealousy, boastfulness, disregard of all rules and sadistic pleasure in witnessing violence: in other words it is war minus the shooting" (Orwell, 1945). In a number of respects, however, this frequently abstracted quotation possesses less resonance, and indeed relevance, unless one places it within the context of the piece in which it appeared. The quote is, in fact, taken from an essay entitled "The Sporting Spirit," which appeared in the December 1945 issue of the socialist periodical *Tribune*. In this essay, Orwell captures the internationalist socialist sensibility of the moment, and particularly its understandable – given the nationalist-inspired genocides of the Second World War – hostility toward expressions of nationalism. Writing in the wake of the Moscow Dinamo (Dynamo) Football Club's legendary tour to the United Kingdom, Orwell confounded the popular sentiment that enveloped this sporting "goodwill" gesture (see Downing, 2000; and Kowalski and Porter, this volume). Orwell argued such international sporting contests, and specifically their propensity to mimic "warfare," for causing "ill-will," and for creating "orgies of hatred," did little more than create "fresh animosity on both sides." Orwell continued:

> If you wanted to add to the vast fund of ill-will existing in the world at this moment, you could hardly do it better than by a series of football matches between Jews and Arabs, Germans and Czechs, Indians and British, Russians and Poles, and Italians and Jugoslavs, each match to be watched by a mixed audience of 100,000 spectators. I do not, of course, suggest that sport is one of the main causes of international rivalry; big-scale sport is itself, I think, merely another effect of the causes that have produced nationalism. Still, you do make things worse by sending forth a team of eleven men, labelled as national champions, to do battle against some rival team, and allowing it to be felt on all sides that whichever nation is defeated will "lose face".

Despite Orwell's warnings, and within the fractious geopolitical landscape created out of the conferences at Yalta (February, 1945) and Potsdam (August, 1945), international sporting competition provided a hitherto unprecedented – and, arguably, cathartic – vehicle for the expression of the new order of nation-based antagonisms within the post-war world. The manner in which the Second World War ended, and specifically the way much of Eastern Europe was left vulnerable to the Soviet Union's expansionist impulses, created a climate of confrontation between the two global superpowers (the USSR and the USA) and their purportedly antithetical economic, political, and cultural systems. Although generally accepted to have begun in 1945, the divergent trajectories of Russian society (from tsarist autocracy to communist command) and the USA (from republican democracy to capitalist hegemony) spoke both to the enduring antipathy between these sovereign nations, and the inevitability of conflict between two burgeoning superpowers – especially given the context of increasingly globalized political, economic and technological relations (Powaski, 1997).

Although it has been described as "the first total war between economic and social systems" (Walker, 1994, p.1), the escalating hostility between the USSR and USA bore little resemblance to the "conventional" global warfare that had immediately preceded, and indeed, preempted it. Mutual recognition of the globally cataclysmic military capabilities possessed by both sides (certainly after the USSR became an atomic power in 1949 with the development of its own bomb) just about prevented the outbreak of a traditional armed conflict between these two increasingly antagonistic foes. Instead, the USSR and the USA, and their respective allies, engaged in a lower intensity, but nonetheless far reaching, Cold War that spanned high-level political wrangling, punitive and beneficent economic policies, competing propaganda initiatives and clandestine intelligence operations. There were also large scale military conflicts between strategically significant surrogate nations backed – to varying degrees, and in varying ways – by the competing superpowers (i.e. the Korean, Vietnam, and Afghani wars) (Painter, 1999; Powaski, 1997; Walker, 1994). However, as well as incorporating multifarious political, economic, and military dimensions, the Cold War was also fought on, and through, the terrain of culture.

As Caute (Caute, 2003, p.1) outlined, as a *modern* imperial struggle between "the *pax Americana* and the *pax sovietica*," the Cold War encompassed an "ideological and cultural contest on a global scale and without historical precedent." In other words, culture became a vehicle through which – in the absence of more conventional forms and frequencies of military engagement – the competing communist and capitalist orders sought to assert their civil, ideological, and moral ascendancy. From the US perspective (and there is every indication that the USSR countered in similarly polarizing fashion), the Cold War became a compelling and authoritative "rhetoric, a narrative, a moral drama propelled by the Manichean myth of apocalyptical struggle between forces of good and evil, between capitalism and communism, between democracy and totalitarianism, rationality and barbarism" (Wang, 2002, p.48). Under such conditions, however, increasingly narrow and exclusive discourses of citizenship became hysterically asserted (Wang, 2002). Framed under the guise of national security, imperatives designed to protect the nation from the risk of invasion and/or from corruption from within, this reactionary rhetoric was produced – and at particular sites, contested – within the public sphere (McConachie, 2003). Hence, the "soft power of culture" (Wang, 2002, p.48) became a major element of the Cold War; it provided an abundant and emotive landscape upon which claims for moral and ideological supremacy were aggressively advanced.

Within what Caute (2003, p.3) described as the "Cultural Olympics," Cold War conflicts were played out over a multitude of cultural "fronts":

> No previous imperial contest had involved furious disputes on genetics, prize-fights between philosophers, literary brawls capable of inflicting grievous bodily harm, musical uproars, duels with paint-brushes, the sending of ballet companies home without a single pirouette performed, defecting cellists, absconding ballet dancers, the hurling of greasepaint between the theatres of divided Berlin, the theft of musical film scores, a great composer yelling hatred into a microphone, a national chess team refusing travel if subject to fingerprinting on arrival, jammed jazz on the airwaves, the erection of iron curtains against the sound of rock, and the padlocking of painters (Pablo Picasso among them).

The sporting tenor of Caute's characterization is far from surprising since international sport in general, and, arguably, the Olympics in particular, provided the most immediate, confrontational and viscerally resonant points of nationalist engagement within the Cultural Cold War (Wang, 2002). For, as Hobsbawm (1990, p.143) noted, "The imagined community of millions seems more real as a team of eleven named people." Thus, and returning to Orwell's prophetic observations, as the Cold War unfolded, international sporting competition provided a context that allowed governing elites to benefit from, and the governed masses to become intoxicated by, "the lunatic modern habit of identifying oneself with large power units and seeing everything in terms of competitive prestige" (Orwell, 1945). Whereas within previous conditions of global conflict and crisis, cultural, and particularly sporting, engagements between rival factions would have been unthinkable – with a few exceptions, such as the much-mythologized impromptu football game which briefly halted the Western front trench warfare during Christmas 1914 (Weintraub, 2001). However, by the mid-twentieth century the globalized institutionalization of sport had created a system of international competitions and events (the pinnacle being the Olympic Games, the FIFA World Cup, and various World championships) that routinely pitted nation against nation, as represented either by teams or individual athletes, – even, or perhaps especially, those with deep-rooted antipathies. Given the systemic maturity of organized sport, and the unavoidable nature of international sporting engagement (if a nation wished to remain in the mainstream community of nations), sporting tours, links and exchanges became natural extensions of the cultural Cold War. Although sport is more regularly mobilized as a means of nurturing positive relations with allied nations, during the Cold War sport brought enemies together, and provided opportunities for initiating and developing diplomatic ties that would otherwise have been harder to instigate, were it not for the apolitical veil of sporting engagement. One particularly idealist advocate of this type of sporting diplomacy clearly articulated the rationale underpinning the Cold War's sporting component:

> Sports exchanges between the United States and Cuba, North Korea, or Iran can break down stereotypes, increase understanding, and confine battles to the playing field rather than the battlefield. They are a "safe" way to ease a country out of isolation, acting as a first step of engagement, if not the first step.
>
> (Goldberg, 2000, p. 63)

Coupled with the "internationalization of sports competition" (Houlihan, 2000, p.217), this practice of sports diplomacy meant the competing factions in the Cold War may have avoided direct military conflict. However, they were regular foes in the sports arena and sporting contests regularly became high profile public spectacles through which the respective merits of the competing social and political systems, ideologies and moral orders were contested in symbolic combat. This process was seen in a number of countries and it began in earnest in the early 1950s – with, for example, the entry of the Soviet Union into the Olympic movement prior to the Helsinki Games in 1952 and the 6–3 defeat of the England football team by "communist" Hungary at Wembley the following year (Beck 2003–4; Kowalski and Porter, 2003–4 and in this volume; Hill, 2003–4). Thereafter, the cultural Cold War helped to define the Olympic Games over 10 Olympiads and a 35-year period, it inscribed numerous other sporting encounters, five Rocky films and much popular culture besides. It is this period and this sport dimension of the cultural Cold War, along with the various issues that they raise, that are the subject of this book.

The chapters deal with the cultural Cold War of sport both chronologically and thematically. In Chapter 1, **Rob Beamish** and **Ian Ritchie** discuss ways in which, particularly in the United States, steroids became the symbol of widespread fears, firstly of Nazism, then of threats to the apparently fundamental distinction between males and females in athletics. The Soviet Union, it was thought, were turning men into women or had become careless of the difference between the two. Thus, in crucial ways, the cultural anxieties of the Second World War are projected onto the Cold War.

In Chapter 2 **Jenifer Parks** discusses one of the great paradoxes of international sport – the entry of the Soviet Union, a country officially opposed both to nationalism and to competitiveness, into the Olympic movement. Drawing on original sources, Parks analyzes the politicking that took place at the highest level of the Soviet Union in the late 1940s and early 1950s and which led to this unlikely event.

Chapter 3, by **Robert Rinehart**, illustrates some of the political-cultural ramifications of the post-Second World war settlement which left the Soviet Union with a huge sphere of influence, and a large number of constituent "satellite nations," East of Berlin. To enforce their authority, the Soviet Union sent troops into Hungary in 1956, the year of the Olympic Games in Melbourne. Rinehart's chapter shows how a water polo match at these Olympics immediately came to symbolize Hungarian resistance to Soviet intervention.

In Chapter 4, **Ronnie Kowalski** and **Dilwyn Porter** highlight the Cold War significance of football in the 1940s and 1950s. With special reference to football relations between England and the Soviet Union (particularly the 1945 tour by Moscow Dinamo mentioned by Orwell) and between England and Hungary, they analyze the ideological undercurrents of these encounters. They suggest that football diminished in its importance in the Cold War after this period because the Soviet Union began to concentrate their efforts on sports that were played by the United States – chiefly, athletics.

Athletics is the subject of Chapter 5, wherein **John Bale** discusses relations between British and Soviet athletes during the period 1945–1960, a time of heightened athletic activity between the two countries. Bale's essay discusses the ideological complexity of these dealings, showing that they were not reducible to simple Cold War antagonism.

Chapter 6, by **Stephen Wagg**, focuses on the ways in which the British sport press adapted to the realities of the Cold War. Analysing coverage of Olympic Games between 1952 and 1972, it suggests that the female "girl next door" athlete who brought home a medal from the Games of the 1950s and early 1960s, was a motif for an imperial, amateur Britishness rapidly being eclipsed by the two superpower protagonists of the Cold War. These protagonists, despite each claiming that they alone upheld the traditional values of the Olympics, both practised sport with science and seriousness and stressed the vital importance of winning. These values are taken up in the two subsequent chapters; both examine the spectre of drugs.

In Chapter 7 **Jeffrey Montez de Oca** examines discourses of the body among politicians and physical educationists in the late 1950s and early 1960s. As he shows, there were widespread fears that young, white masculinity was becoming depleted in the United States during this period. This caused a number of spokespeople to invoke a "Muscle Gap" with the Soviet Union, comparable to the (also frequently invoked) "Missile Gap." Nicely capturing the political rhetoric of the time, as well as the widespread underlying fears, Montez de Oca argues that US policy makers were concerned that this "softness" laid their country open to "communist penetration."

In Chapter 8, **Paul Dimeo** also examines the drug issue in Cold War athletics and makes the case that the preferred view in the West – that the Soviet Union were the drug abusers and the United States and the British were the good guys – cannot be sustained.

Chapter 9 is about the enormous cultural significance in Canadian society enjoyed by the 1972 Summit Series of ice hockey between Canada and the USSR. This, according to the authors of the chapter, **Jay Scherer**, **Gregory Duquette**, and **Daniel Mason**, is an important juncture (for many Canadians it is *the* defining moment) in Canadian sporting history – a signal event, that is to say, in the ongoing Cold War definition of Us (capitalist, liberal democratic, "free") and Them (communist, totalitarian, "oppressed").

Chapter 10 is made up of extracts from **Milton Jamail**'s excellent analysis of Cuban baseball. Baseball is sport culture that Cuba and the United States have in common but baseball relations between the two countries have been constricted by the economic blockade imposed by the US following the Cuban revolution of 1959. "One day," Fidel Castro once said, "when the Yankees come to their senses, we will beat them at baseball." But, so far, the Yankees have not obliged and for Cubans, therefore, in a very real sense, the Cold War goes on. Jamail shows the consequences of this for Cuban baseball.

Chapter 11, by **Damion Thomas**, deals with the vital question of the politics of "race" in the United States during the Cold War. As Thomas shows, the Truman and Eisenhower administrations (1945–52 and 1952–60 respectively) were extremely concerned about the Cold War implications of racism against African Americans. Militant black spokespeople like W.E. Du Bois and Paul Robeson had their passports confiscated while more conservative figures such as the baseball player Jackie Robinson, were encouraged to speak up for the American way of life. Between 1945 and 1968, over 500 athletic goodwill tours featuring African-American sportspeople were sent abroad, basketball and track and field being the preferred sports.

In Chapter 12, **Mary McDonald** suggests the political and cultural significance of the "Miracles" defeat of the all-powerful Soviet ice hockey team by the United States in the Winter Olympics of 1980 at Lake Placid. Engaging directly with Orwell's notion of sport as "war minus the shooting," she argues that sport can promote and strengthen militarism and that the national pride engendered by the "Miracles" victory pre-figured the aggressive foreign policy of the Reagan presidency (1980–88).

Chapters 13 and 14 are based upon fascinating original sources. In the former, **Evelyn Mertin** draws on archival material obtained in Moscow to show how the successive boycotts of the Olympic Games in Moscow in 1980, when the United States and various satellite nations stayed away, and in Los Angeles in 1984, when the Soviet Union and her satellites reciprocated, were handled politically by the Soviet Union. In the latter, **Susan Brownell** analyses the complex ways in which the problem of the "two Chinas" were negotiated in the Olympic movement, following the establishment of the Peoples Republic of China on mainland China in 1949 and the departure of the nationalist government to Taiwan.

Chapters 15 and 16 cover developments in sport and politics *after* the Cold War. Firstly, **James Riordan**, a writer without apparent peer in the field of sport and the Cold War, discusses the impact on Russian sport of the ending of the Cold War and the break-up of the Soviet Union and the proliferation of kleptocratic politics across Eastern Europe. Then **Michael Silk**, **Bryan Bracey** and **Mark Falcous** show how images and memories of the "Miracles" ice hockey game of 1980 have been appropriated by the presidency of George W. Bush and the American right in support of the notion of a perpetual war against "terror" and for "freedom." This war will be seen by many as a continuation of the Cold War, by other means and with different vocabularies.

The final chapter, by **Eunha Koh**, **David L. Andrews** and **Ryan White** examines anti-Americanism in the sport culture of Korea, scene of one of the many "hot" wars fought during the Cold War period.

In the post-Cold War world, (1989 or 1991 onwards, depending on the source), international sporting competition has, among certain circles, been accused of being a little vacuous and contrived. Whilst old/traditional relations and antagonisms continue to flavour some sporting contests (witness the 2005 Ashes series, World War redux every time England plays Germany, the Malvinas/Falklands conflict revisited in and through sporting contests involving British and Argentinian teams), and certainly among the producers of American sporting culture, there is a palpable sense of nostalgia for the Cold War animosities through which otherwise indistinct sporting contests became articulated and experienced as pyrrhic events. Witness one commentator's recent World Baseball Classic:

> The real shame, I think, is that there is no shot at a championship game between the United States and Cuba … you can see how important this tournament is to them. Its a chance to prove something about its baseball, with the subtext of its relationship with the United States where so many Cuban players have defected, of course, over the last decade and a half. I think its safe to say that we all favour a free and stable world, but the Cold War always made the Olympics more intriguing, and I think that's the same thing going on here.
> (Fatsis, 2006)

Similarly, the declining television ratings (a viewership roughly half of that garnered by the television phenomenon of the moment, American Idol) in the US and Canada for the 2006 Turin Winter Olympic Games coverage has been attributed to the lack of a Cold War that drew viewers, in huge numbers, to sports they knew little about nor would have cared much about were it not for the opportunity to defeat the Red machine/menace in the name of the *American way* (Anon, 2006a; Potter, 2006). As the August *Wall Street Journal* commented:

> Today's Games are en route to becoming the least watched in years because they tilt against historical winds – namely, the end of the Cold War and the subsequent waning of nationalist impulses.
>
> Before the Berlin Wall fell, the Olympics were considered, to adapt Clausewitz, politics by other means. Occasionally this was explicit, such as when Cold War opponents boycotted each other's Summer Games in 1980 and 1984. But when enemy countries did agree to participate, geopolitical overtones permeated the Games and produced some of the more memorable Olympic contests. More people tuned in when more was at stake.

Evidently, while the contemporaneous "war on terror" may have been shame-lessly imposed upon, and invoked in order to mobilize, popular sporting practices and sentiments (Silk and Falcous, 2005) this war is, ultimately, a war on an abstraction. "Terror," to adapt Hobsbawm's now famous dictum, is not an imag-ined community and cannot therefore be made more real as a team of eleven, or however many, named individuals. Nothing, it seems, can rival the Cold War for the tension, the ideological import, the sense of Us and Them, nor on occasion the ugliness, that it brought to international sporting encounters.

References

Allison, L. (1994). "The Olympic movement at the end of the Cold War." *World Affairs*, 157(2), pp. 92–97.

Anon. (2006, February 18). "The individual games: Today's Olympics lack the political drama of yesteryear." *Wall Street Journal*.

Anon. (2006, February 21). "The good Ol'(ympic) days." *USA Today*, p.17A.

Beamish, R., and Ritchie, I. (2005). "The spectre of steroids: Nazi proaganda, Cold War anxiety and patriarchal paternalism." *International Journal of the History of Sport*, 22(5), pp. 777–795.

Beamish, R., and Ritchie, I. (2004). "From chivalrous 'brothers-in-arms' to the eligble athlete: Changed principles and the IOC's banned substance list." *International Review for the Sociology of Sport*, 39(4), pp. 355–372.

Beck, P. (2003–4). "Losing Prestige on and off the Field: England versus Hungary 1953–4, *Sport in History*," 23(2) Winter pp. 10–26.

Beck, P. (2005). "Britain and the Cold War's "Cultural Olympics": Responding to the political drive of Soviet Sport, 1945–58," *Contemporary British History*, 19(2), pp. 169–185.

Black, D.R., & Bezanson, S. (2004). "The Olympic Games, human rights and democrati-sation: Lessons from Seoul and implications for Beijing," *Third World Quarterly*, 25(7), pp. 1245–1261.

Caute, D. (2003). *The Dancer Defects: The struggle for cultural supremacy during the Cold War*. Oxford: Oxford University Press.

Conlin, P. (1994). "The Cold War and Canadian nationalism on ice: Federal government involvement in international hockey during the 1960s," *Canadian Journal of the History of Sport*, 25(2), pp. 50–68.

Downing, D. (2000). *Passovotchka: Moscow Dynamo in Britain, 1945*. London: Bloomsbury.

Fatsis, S. (2006). *Dominican Republic, Cuba in Baseball Semifinals, All Things Considered*: National Public Radio.

Goldberg, J. (2000). "Sporting Diplomacy," *The Washington Quarterly*, 23(4), pp. 63–70.

Hill, Jeffrey (2003–4). "Narratives of the Nation: The Newspaper Press and England v. Hungary 1953," *Sport in History*, 23(2), Winter, pp. 47–60.

Hobsbawm, E.J. (1990). *Nations and Nationalism since 1870: Programme, myth, reality*. Cambridge: Cambridge University Press.

Houlihan, B. (2000). "Politics and Sport." In J. Coakley and E. Dunning (Eds.), *Handbook of Sports Studies* (pp. 213–227). London: Sage.

Kowalski, R. and Porter, D. (2003–4). England's World Turned Upside Down? Magical Magyars and British Football, *Sport in History*, 23(2) Winter, pp. 27–4.

McConachie, B. (2003). *American Theater in the Culture of the Cold War: Producing and contesting containment, 1947–1962*, Iowa City: University of Iowa Press.

Orwell, G. (1945, December). *Tribune*, The Sporting Spirit.

Painter, D.S. (1999). *The Cold War: An international history*, London: Routledge.

Potter, A. (2006, March 6). "Hurray! No one's watching," *Maclean's*, 119, p. 8.

Powaski, R.E. (1997). *The Cold War: The United States and the Soviet Union, 1917–1991*. New York: Oxford University Press.

Schillinger, E., and Jenswold, J. (1987). "Three Olympiads: A comparison of Pravda and the Washington Post," *Journalism Quarterly*, pp. 826–833.

Silk, M., and Falcous, M. (2005). "One day in September/A week in February: Mobilizing American (Sporting) nationalisms," *Sociology of Sport Journal*, 22(4), pp. 447–471.

Walker, M. (1994). *The Cold War: A history*. New York: Henry Holt.

Wang, B. (2002). "The Cold War, imperial aesthetics, and area studies," *Social Text*, 20(3), pp. 45–65.

Weintraub, S. (2001). *Silent Night: The Story of the World War I Christmas Truce*, New York: Penguin.

Wilson, J.J. (2004). "27 remarkable days: The 1972 Summit Series of Ice Hockey between Canada and the Soviet Union," *Totalitarian Movements and Political Religions*, 5(2), pp. 271–280.

Yoshimoto, M. (2003). "Hollywood, Americanism and the imperial screen: Geopolitics of image and discourse after the end of the Cold War," *Inter-Asia Cultural Studies*, 4(3), pp. 451–459.

Chapter 1

Totalitarian regimes and Cold War sport

Steroid "Übermenschen" and "ball-bearing females"

Rob Beamish and Ian Ritchie

Shadows over the Cold War Games

From their beginning, the Olympic Games have drawn upon, and also produced, powerful cultural images, rich symbols, and intense emotions. The Cold War Games were not an exception. What set the Games of the Cold War period apart from all other Olympiads was the deeply haunting reality of their immediate past – a reality that created and animated the most ominous images of human history.[1] The post-1945 Games were all conducted under the long shadow of the 1936 Games in Nazi Germany and the realities of the Second World War.

The Second World War (WWII) was the most destructive conflict in human history. There were 50 million direct casualties; millions more died of disease, starvation or personal devastation. Half of the world's major cities were destroyed. In response to the Luftwaffe's bombing of Britain, the Allies razed Dresden and Hamburg with fire and carpet bombing. The marches on and the sieges of Moscow, Leningrad and Stalingrad led to Soviet retaliation during their march on and into Berlin. The brutalization of political opponents, Roma, homosexual men, and the handicapped in the Nazi concentration camps was only the prelude to death marches and the bureaucratically administered, mechanized mass murder of Jews in Chelmno, Sobibor, Treblinka, Belzec and Auschwitz-Birkenau.[2] The technological, scientifically assisted holocaust was not confined to extermination camps once the Allies dropped atomic bombs on the civilian populations of Hiroshima and Nagasaki.[3]

Following twenty years of imprisonment in Spandau, Albert Speer, the last Minister of Armaments in the Third Reich, thought deeply about what he needed to impress upon future generations in his final statement at the Nuremberg Trials. In his memoirs, he wrote:

> The criminal events of those years, were not simply the result of Hitler's personality. The extent of the crimes was also attributable to the fact that Hitler was the first to be able to use means of technology that could multiply their impact.

I thought about the potential future consequences of unrestricted domination coupled with the power of technology – making use of it and also being dominated by it. This war, I indicated [in his final statement at the Nuremburg Trials], had ended with remote-controlled rockets, supersonic aircraft, atomic bombs, and the prospect of chemical warfare. In five to ten years [by 1951–56] one could, with about ten men, annihilate in seconds a million people in the centre of New York, create widespread epidemics and destroy harvests with chemical weapons. 'The more technological the world becomes', [Speer had read in his statement] 'the greater is the danger. ... Nothing can stop unfettered technology and science from completing its work of destroying humankind which they have, in such an insane manner, begun to do in this war'.[4]

The grotesque possibility that post-War science and technology could give a state – any state – such formidable, unbridled power was deeply engrained in the psyche of all who survived the war or grew up in its immediate aftermath.[5]

The emotional impact of the images of waste, devastation and destruction in the Second World War is, however, inseparable from the "master race" imagery that Adolf Hitler and Joseph Goebbels, the coldly calculating Minister of Public Enlightenment and Propaganda, carefully crafted for the Nazi cause.[6] From his early wayward existence in Vienna, through his experiences on the front lines and hospitals during the First World War (WWI), to his political orations in the beer halls of Bavaria, Hitler remained closely attuned to the sentiments, fears and aspirations of the masses in Germany and Austria.[7] Knowing the strength of the traditional belief in authority but aware of how German defeat in 1917 had brought it into question, "the drummer" beat away continually at three themes in his rise to power: Germany had not been defeated in WWI – the "wire pullers" who formed the Weimar Republic had stabbed the army in the back by signing a humiliating armistice; Germany's power and superiority lay in the physical strength and racial purity of the German Volk; and Germany needed a great Führer to return it to its natural and justified glory.[8] Power, pride, racial purity and struggle/combat (Kampf) constituted the central core of Nazi ideology.

Hitler's life experiences also made him keenly aware that public opinion – indeed the beliefs, hearts and souls of the masses – could be captured and shaped by well-crafted and carefully scripted propaganda. As a result, the Nazis constructed imposing, monumentalist or neoclassical styled facilities and integrated the surging energy of mass audiences with meticulously choreographed events, to stage Gesamtkunstwerke – total works of art – in which music, spectator involvement, drama, and architecture were blended into a total, emotion-laden experience.[9] The Nazis were leaders in the exploitation of the emerging mass media technologies – the vast rallies used state-of-the-art public address systems and were carried on radio and shown in cinemas across the country. The mass political rallies, large-scale sporting events, feature films, radio programmes, advertising, political posters, and assiduously organized art exhibitions delivered precisely constructed, carefully crafted images that consolidated Germany's links to its heroic Nordic past, the strength and purity of the Aryan race, and the physical power of the Nazi state. Those messages – projected across Germany and throughout Europe – celebrated a visceral adulation of the Führer, the heroic Aryan warrior, and the fomenting power of the Third German Reich.

Propaganda and imagery were central to the Nazis' orchestration of the 1936 Olympic Games as Hitler and Goebbels welded the Promethian images of Fascist Germany to the Games' rich symbolic power.[10] The Berlin Olympiad allowed the Nazis to demonstrate, before a world audience, the disciplined and disciplining power of the emerging Fascist state. Hitler's entrance into the stadium, teeming with enthusiastic admirers, stiff arm saluting en masse his ascendance to his elevated viewing podium symbolically captured the resilient pride of the German military machine as it rose to increasingly imposing heights. Hitler's interaction with the massed ranks of spectators, the burgeoning swastika banners, and the emotional energy in the stadium reinforced the Nazi leitmotiv of "Ein Volk, ein Führer, ein Reich" (One Racially Pure People, One Leader, One Expansive Empire).

The opening ceremonies in Berlin culminated with the lighting of the Olympic flame with a torch that had been run, in the Games' first torch relay, from Ancient Olympia, across Europe, to the new cradle of advanced civilization – Nazi Germany. The Olympic torch symbolically linked the heroic age of Greece – the racially homogeneous, apogee of ancient civilization – with the Third Reich to which the torch was now passed. Simultaneously, the torch relay rekindled the vivid images and powerful emotions that were created in the imposing, midnight torch procession the Nazi Storm Troopers conducted upon Hitler's January 30, 1933 appointment to Chancellor.[11]

Nazism was a male-based cult that glorified youth, strength and conquest. It emphasized genetic and racial endowment in the natural, Darwinian struggle for the survival of the fittest. While some optimistically felt that Jesse Owens's four gold medals undermined Hitler's political objectives, the German total of thirty-three gold, twenty-six silver and thirty bronze medals, which easily topped the Americans' twenty-four, twenty and twelve, ensured that the Führer's message was not lost on the sympathetic or undecided German follower.

The Games' closing ceremonies were carefully choreographed to remind Germans, and the rest of the world, that the Thousand Year Reich would be resplendent in glories the world had never before experienced. In the final moments, the Nazis replicated the spectacular "cathedral of light," which Speer had introduced at the 1934 Nuremberg Party Congress. Powerful anti-aircraft search lights, placed at forty foot intervals around the Olympic Stadium, shot sharply defined columns of light 25,000 feet straight up into the night sky. Then gradually the columns "converged to enclose the darkened stadium in a temple composed entirely of glowing spirit."[12] The spectacle powerfully linked the glory of Nazi Germany with the majesty of the Olympic Games.

What is most important to remember is that the imagery of German fascism was not merely carefully crafted propaganda. The Nazi Blitzkriegs, their brutalizing occupation of western Europe, the systematic genocide conducted throughout eastern Europe, the "Commissar Order" that required the immediate execution of Soviet political and military leaders, and the wanton destruction of Soviet cities were integral to the reality of Nazism. Nothing was beyond the Nazi leadership's quest for world domination – ideology and reality were one. No one in the post-Second World War period doubted that expansionist, totalitarian leaders would use any means at their disposal to achieve their particular political ends.

Communist totalitarianism and steroid "Übermenschen"

The USSR's highly successful entry into the Olympic Games in 1952 demonstrated, immediately, that the West faced a strong, highly motivated and capable opponent in the Cold War confrontation that would unfold over the next 10 Olympiads. Although no one doubted that the Soviets had some fine athletes, the speed and scale of their success was not normal and therefore could not be natural. Three rumours spread almost immediately.

First, it still remained inconceivable to some that human beings, even Nazi fanatics, could carry out the systematic destruction the Nazi war machine had perpetrated in eastern Europe and the Soviet Union – there had to be something more than fascist aggression behind the devastation. The rumour that the Nazi troops had been injected with steroids was born.

Second, given their own first-hand experience with the Nazi "Übermenschen", allegedly powered with steroid-fuelled aggression, rumours spread that the Cold War "front-line soldiers" of the Soviet Union – their Olympic athletes – were also taking steroids to further Stalin's particular totalitarian aspirations.[13] Worse yet, a third rumour suggested that female athletes from the Eastern bloc were being forced to accept the androgenizing effects of anabolic steroids and other hormone treatments to further communist expansionist goals through victories at the Olympic Games. These rumours continued unabated well into the early days of the Olympic Movement's "war on doping" during the 1970s. Conjuring a popular mythology based on hearsay, and not documented fact, a long string of self-appointed experts and interested observers of Soviet sport in the West drew direct or indirect lines between Nazi steroid experiments and Soviet athletic performances.

Dr Nicholas Wade's 1972 intervention into the debate over steroid use in sport was typical of how the Nazi steroid rumour was used to demonize steroids and their use in high-performance sport during the Cold War.

The first use of male steroids to improve performance is said to have been in World War II when German troops took them before battle to enhance aggressiveness. After the war, steroids were given to the survivors of German concentration camps to rebuild body weight. The first use in athletics seems to have been by the Russians in 1954. John D. Ziegler, a Maryland physician who was the US team physician to the weightlifting championships in Vienna that year, told Science that Soviet weightlifters were receiving doses of testosterone, a male sex hormone. The Russians were also using it on some of their women athletes, Ziegler said. Besides its growth-promoting effect, testosterone induces male sexual development such as deepening of the voice and hirsuteness, which might account for the manifestation of such traits in Soviet women athletes during the 1950s.[14]

In fewer than 150 words, Wade managed to link images of German military aggression, concentration camp horror, rampant Soviet ambition, the male hormonalization and masculinization of female Soviet athletes, and the expert testimony of an American physician.

Robert Windsor and Daniel Dumitru repeated the allegation in *Postgraduate Medicine*, and Fred Silverman did the same in the *Journal of the American Medical Association*.[15] V. Cowart, without reference to Wade, Silverman, or Windsor and Dumitru, claimed that "the first reported use of steroids in a non-clinical setting was during the Second World War when German troops took them to enhance aggressiveness." He continued, "It was only a small step to recognize that enhanced aggressiveness might be desirable in athletic competition, and the Russians took that step in the early 1950s."[16]

These claims, made in reputable scientific and medical journals, transformed a rumour into an apparent medical fact and the claims, never documented more fully than in the unsubstantiated allegations made by Wade, Windsor and Dumitru, and others or Taylor's reference to an interview with Hitler's personal physician, continued to appear in scholarly publications, medical periodicals, medical conference presentations, and newspapers.[17] Those same allegations are now ubiquitous on the World Wide Web.[18]

The Nazi steroid claim has been particularly useful to those who oppose steroid use in high-performance sport and who want to link its use to totalitarian political regimes. Brigitte Berendonk, for example, in her condemning critique of steroid use in East Germany, draws upon recollections of her early life experiences in East and West Germany to affirm that "in many general review articles it was noted that during the Second World War, German army storm troopers had been doped with psychotropic testosterone just a few years after the first chemical identification, synthesis and structural description of these compounds."[19] Similarly, Steven Ungerleider gives the following unreferenced account in *Faust's Gold: Inside the East German Doping Machine*:

During World War II, Hitler issued vast quantities of steroids to the SS and the Wehrmacht so that his troops would better resist combat fatigue and be more ruthless in following any order. As early as 1941, Soviet Red Army observers had noted an unusually passionate fighting spirit among German soldiers, who often seemed eager to die for the glory of the Third Reich.[20]

The fact that the rumours had no substance has never really mattered. Once made, and appearing in scientific publications, the amalgam of steroids, Nazi genocide in eastern Europe, and Soviet ambition was firmly cast into a chilling image. In the long shadow of the Second World War, steroids became, ironically enough, a "juiced up Nazi drug" – they became the "atomic bomb" of Cold War sport.[21] Steroids symbolized the immoral and unprincipled use of science to further totalitarian goals without concern for human consequences. The image of "steroid Übermenschen" had changed from tall, blond, muscular SS soldiers unwaveringly committed to the Führer's will to power, to legions of swarthy, Rasputin-like communists who were equally driven by their allegiance to Stalin and his expansionist dreams.

In the Cold War era, this amalgam of steroids and totalitarian ambition had a further consequence. Ziegler, who was instrumental in the development of the synthetic steroid Dianabol (methandrostenalone) and its use by American Olympians, indicated in 1954 that his Soviet source had confirmed, to Ziegler's satisfaction at least, that the unrestricted pursuit of power led USSR sports leaders to subjugate women to the masculinizing effects of steroids.[22] To compete, the West would apparently have to sacrifice not only its male youth to the Cold War, but women would also be among the casualties. Without tight control, the Olympic Games would become the most visible and public site of extended chemical warfare between nation states.

Steroids, gender ambiguity and sex testing

The USSR's success in the Olympic Games relied heavily on the performances of its female athletes. Three fears emerged from this fact. First, it was possible that Ziegler's source was correct and the Soviets were androgenizing their female athletes with male hormones – a practice most patriarchal, paternalistic sports leaders in the West did not want to replicate. Second, perhaps things were not that bad and it was simply the case that the Soviets were cheating and not all of their "female" athletes were actually women. Since certain female athletes from the USSR deviated significantly from the dominant perceptions in the West of what constituted a "proper" or "natural" female body, either scenario seemed possible. Third, it was also possible that world-class, high-performance sport for women had suddenly and dramatically become the same scientifically rational, technologically assisted, pursuit of the linear record as men's sport. While it turns out that the first and third possibilities were true and the second was not, the fear of all three existed in the popular consciousness of the day.[23]

In a manner that is similar to the way the long shadow of Aryan supremacy, Nazi aggression, and the devastation of the Second World War – especially on the Eastern Front – framed and contoured the response to steroid use by males in the Cold War Games, the fears associated with images of "masculinized" female athletes were also shaped by a long historical past. The presence, impact and success of Soviet female athletes in the first Cold War Games stirred deep seated fears in the West, fears that can only be understood within the long-standing history of clearly demarcated gender and sexual borders that have characterized modern sport and the Olympic Games.

The Olympic Movement has both reflected and reinforced what historian Thomas Laqueur calls the "two-sex model."[24] Sport symbolically conveys the notion that the natural, and by association, the social or cultural constitutions of men and women are determined by their bodies' respective biological, physiological and anatomical structures. As Cheryl Cole points out, "[t]he 'logic' of the sport/body combination, the seemingly free play of bodies in motion, contributes to an illusion that sport and its bodies are transparent, set apart from politics, culture and the economy."[25] The seemingly ahistorical, apolitical nature of sport further reinforces social claims for the two-sex model because sport appears to operate as a "social laboratory" in which "theories" of human nature are tried, tested and proven and the differences between the sexes are demonstrated to be extremely significant in the competitive arenas of social life.

Coubertin set the tone for the Olympic Movement in his numerous justifications for women's absence from the Games. He presented arguments from a naturalistic framework commonplace at the turn of the twentieth century:

> Respect of individual liberty requires that one should not interfere in private acts … but in public competition, [women's] participation must be absolutely prohibited. It is indecent that the spectators should be exposed to the risk of seeing the body of a woman being smashed before their eyes. Besides, no matter how toughened a sportswoman may be, her organism is not cut out to sustain certain shocks. Her nerves rule her muscles, nature wanted it that way.[26]

Coubertin's vision for the Olympic Movement was not an isolated one. John Hoberman points out that there were several internationalist movements at the turn of the century that reinforced a certain idealized male type. The Boy Scout movement, which arose during roughly the same period as the Olympics, attempted to develop and fortify similar notions of universal human traits. The "inventory" of characteristics reinforced by the different movements involved a Eurocentric orientation that claimed political neutrality. The wealthy and those with aristocratic connections determined the direction of the movements. They tended to express an interest in peacemaking or pacifism that was framed in a complex sense of national and international loyalty. The movements also advocated a "citizen of the world" type of supra-nationalism and relied on various symbols, flags and anthems to unify themselves.[27] The idealized chivalrous male figure was regarded as the embodiment of the international movements' goals and this image was crucial to Coubertin's idealized athlete. Gender exclusion was part of the founding ethos of the Games and would continue to pervade the Movement's constitutive practices for years to come.

Other institutional settings excluded women from sport or re-directed them towards more "moderate" exercise. Physical education programs in the West have a long history of regulating activity on the basis of gender, the devaluation of girls' and women's activities, and the normalization of heterosexuality.[28] The form of regulation shifted over time and an interesting historical change in gender relations is evident in the dynamics of women's physical education programs in the USA.

In the early twentieth century, physical education programs were often charged with creating "mannish" students, implying sexual deviance. The deviance that was feared, however, was an "aggressive heterosexual activity outside the norms of feminine respectability."[29] Female athletes were too mannish because they reputedly exhibited men's vigorous and overly heterosexual drives. While many women in physical education departments identified with this image, they did not feel encumbered by it since it existed alongside more traditional notions of female decorum. Female athletes enjoyed the spirited experiences of companionship among female athletes and students too much to be dissuaded by the charge of mannishness.[30]

By the 1920s, however, physical education departments felt the strong chill of growing sentiments opposed to homosexuality and innuendo about the pathology of non-heterosexuality. Under the influence of turn-of-the-century sexology and the normalization of heterosexuality through the medical-scientific gaze, concerns with same-sex perversion began to be expressed in same-sex institutional settings. Factories, hotels, boarding schools, convents, and physical education departments all came under scrutiny. By the 1930s in the USA, non-heterosexual practices were labelled dysfunctional in medical terminology, and lesbian taboos were reinforced in institutional settings. Psychological tests for masculinity and femininity were developed and the presence of "lesbian characteristics" became the litmus tests for female masculinity.[31] The battery of testing techniques included psychiatric and psychological tests and methods, such as free association, questionnaires or interviews; endocrinological measurements of hormone levels; gynecological examinations, including measurements and sketches of breasts and genitals; even photographs were used for morphological descriptions of homosexuality.[32] Under the threat of these taboos, the emphasis in physical education programs changed from one of female companionship to one of heterosexual attractiveness and "moderation."

The shift virtually suppressed all forms of aggressive, masculine competition for women.[33] A 1946 brochure of the Ohio Association for Health, Physical Education and Recreation bluntly stated, "the mannish concept of a physical educator is no longer acceptable."[34]

These normalizing practices took on political significance internationally in the Cold War era because it was during this time that the Eastern bloc female athletic body emerged as a visible challenge to Western normative ideals regarding what constituted "proper" female appearance. Images and perceptions of the sexual body played a vital role in national ideologies and in the inculcation of nationalistic feelings. The Cold War nationalistic imagery was constructed through ideals and symbols generated in relation to the trope of the body politic. Indeed, in the Cold War construction of "imagined communities," images of gender, sexual and familial relations became paramount and reached near-hysterical heights.[35]

In the United States, a super-heterosexualized Cold War family ideal was used as a "psychological fortress" against the fear of communist aggression from without, and communist intervention from within. "The legendary family of the 1950s, complete with appliances, station wagons, backyard barbecues, and tricycles scattered on the sidewalks," American family historian Elaine Tyler May points out, represented "the first wholehearted effort to create a home that would fulfill virtually all its members' personal needs through an energized and expressive personal life."[36] The catchword of the day was "domestic containment," whereby the consolidation of public policy and private behaviour endeavoured to secure a stable home and family, accentuate the benefits of American-style capitalism and its concomitant consumable goods and lifestyles, and maintain psychological security against the perceived threat of communist aggression and intervention. In this climate, communism, the bomb, internal subversion and "non-traditional" women were particularly weighty threats.

The intersection between sexual and domestic practices, on the one hand, and political ideology, on the other, made its way to the highest levels of Cold War diplomacy. In the 1959 "kitchen debate," Vice-President Richard Nixon boasted about the superiority of the American home, its family life and its consumable household products. The idealized American housewife with her domestic role as housekeeper and mother was part of Nixon's claim to US superiority. Soviet women, working for the good of the communist system, Premier Nikita Khrushchev countered, was the mark of a superior social system.[37] While "Rosie the Riveter" in the USA and Europe had been persuaded to help the cause during the War by working in munitions and supplies factories, she was later encouraged to return to "domestic duty" as usual. The dominant imagery of normalized gender and sex roles returned, centring on heterosexuality, the nuclear family, and "gender-appropriate," "biologically natural" behaviour.

Within this context of Cold War sexual rhetoric, Soviet and Eastern bloc female athletes were regarded as troubling challenges to the Western heterosexual imperative – they were portrayed as unfeminine, "Amazons," lesbians or men. The two female athletes who faced the brunt of these attacks were the USSR's highly successful shot and discus thrower Tamara Press and her sister Irina, the world record-holding heptathlete, who were irreverently dubbed the "Press Brothers" by Western journalists and athletes. The extent to which the apparent Soviet threat reached into the USA can be seen in their portrayal in a 1966 edition of *Life* magazine where they were referred to as the "muscular sisters" and juxtaposed to more "properly feminine" Western female athletes.[38]

The redefining of sexual norms in the post-Second World War period set the stage for one of the strangest and arguably most misguided sport policies ever. Once again, it was the Nazi-Soviet association that lurked in the background. At the 1936 Summer Games, Hermann Ratjen posed as "Dora" in the women's high jump although he later admitted to the deception and claimed the Nazis had forced him to it. If Hitler was willing to go that far, why would Stalin not follow? In 1938, a European women's high jump champion was barred from competition because she had ambiguous genitalia; given Soviet aspirations, sports leaders in the West feared that Stalin might also use special competitors to win at the Olympic Games.[39] Although there were very few cases of cheating, rumours combined with Cold War-based sexual ideology fed into a heightened concern with the "politics of sex" in world-class sport. In an attempt to control the unrestrained ambitions of the Communists, the IOC introduced a battery of imperfect, official procedures to check the sex of every female athlete.

Determined to guarantee that there was no room for deception, international sports officials introduced, in the 1960s, procedures that were alternately referred to as "the sex test," "gender verification" or "femininity control." Every female athlete who entered the Olympic program underwent a sex test right up to the 2000 Sydney Games at which time the IOC finally bowed to criticisms that the test was unethical and ineffective.[40]

The defenders of the "sex test" maintained that they were preserving "fairness" and "equity" in sport but the comments of medical officials at the time reveal deeper, underlying attitudes towards women's sport, physically powerful women, and females who did not conform to the Western "norm." During the administration of the first chromatin sex test at the 1968 Games, the chief tester told reporters that the women he tested showed various signs of masculinization because of sports, and that sports had generally made them ugly. R.G. Bunge's comments in the influential *Journal of the American Medical Association* in 1960 are revealing. Bunge facetiously pointed out that he was "not one to fool around with classification," but nevertheless proposed that "Nature's capricious deviation" in some cases had resulted in certain "unfortunate individuals." The author then rhetorically asked his readers "how would a French female feel if she were beaten by a Bolivian contestant who had a vagina and testicles in her labial folds?" – a condition the author later referred to as a "ball-bearing female." The author suggested that the chromatin sex test was necessary to prevent "genetic doping," a metaphor likely made possible by the growing knowledge of drug-use among athletes at the time alongside the known androgenic side-effects of steroids.[41] Indeed, Bunge's article is an early representation of what would later become a commonly assumed link between drug use and sexually ambiguous athletes: both challenged the "natural" order of sport and the idealized "level playing field."[42]

Robert Kerr, a California-based physician who assisted male athletes with their steroid regimes, echoed Bunge's sentiments, although for different reasons. Based on patriarchal, paternalistic grounds, Kerr wanted to protect female athletes in the West from the escalating competition with the USSR. Winning was important, keeping up with the Soviet men was imperative, but protecting the American way of life as it was embodied in the Cold War female ideal, was an even higher good.

> We've been witnessing today, and for the last number of years, how our female athletes are being defeated in certain strength and power sports by Russian and East German women who just seem to have an edge – *a masculine edge. Right now we don't want our women to be defeminized in order to win, but in the next Olympics, or the next after that, will we still be willing to feel the same way? I don't know, I hope in this case that we don't change.*[43]

Women's sport during the early Cold War period was challenging too many conventions; those aspects that could be controlled, had to be regulated; those that could not, would be contained as much as possible. Thus against the background of Cold War rhetoric about the "western way of life," evidence of Soviet success in women's sport, allegations of Soviet drug use and female impersonation, and the fear that without regulation women's and men's sports would soon be indistinguishable, the sports leaders sought to eliminate drugs and alleged female impersonation which, it was felt, would help return women's sport to its more "natural" form. Sex and drug testing both depended upon, and reinforced ideals of the natural body in sport, "unencumbered" by artificial or unnatural factors. Again, the image of the "Amazon," lesbian Communist pitted against "demure" athletes from the West haunted the Western psyche throughout the Cuban Missile Crisis and into the mid-1960s when drug and sex testing were first formally, and simultaneously, introduced into the *Olympic Charter*.

Cold War steroids and sex testing: the reality behind enduring images

W.I. Thomas argued that if people define situations as real, they are real in their consequences.[44] The imagined link of steroid use on the Eastern Front, the total devastation of the Second World War, and the fears of Nazi-styled, Soviet expansion were welded into a single image that horrified sports leaders of the West. The steroid Übermensch who had replaced his Nazi black shirt with a

Communist red one had to be contained and controlled. Although the Americans and other athletes in the West would use steroids from 1954 on, the image of the Eastern bloc, steroid-generated behemoth remained front and centre in the containment policies of sports leaders in the Cold War period. Similarly, the unfeminine, physically imposing, female athletes of the Eastern bloc – the "ball-bearing female" – challenged Western sports leaders' deeply entrenched images of the "biologically natural," gender appropriate appearance and behaviour of female athletes. Cold War sport, if not contained and controlled, would leave female athletes from the West completely exposed to increasing and irreversible masculinization.

From the very first Cold War Games of 1952, Western sports leaders were confronted with images that they themselves conjured of Nazi-inspired steroids, hyper-masculanized female athletes, and an amoral, irrational quest for power and domination. No sports leader and no international or national sport federation ever challenged or deconstructed those images. Instead the images served as the justification for policies of social control. In the face of the crisis environment of the Cold War, the International Olympic Committee and other international sport leaders drew upon another powerful, largely unchallenged image – the "purity of sport" – to justify their efforts to control certain aspects of high-performance sport.

Three major consequences followed. First, rather than embracing the transformation in women's sport that the Soviet women initiated, sport leaders sought to discredit the challenge that increasing numbers of Cold War female Olympians presented to the dominant images of "appropriate" gender appearance, demeanour, and performance. Rather than embracing the women's pursuit of the limits of physical performance in sport, which increasingly dominated male sport, sports leaders tried to contain, control, and redirect women's sport so that it remained "feminine" and projected images appropriate to the dominant ideology of compulsory heterosexuality.

Sex testing suggested that "real" women were not physically powerful, aggressive, and committed to the pursuit of competitive glory. By questioning the biology of female Olympians, sports leaders brought into question women's own self-determination. The attempt to control participants through sex testing was simultaneously an attempt to re-establish and reinforce the dominant Western image of femininity and female appropriate appearance and behaviour. Fortunately, at the time sports leaders were attempting to constrain female athletic imagery, the second wave of the Women's Movement was challenging those very same images in other realms of social life and opening up opportunities that the world of sport could never contain. In the end, the Olympic Movement had to fall in line with the changes the Women's Movement had ushered in during the last quarter of the twentieth century. In this instance, the dominant imagery that motivated policies of containment among female athletes was shattered by the larger social forces of the Women's Movement.

Second, the image of the steroid Übermensch – the "roid-altered, fascist/communist behemoth" – has continued to loom over all discussions of performance-enhancing substances in sport. Although steroids were used – extensively – by athletes throughout the Cold War period, the Frankenstein imagery prevailed and continues to exist. Sanctimonious sports leaders unfailingly support a high-performance sport system that continually pushes athletes to the very limits of physical performance and exposes them to risks and injuries that are far more serious than those that might be associated with performance-enhancing substances, while continuing to control and contain the ways athletes prepare for those assaults on their physiology. For those athletes who are "on the front line" of the ongoing struggle to be the fastest, soar the highest, and be the strongest, there are other images that are far more crucial, meaningful and relevant – the images of shattered dreams, broken bodies, denied opportunities, and unfulfilled promises. Those images, and the deconstruction of the steroid behemoth have not been taken up by people or movements outside sport in the same way the Women's Movement challenged the patriarchal imagery that sports leaders tried to use to control women's sport during the Cold War period. As a result, Cold War imagery still acts as a significant constraining force in policies that control performance-enhancement in high-performance sport today.

Finally, to justify the Cold War policies that attempted to contain performance-enhancing substances and the nature of women's sport, sports leaders invested heavily in a particularly powerful, ahistorical image of sport. Citing Pierre de Coubertin's, IOC President Avery Brundage's and the International Amateur Athletic Federation's images of "the spirit of sport," sport leaders continually drew upon an ahistorical, idealist image of "sport," to support the restrictions they would impose on all those who took part in the Cold War Games. That strategy and the relevant images are still used today.

The World Anti-Doping Agency (WADA), for example, argues that in its battle against certain performance-enhancing substances, it is preserving "what is intrinsically valuable about sport." WADA claims to be protecting "the spirit of sport" which it claims "is the celebration of the human spirit, body and mind."[45] But "sport," in its real material existence, is not an ahistorical abstraction. Sport is a socio-politically established set of real human practices that are constituted and reconstituted within particular socio-historical conditions. One cannot make sound policy or play a genuinely progressive role in the development of high-performance sport without struggling with the contemporary reality of high-performance sport as it is currently practiced. All attempts to force sport to conform to some abstract ideal are ultimately misguided and serve only the interests of those who benefit from the status quo.

The current legacy of the Cold War Games from the perspective of the West includes frightening images of Nazi-inspired communist expansionism, "roid-raging behemoths," and "ball-bearing" females. Only one of those images was ever really critically deconstructed and that was due to forces outside the world of sport. It is not a legacy that many can look back upon with pride.

The long-term and lasting legacy of the Cold War Games could be different: it could entail a commitment to the detailed, critical, socio-historical analysis of high-performance sport as it has actually emerged over the course of the twentieth century. This legacy could involve athletes, sport enthusiasts, and sport scholars who are committed to shaping the world of sport on the basis of the full knowledge of its socio-political reality rather than the commercially motivated images of the sports leaders and politicians of today. If people move beyond dominant imagery and politically inspired definitions to the real world of high-performance sport, the consequences of that action and the changes they would bring would be very real, and would appropriately close the chapter on the Cold War Games.

Notes

1   On the reality and images associated with the Second World War, see E.J. Hobsbawm, *The Age of Extremes: The Short Twentieth Century, 1914–1991* (London: Michael Joseph, 1994) and O. Bartov, *Germany's War and the Holocaust* (Ithaca: Cornell University Press, 2003).

2   See C. Browning, *Ordinary Men: Reserve Police Battalion 101 and the Final Solution in Poland* (New York: HarperCollins, 1992), O. Bartov, *Hitler's Army: Soldiers, Nazis, and War in the Third Reich* (New York: Oxford University Press, 1991), E. Johnson, *Nazi Terror: The Gestapo, Jews, and Ordinary Germans* (New York: Basic Books, 2001) and A. Beevor, *The Fall of Berlin, 1945* (New York: Viking Penguin, 2002).

3   See C. Lawton, *Hiroshima: The Story of the First Atom Bomb* (Cambridge, Mass.: Candlewick Press, 2004), D. Goldstein, *Rain of Ruin* (Washington D.C.: Brassey, 1994).

4   A. Speer, *Erinnerungen* [Memoirs] (Berlin: Verlag Ullstein, 1969), p. 522. To contextualize Speer's comments, see G. Sereny, *Albert Speer: His Battle with Truth* (New York: Alfred A. Knopf, 1995) and J. Fest, *Speer: The Final Verdict*, trans. Ewald Osers and Alexandra Dring (London: Weidenfeld and Nicolson, 2001).

5   See G. Kolko, *The Politics of War* (New York: Pantheon Books, 1990).

6   To understand the extent to which ordinary Germans internalized Nazi's ideology see, V. Klemperer, *I Will Bear Witness: A Diary of the Nazi Years* (New York: The Modern Library, 1998, 1999, 2 Vols) and R. Shandley (ed.), *Unwilling Germans? The Goldhagen Debate* (Minneapolis: University of Minnesota Press, 1998).

7   See I. Kershaw, *Hitler, 1889–1936: Hubris* (New York: Norton Books, 1999).

8   See A. Hitler, *Mein Kampf* [My Struggle] (translated under the auspices of A. Johnson, New York: Reynal and Hitchcock, 1939), pp. 243–69; 303–88, 389–455; 116–62. See also I. Kershaw, *The Hitler Myth: Image and Reality in the Third Reich* (New York: Oxford University Press, 1987) and D. Welch, *The Third Reich: Politics and Propaganda* (New York: Routledge, 1993), pp. 50–89.

9   See T. Clark, *Art and Propaganda in the Twentieth Century* (New York: Calmann and King, 1997) and Speer, *Erinnerungen* [Memoirs], pp. 103–11.

10 See R.D. Mandell, *The Nazi Olympics* (New York: Ballantine Books, 1971) and A. Krüger, *Die Olympischen Spiele 1936 und die Weltmeinung: Ihre aussenpolitische Bedeutung unter besonderer Berücksichtigung der USA* [The 1936 Olympic Games and World Opinion: Their Importance in Foreign Politics with Special Reference to the USA] (Frankfurt/M: Bartels & Wernitz, 1972).

11   On the 30 January 1933 torch procession see Kershaw, *The Hitler Myth*, p. 48.
12   Mandell, *The Nazi Olympics*, p. 312; see also Speer's almost identical description of the effect created at the 1934 Nuremberg Party Rally (Speer, *Erinnerungen*, pp. 96–7).
13   On the similarities between the Nazis and Soviet regimes, see H. Arendt's *The Origins of Totalitarianism* (New York: Harcourt, Brace, 1951), C.J. Friedrich (ed.), *Totalitarianism* (Cambridge, MA: Harvard University Press, 1954) and I. Kershaw and M. Lewin, *Stalinism and Nazism: Dictatorships in Comparison* (Cambridge: Cambridge University Press, 1997).
14   N. Wade, "Anabolic Steroids: Doctors Denounce them, but Athletes Aren't Listening," *Science*, 176 (June 1976), 1400.
15   See R. Windsor and D. Dimitru, "Anabolic Steroids," *Postgraduate Medicine*, 84, 4 (September 1988), pp. 41–2. The Silverman reference is cited in T. Todd, "Anabolic Steroids: the Gremlins of Sport," *Journal of Sport History*, 14, 1 (Spring 1987), 93, n.25. Todd also found the allegation in W. Taylor, "The Case Against the Administration of HGH to Normal Children," presented at the symposium *Ethical Issues in the Treatment of Children and Athletes with Human Growth Hormone*, University of Texas at Austin, 26 April 1986.
16   V. Cowart, "Steroids and Sport: After 4 Decades Time to Return Genie to the Bottle," *Journal of the American Medical Association*, 257, 4 (1987), p. 423.
17   Todd, "Anabolic Steroids," argues that Taylor gained his knowledge of the Nazi use of steroids from Dennis Breo's "Hitler's Final Days Recalled by Physician," *American Medical News*, 11 October (1985). The only relevant reference in Ernst Schenck's interview of his exhaustive study of Theodore Morell's detailed notes is one to Morell's treatment of Hitler's Parkinson's in 1944: "Dr. Morell used the standard medication, belladonna drops, to quiet the tremors, and he also used a testosterone derivative, which was irrational" (p. 40).
18   See, for example, H. Haupt and G. Rovere, "Anabolic Steroids: A Review of the Literature," *The American Journal of Sports Medicine*, 12, 6 (1984), 469; L. Surtees, "Paying the Price … Later," *The Globe and Mail*, 1 April (1989), D1; J. Gomez, "Performance-Enhancing Substances in Adolescent Athletes," *Texas Medicine*, Symposium on Adolescent Health (Feb. 2002) (www.texmed.org/ata/nrm/tme/ texmedfeb02_performance_enhancers.asp) or "Steroids" (2003) (www.electronicref- erences. com/view.php/English/Steroids.htm) "RAW REMARKS: Steroids – Wonder Drug of Wrestling," (http://www.wrestlingdotcom.com/columns/55482600.php).
19   B. Berendonk, *Doping Dokumente: Von der Forschung zum Betrug* [Doping Documents: From Research to Deceit] (Berlin: Springer-Verlag, 1991), p. 227.
20   S. Ungerleider, *Faust's Gold: Inside the East German Doping Machine* (New York: St Martin's Press, 2001), p. 45. See O. Bartov, *Hitler's Army*; A. Beevor, *Stalingrad* (London: Penguin Books, 1999) and Beevor, *The Fall of Berlin* for accurate, factual- ly based, scholarly accounts of German troop behaviour on the Eastern Front.
21   See Berendonk, *Doping Dokumente*, p. 91, "DDR-Staatsplanthema 14.25 – Das Manhattan- Project des Sports" [GDR-State Research Program 14.25 – the Manhattan Project of Sport].
22   B. Goldman, *Death in the Locker Room* (South Bend: Icarus Press, 1984), p. 2.
23   On both this point and the false accusations that men had been clandestinely enter- ing women's events, see I. Ritchie, "Sex Tested, Gender Verified: Controlling Female Sexuality in the Age of Containment," *Sport History Review*, 34, 1 (2003), pp. 80–98.
24   T. Laqueur, *Making Sex: Body and Gender From the Greeks to Freud* (Cambridge/London: Harvard University Press, 1990). See also J. Hood-Williams, "Goodbye to Sex and Gender," *The Sociological Review*, 44, 1 (1996), pp. 1–16.

25   C.L. Cole, "Resisting the Canon: Feminist Cultural Studies, Sport, and Technologies of the Body," in S. Birrell and C.L. Cole (eds), *Women, Sport and Culture* (Champaign, IL: Human Kinetics, 1994), p. 15.

26   Cited in E.W. Gerber, "Chronicle of Participation," in E. Gerber, J. Felshin, P. Berlin and W. Wyrick (eds), *The American Woman in Sport* (Reading, MA: Addison-Wesley, 1974), p. 137. See also C.E. Russett, *Sexual Science: The Victorian Construction of Womanhood* (Cambridge: Harvard University Press, 1989).

27   John Hoberman, "Toward a Theory of Olympic Internationalism," *Journal of Sport History* 22:1 (Spring 1995), pp. 9–10.

28   See, for example, M.A. Hall, *The Girl and the Game: A History of Women's Sport in Canada* (Peterborough, Ontario: Broadview Press, 2002); S. Cahn, *Coming on Strong: Gender and Sexuality in Twentieth-Century Women's Sport* (New York: The Free Press, 1994) or J. Hargreaves, *Sporting Females: Critical Issues in the History and Sociology of Women's Sports* (London: Routledge, 1994).

29   S. Cahn, "Crushes, Competition, and Closets: The Emergence of Homophobia in Women's Physical Education," in Birrell and Cole (eds), *Women in Sport and Culture*, pp. 327–39.

30   S. Cahn, "Crushes, Competition, and Closets," pp. 329–30.

31   Ibid., pp. 327–39.

32   See J. Terry, "Lesbians Under the Medical Gaze: Scientists Search for Remarkable Differences," *The Journal of Sex Research*, 27, 3 (1990), pp. 317–39.

33   Cahn, *Coming on Strong*, pp. 23–6.

34   S. Cahn, "Crushes, Competition, and Closets," p. 334.

35   See, for example, B. Anderson, *Imagined Communities: Reflections on the Origin and Spread of Nationalism* (London/New York: Verso, 1995), E.T. May, *Homeward Bound: American Families in the Cold War Era* (New York: Basic Books, 1988), A. Parker, M. Russo, D. Sommer and P. Yaeger (eds), *Nationalisms and Sexuality* (New York/London: Routledge, 1992) or S. Jeffords, *The Remasculinization of America: Gender and the Vietnam War* (Bloomington/Indianapolis: Indiana University Press, 1989).

36   May, *Homeward Bound*, p. 11.

37   Ibid., p. 16–19.

38   "Are Girl Athletes Really Girls?" *Life*, (7 Oct. 1966), pp. 63–6.

39   M.A. Ferguson-Smith and Elizabeth Ferris, "Gender Verification in Sport: The Need for Change?" *British Journal of Sports Medicine* 25:1 (1991), p. 17.

40   See Ritchie, "Sex Tested, Gender Verified," p. 91.

41   R.G. Bunge, "Sex and the Olympic Games," *Journal of the American Medical Association (JAMA)*, 173, 12 (1960), 196.

42   On the interrelationship between drug testing and sex testing, see C.L. Cole, "Testing for Sex or Drugs?" *Journal of Sport & Social Issues*, 24, 4 (2000), 331–3 and L.R. Davis and L.C. Delano, "Fixing the Boundaries of Physical Gender: Side Effects of Anti-Drug Campaigns on Athletics," *Sociology of Sport Journal*, 9, 1 (1992), pp. 1–19.

43   Cited in Goldman, *Death in the Locker Room*, 81; emphasis in the original.

44   W.I. Thomas and F. Znaniecki, *The Polish Peasant in Europe and America* (New York: Knopf, 1918), p. 79.

45   World Anti-Doping Agency, *World Anti-Doping Code* (Version 3.0, 2003), www.wadaama.org/docs/web/standards_harmonization/code/code_v3.pdf, p. 7.

Chapter 2

Verbal gymnastics

Sports, bureacracy, and the Soviet Union's entrance into the Olympic Games, 1946–1952

Jenifer Parks

On July 18, 1954, the Soviet Union observed its yearly celebration of "youth, strength, health and beauty," the All-Union Day of the Athlete, with special style and spectacle, for this year the Soviets welcomed Avery Brundage, President of the International Olympic Committee (IOC), to their carefully organized festival. Images from the event remained etched in Brundage's mind for years to come, including some seventy high-bar routines performed in unison in a line across the field, and an eight-story human pyramid that resembled "a living bouquet of beautiful flowers." Several events were even presented against a twenty-five foot high "solid wall of water … extending the full length of the stadium." Brundage would later declare that this five-hour carnival of sport "far surpassed in magnitude and beauty anything of its kind,"[1] calling it the "greatest of all festivals of sport and physical culture."[2] Brundage, a conservative, anti-Communist, self-made businessman from Middle America, became a leading voice in praise of the Soviet sports system. His attitude toward his Soviet counterparts had changed dramatically from just two years earlier, when he was the leading voice against the Soviet Union's entrance into the Olympic Games.

Their entrance, during the first years of the Cold War, brought to light underlying tensions between Olympic philosophy, Soviet Communist ideology, and the political goals of the Soviet leadership. While the Olympic ideal promoted peace and understanding among nations, the Soviet leaders saw Olympic participation as an opportunity to show the world the superior technique and training achieved by the Soviet system. Western Olympic organizers assumed a fundamental connection between Olympic ideals and Western-style capitalist democracy, viewing the Soviet system as creating professional athletes, while Soviet organizers saw the IOC's amateurism as an attempt to exclude workers. Furthermore, by entering the Olympic Games in 1952, the Soviet Union broke with the Communist interpretation of sport that favored mass, collective physical culture over competitive, individual sport, which Soviet organizers saw as elitist. How did the Soviet Union come to enter the Olympics in July 1952, given the country's previous opposition to the Olympic Movement, and why did the IOC allow the Soviet Union to enter despite the perceived threat the USSR represented to fundamental Olympic ideals?

My study finds that the Soviet sports administration and sportsmen–bureaucrats played a key role in overcoming these differences, making possible the Soviet entrance into the Olympic Games. In this essay, I examine the pressures the sportsmen–bureaucrats encountered from the Soviet leadership and the international sporting community, and the means they used to negotiate the repressive Soviet system in order to send a team to the Olympic Games. Comparing Soviet internal correspondence with Western sources reveals an unlikely affinity of bureaucratic expediency between Soviet organizers and members of the IOC that helped both sides to overcome the Cold War-induced ideological conflict.

This essay takes advantage of a recently published collection of documents containing sources from the State Archive of the Russian Federation (GARF) and the former Communist Party archive (RGASPI) dealing with the deliberations behind the decision to enter the Olympics.[3] Compiled by Aksel' Vartanian, a Russian sports journalist and respected authority on Soviet and Russian soccer, the collection includes correspondence between members of the IOC, the chairman of the Olympic Organizing Committee in Helsinki, leaders of the USSR Committee for Physical Culture and Sport and the Soviet National Olympic Committee, and members of the Central Committee of the Communist Party and Politburo.[4] I also consider IOC correspondence housed in the Avery Brundage Collection at the University of Illinois.[5] Through analysis of these archival materials I consider the evolution of attitudes surrounding the Soviet Olympic project and the changing relations between the Soviet organizers and the IOC that allowed for the Soviet entrance into the Games.

Soviet Russia and international sports before World War II

On November 25, 1892, French aristocrat Baron Pierre de Coubertin introduced to a gathering of French and foreign dignitaries the idea of reviving the Olympic Games of Ancient Greece. Founded on commonly held ideas of nineteenth-century Western liberalism, this modern Olympic Movement idealized individual liberty within the context of the modern nation-state. Although Coubertin hoped to build a better world through the internationalization of sport, his idealism masked attitudes of superiority characteristic of his socio-economic milieu.[6] Olympic historian John Hoberman compares Coubertin's Olympic Movement to other "idealistic internationalist" movements of the late nineteenth century such as the Red Cross International, the Esperanto movement, Scouting organizations, and the International Council of Women. As Hoberman observes, these organizations possessed "a core repertory of behaviors and attitudes" including Eurocentrism, political neutrality, wealth and aristocratic affiliations, pacifism, and a "problematic relationship between national and international loyalties."[7] Founded in the decades leading up to World War I and motivated by "deep feelings among Europeans that were rooted in anxieties about war and peace," these movements represented for their conservative organizers apolitical and universal remedies to increasing international tensions.[8] Such organizations, the IOC especially, took on an anti-socialist bias as growing worker unrest fueled fears of war and revolution. IOC members probably saw the Russian Revolution as the fulfillment of their worst fears, and their attitudes toward "Soviet Russia" in the twenties and thirties presaged the Cold War tensions that would complicate the Soviet Union's Olympic entrance after World War II.

Nor did Soviet leaders seek Olympic participation in the decades after World War I. Throughout the 1920s, Soviet sports theorists perceived international competitive sports, including the Olympic Games, as elitist and "bourgeois." This class-based view of Olympic sport was not without foundation. Promoting upper-class notions of leisure and sport, Olympic founders distinguished between elite, amateur sport, and professional, worker or lower-class sport.[9] To counteract what they saw as an attempt to prevent workers from competing, Soviet leaders rejected the Olympic Movement and formed the Red Sport International (*Sportintern*) to promote revolutionary class consciousness abroad through athletic meets with Communist sporting organizations.[10]

By the early 1930s, however, presumably to increase their influence in Europe, Soviet leaders encouraged sports organizers to take advantage of the mass appeal of sporting matches and to strengthen the "progressive" (i.e. socialist) elements in national sports federations.[11] A 1933 mandate to "catch up and overtake bourgeois records" strengthened the move toward integration with Western sports, and sports organizers began to implement European tactics and training methods.[12] Numerous sporting exchanges with European nations followed between 1933 and 1938 when the All-Union Committee on Physical Culture and Sport (Sports Committee) applied for permission to join several international sports federations.[13] Yet progress toward joining the international sporting world was immediately halted when the top Soviet governing body, the Politburo, denied the petition after the top-ranked soccer team from the Basque region of Spain defeated six out of seven Soviet teams on a visit in 1937.[14] So, on the eve of World War II, the Soviet leadership severely curtailed international competition as sports officials, athletes, and trainers became victims of the "great terror" when the secret police killed, imprisoned, and exiled millions of Soviet citizens. Participation in the Olympic Games was not on the Soviet Union's political agenda in the years leading to war.

"One rotten apple": amateurism and anxiety in the IOC

While the spirit of unity engendered by the combined Allied defeat of Nazism encouraged many in international sporting circles to seek to bring the Soviet Union into the Olympic Movement in the early post-war years, others feared that Soviet athletics presented a serious challenge to the fundamental ideals of Olympism. If the IOC were to live up to the Olympic ideals of internationalism and maintain its prestige, Avery Brundage, then vice-president of the IOC, admitted, "it [was] necessary that National Olympic Committees be organized in all countries as soon as possible."[15] In this spirit, Lord Burghley, IOC member from Great Britain, visited the Soviet Union in 1947 to encourage the country's participation in the London Games of 1948.[16] On his visit, the Soviet sports committee treated the English visitor to an elaborate Physical Culture Day parade featuring over 20,000 athletes, in an attempt to garner support for Soviet sports internationally.[17] With the reputation of the IOC at stake, Brundage and IOC President Sigfried Edstrom agreed that "young athletes all over Europe [were] crazy to have the Russian athletes participate,"[18] but grew increasingly concerned about articles that had begun to appear in the Western press about the state-run sporting system in the USSR, involving material rewards for athletes who broke records and showed superior results in competition.[19]

This news fueled a debate already raging within the IOC over amateurism. In 1947, a special IOC committee headed by Avery Brundage defined an amateur as

> one whose connection with sport is and always has been solely for pleasure and for physical, mental and social benefits he derives therefrom and to whom sport is nothing more than recreation without material gain of any kind, direct or indirect.[20]

This definition seemed incompatible with the Soviet system where, according to Edstrom, "athletes who are intended for participation in international sport matches are concentrated in training camps ... freed from their jobs, are well paid by the governments and receive – with their families – more and special food."[21] The first hurdle to overcome was the Soviet practice of offering monetary incentives to athletes who broke international records. The Soviet Union ceased giving out cash prizes to athletes in July 1947, but the IOC remained convinced that Soviet athletes were professionals paid by the state and worried that athletes from elsewhere in eastern Europe would have similar state support.[22]

Perceiving astutely that a decision either way could damage the IOC's reputation, Brundage implored Edstrom:

> I urge you to use the utmost care in dealing with the countries behind the iron curtain ... We cannot keep them out but we can be prepared to be just as tough as they are in enforcing our rules and regulations. One rotten apple can do a great deal of damage to the rest of the barrel.[23]

Unable to reconcile the Soviet Union's possible entrance with the Olympic amateur ideal, Brundage found refuge in the IOC's bureaucratic process. Before the Soviet Union formed a National Olympic Committee (NOC) and petitioned the IOC for recognition in 1951, Brundage could avoid dealing with the challenge to the Olympic amateur ideal and focus instead on the more clearly defined rules of the IOC under which no country lacking a National Olympic Committee would be invited to participate in the Olympic Games.[24] Edstrom now made several attempts to persuade Nikolai Romanov, chairman of the Soviet Sports Committee, that the Soviet Union would be allowed to participate in the Olympic Games only if it followed IOC rules and formed a National Olympic Committee.[25] The many missives Edstrom sent to Romanov went unanswered, creating further anxiety for the IOC president and vice-president. Hearing nothing from their Soviet contact, Edstrom and Brundage worried that the Soviet Union might cause embarrassment to the IOC by sending a delegation to Helsinki with or without official recognition. Reminding Edstrom of the Soviet Union's unexpected appearance at the 1946 European Track and Field Championships in Oslo, Brundage stated:

> It would not surprise me if they tried the same stunt at Helsinki in 1952 … Not only the IOC but also our Finnish friends must be prepared for this contingency in order to avoid finding ourselves in the middle of a most embarrassing and dangerous controversy.[26]

Romanov's silence, however, had more to do with indecision within the Soviet party-state bureaucracy than with a plot to enter the Olympics on their own terms.

"If you are not ready …": internal retreat and the need for total victory

Romanov and the other Soviet sports leaders would have to balance demands from the international sporting organizations and the IOC with conditions placed upon them by the Soviet leadership, if the Olympic project were to be realized. How could they make the Soviet-style sports system conform to international standards while promoting the ideological and political goals of Stalin and the Central Committee? Soviet sports administrators promoted the Olympic Games as an arena in which to prove the superiority of socialist sporting methods and the Soviet system, but the receptiveness of the Politburo to Olympic participation remained ambiguous in the immediate post-war years. As sports organizers enquired about the possibility of participating in the 1948 London Games, Soviet leaders pursued an internal policy of anti-Westernism and xenophobia that made international competition of any kind hard to justify.

In 1947, Nikolai Romanov, in a letter to Politburo member Andrei Zhdanov, asked permission to prepare a Soviet team for the 1948 Olympic Games, stressing the huge popularity of the Games throughout the world, the increasing number of countries joining the Olympics, and the idealized message of the Olympic Movement to justify his request.[27] According to Romanov, Stalin believed that even the second place finish of Soviet wrestlers at the 1946 European Championships could discredit the Soviet Union and chastised Romanov for sending a team to the competition: "if you are not ready, then there's no need to participate."[28] From this exchange, Romanov drew the lesson that only the guarantee of first place would induce the Soviet leadership to send athletes to compete abroad. Following Stalin's cue, Romanov couched his request to send a team to the 1948 Olympics in terms of "total team victory." Since Soviet athletes could reasonably hope only for second, third, or fourth place in events such as track and field, boxing, and swimming, where the United States held prominence, Romanov conceded that the Soviet Union could not surpass the United States in medals. Reporting to Zhdanov in 1947 that competing nations observed an unofficial point system based on the first six places in each event, he asserted nonetheless that by competing in every sport on the program and placing in the top six in those sports the Soviet team could secure full team victory based on the "unofficial" points system.[29]

Unfortunately, Romanov wrote these letters just as Zhdanov initiated an ideological campaign against "kowtowing to the West" and the Stalinist leadership purged from their posts, arrested, and imprisoned people for having ties with the West or affinities with Western culture. Student athletes were expelled from prominent sports institutes, and sports educators, scientists, and other officials were arrested during this time.[30] After Zhdanov's death in August 1948, his enemies within the Politburo, Georgii Malenkov and Lavrentii Beria, orchestrated a purge of Zhdanov's former associates in the Leningrad Party apparatus. The increasing influence of Beria, Malenkov, and Mikhail Suslov, who had taken over Zhdanov's position as agitation and propaganda minister, ushered in a period of increasing uncertainty for the Soviet sports program. Before the 1948 World Speed Skating Championships in Helsinki, Romanov cautioned the Politburo not to send a team because he doubted the athletes' chances of a successful performance. The skaters then sent a letter to the Central Committee and the Soviet Council of Ministers denouncing Romanov's position and requesting that they be allowed to compete. The skaters' assurances that they stood to win first place were accepted over Romanov's continued objections, and the team competed, achieving mixed results. Soon after the competition, Nikolai Apollonov, then deputy security chief and head of the secret police run sports club, *Dinamo*, took over as chairman of the sports committee.[31]

The next few years saw contradictory impulses within the Soviet leadership to gain knowledge and expertise from Western countries while isolating its people from foreign influences. International meets occurred rarely during this time as Apollonov's Sports Committee shifted its emphasis away from international competition toward developing a mass participatory sports program.[32] While Romanov had proposed that Soviet athletes face more foreign competitors to prepare for participation in the 1948 Olympics, Apollonov asked only that the Central Committee allow a group of forty-one sports experts to attend an "Olympic Congress" of international sports organizations during the London Games.[33] In the end, the contingent arrived ten days after the start of the congress and comprised only ten experts. Gleb Baklanov, who coordinated physical training for the military at this time, headed the delegation. According to him, the deputy chairman of the Physical Culture Committee detained the group in his office in Moscow and questioned them about their delegation, letting them go only after receiving a phone call. Baklanov did not give the name of the caller but implied that it was a high-ranking Soviet official. Whether this episode is an example of miscommunication or indecision on the part of the Soviet leadership is hard to say, but Baklanov believed it meant that someone important did not want them to go.[34] While the Central Committee issued a resolution in December 1948, charging all sports committees to "help Soviet athletes win world supremacy in major sports in the immediate future,"[35] demonstrating support for Olympic participation, until Romanov's reinstatement as chairman of the Sports Committee in 1951, preparations for Olympic competition appear to have been a low priority for the Central Committee.[36] As a result, when Olympic training began in earnest in 1951, the Sports Committee had to resort to Soviet-style *shturmovshchina* or a rushed, sporadic production spurt.

"Who do we know in Russia?" The Soviet Union joins the "Olympic family"

The 1948 London Games took place as the Soviet Union began to consolidate its sphere of influence in eastern Europe by intensifying its political and ideological control over the region.[37] Promoting a united Communist front in a global confrontation with the West, Soviet leaders hoped to exert influence on international sports organizations through a coordinated effort with eastern European representatives. This goal came into direct conflict with the prevailing effort of the IOC to try to combat nationalism within the Olympic family. The Soviet Union did not introduce a highly nationalistic atmosphere into IOC debates but, rather, the Soviet Union's entrance in the early years of the Cold War took this already present trend to a new ideological level. More importantly, forging new contacts within the Soviet Union represented a challenge to the IOC's traditional way of conducting its affairs.

Officially, IOC members represent the interests of the Olympic Movement to their native countries and do not serve as their nations' representatives to the IOC. Fearing an unwelcome intrusion of state interests, the IOC sought to maintain its independence from state politics by carefully choosing its representatives in Communist countries. As Brundage warned IOC secretary Otto Mayer: "it is essential that we use the utmost care in selecting our representatives to these nations, which are really no longer independent."[38] Edstrom and Brundage's fears that "a coming National Olympic Committee in Soviet-Russia will be a state organization"[39] were well founded. Once formed, the Soviet NOC was headed by Konstantin Andrianov, who also served as vice-chairman of the Soviet Sports Committee. Likewise, the eventual secretary of the Soviet NOC was also head of international sporting relations for the Sports Committee. How could it be otherwise in a centralized economy? The Olympic ideal of an independent movement free from government interference was fundamentally incompatible with the Soviet style of governing.

The real problem, however, was that the IOC traditionally perpetuated itself through social networks that did not extend to the Soviet Union. As Brundage complained: "Aside from all this who do we know in Russia?"[40] Edstrom too agonized over this question, declaring: "The greatest trouble will be to find men that we can have present in the IOC. I do not feel inclined to go so far as to admit communists there."[41] Unlike many of his colleagues, Brundage lacked an aristocratic pedigree, having risen to a position of wealth and prominence through business. This self-made man, however, betrayed the "gentlemen's club" mentality of the IOC when, in a circular letter to IOC members, he waxed nostalgic over the days when

> the care exercised in the selection of the individuals who composed the IOC produced members who, no matter where they came from or what their language, were of the same general type and they were soon welded into what has so often been called the "Olympic Family."[42]

In Brundage's view, the Soviets, "not understanding fair play, good sportsmanship and amateurism," were obviously not of "the same general type" as the current IOC members and would "bring with them nothing but trouble."[43]

Yet the questions over the amateur status of Soviet athletes and the threat of state interference in IOC affairs proved less significant when the matter of accepting a Soviet NOC and Soviet member to the IOC came to a vote.[44] In April 1951, Petr Sobolev sent a telegram to the IOC as secretary of the newly formed Soviet National Olympic Committee, requesting official recognition.[45] It is not clear why, after years of indecision, the Soviets finally decided to form a NOC, but the timing of Sobolev's request roughly corresponds to Romanov's reinstatement as Sports Committee chairman, suggesting that Romanov was instrumental in the decision.[46] The IOC discussed the matter in May. Sobolev's telegram illustrates a keen awareness on the part of Soviet sports administrators of the issues at stake. Earlier attempts by the Soviet Union to gain membership of international federations had included requests for representation on the governing body, that Russian be made one of the official languages, and that "fascist Spain" be excluded from membership.[47] The telegram requesting recognition by the IOC presented no such demands, but stated simply: "We inform you that an Olympic Committee was created in the USSR. This Olympic Committee has examined the rules of the IOC and declares them accepted."[48] Reiterating his concerns over the professional status of Soviet athletes, Brundage presented a full dossier of the reports he had circulated previously on the condition of sports in the USSR. Another committee member suggested that the Soviet NOC be required to present its rules and regulations in order to make sure they conformed to those of the IOC. Lord Burghley of Great Britain, impressed by the elaborate sports parade he had witnessed on his visit to Moscow in 1947, proved to be a leading supporter of the Soviet NOC's recognition. Arguing that they had never asked this of other nations, he spoke out against investigating Soviet sports regulations. Burghley convinced the other members by appealing to the traditions and ideals of the Olympic Movement, stating that "the peace making and international conception of the IOC gives us an obligation to welcome [the Soviet] sportsmen." Ultimately, the IOC members decided to rely on Sobolev's assurances and recognized the Soviet Union's Olympic Committee by a vote of thirty-one in favor with three abstentions and no opposing votes.

Once the Soviet NOC was recognized, the IOC members considered the nomination of Andrianov as a member of the IOC. Oddly enough, there was no discussion over Andrianov's independence from government control or his ability to represent the ideals of the IOC in the Soviet Union.[49] Once Edstrom gave his personal assurance that Andrianov held great influence on sports in the Soviet Union as an athlete and sports official, the only objection was that he spoke neither French nor English, the official languages of the IOC. Once again, Lord Burghley came to the Soviet delegate's defense, declaring that Andrianov was a true sportsman and "that is much more important for us than knowledge of languages."[50] R. W. Seeldrayers, IOC member from Belgium, answered Brundage's declaration that no "stranger" in the form of an interpreter be allowed in private IOC sessions by asserting that other members who spoke Russian could assist Andrianov during meetings. The ease with which the IOC recognized Soviet membership and ratified Andrianov's nomination may seem unexpected, but it reveals the importance of personal ties for securing a positive vote within the IOC. With Edstrom's and Burghley's assurances that they knew Andrianov personally as an athlete and sports official and Seeldrayers' promise that other members would facilitate communication with their new Russian colleague, the IOC members welcomed Konstantin Andrianov into their "Olympic Family" with a vote of twenty-four in favor with five against and five blank ballots.

"Thanks to Great Comrade Stalin": Soviet bureaucracy, the Politburo, and Olympic preparations

Despite the election of Andrianov to the IOC and the recognition of the Soviet NOC, the Soviet leadership continued to withhold permission for a team to be sent to the Games: invitations to compete in both the winter Games in Oslo and the Helsinki Summer Games remained unanswered. As budget constraints and continued avoidance of foreign sporting contacts further jeopardized the Olympic project, Romanov relied heavily on Andrianov and other leaders within the Sports Committee to maintain control over Olympic training measures. In June 1951, the official invitation to participate in the 1952 winter Games set off a flurry of in-house memos and reports deliberating on the Soviet athletes' chances of success.[51] With the decision to compete in either the winter or summer Games still up in the air, Andrianov called on various departments in the sports apparatus to compare their athletes' achievements to those of foreign athletes to assess the state of Olympic training.[52] Setting November 1, 1951, as the deadline, Andrianov hoped to gather all necessary information so that a decision could be reached regarding Olympic participation.

After Romanov decided not to send a team to the winter Games, trainers and department heads tried to make their voices heard through letters to Romanov, Propaganda Minister Mikail Suslov, and even to Stalin's son and personal secretary Vasilii Iosifovich, defending their athletes' preparedness and thereby their personal efforts to train them successfully. For instance, the head of the Department of Skating, Z. V. Kuchmenko, admonished Romanov to reconsider sending skaters to the Olympics because of a "full possibility of a successful appearance in the upcoming Olympic Games."[53] He proclaimed that his skaters had earned the chance to participate in the elite international arena and that the time had come to realize the Central Committee Resolution of 1948. Referencing the resolution of the Central Committee and acknowledging that the "success of Soviet athletes raises the authority and power of the Soviet state even higher,"[54] Kuchmenko couched his appeal within the stated party goals. The head of the Department of International Sporting Affairs, Sobolev, also petitioned Romanov on behalf of Soviet hockey players, insisting that the hockey team had the opportunity to win first place or at least second or third place, thereby increasing the likelihood of the Soviet Union taking the top team spot.[55] Recognizing that success in only one event would not induce the leadership to send a team, Sobolev emphasized the importance of winning a full team victory and requested that Romanov prepare not only a hockey team, but also skaters and skiers to ensure that victory. Sobolev, like Kuchmenko, demonstrated his bureaucratic skill by situating his project within the stated objectives of the Soviet leadership and employing the language of his superior, Romanov.

Not sharing the optimism of his subordinates, Romanov explained to Georgii Malenkov in January 1952 that, without the assurance that the Soviet Union could achieve all-out victory, the Sports Committee "believe[s] that participation in the Olympic Games is pointless."[56] After his report, the leaders of the All-Union Hockey Section and the All-Union Trainer for Hockey along with the coaches of four hockey teams went over Romanov's head to Suslov and urged him to reconsider sending a hockey team to Oslo. The head of the All-Union Skiing Section, the state skiing trainer, and the vice-chairman of the Department of International Sporting Relations sent Suslov a similar plea on January 14. Both letters invoked the Party Resolution of 1948, referring to the "historic decision of the Central Committee." In addition, the authors of these letters used almost identical wording to declare that not sending their respective athletes would be an egregious political mistake.[57] It seems from the formulaic nature of their petitions that these coaches and trainers employed a recognized set of phrases to support their athletes and defend their own positions within the sports apparatus. It also could suggest a coordinated effort to undermine Romanov's authority. These appeals got Suslov's attention: he asked Romanov to re-examine this question.[58]

Unlike the World Skating Championships in 1948 when Romanov's objections to competing were overruled, this time Suslov gave Romanov the opportunity to justify his decision, and Romanov successfully rebuffed the skating and skiing administrators.[59] Romanov's second refusal to reconsider the winter Olympic bid elicited a final entreaty from his underlings, and this time they went right to the top. In a letter to Stalin's son and personal secretary, chairman of the Department of International Sporting Relations Sobolev and his vice-chairman Senkevich argued that Romanov's estimation of Soviet chances was wrong, but that even a second or third place finish would enhance the Soviet Union's image abroad. Furthermore, they warned that "refusal to participate in the Winter Olympics would be widely used in the bourgeois press to promote hostility toward the Soviet Union ... [and] cause us even more damage than an unsuccessful performance."[60] Sobolev and Senkevich made a surprisingly bold move.[61] Speaking out against Romanov, they asserted that the goal of securing full team victory was unnecessary. That they were willing to declare openly their disagreement with the fundamental rationale for Olympic participation betrays a striking degree of maneuverability within the Stalinist system. These appeals by the winter sports administrators could reflect an effort to maintain the committee's attention and resources, but by emphasizing the potential benefits of winning only second or third place, Sobolev and Senkevich acknowledged the relative weakness of Soviet winter sports and very probably undermined their own efforts. That this last petition went unheeded demonstrates that Romanov, gauging correctly that total victory was the only goal, enjoyed the support of important members of the Soviet leadership.

Romanov and the sports administrators now had to guarantee a full team victory under continued restrictions on international competition, and Soviet sports leaders struggled with the question of international experience almost to the eve of the Soviet Olympic debut. On April 30, 1952, less than two months before the opening of the Games in Helsinki, Romanov wrote to Malenkov requesting that the Ministry of Internal Affairs (MVD) provide information to the Sport Committee about the Olympic training of foreign athletes, specifically those from the USA, England, Switzerland, and France.[62] This request strongly suggests that the dearth of foreign sporting contacts continued in the months leading up to the Helsinki Olympics, forcing Romanov to obtain through the MVD what his committee had been unable to get through international competition and trainer exchanges. Working under political and ideological constraints, trainers and bureaucrats maintained their call for more international meets, tried to find out as much as possible about foreign sporting activities, and did everything they could to prepare their athletes.

Romanov's position proved more significant as preparations began in earnest for the Helsinki Games and his committee responded to demands from the Politburo, trainers, and international sporting bodies. In the months leading up to the Helsinki Games, Romanov convinced his superiors in the Politburo to augment the Sports Committee's budget and to fund Olympic training. In February 1952, Politburo member Mikhail Suslov authorized the ministries and departments to release all Olympic athletes from work and school with pay for the six months leading up to the Games and to send doctors and nurses to the training camps. In addition, Suslov endorsed an increase in the number of athletes by 200 and the hiring of another 55 employees to the central administration of the Sports Committee.[63] Then, in May, Romanov appealed to Malenkov for an increase in the daily food expenditure from 50 to 65 rubles for athletes in certain sports – including boxing, soccer, swimming, and long-distance running, among others.[64] This request elicited opposition from the minister of finance, but ultimately Romanov procured 65 rubles per day for each athlete.[65] Romanov's successful petitions for more resources suggest that he was intimately involved in decisions surrounding the Olympics.

In addition to logistics and training, Romanov and the Sports Committee also had the image of the Soviet Union to consider. As the Helsinki Olympics drew near, Romanov wrote to Politburo member Malenkov: "Considering the great responsibility placed upon the performance of Soviet athletes, the committee asks that you help us resolve several questions." Romanov reported that the "bourgeois press" believed that this Olympics would surpass all previous ones and had suggested that the USSR's team was one of "the teams to watch." He also informed Malenkov of the huge influx of foreign tourists expected. According to Romanov, the organizers had sold 50,000 tickets and expected to sell 30,000 more, and they anticipated up to 2000 foreign correspondents to attend with more than 200 from the US. Realizing that participation in such a conspicuous event as the Olympic Games could also open the Soviet Union up to unfavorable publicity, Romanov asked Malenkov to ensure that all information related to international sport be released by TASS (the Soviet news agency) solely with the agreement of the Central Committee department for propaganda and agitation. His stated reason was to "keep secret" and "avoid divulgence" of materials related to the Soviet athletes' training.[66] His statements further indicate that he, like his superiors, wanted control of the Soviet Union's image to rest with the Central Committee and not with Western journalists.

Indeed, Soviet relations with the West on sports matters were marked by a hesitancy to inform the foreign press and Olympic organizers of a training regimen that was characteristic of a closed society. This silence, however, was broken periodically with well organized, strategically timed displays of hospitality designed to further increase the Soviet Union's international prestige. While publicly denouncing the IOC for its bourgeois elitism, Andrianov and the newly recognized Soviet Olympic Committee tried to win IOC President Edstrom over with vodka and caviar.[67] During the Helsinki Games, Soviet organizers hosted the US athletes and coaches to an elaborate banquet replete with steak, wine, vodka, and caviar in a similar effort to garner respect for the Soviet system.[68] The Soviet administrators' image of Western sports as elitist influenced their interchange with IOC members. The Soviet leaders hoped to win friends abroad by catering to the social attitudes of the international sports community. In both the air of secrecy and the displays of generosity, Romanov and the Sports Committee served as the primary conduit of information and the guardians of the Soviet Union's image.

While training progressed in the Olympic camps, the Sports Committee remained busy answering questions, hearing complaints, and solving problems brought to its attention by the trainers on the ground. The committee members found themselves further hampered by interference from non-sporting departments and ministries, and by formalities imposed upon them by international federations. Since the goal was to compete in every sport, each difficulty encountered threatened the entire Olympic debut. For instance, the head of the Department of Water Sports, Nikolai Adamovich, complained from the parasailing camp on the Baltic that the Soviet Ministry of State Security (MGB (precursor to the KGB)) and the MGB of Estonia had refused access for all parasailors to train on the Baltic Sea.[69] Then, in May 1952, he informed the committee that the necessary forms had not been sent to join the international federation for water sports, and that his yachtsmen did not have proof of recognition by the Soviet body for yachting.[70] Similarly, one month before the Games, Andrianov received a note from the Helsinki Organizing Committee reminding him that the Soviet Union had not yet officially joined the International Equestrian Federation.[71] Later Adamovich reported that several of his yachtsmen had not received any salary and threatened to go home if the problem with their pay was not resolved.[72] Similarly, gripes over improper equipment came in from the trainers for shooting, yachting, equestrian events, pentathlon, and fencing.[73] These letters and reports reveal the immensity of the task before the Sports Committee in overseeing the work of hundreds of people under its direction.

The Sports Committee found itself caught between the proverbial rock and a hard place. While having to deal with logistical problems and complaints from the training camps, Romanov and his staff had to convince the Politburo that the Soviet team would win the competition. Athletes and trainers gathered to offer their personal testimonies to the Soviet team's potential, proclaiming that "thanks to the concern for our athletes on the part of the Soviet government, party, and great Comrade Stalin we have been given all the conditions for excellent preparation for the upcoming competition."[74] For Romanov, however, the Soviet Union's chances of victory came down not to sycophantic promises but to an elaborate game of numbers based on the unofficial point system observed by the international press. Romanov predicted that the Soviet team would win eight events and the USA seven in the Helsinki Games:[75] the rest they would split equally, allowing the Soviet Union enough points to win.

Once he submitted his predictions, Romanov again found himself in this uncomfortable position as the Games progressed in Helsinki. To encourage the Soviet and Eastern bloc athletes, the Soviet officials in Finland constructed a scoreboard in the Eastern bloc Olympic village keeping a running tally of the unofficial points as each event ended. Just before the end of the Games, however, the Soviet side took down the scoreboard.[76] The reason for this becomes clear as one looks at discrepancies in the unofficial point totals of the United States and the Soviet Union. At the end of the Olympic Games in Helsinki, *Pravda* (*Truth*), the official newspaper of the Communist Party, proclaimed victory without reference to point totals, reporting simply that the "athletes of the Soviet Union took first place."[77] On the same day, the *New York Times* claimed a win for the USA based on a score of 614 to 553½.[78] Upon his return to Soviet Union, Romanov told the members of the Politburo that while the United States had won more medals in the Games, the Soviet Union tied with the USA in terms of points, with 494. This revised total appeared in the *New York Times* on August 7.[79] Part of the disparity comes from the use of two different point systems. Romanov calculated his results assigning seven points for first place, five for second, four for third, etc., but the United States' system gave ten points for first place. Hours after Romanov's appearance before the Politburo, Malenkov called to confirm the totals. Malenkov put to rest any fears Romanov might have had over his fate by telling him to "Relax. Go home. Rest."[80] After the Games, criticism for poor performance in certain events fell on athletes and trainers, rather than on Romanov and the Sports Committee.[81] Satisfied with the assurance that the United States had not won outright, the Politburo declared its first Olympic Games an adequate success, and Romanov's point tally became the official word for the next fifty years.[82] In October 2002, however, Aksel' Vartanian recalculated the points and found that even by Romanov's point system, the United States came out on top with a score of 495 to 487.[83] The fact that his point totals remained unchallenged for fifty years indicates the security of Romanov's position and the influence he enjoyed in the Politburo.

Conclusion

Burdened by a leadership that was hesitant to open up to the West by sending athletes and trainers abroad, the sports administrators mustered all the resources at their disposal and sent letters to influential figures to convince the Soviet leaders to send their athletes to the Olympic Games. The trainers and sports administrators on all levels demonstrated a degree of maneuverability within the Stalinist system to achieve their own ends. Down the hierarchy of the Sports Committee were other bureaucrats who demonstrated varying degrees of autonomy, finding ways to advance their own projects by relating them to their superiors' priorities. This suggests that the Olympic project got off the ground because individuals were willing and able to step up and make things happen despite operating in a difficult, repressive, and often dangerous environment.

As chairman of the Sports Ministry, Romanov especially displayed great political skill in his dealings with the Politburo, but his approach to the IOC was no less successful. Securing his vice-chairman, Andrianov, as a member of the IOC, allowed Romanov the space necessary to negotiate between the pressures from the Soviet leadership and the international sporting community, and Andrianov's dual role as deputy chairman of the Sports Committee and IOC representative in the Soviet Union allowed him to act as a liaison in Soviet–IOC relations. Key to Romanov and Andrianov's success in dealings with the IOC was their ability to adopt the language of Olympism and their keen sense of the importance of personal connections in the IOC political culture. This bureaucratic skill to co-opt ideological language and to cultivate personal patronage was perfected in the Soviet party-state system and transferred easily to the Olympic venue.

The issues of amateurism and nationalism were never resolved after the Soviet Union's entrance into the Olympic family, but as long as Soviet members of the IOC were able to promote the Olympic ideals, real tensions created by their state-run system proved less significant. The Soviet Union was not kept out of the Games, despite the fundamental political differences it accentuated within the IOC, because Andrianov could assure his fellow members of the IOC that he would "cooperate sincerely with the IOC for the good of the Olympic Movement in his country and for world peace."[84] The ideals of Olympism that sought to "create a sporting fraternity between peoples without distinctions of race, color, religion or opinion" meant that even the anti-Communist Avery Brundage could come to terms with the Soviet Union's entrance once he saw for himself "the vast physical training program and the progress that has been made in the USSR."[85] Dazzled by elaborate sports parades on his visit to the USSR in 1954, Brundage convinced himself that the reports he had heard of grim-faced sporting automatons were unfounded. Becoming a key promoter of the excellence of the Soviet athletes, he remarked: "They weren't forced. They were having a wonderful time."[86] John Hoberman suggests that this "language-by-committee ... serves as a screen behind which the voice of conscience is sacrificed to a myth of global consensus."[87] Yet, as long as Andrianov could proclaim that The Soviet athletes treat the Olympic Games not "as a major battle in the Cold War" but as an international forum for dissemination of the noble Olympic ideas of peace and consolidation of friendship between the nations, he and the IOC did at least give the illusion of working together for peace.

Notes

1   Quoted in John Hoberman, *The Olympic Crisis: Sport, Politics and the Moral Order* (New Rochele, NY: A.D. Caratzas, 1986), 55.
2   Brundage to Andrianov, November 15, 1955, Avery Brundage Collection, University of Illinois Archives Record Series 26/20/37, Box 50.
3   On the 50th anniversary of the Soviet Olympic debut, Vartanian published a collection of over 50 archival documents concerning the Soviet Union's decision to enter the Olympics. Published under the title "Sekretnyi arkhiv Akselia Vartaniana" (The Secret Archive of Aksel' Vartanian), these documents appeared in seven installments in the Russian sports online newspaper entitled *Sport-ekspress* (*Sports Express*). Aksel' Vartanian, "Sekretnyi arkhiv Akselia Vartaniana," Parts 1–7, *Sport-ekspress*, 2002, available from http://www.sport-express.ru. Unfortunately, Vartanian is not meticulous about citing the exact locations of the documents. In his first installment he identifies the following sources: GARF, f. 7576, op. 1, d. 623, and op. 2, d. 408, and RGASPI, f. 17, op. 132, d. 99. He occasionally identifies other locations in his subsequent installments, and I have noted those locations in the appropriate citations.
4   Vartanian has published several books and articles on Soviet sport, particularly soccer, including Aksel' Vartanian, *Sto let rossiskomu futbolu* (Moscow, 1997) and Aksel' Vartanian, "Draki pri sotsializme," *Sportekspress futbol*, no. 27 (1999): 32–35. In the

author's note to his recent AHA article, Robert Edelman acknowledged Vartanian, stating: "I am especially indebted to Aksel' Vartanian, whose vast knowledge of Soviet soccer is unsurpassed. He, too, has been a crucial guide to the archives." Robert Edelman, "A Small Way of Saying 'No': Moscow Working Men, Spartak Soccer, and the Commmunist Party, 1900-1945," *American Historical Review* 107,no. 5 (2002): 1473.

5   Avery Brundage Collection, University of Illinois Archives Record Series 26/20/37 (hereafter ABC).

6   Allen Guttman, *The Olympics: A History of the Modern Games*, 2nd ed. (Urbana and Chicago, 2002), 2.

7   John Hoberman, "Toward a Theory of Olympic Internationalism," *Journal of Sports History* 22, no. 1 (1995): 9–10.

8   Ibid., 11, 12.

9   Guttmann, *The Olympics*, 12.

10   Barbara Jean Keys, "The Dictatorship of Sport: Nationalism, Internationalism, and Mass Culture in the 1930s" (Ph. D. diss.,Harvard University, 2001), 191.

11   Ibid., 207–8.

12   Ibid., 214.

13   Ibid., 224, 244.

14   Ibid., 246–47.

15   Report to IOC by Sydney Dawes, Miguel Moenck and Avery Brundage, April 25, 1949, ABC Box 76.

16   Arthur E. Porrit of the British Olympic Association to Brundage, July 24, 1947, ABC Box 130.

17   Vartanian, "Sekretnyi arkhiv," September 2, 2002; Nikolai Romanov, *Trudnye dorogi k oliimpu* (Moscow, 1987), 42.

18   Edstrom to Brundage, December 4, 1946, ABC Box 42.

19   Edstrom to Brundage, December 7, 1945, ABC Box 42.

20   Sydney Dawes' report of IOC meeting with international federations, June 16–17, 1947, ABC Box 75.

21   Edstrom to Brundage, November 12, 1947, ABC Box 149.

22   James Riordan, "Rewriting Sports History," *Journal of Sport History* 20, no.3 (1993): 248; Brundage to Mayer, February 10, 1951, ABC Box 46.

23   Brundage to Edstrom, October 30, 1947, ABC Box 42.

24   "The Position of Soviet Russia," *Bulletin du Comité International Olympique*, no. 25 (1947): 26.

25   Edstrom to N. Romanov, November 25, 1946, ABC Box 42.

26   Brundage to Edstrom, July 12, 1950, ABC Box 149. Edstrom had invited the Soviet Union to become a member of the International Amateur Athletic Association and to participate in the competition, but he received no reply prior to the arrival of the Soviet contingent in Oslo. Edstrom to N. Romanov, November 25, 1946, ABC Box 42.

27   As head of the propaganda and agitation section of the Central Committee, Andrei Zhdanov and later Mikhail Suslov oversaw the work of the Sports Committee, but as secretary of the Central Committee in charge of hiring Party cadres, Georgii Malenkov appointed the Sports Committee chairman.

28   Romanov, *Trudnye dorogi*, 64.

29   Romanov to Zhdanov, 1947, "Sekretnyi arkhiv," September 2, 2002.

30   For some idea of the scope of such purges in the sports bureaucracy see Riordan, "Rewriting Sports History," 250.

31   Romanov, *Trudnye dorogi*, 66–69. Soviet women won their events, but no one on the men's team came in third place with no one ranking higher than 12th place in individual events. While the reason for Romanov's removal remains unclear, it is generally assumed that he was dismissed because of the World Championship results. See Romanov, *Turdnye dorogi*, 70; Riordan, *Rewriting Sports History*, 249.

32   Ibid., 152. Between 1948 and 1950, even socialist sporting contacts, common since the late 1920s, occurred less frequently. For example, the Soviet track team ceased to compete in the *l'Humanite* (*Humanity*) competition organized by the French Communist Party in which the USSR had taken part, with the exception of the war years, since 1935. "Pobeda sovetskikh legoatletov," *Fizkul'tura i sport*, April 1951, 1. Robert Edelman notes in his study of Soviet soccer that Soviet teams ceased to play foreign opponents between 1948 and 1950, asserting that Malenkov, Beria, and Suslov exerted more control over sports than Zhdanov had. See Robert Edelman, *Serious Fun: A History of Spectator Sports in the USSR* (New York, 1993), 96.

33   Romanov to Zhdanov, 1947, and Apollonov to Mikhail Suslov, July 7, 1948, "Sekretnyi arkhiv," September 2, 2002.

34   Gleb Baklanov, *Tochka opory* (Moscow, 1971), 216.

35   This statement became a battle cry in sports reporting after the resolution. I have used James Riordan's translation. See Victor Peppard and James Riordan, *Playing Politics: Soviet Sport Diplomacy to 1992* (Greenwich, CT, 1993), 62. Riordan maintains that the resolution was issued in 1949, but Apollonov gives the date as December 27, 1948. Arakadii Apollonov, "Stalinskaia zabota o protsvetanii fizicheskoi kul'tury v SSSR," *Fizkul'tura i sport*, December 1949, 4.

36   The circumstances around Romanov's dismissal and reinstatement remain mysterious. Despite his removal as chairman, Romanov remained active in the Sports Committee's work and was appointed vice-chairman upon Apollonov's recommendation. Romanov, *Trudnye dorogi*, 71.

37   Vladislav Zubok and Constantine Pleshakov, *Inside the Kremlin's Cold War: From Stalin to Khrushchev* (Cambridge, Mass., 1996), 110–11.

38   Brundage to Mayer, January 19, 1952, ABC Box 46.

39   Edstrom to Brundage, December 7, 1945, ABC Box 42.

40   Brundage to Edstrom, April 6, 1947, ABC Box 42.

41   Edstrom to Brundage, September 3, 1947, ABC Box 42.

42   Brundage to members of the IOC, January 30, 1954, ABC Box 70.

43   Brundage to Edstrom, September 27, 1948, ABC Box 43.

44   45th session of the IOC, Vienna, May 7, 1951, ABC Box 90.

45   Sobolev to Edstrom, telegram, April 23, 1951, "Sekretnyi arkhiv," September 16, 2002.

46   The exact date of Romanov's reinstatement as chairman of the Sports Committee is unclear, but Romanov states in his memoir that his replacement Apollonov "was recalled to his previous post" in December 1950, and that he was reinstated "within a short time." Romanov, *Trudnye dorogi*, 72.

47   N. Romanov and B. Chesnokov to International Amateur Wrestling Federation, January 29, 1947, and N. Romanov and A. Morosov to International Amateur Athletic Federation, January 29, 1947, ABC Box 42. See also, Apollonov to Suslov, June 1948, "Sekretnyi arkhiv," September 2, 2002.

48   Sobolev to Edstrom, telegram, April 23, 1951, "Sekretnyi arkhiv," September 16, 2002.

49   Ibid.

50   Ibid.

51   President and General Secretary of the Oslo Organizing Committee to NOK USSR, telegram, June 1951, "Sekretnyi arkhiv," September 23, 2002.

52   Von Frenckell to Andrianov, November 22, 1951, "Sekretnyi arkhiv," September 30, 2002. Andrianov to Sports Committee, memorandum, October 1951, "Sekretnyi arkhiv," September 23, 2002.

53   Kuchmenko to Romanov, November 23, 1951, "Sekretnyi arkhiv," September 23, 2002.

54   Ibid.

55   Sobolev to Romanov, December 17, 1951, "Sekretnyi arkhiv," September 23, 2002.

56   Romanov to Malenkov, report, January 12, 1952, "Sekretnyi arkhiv," September 23, 2002. Vartanian states that this report was to Suslov, but the document itself quoted by Vartanian indicates the report was sent to Malenkov. Because the wording of this report is similar to a later one sent by Romanov to Suslov, it seems logical that Romanov was the author of the January 12 report. In his reference to the later report, Vartanian states that Suslov underlined in red a certain sentence. This suggests that the reports could have been sent to Suslov who then forwarded them to Malenkov. It seems clear, however, that Romanov authored both reports.

57   Korotkov, Tarasov, Babrov, Egorov, and Chernyshev to Suslov, January 14, 1952, "Sekretnyi arkhiv," September 23, 2002. Andreev, Khimichev, and Senkevich to Suslov, January 1952, "Sekretnyi arkhiv," September 23, 2002.

58   Suslov to Romanov, Stepanov, and Suzhkov, January 15, 1952, "Sekretnyi arkhiv," September 23, 2002.

59   Romanov to Suslov, January 1952, "Sekretnyi arkhiv," September 23, 2002.

60   Sobolev and Senkevich to V. I. Stalin, January 1952, "Sekretnyi arkhiv," September 23, 2002.

61   Vartanian suggests that Andrianov was behind this letter, but his evidence for this assessment is unclear.

62   Romanov to Malenkov, April 30, 1952, "Sekretnyi arkhiv," September 30, 2002.

63   Stenogram of meeting with Suslov, February 9, 1952, "Sekretnyi arkhiv," October 7, 2002.

64   Romanov to Malenkov, May 20, 1952, "Sekretnyi arkhiv," September 30, 2002.

65   A. G. Zverev to Suslov, undated, "Sekretnyi arkhiv," September 30, 2002. Vartanian does not cite the source of this total.

66   Romanov to Malenkov, April 30, 1952, "Sekretnyi arkhiv," September 30, 2002.

67   Edstrom to Andrianov May 29, 1951, "Sekretnyi arkhiv" September 16, 2002.

68   "Soviet Hospitality Goes Unreturned," New York Times, 28 July 1952.

69   Adamovich to Sports Committee, undated, "Sekretnyi arkhiv," October 7, 2002 (GARF, f. 7576, op. 20, d. 1).

70   Adamovich to Sports Committee, May 8, 1952, "Sekretnyi arkhiv," October 7, 2002.

71   Balkama to NOK USSR, June 16, 1952, "Sekretnyi arkhiv," October 7, 2002.

72   Vartanian, "Sekretnyi arkhiv," October 7, 2002. Vartanian does not provide particulars on this report, but cites it as part of a summary report compiled at the yachting training camp.

73   Chekarev to Semichastnoi, June 27, 1952, "Sekretnyi arkhiv," October 7, 2002.

74   Ibid.

75   Romanov to Suslov, report, May 10, 1952, "Sekretnyi arkhiv," October 21, 2002.

76   "Olympic Arithmetic," New York Times, August 3, 1952, sec. 4, p. 2E.

77   "Na olimpiiskikh igrakh," Pravda, August 4, 1952, 4.

78   "Unofficial Scores," New York Times, August 4, 1952, 19.

79   Harrison Salisbury, "Russians Recount then Recant," New York Times, August 7, 1952, 16.

80   Romanov, Trudnye dorogi, 283.

81   Harry Schwartz, "Moscow Berates Olympics Losers," New York Times, September 20, 1952, 1.

82   "The 50th anniversary of the Helsinki Olympics," Online Pravda, July 19, 2002, available from http://english.pravda.ru.

83   Vartanian, "Sekretnyi arkhiv," October 21, 2002.

84   45th session of the IOC, Vienna, May 7, 1951, ABC Box 90.

85   Brundage to Andrianov, November 9, 1954, ABC Box 113.

86   Hoberman, Olympic Crisis, 55.

87   Hoberman, Olympic Crisis, 7.

Chapter 3

Cold War expatriot sport[1]

Symbolic resistance and international response in Hungarian water polo at the Melbourne Olympics, 1956

Robert E. Rinehart

Cold War sport: an introduction

As the Soviet Union took its place upon the world sport stage, particularly in the early 1950s, it was also solidifying its grasp upon so-called "satellite nations," post-Second World War, such as Poland, Yugoslavia, and Hungary. Similarly, as the sports scene coalesced for the United States and the Soviet Union (as primary post-Second World War players), both nations' "satellite spheres" supported a sport rhetoric that proposed that success in the sports realm reflected superior managerial, geopolitical, and fiduciary ideology. As such, one of the fundamental ways that the Cold War rhetoric was staged in sport was during the 1956 Hungarian Revolution and the Melbourne Summer Olympic Games. In particular, much of the antecedents to the water polo match between the Soviet Union and Hungary created and intensified the symbolic nature of sports contests from representative of national pride to instilling national pride.

As expatriots from Hungary flowed to other nations, they – like diasporic peoples everywhere – established nostalgic- and ethnic-based communities. These communities led to support, both symbolic and real, of their home countries. It is not surprising, therefore, that the 1956 Hungarian Revolution coalesced Hungarian expatriots, water polo players, and other fans as a symbolic gesture against the Soviet Union's policies.

Weaving the threads: national identity

Nationalism or national character may emerge slowly, generationally, with small and large turning points serving to direct the evolution of a national *je ne sais quoi*. Andrews has argued passionately for the emergence of a Welsh national identity through Wales' cultural alliance with rugby at the turn of the century.[2] Dyreson linked an internationally emerging United States with the international forum of the Olympic Games, and pointed out American athletes' proselytizing in the political–cultural arena.[3] And Hobsbawm, Trevor-Roper, and Lowenthal, in differentiated ways, all point to the use of invented tradition in [re]constituting the past.[4] Scholars have thus examined the *gradual* emergence of a national identity through sport (e.g. rugby in Wales) or a system of sport (e.g. Olympism in America), or, indeed, the cultural or political nature of how nations themselves determine just what their "'national sport'-concept is."[5]

Just as surely, however, national identity may crystallize around a highly charged moment. If the metaphor of evolutionary change may be extended, these crystallized moments of national identity might be seen as clear and dramatic mutations of the original which, in retrospect, are epiphanic definers of a new way for nation-builders or citizenry to view the world.

In this paper, I intend to examine one crystallization of national identity for Hungarians during the time of the 1956 Summer Olympics, held in Melbourne, Australia. Because resistance may be both symbolic and real, I begin by examining resistance literature – and resistance in sport particularly – and provide a brief theoretical discussion of signs and symbolism. I continue with an overview of Hungarian life (including sport) up to 1956, which serves to demonstrate two major points: 1) that Hungarians highly value[d] their sport, and 2) that football (soccer), while considered by many the Hungarian national sport, was not, in fall of 1956, aptly prepared to provide symbolic resistance to the Soviet occupation. Finally, I frame the Olympics within the context of the Hungarian Revolution, show the nature of expatriate nationalism, and speculate as to the import of the Hungarian men's water polo team's victory over the Soviet Union, most especially for the athletes and expatriates of Hungary.[6]

Signs

Dick Hebdige's examination of style as a form of signification serves as a starting point for a discussion of collective, albeit polysemous[7] readings of signs as determined by the reader. However, tying signs and their signification – in terms of their audience – to acts of resistance is quite another issue. As Scott puts it, in studying south-east Asian peasant revolutions, there has been an "inordinate attention to large-scale … insurrection"[8] yet less scholarly interest in more subtle – and symbolic – forms of resistance.

According to Scott, there appear to be at least two categories of peasant rebellion and revolution that historians have examined. The first is large-scale peasant revolutions, which

> … are few and far between. Not only are the circumstances that favor large-scale peasant uprising comparatively rare, but when they do appear the revolts that develop are nearly always crushed unceremoniously. To be sure, even a failed revolt may achieve something: a few concessions from the state or landlords, a brief respite from new and painful relations of production and, not least, *a memory of resistance and courage that may lie in wait for the future*. [emphasis added][9]

The second form of peasant "rebellion and revolution," which Scott calls resistance, is made up of subtle,

> ... quiet, unremitting guerrilla warfare that [takes] place day-in and day-out. [This includes such forms as] foot dragging, dissimulation, feigned ignorance, false compliance, manipulation, flight, slander, theft, arson, sabotage, and isolated incidents of violence ...[10]

I suggest that there is at least one other form of rebellion and revolution, a symbolic form that finds one of its most profound incarnations through sport. This is a middle area[11] between outright, open rebellion and underground, passive resistance, and it involves the socially accepted practices of symbolically "killing" one's enemy and regaining one's land while being monitored by the world according to the rules of sport. Such a middle-area practice was enacted at the 1956 Summer Olympics, in a water polo contest between the Soviet Union and Hungary. This match came to signify anti-Soviet sentiment to many athletes, Hungarian expatriates, Hungarian nationalists, and much of the Western world press.

Resistances

There exist at least three basic forms of resistance to a dominant culture through sport: political, colonial, and cultural resistance. While a subordinate culture may overtly submit to the prerogative of the dominant culture, there may remain overt or covert "oppositional aspects of sport"[12] that illuminate forms and degrees of resistance to the dominant culture.

These three forms of oppositional resistance are not mutually exclusive. Political resistance in sport may emerge when a group feels that a sporting event can be used as an effective tool for political change. There may be planned or spontaneous political resistance: the key element is the attempt at effecting change.

The 1972 Munich massacre and the "Black Power" salute at the Mexico City Olympics in 1968 are cases of political resistance/rebellion surrounding sport. To me, the photograph of a victorious yet somber Hungarian water polo team is also an example where "... objections are lodged, the contradictions displayed ... at the profoundly superficial level of appearances: that is, at the level of signs."[13] In a broader though more subtle sense, the use of an international forum to exact political gain, whether spontaneous or planned, serves every bit the same purpose, and is not "superficial," but, rather, is the more profound, accurate depiction, "representative of human life."[14] As some Hungarian athletes said, "We had a duty to come to Melbourne and tell the world about our wonderful revolution."[15]

Colonial resistance emerges when colonized peoples struggle to retain their cultural heritage, in sport as in other societal institutions.[16] Donnelly notes that "expression of nationalism through sport"[17] falls into this category; "more subtle forms of cultural hegemony" in culturally diverse societies may induce "attempts to retain or revive traditional cultural forms."[18] Political and colonial resistance are implicated in cultural resistance, with the added possibility of the emergence of new cultural forms.

Observation of resistant behaviors may not tell the whole story, and may require intertextual analyses. Overt, confrontational resistance may prove geno-cidal: as a result, the "weapons of the weak ... are deliberately nonconfrontational in style."[19] Thus, acceptable gestures are directed at domi-nant cultures, with the intent to gradually erode dominance:

> ... whenever an autocratic or totalitarian system of government prohibits the expression of overt opposition, antagonism against the regime is likely to find expression through other channels and in forms approved or at least tol-erated by the rulers.[20] ... [This was demonstrated] during the summer of 1954, [when] the unsportsmanlike behavior of the Soviet water polo team had given rise to anti-Soviet demonstrations in Budapest.[21]

Thus, colonial and political resistance to a dominant culture or ideology may evi-dence itself broadly; it may evolve slowly over time and/or crystallize in a single event or moment; and it may be covert or overt, directly oppositional or tangen-tial, direct or circumlocuted. The sport of water polo served as an impetus for public demonstrations known as "disguised antagonism."[22]

Post-Second World War Soviet occupation of Hungary, to 1956

Hungarian nationalism in the face of Soviet occupation after the Second World War took on gradual yet dramatic form. Neighbored by Czechoslovakia, Austria, Yugoslavia, and Rumania, with the Soviet Union an omnipresent force, Hungary had a proud and fairly homogeneous citizenry, which was deeply interested in sport.[23] In Budapest, the Danube River neatly cleaves Buda and Pest in almost equal halves. Folklore ties this Danube presence to many of Hungary's late nineteenth and early twentieth century Olympic victories in swimming and aquatic sports.[24]

Between the Second World War and the Hungarian Revolution of 1956, a Hungarian underground certainly existed. The pre-Revolution incarceration of many intellectuals, students, and writers evidences opposition to Soviet incur-sion. While forces oppositional to the dominant Soviet ideology were at work from 1945 on, their effects were largely driven underground and inward through a systematic program of exile, imprisonment, and execution orchestrated by the Soviet-installed regime.[25]

Hungarian resistance prior to the 23 October Revolution, according to Hungarian popular idiom, consisted of "'those who have been there, those who are there, and those who are heading there.' By 'there', they meant prison."[26] The uprising was "powered" by blue-collar workers, not just a few disgruntled students. Popular and humorous rhetoric was cynical, but pithy.[27] Mutterings of the people demonstrated anxiety and verbal resistance; the Hungarian Revolution erupted from such mostly private demonstrations.

Similarly, Hungarian resistance through sport imitated peasant resistances and day-to-day impediments to the system. Athletes performed their athletic jobs steadily; in retrospect, however, they appear to have likewise bided their time. Hungary was, at least superficially, an orderly society. Despite this, "Revolutionary newspapers like Truth were printed even when the Russians returned [after the Revolution]."[28] Fear of the secret police enforced the apparent order, yet public (but anonymous) disavowals of the Soviet presence were common. In fact, at the European basketball championship in 1955, "when the Soviet team padded out into the arena there were catcalls from the audience; there were many arrests, and news of the demonstration grapevined all over the country."[29]

Rabid sports fans, the Hungarians followed club and national sport intently. Indeed, "The Hungarians' love of viewing and participating in sports is matched only by their delight in talking about them. It probably is the most popular topic of casual conversation on the street, at work, in cafés, and in the home."[30] In 1986, an editorial in the "Hungarian Digest" stated that, while "interest in soccer and attendance at soccer games has fallen back somewhat … everybody seems to be an expert, and soccer is more often than not the object of passionate debate, even enthusiastic demonstration of patriotism."[31] Sport has always contributed greatly to the warp and weave of the Hungarian cultural fabric.

Post-Second World War Hungary supported water polo, swimming, fencing, wrestling, and soccer football. The Hungarian soccer team of the 1950s, called the "Golden Team" by Hungarians, captured the gold medal in the 1952 Olympics yet failed to win the 1954 World Cup. The goalkeeper of that defeated 1954 team, Gyula Grosics, said: "… we were far more than mere soccer players: we represented a country and our results could secure Hungary more favorable treatment both politically and economically. When we failed to become world champions, we fell from grace overnight."[32]

The World Cup, held in 1954 and 1958, did not coincide with the October Revolution of 1956. In addition, an Olympic preview from 1956 reported: "In September … the Hungarians announced that the [soccer] team was being withdrawn from the Olympic competition; … there have been rumors of crippling personal dissensions within the team."[33] If sport was to be a medium for timely resistance against the Soviets, the 1956 Melbourne Olympics (in November, during the Australian summer) was the most opportune event. The great investment Hungarians had in soccer (socially, emotionally, financially), would logically have encouraged the Soviets to anticipate soccer, not water polo (if they anticipated sport as a site of resistance at all), as a site of symbolic resistance – yet the Hungarian Olympic soccer team had withdrawn.

So, even though soccer football was and is considered the Hungarian national pastime, the Hungarian Revolution and the World Cup did not mesh, nor did a significant "political" opportunity in sport arise for the soccer team soon after the Revolution. It did, however, for the bulk of the Hungarian Olympic Team, and no more fortuitously, as fate would have it, than for the water polo team. It is this "wrinkle in time" that made water polo a focal point of nationalistic and patriotic fervor for Hungarians – including expatriates – everywhere.

To assume that the Hungarian Olympic water polo team took on greater importance than the crushing of the Revolution by the Soviets would be grossly inaccurate. War has been, and remains, much more compelling to most people than sport.[34] Nonetheless, by the end of 1956 when an estimated 200,000 Hungarian refugees escaped,[35] any decisive Hungarian victory, especially in sport, was bound to rouse the spirit of Hungarians. According to Western sources, prior to 1956:

> much more deeply resented by the captive population [was] the pressure on their teams to allow Soviet teams to beat them. ... [Sports] provided a most amusing example of the rawest and most blatant pressures applied by a physically dominant nation, sugar-coated in ideological double-talk.[36]

The occupying force's control over the Hungarians thus was carried over into sport, and the skirmishes turned into ideological verbal matches.

The Hungarian water polo team was highly successful internationally. From 1926, when Hungary's national team took first in the European championships in Budapest, to the Melbourne Olympics in 1956, Hungary won six of eight European championship titles and four of six Olympic gold medals.[37] The water polo teams of Hungary were "masters in this game since [at least] the end of the Second World War."[38] Considering the dampening effects of the post-Second World War occupation by the Soviet Union on Hungarian national life, which included intimidation in many forms, this success is remarkable.

Molotov cocktails and polo balls: the Hungarian revolution and the Olympics, 1956

In October of 1956, athletes' dedication to their sports and hopes for Olympic glory suddenly seemed less important than their sense of national pride. An interview with two Hungarian athletes illustrates this view. The first:

> When October 23 came, ... our hearts leaped and sport and the Olympics were forgotten. A yearning for national independence, a decent democratic life and freedom and dignity took their place. None of us was thinking of physical condition, training, sleep, departure dates or gold medals.[39]

The second athlete's comments:

... [on the ship over] there was no clash between Hungarians and Russians, but this was perhaps due to the fact that at no stage of the voyage were we aware of what really had happened in Hungary. After what I heard on my arrival in Melbourne, I will never mix with those butchers again.[40]

Clearly, the revolution became foremost in the athletes' minds. But their sense of the influential power of the Olympic Games as a forum for lodging complaints symbolically is clear as well. This sense may be seen in their comments and in the resistant acts they employed during the highly-visible Olympic Games.

Athletes felt that the continuing effort to educate the Western world of "Hungarians' right to Hungary," where "the strength of the fallen somehow fired those who lived, and ... continues to fire them in their spirited exile. ..."[41] partially lay with themselves, that they might contribute to an articulation of cultural, physical, monetary, and popular inspiration. The ideology that sport can serve as a powerful reminder of a strength of spirit and hope in resistance is one to which many athletes subscribed – including those athletes previously quoted. The Hungarian Revolution was a spontaneous uprising of students, but more than that, it was inspired by Western models and hope of Western intervention.[42] The encouragement of Radio Free Europe (RFE) was significant:

Of one thousand refugees to be expertly sampled in December 1956 as to why, given that the uprising was triggered by other causes, they personally joined in, *ninety-six* percent will state that they expected the West to come to Hungary's aid, and seventy-seven percent will say that they anticipated actual military intervention. ... Of course, when the balloon goes up, both [Secretary of State John Foster] Dulles and [President Dwight] Eisenhower will indignantly deny responsibility.[43]

For the Hungarian people to expect intervention was not mere wishful thinking. In fact, propaganda leaflets were dropped by Western sympathizers via balloons which "talked of a resistance movement being raised in Hungary."[44]

From post-Second World War until the very recent *perestroika*, Hungary was – with this eleven-day exception during the 1956 Hungarian Revolution – a satellite of the Soviet Union, though yearning for self-determination. The events of the night of 23 October, 1956 resulted from the spontaneous foment and grassroots resistance of Hungarian students responding negatively to Erno Gerö's speech in which he "incited the crowd by his reckless words."[45]

In the shadow of the Hungarian Revolution, the Melbourne Olympic Games were held. By early November 1956, Spain, Switzerland, and the Netherlands had all withdrawn from the Olympics in support of Hungary.

It was a volatile time, and athletes were not immune. The Revolution's significance, their place in it, and their decisions to participate in athletics during such a time weighed heavily. Expatriated Hungarians cited the "Hungarian athletes ...

fighting on the rebel side"[46] and Hungarian athletes arrived in Melbourne to a crowd of 500 cheering Free Hungarians. A water polo player, Martin Nikolas, announced, "There are no Communist party members in this group."[47]

Indeed, the "touchstone for genuine national feeling in Hungary is still, and will remain for a long time to come, the attitude towards the revolution of 1956."[48] Hungarians divided into supporters of the regime or of the revolution.[49] Furthermore, the "national awareness of the masses"[50] demonstrated that they did not accept the government's hastily constructed reasons for the revolution. The masses were being physically, but not intellectually, suppressed.

In the 1950s, the international press and media largely reproduced and reinforced their own chosen (dominant) ideology. When discussing this issue, for example, the *New York Times*, on 10 November 1956, carried linked news items regarding the proposed Olympic withdrawal of six nations. In one, Avery Brundage, then International Olympic Committee (IOC) president, said, "Every civilized person recoils in horror at the savage slaughter in Hungary, but that is no reason for destroying the nucleus of international cooperation. ... The Olympic Games are contests between individuals and not between nations. ..."[51]

Further on in the news piece, J. Lyman Bingham, "the executive director of the United States Olympic team, called the withdrawals 'ridiculous.' 'This is a track meet, not a political rally,' he said. 'To withdraw from the Olympics is ridiculous.'"[52]

But nationalism, political maneuverings, and the contest between nations, not just individuals, has had historical precedent.[53] Up to that time, one of the most blatant was Hitler's 1936 Olympics. Many of the Hungarian athletes reported having fought against the Soviets. They were frustrated and anxious for their families' welfare back home. Reports from the Olympic Village indicate that "athletes sat around in groups talking in church whispers. Some still wore a black ribbon across the Hungarian flag on their track suits."[54] The choices were limited: defect and withdraw from the Olympics, or compete with honor. The water polo team chose the latter alternative.

Sport as metaphor: Hungarian resistance and Olympic water polo

The 1956 Hungarian water polo team, ready to defend its 1952 Olympic gold medal, was made up of athletes torn between yearning for a free Hungary and fearing reprisals. Ship-board radio reports of Soviet fighting in Budapest exacerbated the athletes' anxiety as the Soviet steamer *Gruzia* carried members of the Hungarian team to Melbourne. Still they carried on, though:

> all but 12 members of the team [were] married and parents of children ... even they realized at this crossroads that we had a duty to come to Melbourne and tell the world about our wonderful revolution. It was that feeling which brought us here.[55]

Other athletes had been "involved in the fighting and … they told us how they had manned machine guns and barricades, fought secret police and Soviet troops and helped carry wounded."[56] Such commitment to the revolution carried over to an arena in which nationalistic pride could be demonstrated with less ruinous consequences. The water polo venue became just such a synchronic event.

The Hungarian water polo team was bracketed in Group B. Group A included Yugoslavia and the USSR.[57] The top two teams in each group qualified for the final group. Final qualifiers were, from Group A, Yugoslavia (3–0) and the Soviet Union (2–1); from Group B, Hungary (2–0) and the US (1–1); and from Group C, Italy (2–0) and Germany (1–1).[58] Each team was then to play the other survivors.

The Hungarians dominated Italy (4–0), Germany (4–0), and easily beat the United States (6–2). Following their victory over the Soviet Union (score 4–0, called), which had practically assured them of the gold medal,[59] they squeaked out a win over the Yugoslavs (2–1).

The Hungary–Soviet match could have been viewed as just another game. After all, the Hungarians were practically guaranteed the gold. Prior to the game, the world press and Australian media downplayed the happenstance of Hungary versus "Russia," yet their soothing words did not convince. The significance of the match was hinted at when 5,500 spectators, many of them Hungarian expatriates, jammed into the natatorium.[60] Additionally, a Hungarian refugee "said he was carrying 'Stay in Australia' messages to some of the Hungarian Olympic team."[61] Clearly, this was not going to be a typical Olympic moment.

The game itself deteriorated from its opening. Reports indicate that this game was not ordinary, even by current water polo standards.[62] Melbourne writer, Ken Knox, for example, asserted, "I am not trying to excuse yesterday's incidents but I am certain it was the inconsistent refereeing which touched off the displays of temper." Mr. Knox continued, "when you also have – as yesterday – political feelings among players and a demonstrative crowd, serious trouble is inevitable."[63]

This is how it was reported: "The game was a minute old when Russia's Peter Mchvenieradze hammer-locked a Hungarian player and wound up in the penalty box."[64] "The crowd showered him with catcalls,"[65] and, as the second half began (with Hungary leading 2–0), "Russia's Boris Markarov delivered a haymaker to the right eye of Hungary's Antol Belvari,"[66] "and the ball was all but disregarded as fighting broke out all over the pool."[67] Throughout the match, fighting above and below the surface of the water was going on, and, at one point, the "crowd went wild as the short-handed Hungarians [playing man-down][68] held off the Russian attack."[69] In the final minutes, "a Russian hit a rival, Ervin Zador, such a vicious and violent blow over the right eye that it split his brow and stained the water red."[70] The partisan crowd became incensed, the police were called to quell a potential riot, and the "Hungarian officials and reserve players stood on the side of the pool screaming abuse at the Russians."[71]

After the game, a bleeding Zador decided to stay in Australia. He was joined by four other players, including the brilliant Gyorgy Karpati. One of the defectors,

Miklos Martin, said of the Soviets, "'They play their sports just as they conduct their lives – with brutality and disregard for fair play.'"[72]

Perhaps in part because the Australian media were interested in putting on a good show at their Olympics, the game's intensity was downplayed in the press and in later historical reports. Fighting between the Hungarians and Soviets in the water polo match was seen as an aberration: Avery Brundage "brushed aside such incidents as the bloody water polo match between Russia and Hungary. [He said] 'People are only human and these conflicts have been at a minimum.'"[73] Further, Mandell demurs, "The Olympic Games of 1956 closed rather harmoniously. So many dissidents had left. Happily there had been only one confrontation between the Hungarians and the Soviets."[74]

"God save Hungary": expatriate reaction

Many of the "older generation of Hungarian refugees, fascist exiles who had fled Hungary at the end of the Second World War"[75] had established themselves in Western countries, including Australia. Additionally, during the week after Soviet troops attacked Budapest on the early morning of 4 November, an estimated 200,000 refugees fled Hungary.[76]

While the official (that is, the one sanctioned by the Soviets) revolutionary government discouraged overt foreign intervention in the Revolution, many of the people anticipated aid.[77] At first, intellectuals and expatriates were not so sure.

> [D]emonstrators and the subsequent freedom fighters were acting instinctively, led by their hatred of the regime and its representatives. Finally, when Soviet forces intervened, this fact aroused nationalist passions even among those who up to that point had remained unmoved by events.[78]

RFE broadcasts, while not "foment[ing] the revolt,"[79] may have excited some hope for intervention. Certainly, expatriates' nationalistic responses were flavored by the Western press.[80]

Many expatriates, living in Western countries and physically removed from Hungary, demonstrated their support. In Melbourne, 500 former Hungarians greeted the Olympians. They brought "crepe-draped Hungarian flags," which they "dipped in mourning as members of Hungary's Olympic team arrive[d] in Australia."[81] These were the tri-color "national flags" raised during the Revolution, with cut-out hammer-and-sickles representing the expulsion of the Soviet presence.[82]

The symbolic gestures of the expatriates carried over to the athletes' behaviors. The athletes wore uniforms with black arm bands or "proudly wore the emblem of the revolt on their breast pockets."[83] The water polo team, on the award podium

... stood with tears streaming down their faces and sang their national anthem during the victory ceremony. Olympic officials departed from procedure and played the slow and sad Hungarian anthem from start to finish. Just before that, Hungarians in the crowd jumped and shouted for joy while the players embraced.[84]

The Australian Hungarians cheered them not only for the gold medal, or for the victory over the Soviets, but for their courage. Of the estimated 200 "athletes from Hungary, Czecholslovakia and Yugoslavia [who] elected not to return to their homelands,"[85] the world press averred:

> ... these athletes are not pitiful creatures. They are proud men and women who have attained recognition at home and honor abroad. Their flight is therefore the more impressive, because it is completely rational. They cannot stomach the regime in Budapest. Neither can we.[86]

Since the Revolution had been, for all intents and purposes, quelled by the Soviets with little material assistance from the West, words and opinion were the last resort. The athletes' decisions to publicly demonstrate their loyalties were courageous and poignant, and transcended material self-interest:[87]

Expatriates understood their fellow Hungarians' choices. One, citing fundamental political differences with a friend who chose to remain in Hungary, wrote, "We parted as good friends, and I wished him luck. I do not know whether he has since changed his mind. I have not changed mine."[88]

Australian Hungarians at Essendon Airport in Australia parted sadly with those athletes returning to Hungary. "Tears flowed profusely when the first plane took off yesterday. A small group of Hungarian refugees at the airport stood at attention and sang the old national anthem, 'God Save Hungary.'"[89] The athletes' decisions to remain or to return home were private,[90] yet they received worldwide coverage in the English-speaking press and became public, political decisions. And yet more refugees poured into Sydney.[91] Eight of the eleven water polo team members would "not go back to Hungary,"[92] and remained in Australia.

The 1956 Melbourne Olympics created high visibility and opportunity for Hungarian athletes, which meant that their participation and subsequent victories could form oppositional signs of political resistance to the Soviet regime in Hungary. The athletes believed they could demonstrate Hungary's resilience to the world. Additionally, expatriates exploited every symbolic opportunity (when greeting the team's arrival, at the swimming pool, during the water polo awards ceremony, and at the airports) to show the world Hungarian tenacity and pride.[93]

Flickering hope: a conclusion

The Hungarian water polo team's victory over the Soviet Union and its nearly anti-climactic garnering of the gold medal at the Melbourne Olympics demonstrated more than a simple victory of a proud and capable water polo team. It contained symbolic messages. The victory, and the context surrounding it, restated to the world that the politically significant terrain of sport still nourishes forms of resistance.

Until very recently, open and public discussion about the Hungarian Revolution has been a taboo subject. Most discussion was done in private. As well, the biases of popular ideology and the its reinforcement made the Revolution difficult to discuss.[94] The widespread support for the Hungarian Revolution evidenced itself in many, varied sites[95] – the "contested terrain" of symbolic resistance. Such resistance was most profoundly effected in the streets of Budapest during the Revolution,[96] but also emerged, particularly for expatriates of Hungary, in places such as the water polo venue at the 1956 Olympics.

The Hungarian water polo victory was a bittersweet one for Hungarians: 45 of the 175 Olympic team members, including an official from the Hungarian Olympic Committee, sought political asylum after the Games. Yet, this exodus itself served one of the same functions as everyday peasant resistance does: it managed to tell the "haves" that they could not control the freedoms of the "have-nots."

The Olympic water polo victory served to coalesce, if not a whole nation embroiled in life and death, then at least the Hungarian refugees and athletes. At minimum, as a form of political resistance, the Soviet–Hungarian water polo match became a fragment for Hungarian collective memory,[97] a tiny taste of satisfaction for Free Hungarians in Australia and for soon-to-defect athletes. The water polo victory largely became an *indirect* icon for the revolutionary movement, and a symbolic sign of resistance to "those butchers,"[98] the heretofore "physically dominant"[99] Soviet Union.

Photographs of successful Hungarian water polo teams clearly show the players' feelings. The Hungarian water polo gold medal teams (1932, 1936, 1952) are portrayed as bemusedly jubilant, smiling, cocky, arrogantly intense, and confident.[100] In the photograph of the 1956 Hungarian gold medal winners, team members hold their medals unsmilingly. In fact, one player has his head bowed, while two others look extremely pensive.[101] The mood of the team is reflective of the inner turmoil they are feeling.

To determine the significance of the water polo victory would be akin to deciding which one of thousands of bits of glittering glass actually turned a mosaic into a piece of art. Yet, to the post-Revolution Hungarian expatriate and Olympic athlete, there must have been satisfaction in the victory itself, followed by word-of-mouth reportage of the victory over the Soviet Union's water polo team. As well, the subsequent defection of more than a quarter of their Olympians likely carried the message that the fire of the Revolution was alive.

During the Hungarian Revolution there was grass roots and large-scale revolution in Hungary itself. But, in part out of fear for their families remaining at home, the athletes' (and expatriates') acts of "rebellion and revolution" within the sporting milieu remained, for the most part, within the rules structure. The overt violence I have discussed in this paper (particularly the altercation resulting in Hungarian Ervin Zador being cut above the right eye) was directed from Soviet to Hungarian athlete. However, there was symbolic significance in these acts – from the easily recognized photo of a bleeding Ervin Zador, to the water polo victory of a supposedly humbled satellite of the Soviet Union, to the expatriate prideful reaction to the Hungarian Olympic team. These signs of resistance came to signify Hungarian anti-Soviet sentiment to the world and to and for thousands of Hungarian expatriates.

Furthermore, the significance of grass-roots resistance stemming from symbolic acts of resistance cannot be overestimated. Chantal Mouffe interprets Gramsci's "new collective will [which] must be formed through moral and intellectual reform."[102] While Gramsci saw hegemony as being driven by an intellectual elite, by definition, the mass of people must accede to dominant ideology. Thus, the significance of symbolic gestures of resistance, while (and perhaps *because*) not easily documented, may have much more importance than previously thought. According to Scott, it seems that grass-roots resistances employ time in order to wear down opposition. But for time to remain an effective tool, key symbols must hold significance for the oppressed.

Anything that reinforced a notion of difference (such as the superiority of the Hungarian over the Soviet water polo team) burned brightly for Hungarians. This ember of hope was reinforced in the Western press. According to the Manchester *Guardian Weekly*:

> The thing that Soviet power has quite failed to attain is to make a subject State go back on its own revolution and consent to the re-establishment of the old order. ... Physical power lies – mostly held in reserve – with the Soviet troops. Political power lies scattered amid the rubble and the broken promises, waiting to be picked up.[103]

As this statement implies, resistance to force uses time and cultural memory as tools for success. Ferenc Váli, an expatriated Hungarian author, in 1966, wrote of Hungary's wait for a "traditional nationalism":

> The pessimism of society is a current topic of Hungarian sociological-political articles. ... in the wake of the 1956 uprising to the present [1966] ... [m]uch evidence available demonstrates that the alienation from public affairs, from politics and the affairs of party and state, is the reaction against the concepts and ideology of the communist regime. It is not an indifference towards the interests and future of the nation, it is not an attitude devoid of

national feeling. ... Even in the background of complete nihilistic attitudes nationalism may even more prevail.[104]

The Hungarian people, according to Váli, had gone underground with their hopes of a "traditional nationalism." If Western-style, traditional nationalism was to prevail in Hungary, shared and crystallized cultural moments in time like the Olympic water polo matches between the Soviet Union and Hungary might serve to keep it alive, albeit simmering below the surface.

Yet the coalescence of the rich tradition of Hungarian Olympic water polo with the team's victory over the Soviet Union in December of 1956 provided some inspiration.[105] The win became a symbol, much like Scott's "quiet, unremitting guerrilla warfare,"[106] which served to diminish the fact of the Soviet Union's brutal military superiority over Hungary. This crystallized moment of resistance became a sign that could easily be alluded to and called upon as a cultural icon for the anti-Soviet sentiment felt by expatriated Hungarians. A case for the recognition of cultural icons as forms of resistance is cited by Allen Guttmann:

> "Every Tunisian sports victory against the European sports organizations," wrote Ben Larbi Mohamed and Borhane Errais, "contributed to the destruction of the myth of colonial power."[107]

As Morgan puts it, the water polo victory and the context surrounding it, became "collectively oppositional. ... [this type of action] represent[s] 'counterhegemonic' assertions that are based in a recognized opposition of interest."[108] From without and within Hungary, small, guerrilla-like resistances like the 1956 Hungarian Olympic water polo victory in Melbourne, Australia, continued to erode remaining Hungarian respect for the Soviet-directed regime.

Notes

Editors' note: This chapter, in slightly different form, was originally published in the *Journal of Sport History* 23(3): 120–139.

1 "Hungarians beat Russian team, 4–0," New York Times, 6 December 1956, p. 49.
2 David L. Andrews, "Welsh Indigenous! and British Imperial? – Welsh Rugby, Culture, and Society 1890–1914," *Journal of Sport History*, 18, Winter 1991: pp. 335–349.
3 Mark Dyreson, "America's Athletic Missionaries: Political Performance, Olympic Spectacle and the Quest for an American National Culture, 1896–1912," *Olympika: The International Journal of Olympic Studies*, 1, 1992: pp. 70–91.
4 See Eric Hobsbawm, "Introduction: Inventing Traditions," in *The Invention of Tradition*, ed. Eric Hobsbawm and Terence Ranger, (Cambridge: Cambridge University Press, 1983),1–14; Hugh Trevor-Roper, "The Invention of Tradition: The Highland Tradition of Scotland," in *The Invention of Tradition*, ed. Eric Hobsbawm and Terence Ranger, (Cambridge: Cambridge University Press, 1983), pp. 15–41; David Lowenthal, *The Past is a Foreign Country*, (Cambridge: Cambridge University Press, 1985), pp. 336–337.

5 See Matti Goksøyr, "Our Games - Our Virtues? – 'National Sports' as Symbols: (An Attempt to Establish Idealtypes"), paper given at the 3rd Annual International Society for the History of Sport and Physical Education, July 1995, Capetown, South Africa.

6 Since the major focus of this paper is on the symbolic power of the Hungarian–Soviet Union match on Olympic athletes and Hungarian expatriates, English-language material provided the primary sources for this paper. An equally interesting angle on this "crystallized moment" would be to explicate home reaction (war tends to obliterate, among many taken-for-granteds, communications) of Hungarians involved in the Revolution to their country's Olympic defeat of the Soviets.

7 "Whereby each text is seen to generate a potentially infinite range of meanings": Dick Hebdige, Subculture: The Meaning of Style, (London: Methuen and Co. Ltd., 1979), 117.

8 James C. Scott, Weapons of the Weak: Everyday Forms of Peasant Resistance, (New Haven: Yale University Press, 1985), p. 28.

9 Scott, Weapons of the Weak, p. 29.

10 Jim Scott, "Everyday Forms of Peasant Resistance," in Everyday Forms of Peasant Resistance in South-East Asia, eds. James C. Scott and Benedict J. Tria Kerkvliet (Totowa, NJ: Frank Cass and Company Limited, 1986), p. 5.

11 See Milton J. Esman, "Commentary," in Everyday Forms of Peasant Resistance, ed. Forrest D. Colburn (Armonk, NY: M. E. Sharpe, Inc., 1989), p. 223 and his note 5.

12 Peter Donnelly, "Resistance Through Sports: Sport and Cultural Hegemony," in Sports et Sociétés Contemporaines: Proceedings of the VIIIe Symposium de L'ICSS in Paris 6–10 July, 1983, (Paris: Société Française De Sociologie Du Sport, 1983), 398. Much of this discussion is drawn from Raymond Williams, "Dominant, Residual, and Emergent," in Marxism and Literature, (Oxford: Oxford University Press, 1977), pp. 121–127.

13 Hebdige, Subculture, p. 17.

14 Jerome Bruner, Acts of Meaning, (Cambridge, MA: Harvard University Press, 1990), p. xiii.

15 "Hungary's Heroes in their Hour of Staggering Strain," Sports Illustrated, 3 December 1956: p. 22.

16 See, for example, Victoria Paraschak, "Organized Sport for Native Females on the Six Nations Reserve, Ontario from 1968 to 1980: A Comparison of Dominant and Emergent Sport Systems," Canadian Journal of History of Sport, 21(2): pp. 70–80.

17 Donnelly, "Resistance Through Sports," p. 399.

18 Donnelly, "Resistance Through Sports," p. 400.

19 See Esman, "Commentary," p. 222.

20 Ferenc A. Váli, Rift and Revolt in Hungary, (Cambridge, MA: Harvard University Press, 1961), p. 207.

21 Váli, Rift and Revolt in Hungary, p. 209.

22 Ibid.

23 Sandor Molnar, "Physical Education in Hungary," (Monograph #2), in Physical Education Around the World, ed. William Johnson (Indianapolis, IN: Phi Epsilon Kappa Fraternity, 1968), 18–25; F. Mezö, Golden Book of Hungarian Olympic ChampionsI, (Budapest: És Könyvkiadó, 1955).

24 As early as 1896, popular myth linked Hungarian aquatic prowess to the Danube River: Hungarian hero Alfréd Hajós, the Athens' (1896) gold medalist, was, it is said, spurred on to swimming glory at age 13 by the drowning of his father in the waters of the Danube. See Mezö, Golden Book of Hungarian Olympic Champions.

25 David Ray, ed., From the Hungarian Revolution: A Collection of Poems, (Ithaca, NY: Cornell University Press, 1966).

26 David Irving, Uprising! (London: Hodder and Stoughton, 1981), p. 7.

27 For example, "'What is the difference between Communism and slavery?' 'Easy. At the time of slavery there was no telephone or radio.'" Irving, *Uprising!*, p. 58.

28 Irving, *Uprising!*, [photo caption] 321-m.

29 Irving, *Uprising!*, p. 165.

30 A. Handler, *From the Ghetto to the Games: Jewish Athletes in Hungary*, (Boulder, CO: East European Monographs, 1985), p. 129.

31 "Letter to the Reader," *Hungarian Digest*, 3, (1986), p. 3.

32 Quoted in István Zsiday, "Myth and Reality", *Hungarian Digest*, 3, (1986), p. 76.

33 "Before the Olympics: A Review of Sports in the Satellites," *News From Behind the Iron Curtain* 5 (1956): p. 18.

34 See, however, Avery Brundage's and J. Lyman Bingham's comments on p. 52 of this book.

35 Irving, *Uprising!*.

36 "Before the Olympics," p. 15.

37 B. Rajki, *Water Polo*, (London: Museum Press Limited, 1958).

38 W. J. Juba, "Introduction," in *Water Polo*, B. Rajki (London: Museum Press Limited, 1958), p. 5.

39 "Hungary's Heroes in their Hour of Staggering Strain," *Sports Illustrated*, 3 December 1956: p. 22.

40 "Hungary's Heroes," p. 23.

41 Ray, *From the Hungarian Revolution*, viii.

42 Ferenc A. Váli, *A Scholar's Odyssey*, (Ames, IA: Iowa State University Press, 1990).

43 Irving, *Uprising!*, p. 158.

44 Irving, *Uprising!*, p. 155.

45 Váli, *Scholar's*, p. 216.

46 "Hungary Will Send Team to Olympics," *New York Times*, 30 October 1956, 49.

47 "Nations That Withdrew Urged to Return to Olympic Games," *New York Times*, 10 November 1956, p. 22.

48 Ferenc A. Váli, "The Regime and The Nation: Resistance and Coexistence," in *Ten Years After: The Hungarian Revolution in the Perspective of History*, ed. T. Aczel (New York: Holt, Rinehart and Winston, 1966), p. 149.

49 During the Revolution, a few of the Soviets, as well, were sympathetic to the Hungarian people. On 25 October 1956, for example, Italian Ilario Fiore wrote,
   It appeared that the Russian army, after twenty-four hours of procrastination, had finally decided to wipe out the rebels. The procession of Hungarians moved slowly towards the tanks, and then suddenly the "miracle" occurred: the Russians got down from their tanks and beckoned to the Hungarians, as though inviting them to come on without fear. They mingled, they talked, and finally the civilians were seen to mount the tanks with the soldiers ...
   (Cited in Irving, *Uprising!*, p. 344)
   But many of the sympathetic Soviets were later executed.
   Certainly, this ambivalence between the Soviet and Hungarian *people* may have contributed to the curiosity reported, that "the Hungarians, on the [water polo] winners' rostrum, applauded the Russians as they received their medals." British Olympic Association, *Official Report of the Olympic Games XVIth Olympiad*, (London: World Sports, 1956), p. 70.

50 Váli, "The Regime and the Nation," p. 149.

51 "Nations that Withdrew," p. 22.

52 Ibid.

53 For further discussion of this "Olympics as political maneuvering" concept, see, for example, Wendy Gray and Robert Knight Barney, "Devotion to Whom? German-American Loyalty on the Issue of Participation in the 1936 Olympic Games," *Journal*

of Sport History, 17(2) 1990: pp. 214–231; Steven R. Wenn, "A Suitable Policy of Neutrality? FDR and the Question of American Participation in the 1936 Olympics," *The International Journal of the History of Sport*, 8(3) 1991: pp. 319–335; for a slightly different view, see Bill Murray, "Berlin in 1936: Old and New Work on the Nazi Olympics," *The International Journal of the History of Sport*, 9(1) 1992: pp. 29–49. Brundage himself, after the Melbourne Games, asked that the IOC be considered for a Nobel Peace Prize, citing previous "Pax Olympica" (my term) efforts of the IOC ("Olympic Committee Bids for Nobel Peace Prize." *New York Times*, 8 December 1956, p. 23.)

54 "How Foul Can the Games Get!," *Daily Mirror*, 7 December 1956, p. 19.

55 "Hungary's Heroes in their Hour," p. 23.

56 Ibid.

57 Group A included Rumania and Australia; Group B included the United States and a combined Great Britain and Northern Ireland team; Group C was made up of Italy, Germany, and Singapore.

58 Organizing Committee, *Official Report of The Organizing Committee for the Games of the XVI Olympiad Melbourne 1956* (Melbourne: W. M. Houston, Government Printer, 1958).

59 *Sports Illustrated* (17 December 1956), *The Melbourne Herald* (7 December 1956), and the British Olympic Association (1956) all report that the Hungarians played the Yugoslavs last to win the gold; *The Official Report of the Organizing Committee for the Games of the XVI Olympiad Melbourne 1956* indicates a more dramatic chronology, with the Soviets and Hungarians playing for the gold. This appears to be a mistake: the *United States 1956 Olympic Book* (New Haven, CT: United States Olympic Association, 1957, p. 191) cites the results of the contest for the gold medal as Hungary 2, Yugoslavia 1, and the "Final Round," the one prior to the medal round, concluding with the Hungary/Russia [sic] match. The reason that the victory over the "Russians" "practically assured" the Hungarians of the gold was because Yugoslavia and Germany tied 2–2 in the Final Round. At any rate, the Hungarian-Soviet match was uncommonly bloody, even by water polo standards, to many signifying oppressed versus oppressor, with the oppressed winning the sympathies of a partisan crowd.

60 "Hungarians Beat Russian Team, 4–0," *New York Times*, 6 December 1956, p. 49.

61 "Messages for Team Brought," *The Melbourne Herald*, 3 December 1956, p. 3.

62 "Russians in Rough Game," *The Melbourne Herald*, 6 December 1956; Ken Knox, "Polo Clash Not Players' Fault," *The Melbourne Herald*, 7 December 1956, p. 30; "A Sweet and Bloody Victory for Hungary," *Sports Illustrated*, 17 December 1956: 22–23; "Hungarians Beat Russian Team, 4–0," *The New York Times*, 6 December 1956, p. 49; "Fire in the Ashes," *The Manchester Guardian Weekly*, 13 December 1956, p. 1; "Olympic Games Water Polo Incident," *The London Times*, 7 December 1956, p. 10; and Peter Wilson, "How Foul Can the Games Get!," *The Daily Mirror*, 7 December 1956, p. 19.

63 Knox, "Polo Clash," p. 30.

64 "A Sweet and Bloody": p. 22. I am grateful to an anonymous reviewer for pointing out that the term "penalty box" is not appropriate to water polo; perhaps this misappropriation of the term by this journalist serves to indicate the lack of knowledge of the sport of water polo.

65 "Hungarians Beat Russian," p. 49.

66 "Hungarians Beat Russian," p. 49.

67 "A Sweet and Bloody": p. 22.

68 "Man down" or "man up" are water polo terms signifying imbalance of number of players, generally due to ejection for some sort of foul.

69 "Hungarians Beat Russian," p. 49.

70 Wilson, "How Foul," p. 19.

71 Ibid.

72 "A Sweet and Bloody:" 23.

73 "Olympic Committee Bids." p. 23

74 Richard D. Mandell, *Sport: A Cultural History* (New York: Columbia University Press, 1984), 249.

75 Bill Lomax, *Hungary 1956* (New York: St. Martin's Press, 1976), p. 128.

76 Irving, *Uprising!* p. 546.

77 Irving, *Uprising!* pp. 475–479 and 154–164.

78 Váli, *A Scholar's*, p. 219.

79 Ibid.

80 See B. Lotze, "While the World Was Watching: Coverage of the Revolution in German and American Newsmagazines," in *War and Society in East Central Europe, Vol. XI: The First War Between Socialist States: The Hungarian Revolution of 1956 and Its Impact,* ed. B. K. Király, B. Lotze, and N. F. Dreisziger (New York: Brooklyn College Press, 1984). In this analysis of coverage of the Hungarian Revolution by three newsmagazines (*Time, Newsweek,* and *Der Spiegel*), Lotze found that the two United States' publications viewed the revolution as "an uprising against communism. … [while] *Der Spiegel* sees the significance of the events in the fact that one socialist country has rebelled against another" (p. 446). These, she infers, reflect nationalistic ideologies.

81 "Hungary's Heroes in Their Hour": p. 22 [photo caption].

82 Irving, *Uprising!*

83 "45 Hungarians Stay Behind in Australia as the Olympic Athletes Start for Home," *The New York Times,* 8 December 1956, p. 3.

84 "Hungary Retains Water Polo Title," *The New York Times,* 8 December 1956, p. 23.

85 Harry Gordon, *Australia and the Olympic Games* (St. Lucia, Queensland: University of Queensland Press, 1994), 223.

86 "Hungarian Sidelight," *The New York Times,* 9 December 1956, p. 8E.

87 Athletes on the Hungarian Olympic team, by challenging the system, were sacrificing security for their families and friends, but also lucrative financial situations. See "Before the Olympics": 14: "… a player would have a token job at which he [sic] would put in a few hours of work or none. From this he draws an excellent salary. In addition, he has special bonuses (called in Hungary, 'calory money') … It is estimated that an average Hungarian 'Ace Athlete' earns 2–3,000 *forint* a month; a Class I soccer player, 4–5,000 *forint* (the average industrial worker earns less than 1,000 *forint* a month)."

88 Váli, *A Scholar's*, p. 242.

89 "45 Hungarians," p. 3.

90 "Most of those going back to Hungary … are doing so because they have wives and children at home, and not because they approve of the Soviet-supported Government in Budapest": "45 Hungarians", p. 3.

91 "Hungarians Sob in Airport Welcome", *The Melbourne Herald,* 3 December 1956, p. 1.

92 "This Team Won't Go Back to Hungary", *The Melbourne Herald,* 7 December 1956, p. 1.

93 Unfortunately, according to Stephen Wenn, "The Olympic Movement and Television, 1936–1980: Critical Dates", handout from panel discussion ("The Impact of Television on the Olympic Movement") at the North American Society for Sport History annual meeting, Long Beach, CA, May 27, 1995: "[when] international television networks refuse to pay the 1956 Melbourne Organizing Committee for the right to use delayed newsreel footage … [there was a] virtual television blackout." For

the Hungarian athletes, this, of course, resulted in less visual impact upon the world's Olympic audience.

94 Lomax, *Hungary 1956*, p. 17: "In the West, the uprising was presented as a national rebellion against communist dictatorship, while in the East the communists saw it as an attempt to overthrow socialism and restore Western-style capitalism. Both these viewpoints ignored the real issue of Hungary – that it was a social revolution aimed not at restoring a previous régime but at creating a radically new social order, one that would be both more democratic than the capitalist West and more socialist than the communist East." In fact, Lomax argues against Zinner and Kecskemeti (cited in Lomax), who, he says, view "the mass revolution of workers, peasants and youth … [as] a secondary development and not an activating force."

95 The fact that its participants consisted of the people, Olympic athletes as well as writers and factory workers supports a social heteroglossic, polyphonic view as proposed by M. M. Bakhtin, "Discourse in the Novel", in *The Dialogic Imagination*, ed. Michael Holquist, trans. Caryl Emerson and Michael Holquist (Austin, TX: University of Texas Press, 1981), p. 263. See, for varied sources, e.g. *Ten Years After: The Hungarian Revolution in the Perspective of History*; Lotze, "While the World Was Watching: Coverage of the Revolution in German and American Newsmagazines"; Ray, *From the Hungarian Revolution: A Collection of Poems*.

96 *Time* magazine cited the Hungarian Freedom Fighter as their Man of the Year for 1956.

97 This whole paper serves as evidence for this point; however, see, for example, Váli, "The Regime and the Nation"; Ray, *From the Hungarian Revolution*; Lomax, *Hungary 1956*.

98 "Hungary's Heroes": p. 23.

99 "Before the Olympics": p. 15.

100 Mezö, *Golden Book*.

101 Several crew members of the celebrated US naval vessel Pueblo demonstrated resistance to capture by extending their middle fingers to the photographer.

102 Chantal Mouffe, "Hegemony and Ideology in Gramsci", in *Culture, Ideology, & Social Process: A Reader*, ed. Tony Bennett (London: Barsford Academic and Educational Ltd., in association with the Open University Press, 1981), p. 225.

103 "Fire in the Ashes," p. 1.

104 Váli, "The Regime and the Nation," p. 142.

105 Hungarian prowess in the pool has been legendary, and continues to this day: on a water polo tour to Australia and New Zealand, this author met several outstanding water polo coaches who were Hungarian. Additionally, Hungarian innovations in swimming (e.g. the over-the-water recovery of the arms in the "Hungarian breaststroke") and water polo (the high-finesse at ball-handling) have been legend (see, e.g. "Mixed Bag").

106 Scott, "Everyday Forms of Peasant Resistance," p. 5.

107 Ben Larbi Mohamed and Borhane Errais, "Un Siécle d'Histoire du Sport en Tunisie, 1881–1981", in *Geschichte der Leibesübungen*, ed. Horst Überhorst, 6 vols (Berlin: Bartels & Wernitz, 1971–1989), 6:277, 283–84, cited in Allen Guttmann, *Games and Empires: Modern Sports and Cultural Imperialism*, (New York: Columbia University Press, 1994), p. 69.

108 William J. Morgan, *Leftist Theories of Sport: A Critique and Reconstruction* (Urbana: University of Illinois Press, 1994), p. 100.

Chapter 4

Cold War football

British–European encounters in the 1940s and 1950s

Ronnie Kowalski and Dilwyn Porter

Sport, as Kim Philby discovered, was embedded in the tortuous story of East–West relations even before the Cold War had begun. Retreating into the darkness of a London cinema after a clandestine meeting in the autumn of 1945, the British Secret Intelligence Service official and double agent found himself watching a newsreel item covering the arrival of the Dinamo Moskva (Moscow Dynamo) footballers at the start of their British tour. There, smiling back at him from the screen, was his contact from the Soviet embassy, who had been at the airport as part of the official welcoming party.[1] This trivial incident, of no significance at the time to anyone but Philby himself, reminds us that sport, in its own way, was as important a part of Cold War international relations as diplomacy and espionage. Peter Beck's recent work on the history of Cold War sport underlines this point. While conceding that the nature of the conflict was primarily "politico-ideological," he argues that "[s]port became a high-profile battlefield upon which representatives from both sides of the 'Iron Curtain' competed (in the full glare of the modern media and before a global audience) for primacy." In short, sport was one manifestation of the "Cultural Olympics" in which the Cold War protagonists were more or less permanently engaged.[2]

This essay will examine the ways in which encounters on the football field between teams from Britain, the Soviet Union and eastern Europe after the end of the Second World War reflected Cold War tensions. Notwithstanding the lip service paid by both sides of an increasingly divided Europe to the idea that sport in general could act as a means of cementing or promoting international friendship (peaceful coexistence and *détente* as it later was called) other political considerations were paramount. They were most pronounced in the communist East where the various regimes invested in significant propaganda campaigns on the back of sporting successes. Their purpose was to vindicate the achievements of communism, domestically and internationally. In Britain, the government since the 1930s increasingly had recognised that there was a connection between sport and politics. Yet it had not exploited sport as systematically for propaganda purposes. In part, its failure to do so can be explained by the fact that in Britain sport remained autonomous: it was not sponsored by the state. In the other part, the government had few major successes to crow about.[3]

The following analysis will focus on key episodes in the evolution of Cold War football between the mid-1940s and the mid-1950s: the Dinamo Moskva tour of Britain in the autumn of 1945; and the clashes between British and Hungarian national and club sides in 1953 and 1954. Olympic football where, between 1952 and 1960, Great Britain's amateurs competed against state-sponsored "amateurs" from the Soviet bloc, supplies an additional theme. While the Cold War continued, with ebbs and flows, until Mikhail Gorbachev embarked on his "new course" in Soviet relations with the West in the late 1980s, football never again attained the political significance that it had between 1945 and 1954. There are two reasons why this was the case. After the mid-1950s, with but few exceptions, communist teams were not serious contenders for the major prizes in World and European football: the World Cup; the European Nations' Championship; and the various European (club) cup competitions. Secondly, for the communist states, the Olympic Games, especially the track and field events, became the primary focus of sporting diplomacy and propaganda after their surprisingly successful debut in 1952.

The origins of the Dinamo Moskva tour of 1945

The tour appears to have grown out of an approach made, some time in 1944, by Stanley Rous, secretary of the Football Association (hereafter FA), to Ivan Maisky, Soviet ambassador in London. It subsequently was discussed by, amongst others, the Foreign Secretary, Anthony Eden, and Mrs Churchill, prior to her visit to the Soviet Union at the end of the war.[4] Philip Noel-Baker, a junior minister in the wartime coalition and himself a former Olympic athlete, firmly believed that sport was a means of cementing harmonious relations with the Soviet Union and vigorously supported the tour. The Foreign Office (FO) grudgingly concurred, though it cautioned that "it would take much more than a football match to break down the real barriers which the Soviet Govt. firmly believe in." Frank Roberts, the British *chargé d'affaires* in Moscow, also supported the tour as an "opportunity to promote closer Anglo-Soviet relations."[5] In reality, the FO had become increasingly suspicious of Soviet expansionist designs at the end of the war. But it was reluctant to antagonise the British public, where a solid core of sympathy for the Soviet Union had grown as a result of its enormous contribution to the defeat of Nazism, by reverting to pre-war diplomatic hostilities.[6] Its reluctance to do so arguably explains why the government gave its blessing to the official invitation sent by the FA to Moscow for a Soviet team to tour Britain. The inspiration behind this invitation again had been Rous who had urged the FA to act after he had met Revenko, secretary to the All-Union Committee of Sport and Physical Education, in London in October 1945.[7]

The evidence available makes it more difficult to determine precisely why the Soviet Union, which had largely shunned competition with the West in the inter-war period, agreed to the tour. There is little doubt that it could not have taken place without the sanction of the highest Soviet authorities, presumably Stalin himself. His personal approval was later required before the Soviet Union could compete in the Helsinki Olympics. The rhetorical justification offered at the time by Adrianov, the vice-president of the All-Soviet Committee for Physical Culture, that its purpose was "to establish closer and more friendly relations in the field of sport," was facile.[8] Ten years after the tour, the Soviet sporting journal, *Fizkul'tura i sport,* revealed the true reason. It was seen as the most effective means by which the Soviet Union could launch itself as a major power in world sport and in so doing demonstrate the vitality, even the superiority, of the Soviet system both at home and abroad.[9] What remains puzzling is what motivated the Soviet government in the autumn of 1945 to abandon its reluctance to compete with the West, and especially to send a team to the so-called "home of football" where the risk of defeat might jeopardize its emerging grand designs for sport. While no definitive answer is possible, it is not unreasonable to speculate that earlier "unofficial" encounters had provided some grounds for confidence. In 1944, a team drawn from the Soviet garrison in Tehran had soundly beaten its British counterpart. More importantly, in Berlin on 30 September 1945, a Red Army side had defeated a good British garrison team, drawn largely from professional footballers then serving in the armed forces.[10]

Yet the Soviet government took pains to guarantee that its first officially sanctioned assault on "the bourgeois fortress" of football would not founder. Moskva Dinamo was the chosen instrument of this foray. As champions of the Soviet League, it was the best-equipped club side for the purpose. Political considerations played an important part too. That it was progeny of the Soviet security forces (within the Soviet Union Dinamo was widely known as the *gorodviki*, "the secret policemen") meant that it was the least likely to embarrass the regime either on or off the field.[11] Moreover, in an effort to ensure that Dinamo suffered no inopportune defeats, several guest players were drafted into the squad, most notably Vsevolod Bobrov, the Soviet Union's leading goalscorer from TsDKA, the Red Army team.[12] The Dinamo players no doubt welcomed such reinforcement of their ranks. Anecdotal evidence suggests that teams incurring the displeasure of the regime could expect to be disbanded and their members sent back to the factories, collective farms or, even worse, the labour camps.[13] Finally, some of the fourteen conditions tabled by the visitors on their arrival in Britain betrayed the anxiety of both Dinamo and Soviet Embassy officials that the tour should proceed successfully. Less than truthfully they insisted that as Dinamo was simply a club side it only would "play matches against clubs." Any fixtures with the English, Scottish or Welsh national teams were ruled out, presumably to minimize the risk of defeat.[14]

The Dinamo Moskva tour

There is no doubt that the visit of the "mysterious" Russians attracted enormous interest both from the British public and press. "Mystery" was a central part of this attraction, at a time when British football remained highly insular and world football was regarded as "largely an irrelevance" compared to domestic competition.[15] Moreover, the Britain that Dinamo visited had just come through six years of war. It was in the throes of demobilization and its people were suffering the rigours of post-war austerity. "Conditions of everyday life," as Paul Addison has observed, "were shabby and constricting." Football, then an affordable spectator sport for all, was at the height of its popularity. In combination with respect and admiration for the Soviet Union's heroism and achievements in the war against Nazism, it is little wonder that the tour captured the imagination of supporters in London, Cardiff and Glasgow who filled to capacity (and more) the grounds where Dinamo played.[16]

Dinamo performed with unexpected aplomb and success: first drawing 3–3 with Chelsea; then hammering Cardiff City 10–1; defeating Arsenal 4–3; and finally drawing 2–2 with Glasgow Rangers. The quality of their performances certainly surprised the press pundits and heightened interest in every move the Russians made.[17] Popular enthusiasm was particularly evident in industrial and working-class South Wales where, according to the *Western Mail*, "[t]he Red Flag with its hammer and sickle flew everywhere" in honour of Dinamo's visit. Similarly, on industrial Clydeside in the west of Scotland, Dinamo's cruise down the river to see the shipyards that had contributed so much to the war effort evoked cries of "Good old Joe Stalin" from many workers.[18] Yet such instances of enthusiasm should not blind us to the growing tensions surrounding the tour. It began inauspiciously. The arrival of the Dinamo party, at very short notice, on 4 November was an embarrassment for Rous who had been unable to keep scarce hotel rooms in London on hold. In consequence, the best that could be arranged for some of the party was accommodation at Wellington Barracks until more comfortable arrangements could be made elsewhere. The Barracks were, as Rous conceded, "bare and uncomfortable." Boris Karavsev, cultural attaché at the Soviet Embassy, complained of insufficient bed linen and water for showers. Siniavskii, the radio commentator accompanying the party, swiftly made political capital from this incident. He accounted for the difficulties of accommodation to his listeners by reference to London's post-war housing problem. The reaction of the Soviet Union's estimated 25 million homeless to this explanation remains indeterminable.[19]

Other seemingly trivial controversies dogged the tour as it progressed. The first instance concerned the fixture with Chelsea. On 13 November, *Krasnaia Zvezda*, the Red Army paper, spuriously reported that Chelsea had just signed Tommy Lawton, England's centre-forward, to strengthen the team with the Dinamo fixture in mind.[20] After Dinamo had drubbed third division Cardiff City by a score of 10–1 – (the Soviet press reported that Cardiff were the champions of South Wales and had an imposing reputation in world football) – Trevor Ford, the Welsh international forward, alleged that the scale of the defeat could be attributed to a pre-match warning from the officials that had prevented the home side from adopting its natural, rather physical approach. The upshot, he explained some years afterwards in his autobiography, was that "the Reds [had made] political capital out of a game that had been Britain's pride and joy. That was why, years later, I so thoroughly enjoyed seeing Wolves whip Spartak [Moskva]." The claims of the Soviet press and Ford should both be treated with scepticism. Lawton, though he made his debut against Dinamo, remained at Chelsea until November 1947. Ford himself did not play in the match at Cardiff. And Cyril Spiers, City's manager, had conceded at the time that Dinamo was "the finest football machine he had ever seen."[21]

Further disputes arose before and after the match with Arsenal, regarded by Dinamo as its most important fixture. Mikhail Semichastnyi, the Dinamo captain, issued a press statement before the game in which he argued that the guest players drafted in by Arsenal essentially meant Dinamo would face not a club side but a representative English XI. One plausible reason for Semichastnyi's intervention was that the Dinamo players were anxious to ensure that Moscow would not penalise them unduly should they be defeated.[22] Acrimonious exchanges escalated after the match, which no one had really seen as it was played in thick fog. Both sides complained of foul play. Dinamo was accused of late-tackling and shirt-pulling. In response, Mikhail Iakushin, the Dinamo coach, claimed that "the English" had resorted to physically robust "methods which are considered unsporting by us," a claim that was widely reported and much resented.[23] Interest in and sympathy for Dinamo (and the Soviet Union) did not evaporate overnight but the atmosphere surrounding the tour became increasingly sour and this was reflected in increasingly hostile coverage of Dinamo in most of the British press.

Dinamo's final encounter, with Glasgow Rangers, did little to dispel this growing animosity. On its eve, Dinamo again feigned ignorance of the British transfer system, and categorically refused to take the field with a Rangers side including Jimmy Caskie. He had been bought two days earlier from Everton, so Dinamo attested, just to play against them. Having already sold 90,000 tickets, Rangers had little choice but to bow to Dinamo's pressure.[24] The match itself was dogged with controversy. At one point in the second half, Dinamo had twelve players on the pitch, having brought on a substitute without taking anyone off, while neutral observers were sceptical about the second penalty awarded to Rangers. Mutual recriminations soon followed, with Dinamo accused of persistent body-checking and Rangers of over-robust tackling. Anatolii Salutskii, in his biography of Bobrov, commented that the game had been far from "comradely," with the atmosphere, both on and off the field, threatening.[25]

Consequences

As relations between Dinamo and their hosts deteriorated, it was little surprise that the idea of climactic encounter with a "British" or "English" representative team, though eagerly touted by the British press, was ruled out by Moscow. Nor was it in the interests of the Soviet government to prolong the tour. Each additional match would increase the risk of defeat and so vitiate the extensive and varied propaganda campaign mounted in the Soviet Union on the strength of Dinamo's successes. In *Izvestiia*, the celebrated composer Dmitrii Shostakovich, who was in truth a "keen fan," praised Dinamo's achievement as testimony to the vitality of Soviet society. Special film reports of the matches were prepared for cinema distribution across the country.[26] As *Krasnyi sport*, the leading Soviet sports paper, noted on the eve of the team's return to Moscow, there were important lessons to be drawn from the tour. "It is a triumph for our school of football," it stressed, "which is based on collectivism, organisation and the unbending will for victory, the characteristic qualities of Soviet man." Ultimate credit for this triumph was attributed to the Communist Party, which had nurtured these qualities.[27] Though it is impossible to assess the impact of this campaign on the Soviet people, it signified the importance that the regime had begun to attach to sport as a vehicle for its propaganda.

It was hoped, moreover, that the tour would yield significant advantages abroad, by encouraging British goodwill towards the Soviet Union. To some extent it may have succeeded in that Dinamo's visit provided a convenient focus for those already well disposed towards the Soviet Union and anxious about the rapid deterioration of post-war relations with Britain's former ally. But surviving pro-Soviet sympathies owed little to the British press, which, with the exceptions of the *Daily Herald* and the *News Chronicle*, became increasingly hostile to Dinamo as the tour progressed.[28] The Dinamo party's reluctance to talk to journalists led the right-wing *Daily Mail* to depict the Russians as secretive, sullen and suspicious. On the left, the staunchly pro-Labour *Daily Mirror*, described Dinamo in a similar way, in all probability taking its cue from Ernest Bevin, the foreign secretary in the recently elected Labour Government, who had scant sympathy for the Soviet Union.[29] There is no doubt that Dinamo's visit did little to mitigate the developing hostile trend in British public opinion which tended, after the Potsdam Conference of July–August 1945, to follow the Foreign Office and service chiefs down what Peter Hennessy has described as "an ever-grimmer road of East-West confrontation." By September 1946, a Gallup poll indicated that 41 percent of those questioned were "less friendly" towards the Soviet Union than they had been a year earlier; only 9 percent were "more friendly."[30] Whether the tour created "fresh animosity on both sides," as George Orwell, another critic of the Soviet Union concluded, is far less certain. Arguably he exaggerated the political significance of what he called "the vicious passions that football provokes."[31] Some fifty years later ,Victor Peppard and James Riordan offered a more measured judgement of the Dinamo tour. It had served its purpose in gaining international credibility for Soviet sport generally. As an instrument of Soviet propaganda, however, it was at best a qualified success and had not served to improve relations between Britain and the Soviet Union. Finally, and without denying its political import, they pointed out that sport "is not the real substance of politics." As such, it "is unable to reconcile fundamental differences between opposing political systems, especially when one or both are determined not to find accommodation and common ground."[32]

It was not until the autumn of 1954, when Arsenal again played Dinamo in Moscow, that the British–Soviet football connection was renewed. No doubt British insularity was partly responsible for this nine-year gap. In addition, as the Cold War intensified in the late Stalin period, the Soviet leadership retreated to its previous position with regard to sporting competition with the West – at least until it had fully prepared its sportsmen and sportswomen for their dramatic entry into the Helsinki Olympics. Thereafter, football in general rarely again served as an important surrogate for East–West rivalries. Even in 1958, when the Soviet Union first competed in the World Cup, little overt political significance was attached to the event, despite Soviet victory over England. One major exception, when football became more than a game, were the years 1953 and 1954 when a series of high profile contests between British and Hungarian sides took place.

The Hungarian challenge

With football relations between Britain and the Soviet Union effectively suspended between Dinamo's tour of 1945 and Arsenal's visit to Moscow in November 1954, any contacts between Britain and other countries in the Soviet bloc were likely to seem more significant. This was especially so in respect of links with Hungary, winners of the Olympic tournament at Helsinki in 1952 and widely recognized at the time as the rising power in world football. Though clearly of less central importance in the context of the Cold War than British-Soviet relations, the suspicion and hostility that characterized diplomatic contacts between London and Budapest, once communist rule had been established there in the late 1940s, should not be underestimated. The fall-out following the arrest, in November 1949, of Edgar Sanders, a British businessman accused – with some justification it now seems – of spying, was especially severe. After "confessing" at a show trial in February 1950, Sanders was sentenced to thirteen years' imprisonment, prompting the *Economist* to claim that "the normal conduct of business behind the Iron Curtain is now virtually impossible."[33] Trade relations between Britain and Hungary were severely disrupted as a result of the ban on Hungarian imports that followed, the intention being to punish the regime in Budapest by closing down a source of much-needed hard currency. When this pressure resulted in Sanders being released in August 1953, it generated a further wave of hostility in the British press. The *Daily Herald*, then a mass-circulation newspaper selling almost two million copies daily, ran the story of Sanders' ill treatment at the hands of the Hungarian authorities for five consecutive days.[34]

Moreover, it was by then clear that the government in Budapest was likely to be as assiduous as the Soviet Union in using sport for propaganda purposes. Under the Stalinist hard-liner, Matyas Rakosi, Hungarian sport had been reorganized and brought under central direction. Indeed, "the entire organisation of sport [had been] reshaped to fit the new ideological requirements."[35] One element of this process was the transformation, in 1949, of the Kispest football club into Honved, the team chosen to represent "the people's army." Honved's extraordinarily privileged players, along with those from MTK ("Red Banner"), sponsored by the state security police, supplied the core of the Hungarian national side that triumphed at the 1952 Olympics. The successes achieved by what became known as "the golden team" could not alleviate the grim reality of everyday life under Rakosi's government, with its relentless concentration on production rather than consumption. They were, however, very important to a regime that became increasingly desperate to promote a positive image of itself both at home and abroad.

The crisis that led to the fall of Rakosi in July 1953 provided anti-communist propagandists in the West – "the psychological warfare boys" as they were referred to by Britain's Communist Party newspaper – with an opportunity to suggest that the people's republics of eastern Europe were "cracking up."[36] At this time, it has been noted, there was "an extraordinary gap between popular hatred for the [Hungarian] regime and professed solidarity with it."[37] Imre Nagy's incoming government, desperately seeking to buy a little time, was happy to associate itself with the continuing success of the national football team and the patriotic sentiment that it aroused. Sport became an integral part of an heroic story often repeated in official publications both before and after the Magyars' famous 6–3 victory over England at Wembley in November 1953. Hungary, its workers were constantly reminded, had emerged from the Second World War "devastated, run-down and near bankrupt but with an iron determination to make itself not only prosperous but one of the fittest nations in the world."[38] To this extent, sports journalists on popular newspapers in Britain, like Peter Wilson of the *Daily Mirror* and Desmond Hackett of the *Daily Express*, who were inclined to sift events through an ideological filter, read the situation in Hungary correctly. "I do hope most sincerely that we beat the Hungarians," wrote Wilson before the match at Wembley, "... because I have visited Hungary and I know how they, like other totalitarian states that I have seen, regard a sporting triumph as a justification for their 'superior' way of life."[39]

Origins of the 1953–54 England–Hungary matches

The dismal particularities of British–Hungarian diplomatic relations, along with the intensification of the Cold War generally, help to explain why it took so long for British–Hungarian football relations to be re-established after 1945. It is important to note that sporting contact between the two countries was long established. England had sent an international side to play against Hungary as early as 1908, and there had been matches at full international level as recently as 1934 and 1936. Scotland, rather less inclined to travel abroad than England, had played in Budapest in 1938. British football, moreover, was well regarded in Hungary, largely on account of the legacy of Jimmy Hogan, an Englishman, who had coached MTK/Hungaria with great success during the First World War and again in the mid 1920s.[40]

Yet, when the Hungarian Football Association requested full international fixtures with England in 1946, and again in 1948, they were refused. Stanley Rous, FA secretary and an increasingly important presence at FIFA after he became its secretary in 1950, was especially anxious that England should engage with the global game after the war. It was July 1952, however, before he was able to issue a slightly tentative invitation to the Hungarians. "I'll do my best," he is reported to have said after watching Hungary beat Sweden 6–0 in the Olympic semi-final, "to bring about a meeting between Hungary's and England's best players in the near future."[41] If this is an accurate record, it suggests that Rous – perhaps recalling the Dinamo tour – anticipated some difficulties before arrangements could be finalized. It was a further nine months before a formal invitation was forthcoming in respect of the match that eventually took place at Wembley in November 1953. Significantly, Sandor Barcs, president of the Hungarian Football Association, who claimed that he and Rous had shaken hands on the deal at Helsinki, later recalled that it had taken some time to persuade nervous government officials at home that the match with England should go ahead. At one point he was asked directly, "Do you guarantee that we will win the game if you get permission to play in England?"[42] This suggested a degree of paranoia but was also indicative of the anxieties of a regime determined to protect a major propaganda asset. When Ferenc Puskas and his colleagues finally arrived at Wembley, they came as Olympic champions and were undefeated in their previous twenty-three international matches.

Wembley 1953 and Budapest 1954

For once the Fleet Street hacks could be excused their hyperbole. As far as they were concerned, England versus Hungary at Wembley on 25 November 1953 was "the match of the century." On the day, the English, who liked to regard themselves as the masters of the game that they had given to the rest of the world, were outplayed. Though there had been some recognition before the match that England, previously unbeaten at home against continental opposition, would be severely tested, both the scale of the defeat and the manner in which Hungary had achieved victory, were truly astonishing. "6–3," ran the News Chronicle headline on the morning after the match above a photograph of Gyula Grosics, the Hungarian goalkeeper, walking on his hands: "NOW THE WORLD IS REALLY

UPSIDE DOWN." It was a measure of Hungary's superiority that Peter Wilson, in the *Daily Mirror*, set his ideological reservations aside to acclaim "these new streamlined champions of Europe and, dare I say, the world."[43] Grosics, Hidegkuti and Puskas – especially Puskas – became well-known in England, almost overnight. Collectively, the Hungarians had administered a huge shock to the small world of English professional football. As George Robb, England's left-winger, who had the misfortune to play his one and only full international that day at Wembley, later reflected: "It changed our attitude. We weren't the governors any more."[44] This message appears to have reached Glasgow. The sight of England humbled may not have been entirely unwelcome north of the border but some Scottish sports journalists were quick to point out that the "magical Magyars," as they were often called, had exposed weaknesses afflicting British football generally. "We'd only begin to measure up to these continental crackshots," observed Jack Harkness in the *Sunday Post*, "if the Government took the game over, appointed a Minister of Sport, and ran the game the way Hungary and others run it."[45]

For the fiercely right-wing and anti-interventionist *Sunday Post* even to hint in passing that such an outcome might be desirable was an indication of the immediate impact of Hungary's victory on the professional game and those who wrote about it in the newspapers. It no doubt shook many – though by no means all – of those characterized by Malcolm Allison, a professional footballer with unusually radical views for the 1950s, as "the dim, bland men whose voices were most powerful in English football." As the football journalist, Brian Glanville, later explained, "this match gave eyes even to the blind."[46] For a few followers of "the people's game" the lessons to be drawn were essentially political. Rogan Taylor, who watched the match on television as an eight-year-old in Liverpool, recalled that communist neighbours were convinced that what had transpired at Wembley was a victory for "socialist football," the triumph of the collective over a collection of individuals.[47] Though this was undoubtedly a minority view in Britain, it coincided precisely with the post-match analysis disseminated by the party propagandists in Budapest. George Labouchere, head of the British legation in Budapest, reported that the Wembley victory had been acclaimed "at great length" and that the press there had been "at pains to show that it represents a victory for the Communist nature of the Hungarian state."[48] Puskas's speech to the crowd that greeted the team on its return to Budapest, as recounted by official Hungarian sources, seems contrived and suspiciously well rehearsed, but was clearly designed to make the same point. "We thank the party, the government and our people," he was reported as saying, "for making it possible for us to prepare undisturbed for the greatest sporting task of our lives."[49]

Though diplomatic relations between England and Hungary improved a little before the return fixture in May 1954, they remained generally cool. A British European Airways spokesman observed that the "Elizabethan" in which the English team had travelled had been "the first British plane [to land] in Budapest for two years." It was a mark of the extent to which football's world order had changed that the British press was unanimous in predicting a comfortable Hungarian victory. "It will be the biggest shock of post-war European football," observed Clifford Webb in the *Daily Herald*, "if England manage to humble Hungary here on Sunday." Peter Wilson, writing after the event, claimed that his pre-match prediction had been only two goals out: "I thought it would be 8–2 in favour of Hungary."[50] In the end it had been 7–1 and that was bad enough. It remains the heaviest defeat suffered by England at full international level. This outcome supplied an opportunity that the propagandists in Budapest exploited assiduously for both internal and external consumption. The match itself, staged at the recently constructed People's Stadium, had been something of a state occasion with prominent roles assigned to Imre Nagy and to Istran Dubi, the Hungarian president. A special newspaper bearing the headline "NEW WORLD FAME FOR HUNGARIAN SPORTSMEN" was on sale in the streets of Budapest shortly after the match ended.[51] All this was predictable enough given the nature of the Hungarian regime and its determination to associate itself – and state socialism – with sporting success. Live radio commentaries – broadcast not just in Hungary and England, but in Bulgaria, Czechoslovakia, East Germany and Poland, as well as in Austria and Italy – helped to spread the message. Moreover, English embarrassment was compounded by a BBC own goal. Charles Buchan, a former England captain, employed to supply intermittent summaries as the match progressed, sat in the commentary box "passing remarks and groaning every time something went wrong." Only later did he realise that a live microphone had picked up these comments and broadcast them to listeners at home.[52]

Consequences

Dinamo Moskva's 1945 tour and Arsenal's long-delayed visit to Moscow in 1954 left behind a residue of bitterness and bad feeling that seemed to reflect the state of the political relationship between Britain and the Soviet Union. After the Dinamo–Arsenal game, which Dinamo won 5–0, Jimmy Logie, the Arsenal captain, had refused to shake the referee's hand, thus prompting the accusation that he had lent himself "to those who want to make capital against the Russians."[53] By contrast, the immediate aftermath of the England–Hungary matches in 1953 and 1954 was remarkably benign. There was some irritation about the way in which the Hungarian victories were exploited for propaganda purposes and Frank Coles of the *Daily Telegraph* was moved to suggest that England should in future avoid matches "against obvious world beaters like Hungary."[54] Some in officialdom agreed. Labouchere advised the FO that "it would be better to avoid arranging [contests] with countries such as the Satellite states whose propaganda made largely at the expense of our prestige it cannot be our policy to further." The FO declined his advice, arguing that "[i]t would be *much worse* propaganda if it got around that the West would not make fixtures with the Iron

Curtain because they were afraid of losing." [55] British public opinion, however, seemed relatively unperturbed by the heavy defeats that England had suffered. Indeed, Puskas later recalled "the way everyone we encountered in England hailed the victory without resentment."[56] Back in 1945, it has been suggested in relation to the Dinamo tour, a foreign victory over a British team would almost inevitably have been greeted with a chorus of complaints about cheating. There is no evidence of such a reaction after the England–Hungary matches. "But, no, there we were", recalled George Robb, reflecting the view of the English players. "We were walloped and all credit to the Hungarians."[57] Moreover, it was clear to the millions who had watched the match on television that Hungary's victory at Wembley had been both fair and square. "The game had not been played in Europe but in London; the refereeing had been quite adequate; the margin did not unjustly reflect the play," noted football journalist Brian Glanville.[58] Perhaps, also, it was a little easier to accept a defeat inflicted by Hungary, a communist state but one without superpower pretensions, than a defeat inflicted by a team from the Soviet Union.

In addition, it is important to remember that British people in general, and the English in particular, had many reasons to be cheerful in 1953–4 as they moved from the period of post-war austerity towards the threshold of a modern consumer culture. "The miracle has happened," declared the *Economist* a few weeks after the Budapest fiasco, "– full employment without inflation."[59] And even for those who were inclined to measure national prestige in terms of sporting success, the signs were generally very positive. After all, the summer of 1953 had seen England regain the Ashes by beating Australia at cricket and a British Empire Expedition, led by Sir John Hunt, conquer Mount Everest. A year later, just a few weeks before England conceded seven goals in Budapest, Roger Bannister ran the first sub-four-minute mile, a sporting achievement so significant that even the *Daily Worker* was obliged to wax patriotic. "Hold your heads high this morning, Britain, and shout praise for Roger Bannister, Athlete of the Century."[60] In this context, the "New Elizabethan" era proclaimed by the popular press at the time of the Coronation appeared to have some substance and the disappointing performances of the English football team could be set aside as a mere aberration. There were some journalists who had characterized the matches in ideological terms. Bob Ferrier, Peter Wilson's colleague at the *Daily Mirror*, before the match at Budapest had informed readers that the contrast between Hungarian and English football was "as stark as that between the Sovietised State and the eternal freedom of Britain."[61] In the optimistic climate of 1953–4, however, any collateral damage resulting from the triumph of socialist football, Hungarian-style, at Wembley and the People's Stadium, Budapest, was minimal.

It was minimized still further in November and December 1954 when Wolverhampton Wanderers, the current English champions, within the space of a few weeks, defeated both Moscow Spartak and Honved in two high-profile challenge matches, both of which were televised. Spartak, according to

Glasgow's *Daily Record,* had been "hammered and sickled."[62] Given the comprehensive drubbing that Hungary had inflicted on England only six months previously, and their 4–2 victory, albeit less convincing, against Scotland only a week before, the Honved fixture was seized upon by the media as an opportunity to re-establish the international credentials of English football. The style of play favoured by the Wolves was recognizably and uncompromisingly English; it was direct, physical and based on the long ball. This had proved especially effective in the conditions often experienced in an English winter and Stan Cullis, the Wolves manager, left nothing to chance by ordering the pitch to be watered before the game. According to Ron Atkinson, a Wolves apprentice at the time, Cullis wanted it to be "nice and heavy."[63] As the pitch became heavier on the night – the *Daily Mail* described it as "like a cattle ground at the end of a four day show in the rain" – Honved's neat passing movements broke down and the Wolves recovered from a two-goal deficit to secure a dramatic 3–2 victory. What this proved, according to Desmond Hackett in the *Daily Express,* was that "English soccer ... the genuine, original, unbeatable article, is still the best of its kind in the world."[64] Some extravagant claims were made after the Wolves–Spartak and Wolves–Honved matches including the most extravagant of all, that Wolves were now "champions of the world," a claim from which Cullis, sensibly, sought to disassociate himself.[65] As many words were now expended in praise of the traditional English style of football as had been used to condemn it after the internationals at Wembley and Budapest. The media overreaction was understandable after the Hungarians had given the English such a miserable time over the previous 12 months but it was now possible for those who so wished to believe that the balance had been redressed. A few weeks before Wolves' win over Honved, England had defeated the reigning world champions, West Germany, at Wembley. After Honved's defeat in the mud at Wolverhampton, continental football – and socialist football in particular – lost its mystique and, along with it, much of its ideological significance.

Olympic football

After 1952, when the Soviets made their debut at Helsinki, Cold War rivalries were symbolically represented through sport at each Olympic Games. The Olympic football competition, though massively overshadowed by FIFA's World Cup, created additional opportunities for encounters between teams representing Britain and the Soviet bloc on the football field. Great Britain had dominated Olympic football in the early years of the twentieth century but made little impression at Helsinki, Melbourne (1956) and Rome (1960). These tournaments were dominated by teams from eastern Europe – Hungary winning in 1952, the Soviet Union in 1956, Yugoslavia in 1960, and Hungary again at Tokyo in 1964, when no British team was entered. There were only three matches between Great Britain and east European opposition in this period, and these were all against Bulgaria. A 2–0 victory for Bulgaria in Sofia was followed by a 3–3 draw at Wembley in the 1956 qualifying tournament. Having been eliminated, the British team was then invited to Melbourne after a number of entrants had withdrawn, only to be eliminated by Bulgaria for a second time, losing 6–1 in the second round.

Reports of the Great Britain–Bulgaria matches in the British press often resorted to the stereotypes that had featured in coverage of the Dynamo tour of 1945. Thus Geoffrey Green in *The Times*, after the draw at Wembley in May 1956, while acknowledging the superior technique of the Bulgarians, observed that "as a team, they bore the stamp of being too highly drilled, an automaton unable to extemporise, or adjust itself to changing circumstances."[66] This resurfaced in the official report on the Melbourne tournament written by Willy Meisl for the British Olympic Committee. The Soviet team had won yet "they still lack[ed] individual initiative and [were] absolutely stumped when faced with any 'unusual' situation or tactic." Meisl's description of Lev Yashin, the Soviet Union's famous goalkeeper, betrayed an underlying *angst*, reflecting frustration at the failure of the Western powers to deter the invasion of Hungary that had taken place a few months earlier. Yashin, it seemed, viewed the penalty area much as the Soviet leadership viewed eastern Europe, as his particular sphere of influence: "he feels sacrosanct in this area, parading it at his leisure." Meisl, Austrian by birth and normally not an admirer of the more physical aspects of the British game, "longed for a spirited forward – a Lofthouse or a Ford – to bring him down to earth."[67]

There was, however, no possibility of Nat Lofthouse, Trevor Ford or any other British professional appearing at the Olympic Games where only designated amateurs were allowed to participate. The players who represented Great Britain, drawn from senior amateur clubs in England and Scotland, were capable of delivering the occasional outstanding performance, notably a 2–2 draw against an Italian side that included Burgnich, Trapattoni and Rivera during the 1960 tournament in Rome. Their failure, however, to mount an effective challenge to the supremacy of teams from the Soviet Union and eastern Europe was due to the inability of the International Olympic Committee to ensure that its football tournament was played on a level playing field. "Even by 1952," Stanley Rous recalled, "the Olympic final in Helsinki was between perhaps the two best professional teams of the day, Puskas's Hungarians and the Jugoslav national side."[68] The representative sides sent to the Games by east European countries were composed of "amateurs" who were, in effect, state-aided professionals. Even after 1960, when the rules were modified to exclude players who had previously represented their countries in the World Cup, teams sent to the Olympics by countries from the Soviet bloc were "merely stepping stones for players destined for higher things in the international soccer world."[69] The Hungary–Yugoslavia final, wrote Bernard Joy of the London *Evening Standard*, who had played for Arsenal against Dinamo in 1945, had featured teams that were "professional" in all but name. "These players were given 'paper' jobs," he complained, "named students or army officers, paid a fat salary and played football whenever and wherever they liked."[70] Though this overestimated the autonomy of eastern Europe's state-aided footballers, Joy was essentially correct. "To compete on equal terms," he observed in 1960, "we should have to register our full international side as amateurs, persuade a firm or Government Department to put them nominally on the staff, pay higher wages than they earn now and have no restrictions on their playing and training."[71] With Olympic officialdom determined to fudge the definition of amateurism in order to maximize the number of participant countries, this remained a persistent, if minor, cause of contention in Cold War football relations through to the early 1960s.

Conclusion

Sport remained a surrogate battleground for East–West politics as long as the Cold War itself endured. Yet, after the mid-1950s, football itself increasingly receded into the background of East–West sporting rivalries. When England met the Soviet Union at full international level for the first time in May 1958, just prior to the World Cup finals in Sweden, British press coverage was relatively restrained. Even Desmond Hackett of the *Daily Express,* who was noted, according to Stephen Wagg, for his "patriotic venom," confined himself to complaints about the referee and the occasional ideologically loaded aside about the inconveniences of the Soviet system. Having flown from Budapest to Moscow in two hours, he griped, "it then took us 3 hrs. to do the 75 yards from the Customs shed to the car." A few weeks later, after a 1–0 defeat had eliminated "our boys" from the tournament, Hackett directed his venom exclusively at the English selectors, "the mourners at the funeral of the team whose chances they killed," and spared the Soviet victors from criticism.[72]

Thereafter, despite victories in Olympic football, Soviet and east European teams rarely became serious challengers for the major titles in the European and World game. Admittedly, the Soviet Union did win the first European (Nations) Championship in 1960 but victory was devalued by the absence of England, Italy, Scotland, Sweden (World Cup runners-up in 1958) and West Germany. Soviet teams did contest the finals of the same championship in 1964 and 1972 but lost to Spain and West Germany respectively. In the World Cup, the best that the Soviet Union achieved was to reach the semi-finals in 1958 and 1966, while a much underrated Czechoslovakian side was defeated by Brazil in the 1962 final. Such a record of achievement was respectable enough yet ultimate triumph in the most significant football competitions, national and club alike, continued to elude teams from the Soviet Union and eastern Europe. Dinamo Kiev did win the European Cup-Winners Cup in 1975 and 1986, as did Dinamo Tbilisi in 1981, but this competition was very much the poor relation of the European (Champions) Cup.[73] Failure "to storm the heavens" of world football, to use an old revolutionary metaphor, was one reason why the Soviet Union in particular attached less significance to it after the early years of the Cold War. The other reason was that football was of no significance to its major adversary, the United States. Hence, if the Soviet government was to utilise sport "to demonstrate in practice the superiority of the socialist system" it had to concentrate its efforts in areas that did matter to the United States. The Olympic Games supplied one such arena. The regular track and field meetings between the "superpowers" that began in 1958 also assumed increasing importance in Soviet sport diplomacy.[74]

Notes

1 G. Borovik, *The Philby Files: the secret life of the masterspy – KGB archives revealed*, (London: Little, Brown, 1994), pp. 261–2.

2 P. Beck, "Britain and the Cold War's 'Cultural Olympics': Responding to the Political Drive of Soviet Sport, 1945–58," *Contemporary British History*, 2005 vol. 19 (2), pp. 169–70.

3 P. Beck, *Scoring for Britain: International Football and International Politics, 1900–1939*, (London: Frank Cass, 1999).

4 The Football Association, London. Minutes of the Council, 1943–6, 14 January 1946, "A Report of the Visit of Dynamo F.C.," Moscow, November 1945 (hereafter "Rous report").

5 Cited in Beck, "Cultural Olympics," p. 171.

6 P.M.H. Bell, *John Bull and the Bear: British Public Opinion, Foreign Policy and the Soviet Union, 1941–1945*, (London: Edward Arnold, 1990); A. Foster, "The British and the Coming of the Cold War," in A. Deighton (ed.), *Britain and the First Cold War*, (Basingstoke: Macmillan, 1990), pp. 18, 28.

7 Rous report; J. Schleppi, "A History of Professional Football during the Second World War" (unpublished Ph.D. thesis, Ohio State University, 1972), p. 272.

8 Adrianov interview, *Daily Worker*, 8 November 1945.

9 *Fizkul'tura i sport*, 1955 (No. 7), pp. 2–3.

10 *Russia Today*, October 1944; *The Times*, 1 October 1945.

11 *Entsiklopedicheskii slovar' po fizicheskoi kul'ture i sportu* (Moscow, 1961), p. 259; A. Salutskii, *Vsevolod Bobrov* (Moscow: Fizkul'tura i Sport, 1984), p. 9.

12 Salutskii, *Bobrov*, pp. 9–10.

13 A. Ekart, *Vanished without Trace: The Story of Seven Years in Soviet Russia*, (London: Max Parrish, 1954), p. 206.

14 Rous report.

15 P.M. Young, *A History of British Football*, (London: Stanley Paul, 1968), p. 183.

16 P. Addison, *Now the War is Over*, (London: Jonathan Cape, 1985), pp. 113–14; *Glasgow Herald*, 29 November 1945.

17 A detailed account of the matches played can be found in R. Kowalski, D. Porter, "Political Football: Moscow Dynamo in Britain, 1945," *The International Journal of the History of Sport*, 1997 vol.14 (2), pp. 107–113. See also D. Downing, *Passovotchka: Moscow Dynamo in Britain, 1945*, (London: Bloomsbury, 1999).

18 *Daily Herald, Western Mail*, 16 November 1945; *Komsomol'skaia pravda*, 20 November 1945; *Glasgow Herald, Bulletin and Scots Pictorial*, 28 November 1945.

19 S. Rous, *Football Worlds: A Lifetime in Sport* (London: Faber and Faber, 1978), pp. 119–20; Karavsev's complaints in *The Scotsman*, 6 November 1945; Siniavskii's report in *Soviet Weekly*, 22 November 1945. Ironically, when Arsenal visited the Soviet Union nine years later their flight was diverted to Minsk where they spent an uncomfortable night in basic dormitory accommodation.

20   *Krasnaia zvezda*, 13 November 1945.
21   T. Ford, *I Lead the Attack*, (London: Stanley Paul, 1957), p. 57; Spiers' conclusion is cited in S. Matthews, *Feet First Again*, (London: Nicholas Kaye, 1952), p. 82.
22   *Daily Mail*, *Daily Express*, 21 November 1945.
23   Iakushin's allegations on Moscow Radio reported in *Daily Mail*, 23 November 1945; of many Soviet reports see, for example, *Komsomol'skaia pravda*, *Krasnaia zvezda*, 22 November 1945.
24   *Bulletin and Scots Pictorial*, 27 November 1945.
25   *Daily Mail*, 29 November 1945; Salutskii, *Bobrov*, pp. 60–1.
26   *Izvestiia*, 22 November 1945; *Pravda*, 18, 28 November 1945.
27   *Krasnyi sport*, 4 December 1945.
28   *Russia Today*, June 1946.
29   *Daily Mail*, 6 November 1945; *Daily Mirror*, 13 November 1945.
30   P. Hennessy, *Never Again: Britain 1945–51*, (London: Jonathan Cape, 1992), p. 246; G.H. Gallup (ed.), *The Gallup International Public Opinion Polls: Great Britain 1937–1957*, (New York: Random House, 1975), I, 139.
31   G. Orwell, "The Sporting Spirit," *Tribune*, 14 December 1945.
32   V. Peppard, J. Riordan, *Playing Politics: Soviet Sport Diplomacy to 1992*, (London: Jai Press, 1993), p. 58.
33   *Economist*, 26 February 1950; for Sanders case, S. Dorril, *MI6: Fifty Years of Special Operations*, (London: Fourth Estate, 2000), pp. 176, 178.
34   *Daily Herald*, 1–5 September 1953.
35   M. Hadas, "Football and Social Identity: The Case of Hungary in the Twentieth Century," *The Sports Historian*, 2000 vol. 20 (2), p. 51.
36   *Daily Worker*, 6 July 1953.
37   C. Gati, "From Liberation to Revolution, 1945–56," in P. Sugar (ed.), *A History of Hungary*, (London: Tauris, 1990), p. 374.
38   G. Szepesi, L. Lukacs, *The Match of the Century*, (London: Hungarian News and Information Service, 1954), p. 6.
39   *Daily Mirror*, 24 November 1953.
40   N. Fox, *Prophet or Traitor? The Jimmy Hogan Story*, (Manchester: Parrs Wood Press, 2003), pp. 74–81.
41   Rous quoted in Szepesi, *Match of the Century*, p. 6.
42   Barcs quoted in R. Taylor, A. Ward (eds), *Kicking and Screaming: An Oral History of Football in England*, (London: Robson Books, 1996), pp. 95–6.
43   *News Chronicle*, *Daily Mirror*, 26 November 1953.
44   Robb quoted in *Evening Standard*, 30 November 1998.
45   *Sunday Post*, 29 November 1953.
46   M. Allison, *Colours of My Life*, (London: Everest Books, 1975), p. 27; B. Glanville, *Soccer Nemesis*, (London: Secker and Warburg, 1955), p. 182.
47   R. Taylor, K. Jamrich, *Puskas on Puskas: The Life and Times of a Footballing Legend*, (London: Robson Books, 1997), pp. 11–112.
48   National Archives: Hungarian Political Summary, 21 November – 4 December 1953, FO371/106260/26.
49   Szepesi, *Match of the Century*, p. 24.
50   *Daily Herald*, 22 May 1954; *Daily Mirror*, 24 May 1954.
51   *Daily Worker*, 24 May 1954.
52   C. Buchan, *A Lifetime in Football*, (London: Phoenix House, 1955), pp. 209–10.
53   *Daily Worker*, 11 November 1954.
54   *DailyTelegraph*, 25 May 1954.
55   Cited in Beck, *Cultural Olympics*, p. 177.
56   Taylor, Jamrich, *Puskas*, p. 107. See also Winner, D., *Those Feet: A Sensual History of English Football*, (London: Bloomsbury, 2005), pp. 126–7.

57   D. Porter, "'The Match of the Century': George Robb Interviewed," *Sport in History*, 2003–4 vol. 23 (2), p. 67.
58   Glanville, *Soccer Nemesis*, p. 182.
59   *Economist*, 4 July 1954.
60   *Daily Worker*, 7 May 1954.
61   *Daily Mirror*, 22 May 1954.
62   *Daily Record*, 18 November 1954.
63   *Guardian*, 23 May 2003.
64   *Daily Mail*, 14 December 1954; *Daily Express*, 17 December 1954.
65   See G. Green, *Soccer in the Fifties*, (London: Ian Allen, 1974), p. 51. For Cullis's denial *Express and Star* (Wolverhampton), 15 December 1954; *Daily Mail*, 16. December 1954.
66   *The Times*, 14 May 1956.
67   British Olympic Association, *Official Report of the Olympic Games, XVIth Olympiad, Melbourne 1956*, (London: World Sports, 1957), pp. 47–9.
68   Rous, *Football Worlds*, p. 123.
69   *British Olympic Association, Official Report of the Olympic Games, XVIIIth Olympiad, Tokyo 1964*, (London: World Sports, 1964), p. 71
70   B. Joy, "Hungary's Year (1952)," in A.H. Fabian, G. Green (eds), *Association Football*, vol. 4 (London: Caxton Publishing Co.,1960), p. 475.
71   B. Joy, "A Dull Olympiad (1956)," in ibid., pp. 480–1.
72   See *Daily Express*, 14 May, 18 June 1958. For Hackett see S. Wagg, "Playing the past: the media and the England football team," in J.Williams and S. Wagg (eds.) *British Football and Social Change: Getting into Europe*, (Leicester: Leicester University Press, 1991), p. 222.
73   G. Oliver, *The Guinness Book of World Soccer: the History of the Game in over 150 countries*, (Enfield: Guinness Publishing, 2nd ed., 1995), pp. 116, 500–1.
74   Peppard, Riordan, *Playing Politics*, pp. 73, 75–6.

Chapter 5

"Oscillating antagonism"

Soviet–British athletics relations, 1945–1960

John Bale

The twins, Norris and Ross McWhirter published, edited (and in large part wrote) the first issue of their magazine, *Athletics World*, in March 1952.[1] Among the magazine's objectives was to "try always to provide pictures of the 'mystery' men or women of whom much has been heard but of whom pictorially little or nothing has been seen."[2] The McWhirter twins exemplified their objective by stating that a "formidable Russian girl," who the previous year had achieved the world's best-ever result for the 800 metres, would be the first "mystery" person to appear in their pages.[3] The twins' statement was symbolic in various ways. For a start, the adjective "formidable" could be read as a way of labeling not only the athlete but also the state that she represented. Additionally, the significance of *seeing* what Soviet athletes looked like suggested a degree of difference and the possession of qualities that could not be fully appreciated by simply *reading* about such athletes: they were shrouded in mystery and had to be seen to be believed. Additionally, by exemplifying the "mystery" athletes by using a Soviet runner, the McWhirters were seeking to bring into the world's sports system representations of the Soviet Union *via* texts on Soviet athletes, their performances and their results. This was necessary to satisfy the ambitions of their magazine to provide "*complete* coverage of track and field athletics."[4] In their own small way, therefore, the twins were engaged in thawing the Cold War by accommodating textually (at least) the Soviet athletes within international sport.

That the McWhirters felt the need to bring the Soviet athletes – rhetorically and visually – into the global fold resulted from the relative paucity of information about east European sport available to the UK athletics press. But it was not only written and visual representations that the McWhirters craved. There was a need also for numbers that would enable track fans and athletics authorities to compare statistically the "West" with the "East." The collection of annual athletics statistics would serve to reveal and compare the athletic "output" of nation states, the distribution of their athletes between events, and rates of change in athletic "production."

Reporting athletics results from the Soviet Union in the early 1950s was difficult. The international Association of Track and Field Statisticians (ATFS) had been established in 1950. Norris McWhirter was a founding member but there were no Soviet members of the Association until 1958.[5] The 1953 edition of the ATFS *International Athletics Annual* (a sort of athletics *Wisden*) included the admission that "major difficulties confronted the compilers of the various lists in connection with performances made in the USSR. Owing to the dearth of information obtainable from official USSR publications – particularly in the weeks prior to the 1952 Olympics – several USSR performances are most probably missing."[6] This implied that the Soviet Union was not yet fully a part of the global athletics system and reflected the existence of a sporting Cold War.

The period under consideration in this essay is the late 1940s and 1950s, a period in which the Cold War – "a stand-off situation rather than direct conflict"[7] – was showing signs of thawing. According to Fred Halliday, most of the period covered here was one of "oscillatory antagonism," a mixture of crises and summits that included hot, cold and thaw elements.[8] These meteorological metaphors, I believe, can be used in exploring the objectives of this paper. They certainly apply to the attitudes of *individual* athletes and journalists as well as to *national* attitudes and it is the voices of both of these categories that I explore below. In the 1950s and early 1960s the athletic relations between the USSR and the UK were certainly not free from cold blasts but there were also periods of thaw. It became "cold" when no contact existed or when previous contact was withdrawn and "warm" when nations engaged with one another according to the Coubertinian model. But it was not a case of the essentialist hot–cold binary that was often destabilised by different attitudes at different times or different attitudes at the same time.

My paper is divided into two broad sections. The first briefly reviews the chronology of the growth of the "contact zone" between British and Soviet athletics and athletes. Secondly, in the bulk of the chapter, I explore the ways in which British writers on athletics (journalists and athletes) represented the Soviet Union (and some Eastern bloc nations) during the period.

Athletic contacts

The most well-known sporting contacts between the Soviet Union and Britain in the early post-war years were the visits of the Moscow Dynamo football club in late 1945.[9] The notion that sports could represent national, political as well as sporting prowess was not new and nations on both sides of the "Iron Curtain" sought to employ sport in the national interest and in the formation of positive images.[10] British athletes came into contact with those from the Soviet realm in three main contexts during the period under discussion. First, there were major international events such as the Olympic Games and European Championships in which UK and Soviet athletes would engage in athletic contact but in which there was a minimum amount of social engagement. The USSR made its post-war entry into international championship athletics in 1946 when, along with Czechoslovakia and Hungary, they entered teams in the European

Championships at Oslo. The Soviet Union team was invited even though they were not members of the International Amateur Athletics Federation (IAAF), membership of which was also a requirement for taking part in the Olympics. But there was no reply to the invitation. Immediately before the start of the championships, the Russians arrived without notice. They were allowed to compete, despite the well-known strictness of Avery Brundage in his usual interpretation of rules. Sigfrid Edström, the founder of the IAAF and influential member of the International Olympic Committee (IOC), made it clear that it was an exceptional gesture of goodwill.[11] It was an odd, but warm, gesture that enabled the Soviet Union to take part. It was clear that the grandees of the IOC had a stronger commitment to Olympism than to their opposition to communism. As it happened, the Soviet team produced some excellent results, notably in the women's field events. The Czech runner Emil Zátopek made his first appearance in a major championship but became more visible in the 1948 Olympics in which several east European nations competed, despite the communist take-over of Czechoslovakia in February of that year. The USSR was affiliated to the IAAF in 1947 but did not join the Olympic movement until after the 1948 Olympics. Their first Olympic appearance since 1912 (as Russia) was in 1952 at Helsinki.

The second kind of contact included more modest international events, namely dual competitions in which the UK competed against the USSR or its satellites. Eastern European states competed against each other and the major communist bloc meeting in the "International World Youth Games." By 1952, neighbours Austria and Hungary competed in Budapest and a Swedish team competed against Yugoslavia in Belgrade. The first international match between the USSR and the UK (named "Moscow" *versus* "London") took place in London in 1954. Following this successful *entente*, subsequent fixtures were arranged between the UK and the USSR, held in London and Moscow. Additionally, by the mid-1950s individual athletes from the Soviet Union and rather more from their satellites such as Hungary, Poland and Czechoslovakia competed in west European "open" meetings that did not involve international teams.

The third level of contact is rather harder to identify. It is the extent of interpersonal dialogue that individual athletes from the respective nations had with each other. In the kinds of major championships noted above, there was always the possibility of defection or corruption by too much contact with capitalist competitors. As a result, the Soviet athletes' accommodation was, in the 1950s especially, segregated from that of the other nations. In the 1952 Olympics at Helsinki, for example, groups of countries shared different Olympic "villages," each nation's athletes being in a separate building. The Soviet Union and its allies demanded that they shared a separate village from the other teams.[12] The UK men's team, in contrast, was at a different "camp" with 60 other nations' teams and shared a building with the Australians.[13] By 1956 at Melbourne, however, Stalin was dead and a somewhat warmer attitude was prevailing. The Soviet team initially wanted to have their team based on a Soviet ship but persuasion led them to occupy the same "village" as all the other nations. Australians read it as their refusal to allow them to occupy a separate village[14] and the Soviets as a gesture of goodwill and international friendship.[15] Their accommodation was across the road from the building housing the USA team.[16]

However, isolationist tendencies continued to exist. The Official Report of the Melbourne Games records that the Soviet team wanted all meals an hour later than originally planned "as it selected training times during normal meal hours when training facilities were freely available. Arrangements were made to meet Russian requests."[17] The barely concealed code here was that the Soviets wanted the training area to themselves. The isolated nature of the Soviet teams symbolised the isolationism of the "Cold War" but, as I show below, this was not necessarily always the case, or the perception.[18]

Cold War rhetoric was not consistent. This may have been in part the result of the Western convention that politics should not intrude on sport. Warm feelings were sometimes expressed but often east Europeans were seen stereotypically or as suspect in some way. Representations of east European sports-workers fluctuated between hot and cold.

Negation

Even without Cold War politics it is unlikely that those writing about Soviet–British sporting relations would be consistent in their representations. And it is intriguing to conjecture the extent to which political rhetoric was internalized by sports writers, athletes and spectators and then applied to individuals and national teams. Opinions changed over time and varied within the context of particular situations. It is the fractured nature of British attitudes towards the Soviet Union and its satellites rather than the consistency of policy and attitudes that was common during the 1950s. Negative rhetoric implies a degree of antagonism or of coldness; warmth is implied in positive rhetorics that might be idealistic or romantic.

Using mainly the pages of the McWhirters' *Athletics World*, I will show how the written representation of Soviet sports-workers carried strong negative connotations. The McWhirter brothers were wealthy sons of the chief executive of both Associated and Northcilffe newspapers. They were educated at Marlborough and Oxford. Each of them was a good enough athlete (sprinters) to be elected to the élite Achilles Club for ex-Oxbridge "blues." Politically they were far to the right of centre. Indeed, Ross dabbled in extreme rightist organizations. It is hardly surprising that they were rabid anti-Communists, opposed trade unions and championed "the true humanity of the market."[19] Emphasis on the McWhirters is not only a matter of convenience. The fact that they were politically opposed to the Soviet Union puts them at the polar extreme in the warm–cold spectrum and presents an excellent example of what rhetorical "coldness" means in the context of the cultural cold wars of the 1950s.[20]

Rhetoric is rarely homogeneous and even the representation of Soviet athletics by the McWhirters was at times ambivalent. On the one hand, they required "objective" data in the form of statistics that could be easily ranked in order to establish the relative contribution of the USSR to world sport. Track and field results can be read as a universal currency that athletes from different nation states can readily comprehend. The statistics measured space and time and provided records of achievement. Walter Benjamin compared such records to the industrial science of Taylorism,[21] not unlike the "cult of the record-breaking Stakhanovite super worker" of the Soviet Union.[22] Here we see the McWhirter twins accepting both the reduction of human beings to statistics *via* their ranking lists while at the same time welcoming the Soviet athletes into the world of quantified sport. Through their *quantification* and statistics a sort of objectivity could be achieved but – another contradiction – in their *writing* of Soviet athletes they felt free to indulge their subjectivity to excess (as will be shown below). The labelling of the Soviet woman runner as "formidable" is mild compared with some of their more expressive appellations. Despite the McWhirters' desire to improve coverage of the Soviet athletes in their magazine, the negation of Soviet athletics featured prominently in its pages. These were, I suggest, a reflection of their political views.

Several themes can be seen running through the British discourse on Soviet athletes as represented mainly in *Athletics World*. The first was that significant Soviet results were the result of cheating or that they were achieved through unfair advantages. Having obtained Soviet data, the statistics could be scrutinised. Soviet athletes were also negatively stereotyped. A photograph, printed in the middle of the first page of the first issue of the magazine was hyperbolically dubbed "the most controversial picture of the year." It showed the Soviet steeplechase runner Vladimir Kazantsev "shattering" the previous world's best time for the 3,000 metres steeplechase in Moscow the previous year. His time was stated to be 8 minutes 49.8 seconds, beating the previous best performance (by a Swede) by nearly ten seconds.[23] There was, however, a sting in the tail. The McWhirters quoted the opinion of the British chief coach, Geoffrey Dyson, who stated that in the photograph "the barriers appear to be less than the standard 3 feet in height. The wearing of socks in an event involving seven water jumps is puzzling."[24] However, later in 1952 Kazantsev proceeded to gain a silver medal in the Olympic steeplechase and achieve excellent results at 5,000 metres. In the 1952 Olympics, "Comrade" Kansantsev as he was called, was said to have a "curious swaying action" and faced the American Horace Ashenfelter who was written as "a tall powerful FBI agent."[25] The respectively negative and positive imagery was enhanced by the thought of an FBI man chasing (and beating) a member of the Soviet system.

Doubt was also raised about a report in 1962 that reported a sprint result made by the Georgian, Leven Sanadze. He was said to have recorded what the McWhirters called "a rather mysterious" result at Tblisi where he returned a time of 10.3 seconds for the 100 metres that equalled the European record.[26] It was not made clear why this result should have been mysterious and, like Kazantsev, Sanadze produced a world-class time the following year. The fact that in both cases his results were achieved in Soviet Georgia may have created the doubt surrounding them.

Inscrutability was a quality that UK journalists were known to apply to the Soviet athletes. In a review of prospects for the 1952 Olympics *Athletics World* noted that high jumper Galina Geneker was "Russia's inscrutable human calculating machine," such was the meticulous monitoring that she applied to her opponents during the competition.[27] In the report of the women's events at the 1952 Olympics, the McWhirters appeared surprised at the Soviet shot-putter, Galina Zybina "whose peaches and cream complexion seemed more befitting an usherette than a muscle moll" but nevertheless possessed "not inconsiderable muscles." Following her Olympic victory with a world record result, she was said to have "tidied her flaxen tresses ready for the victory ceremony and heroineship of the Soviet Union."[28] She was later referred to as a "blonde bombshell"[29] with a "nutcracker handshake sufficient to bring any man to his knees."[30] Reporting her competition, a better throw by a German athlete was described as a "piece of Western aggression." Mocking Soviet women was typified by the description of the high jumper, Chudina: "Her massive gold signet ring must have put her in the category of jumping 'with weights' but her wasteful style [...] proved her downfall" in finishing second.[31] The Soviet long jumper Nina Tjurkina, was described as a "dumpy blonde,"[32] a negative description that typified the twins' way of describing Soviet women: A javelin thrower was "buxom" and "sloe-eyed";[33] a European champion sprinter was "unpulchritudinous."[34] A content analysis of the McWhirters' coverage of the women's events at the 1952 Olympics reveals that negative descriptions were *only* used to describe Soviet athletes.

The negation of Soviet athletes often focused on the state aid that was known to support talented athletes in the Soviet bloc.[35] Such aid included boarding schools for talented athletes.[36] The May 1956 issue of *Athletics World* alluded to the "Russians £30,000,000 drive to 'win the Olympics'" and the editorial was explicit in its condemnation of the Soviet system:

> Russia's mass physical education drive, doubtless of great sociological benefit in the drab lives of her own people, must produce great champions. They may spur the champions in non-state controlled countries to greater things. But, unfortunately, the standards reached by these full-time state athletes may become so divorced from those capable of being achieved by ordinary "part time" athletes that discouragement rather than inspiration might follow.[37]

The Soviet system, therefore, was seen to provide their athletes with an unfair advantage but it would be so great that numbers willing to make the effort to compete against them at the highest level would be diminished.

Stalin died in 1953 and the prospect of greater warmth in East–West relations seemed likely. Even Norris McWhirter's report of the 1956 Games was much more sober and avoided the excessive chauvinism of his 1952 reports.[38] Nevertheless, the McWhirters' continued regularly to allude to the USSR as "Russia" suggesting that they could not bring themselves to accept the use of the word "socialist" – or that they simply chose to ignore the events of 1917.

Toward idealisation

Athletics World was not the only athletics magazine available to fans during the 1950s. A pre-existing magazine, *Athletics Weekly,* also sought to provide athletics coverage but tended to be more parochial and dealt mainly – but certainly not entirely – with British events. It employed a *Daily Worker* correspondent, a communist named Armour Milne. His job was to cover athletics in eastern Europe. The *Weekly* employed less flamboyant language than that used by the McWhirters. Even so, the editor was forced to defend Milne from time to time against readers who saw reds under every bed.[39]

While the previous section has illustrated negative attitudes towards the Soviet Union and its athletes, it is clear from the writings of athletes and journalists that there was more than a degree of "warmth" in what is more generally read as the "Cold War." Bill Nankeville, who preceded Roger Bannister as Britain's top mile runner, observed that in "the world of diplomacy it is believed that an impregnable iron curtain divides East and West. But the world of sport had reduced that impregnable iron curtain to a flimsy partition, which can be breached at will."[40] This somewhat idealized view of world sport was illustrated by his view of a Soviet team's visit to London in 1954. He noted that "Russian athletes came, saw and conquered our hearts," mediated by television that greatly assisted in the symbolic abolition of frontiers.[41] Nankeville's positive attitude towards the Russians was amplified by an allusion to judging the Russian athletes by their ability, not by their politics. He read newspaper reports of the Russians being "Red athletes" as an insult and that the Russian distance runner, Vladimir Kuts should not be sneered at because he was a "communist."[42] Indeed, even Roger Bannister (a good friend of the McWhirters) refused to criticize the Soviet system – one that many would have regarded as "almost professional."[43] He wrote, "We must, I think, realise that countries will organise their sport in different ways [...] We must leave the choice to them."[44] He was sure that athletics would safeguard itself from corruption, simply because it had "an individual not a national basis."[45] In suggesting this he ignored (or was unaware of) the explicit statements from Soviet sports leaders that "[e]ach new victory is a victory for the Soviet form of society and the socialist sports system: it provides irrefutable proof of the superiority of socialist culture over the decaying culture of the capitalist states."[46]

A fellow member of the Oxbridge-only Achilles Club, Philip Noel-Baker, presented a much warmer view of the Soviet system. Noel-Baker was a winner of the

Nobel Peace Prize in 1959, for his promotion of disarmament and world peace, having previously been Secretary of State for Commonwealth Relations in Clement Attlee's post-war Labour government, and earlier a silver medallist in the 1920 Olympic 1,500 metres. He greatly admired the Soviet system of sport and indeed likened it to the lavish provisions for sport in the British private schools and the ancient universities. "But," said Noel-Baker, "the Russians do it for *all* their children, *all* their citizens."[47] He lauded the Soviet system of State organization, their desire to develop specialized talent (contrasting it with the "clumsy efforts of the [British] untrained, uncoached all-rounder").[48] He admired the awarding of the national honour, Master of Soviet Sport, the availability of athletic facilities to all, and greatly welcomed the entry of the USSR into the world of international sport.[49]

Gordon Pirie praised the communist system *per se*, particularly for its attitude to "amateurism." He wrote:

> In all [sic] Communist countries, of course, the jobs which 'amateur' athletes have are purely nominal. These jobs keep them in reasonable comfort but do not interfere in any way with their athletics. There are State training camps where athletes are trained and kept with exclusive attention to athletics. Russian athletic stars are sent to the Black Sea resorts to train in mid-winter.[50]

He contrasted the Soviet system with "the hypocrisy of British athletics" that lacked adequate support and was a system based on "out-of-date conceptions inherited from the past."[51] These views represent the warm end of the spectrum of attitudes towards Soviet athletics.

Chataway and Kuts

Most athletics fans will recall 1954 as the year in which Roger Bannister ran the mile in less than four minutes. At the end of the year's athletic season, however, an epic race occurred at the White City Stadium in London that marked the first appearance of a Soviet athletics team in the UK. It was held on the evening of 13 October and it was nominally presented as a match between London and Moscow though the athletes' affiliation with the respective cities was treated loosely. The highlight of the meeting was the 5,000 metres in which the world record holder, Vladimir Kuts, faced the British runner, Christopher Chataway.

In his description of the race, Norris McWhirter preferred to use military appellations, referring respectively to the "ex-marine of the Red Navy" competing against the "ex-Lieutenant of the British army."[52] He also drew attention to the alleged superiority of the Soviet sports system over that of the UK: "Could a spare-time amateur businessman who trains 35 miles a week live with the full-time

'State' athlete who trains 135 miles a week in this waging of 'total' sport?"[53] The hyperbole was taken further. Chataway won the race in a new world's record time after he "had switched over to the super human." The "brilliant" Kuts "trotted on to commune with himself in the desolate loneliness of a beaten man."[54] Here McWhirter, with his military allusions, highlighted the Cold War. But while stereotyping Kuts as a "state" athlete he also acknowledged him as a great runner. The rhetoric is again ambivalent.

Pirie and Kuts

One of Chataway's contemporaries was Gordon Pirie, arguably one of the greatest British athletes of all time and a world record holder at six miles, 3,000 metres and 5,000 metres. His report of a visit to Moscow in 1955 for the first ever "away" international match against the Soviet Union supplies some contrasting British images of the Soviet world. As noted earlier, Pirie was prepared to go beyond sporting descriptions and take in the urban infrastructure, retailing and the sociability of the Russian people. He claimed that "except for the surrender of our passports, we were 'free in Russia,' though the accompanying journalists were not. They suffered a long delay, apparently to show that they weren't really welcome."[55] He described the meals at the Moscow hotel at which he stayed as "shocking. The service was even worse."[56] He also suggested that he had been deprived of a meal and had to take part in a march-past before his 10,000 metres race. His opponent Kuts, on the other hand, was "lucky, having his meal and resting. [...] This was downright bad sportsmanship or first-class gamesmanship."[57] Additionally, Pirie complained that if "the slightest thing is out of place when the Russians visit other countries they withdraw from the match like spoiled school children."[58] Furthermore, Pirie was also able to point out that "gross forms of professionalism" are "quite undisguised in Iron Curtain States,"[59] reinforcing his comments on the Soviet system noted above though the word "gross" carries somewhat negative connotations.

In the Olympic year of 1956, Pirie had two important races with his Russian adversary. In June, he contested a 5,000 metres race in Bergen, Norway. Kuts was the world record holder but Pirie defeated him by about twenty metres in a world record time. He was photographed after the race with his arms around Kuts's shoulders. Pirie was smiling and Kuts was holding his hand. It reflected a spirit of camaraderie.[60] The image was communicated to the Norwegian population in *Bergens Tidende* but did not appear in the British press. After the race, the runners ran a lap of honour together and via the public address system Pirie sportingly acknowledged the part that Kuts had played in the race.[61] At times the impression was given that there really was camaraderie between athlete from East and West.

Pirie's attitude towards Kuts was somewhat different following the next race between the two athletes. This was at the 1956 Olympic Games at Melbourne.

Kuts had already defeated Pirie in the 10,000 metres and Pirie magnanimously stated that he didn't think it possible that he could ever beat Kuts over that distance.[62] However, in the 5,000 metres he had a better chance and, indeed, finished second to win the silver medal. The two athletes were again photographed after the race, hugging each other closely and having broad smiles on each of their faces. The image of international friendship was soured however when, a few years later, Pirie suggested that Kuts's successes were due to drug-taking or hypnotism.[63]

Pirie's comments on his 1955 and 1956 experiences reveal an image of both negative criticism and feelings of friendship towards the Russian people. It is an ambiguous discourse, reflecting warmth and coldness towards the Soviet Union and one of its athletes. However, it is impossible to detect whether comments about individuals are influenced by the national affiliation of the athletes concerned. Pirie makes some negative noises about the state of Soviet society and about one of its representatives.

Nina and the five hats

From the relatively hot position of Nankeville and the warm and cool comments of Pirie, I now want to move to a much cooler situation that surrounded the first visit of a full USSR athletics team to London in late August 1956. *Athletics Weekly* heralded this as "both historic and memorable." Travelling abroad conferred special treatment for the Soviet athletes and as a result it can be argued that such visits solidified their loyalty to the Soviet Union. On the other hand, such travel would expose them "to a world at odds with Soviet propaganda," leading to an undermining of their beliefs.[64] Barbara Keys avers that they were monitored by the secret police while abroad.

The visit of the full might of the USSR for a match with Britain is "quite out of the ordinary." It would be the "greatest attraction in Britain since the Olympics of 1948"[65] and the meeting was a sell-out, showing the considerable public interest in East–West sport.[66] However, a disaster occurred during the week leading up to the event. Nina Ponomereva, one of the Soviet discus throwers, was charged with stealing five hats worth £1 12s 11d from C. and A. Modes, a store on Oxford Street in London's west end. As a result, the Soviet team withdrew from the White City event. The British team manager claimed that the financial loss had been £25,000. This was a Cold War situation that coincidentally took place near the time of the Soviet invasion of Hungary. Ponomereva was accommodated in the Soviet embassy but did not turn up in court the following day. A warrant was issued for her arrest and she surrendered to the Metropolitan Police. She was eventually tried and claimed that she had paid for the hats but no receipt could be discovered. Nina was found guilty but was freed on paying £2 costs and quickly returned to the USSR. It should be added that this was a case of British justice *not* being independent of the government. As

David Caute puts it, the attorney general could have dropped the proceedings at any time as being "not in the public interest" but the decision to pursue the charge was taken at Cabinet level.[67]

The UK response to the withdrawal of the Soviet team was mixed. Rather than attack the behaviour of the Soviet decision to withdraw, Chris Chataway and Chris Brasher wrote to the *Evening Standard* suggesting that the charge against Ponomereva was "an unbearable blow to the pride of all Russian athletes."[68] The editor of *Athletics Weekly*, P.W. Green, was highly conciliatory, arguing that the British authorities had handled the affair in a "ham fisted" way. He suggested that Ms Ponomereva might have mistaken the shop for a self-service store of the type commonly found in Moscow. The taking of the hats may not have been deliberate. But even if she had deliberately stolen them, no charges needed to have been made against her. Here, however, Green adopted mildly anti-Soviet rhetoric by noting that because "of the way the Russians are so ready to see signs of ulterior motives reflecting discredit on the Soviet Union, or causing trouble between East and West, even when they did not exist," alternative approaches should have been adopted.[69] The incident could have been left to the Russians or it could have simply been treated as a breach of etiquette or misunderstanding. The Soviet team was withdrawn from the match despite the British Board dealing with the situation "on a very high level." Green continued, "It was a complete deadlock and everyone knows how well the Russians can dig their feet in when they want to!"[70]

The Scotsman argued that the Soviets have "an Oriental regard for 'Face'" and that for them "everything is political, and is viewed in terms of propaganda." And in Britain the law is the law and Nina had "no claim to diplomatic immunity."[71] The Soviet *chargé d'affaires* in London stated that the incident exerted "an adverse effect on the possibilities of the two countries drawing closer together."[72] *Pravda* claimed that the "criminal" British police were holding Ms Ponomereva incommunicado while the team manager said that the British attitude was "dirty provocation." *Izvestiya* stated that the "provocation of the British would mean that a trip planned by the Bolshoi Ballet could not be undertaken."[73] However, the British communist newspaper, the *Daily Worker*, condemned the decision to withdraw from the event as "regrettable." It was the first time that the paper had editorially criticized a Soviet action.[74] Additionally, the eminent historian, communist Eric Hobsbawm, complained that this was the only example that the Communist Party of Britain could give that illustrated its opposition to a Soviet policy.[75] In other words, criticizing the stealing of hats was easy; criticizing the invasion of Hungary was rather more difficult.

The national mood may have been caught in a dialogue carried in the "Letters to the Editor" column in *Athletics Weekly* following an announcement in early 1957 that a UK *vs* USSR athletics meeting would be planned for the upcoming season. The observations ranged from:

Unless they [the USSR] make a public apology for the filthy things they said about us in their press, I for one, would be disgusted to think that could sink so low in national pride ever to invite them here again for a match.[76]

to:

I welcome every opportunity offered for friendly competition on the field of sport, for by closing the door a chance is lost of breaking down prejudice and misunderstanding. It may well be that we deplore the actions of governments and nationals of other countries but we shall never improve matters by refusing to even try to be friends.[77]

This brief dialogue certainly illustrated the fractured nature of Cold War rhetoric.

A footnote to the Nina Ponomereva incident is, I think, worth adding. On the Sunday following the scheduled White City meeting, two members of the Soviet team took part in a non-publicized and impromptu hammer-throwing competition against British opposition at the annual meeting of the "Hammer Circle" – an organization of hammer throwers – at Bisham Abbey in Buckinghamshire.[78] This modest union of athletes from both nations revealed a sign of thaw within the overall coldness of the general withdrawal. And to show that coldness could be matched by warmth, the Soviet Union sent a fencing team to London despite the dispute – and the Bolshoi Ballet came too.

Personal contact

In the course of international travel, meetings were invariably arranged for the British athletes to meet their Soviet hosts. The example of the mixing of the hammer throwers noted above is an example, if an unusual one. More commonly, such meetings encouraged the trappings of diplomacy. On foreign visits athletes were able to experience (or suffer) banquets at which party functionaries made statements about "peace and friendship."

The 1952 Olympics enabled the British athletics team to officially meet their Soviet opponents. Roger Bannister provided a detailed account of his visit to the Soviet training camp where the meeting was held, located twenty miles away from the Olympic Village where teams, other than those of the Soviet empire, were accommodated.[79] He felt embarrassed to find a huge portrait of Stalin with smaller images of the leaders of Soviet satellites. The entire evening was, thought Bannister, "a bewildering alternation of planning and confusion – of friendliness and distrust."[80] He talked with an interpreter. Bannister said, "I felt he was being frank and we were establishing a genuine understanding." But once the various speeches started he found it "difficult to believe in the sincerity of the Russians, or indeed the sincerity with which we welcomed their gesture of friendship."[81] The suspicion Bannister felt suggests coolness in the relationship despite his apparent acceptance of the "total" nature of Soviet sport noted earlier.

Reports of British engagements with Soviet athletes could, unsurprisingly, be reduced to chauvinism and sexism. Norris McWhirter seemed pleased to admit that, on a visit to Moscow as an athletics journalist, he was able to meet the Soviet team at a reception at the British embassy. However, his apparent desire to insult and mock the Soviet athletes with his sixth-form humour was illustrated by his meeting with shot-putter Tamara Tyshkyevich, referred to as "the behemoth woman." He further described her as a "cylindrical damsel whose vital statistics were, as near as no matter, 50–50–50." He also noted her "teeth which were capped not with capitalist gold but with proletarian steel."[82]

More sober descriptions and more friendly associations matched such extreme attitudes, of course. Occasionally, presentations of gifts were set up and before he left Moscow after the 1955 international meeting, Gordon Pirie received "a fine box of chocolates [...] as a friendly gesture" from his adversary, Vladimir Kuts.[83] On another occasion, he was presented with a Soviet tracksuit with the initials CCCP (cyrillic version of USSR) on the front. He was happy to be photographed posing in it and it appeared in *Athletics World*.[84]

If the other nations of the Eastern bloc are included, considerable dialogue at the individual level can be recognized. Gordon Pirie, for example, developed a "warm" relationship with the Czech star, Emil Zátopek, and was photographed training with him. Zátopek was Pirie's hero and a close bond developed between the two long distance runners. They exchanged letters on matters of training and racing and Pirie had a picture of Zátopek on his bedroom wall.[85]

Indirect contact: Zátopek and a sanitized Soviet sphere

Contact with east European athletes did not come solely from personal meetings such as those noted above. The Cold War was also fought in the cultures of magazines, books, drama, dance and music.[86] The somewhat paradoxical aim of the early writings of the right-wing McWhirters exemplified the use of the written word, the photograph and the statistic to welcome Soviets textually into the Western realm. In the Soviet Union too, profiles of Western sports stars were often included in the popular press, notably the thrice weekly *Sovietski Sport*. In preparation for the 1965 Olympics, it devoted up to two of its seven pages to international sports events and athletes. According to Keys, some of this coverage was remarkably positive.[87]

At the same time as the West was beaming jazz into eastern European radio stations,[88] an impressive book on a Czech distance runner, Emil Zátopek, was being sold to British and American athletics fans. Dramatic (and perhaps unique) warmth in cultural relations was found in the English language publication of *Zátopek the Marathon Victor*. This was *not* a British publication but a biography written by Frantisek Kozik, published in Prague.[89] I am unaware of any other English language *sporting* book published in eastern Europe during the period dealt with here. It was something of a propaganda success for the publisher (i.e. the state) as it promoted Czechoslovakia and, explicitly and implicitly, the Soviet bloc. However, its impact was probably limited as it was mainly read by athletics *aficionados* and was not retailed in high street bookstores.

Zátopek had made his international debut in the 1946 European Championships in Oslo. He finished fifth in the 5,000 metres, won by Britain's Sydney Wooderson. In the 1948 Olympics, Zátopek won the 10,000 metres and finished second in the 5,000. In the 1952 Games he won both the above races and the marathon. During his career he also broke numerous world records. Many athletics fans still revere him as the greatest ever distance runner. Kozik's book is in large part propaganda. Zátopek was represented as an ambassador who was fighting for not only "victory on the track, but also for the mutual understanding of all the peoples of the world in the desire to live together in friendship."[90] The book promoted the Soviet Union. For example, the enormous amounts spent on physical culture had paid off with the physically fit Soviets' defeating "the enemy and the liberation of their country."[91] The Soviet annexation of Czechoslovakia in 1948 was sanitized as a series of "political events" through which state control of all sports organizations was established. While in Dresden in 1950, Zátopek gazed admiringly at a statue of the Nazi 800 metres world record-holder, Rudolf Harbig, who was killed during the Second World War. The Czech is recorded as stating that "at the very thought of him we should shout the louder: may there be no more war!"[92] On a visit to compete in Moscow, he claimed to have witnessed "magnificent buildings, busy streets filled with modern cars [...]. The shop-windows and department stores [...] were full of goods." His hotel had "spacious, comfortable rooms."[93] At the 1952 Olympics the, Czech team shared the Otaniemi Olympic village with the other east European teams. Kozik's account of life at the village is somewhat different from Bannister's, noted earlier. He claims that "within a short time there was no barrier between Otaniemi and Käpilla" where the other nations of the world were based. A "comradely life" existed and east and west Europeans mixed: "there were no more separate training grounds."[94] And US athletes, after visiting the Soviet village, were said to have stated, "We are delighted to find that we are all so alike." The Soviet riposte was, "Convey our greetings to all those in your country who are of good will."[95]

Kozik, then, was engaged in a charm offensive, presenting the Soviet Union (and the Eastern bloc *per se*) to British and American audiences as a peace-loving country, a state that was prosperous and one whose athletes willingly mixed and mingled with American visitors at the Olympics. Whether the relatively small number of British readers believed any of this or not (especially if they had read Gordon Pirie's view of Moscow) is unknown but the Czech publishers had done their best. They presented eastern Europe as a peace-loving bloc with a sports system that produced athletes that could defeat the best the West could offer.

Concluding comments

Post-war international sport has been described as a paradox.[96] On the one hand, the Soviet Union expanded its sporting contacts, illustrated above by the growth of its presence and success in world athletics. Its entry into the Olympic Games and European athletics championships and the concomitant awareness of Soviet athletes by the West exemplified this presence. On the other hand, it continued to adopt a degree of sporting isolationism with its athletes rarely competing internationally, except, with satellite nations and in the aforementioned championships.

The rhetoric surrounding the political Cold War was inevitably transferred to a sporting Cold War. This was manifested in attitudes toward Soviet sports-workers that, in different ways, could also be seen as ranging from hot (favorable) to cold (unfavorable), though often ambiguously. Soviet athletes could be admired; they could also be negated. And as individuals could be admired, the state that supported them could be disdained. As with any discourse (meaning the arena in which knowledge is produced and formed[97]), that surrounding the east European athletes in the post-war period was fractured and far from homogeneous.

Notes

1   The McWhirters' debut publication was *Get to Your Marks!*, Kaye, London, 1951, a detailed and statistically inclined history of British athletics.
2   "Sand and Cinders," *Athletics World*, 1, 1, 1952, p. 2. For a description of the founding and early days of the magazine see Norris McWhirter, *Ross*, Churchill Press, London 1976, pp. 106–107. A decade later the McWhirter twins would be famed as the editors of the *Guinness Book of Records*.
3   Ibid.
4   *Athletics World*, 1, 1, 1952, p. 1.
5   R. L. Quercetani (ed.), *International Athletics Annual, 1958*, World Sports, London, 1958, p. 4. The ATFS have published annuals since 1950. The Association is made up of amateur collectors of athletic results. In some countries, national federations statutorily collect comprehensive data on athletic performances but in others no such "official" statistics are collected and it is amateur collectors who monitor and collect results. It is impossible to know how comprehensive such data are, especially for the period under discussion here.
6   R. L. Quercetani and Fulvio Regli (eds.) *International Athletics Annual 1953*, World Sports, London, 1953, p. 5.
7   Peter Taylor, *Political Geography*, 2nd ed., Longman, London, 1989, p. 70.
8   Ibid, p. 71.
9   Peter Beck, "'The most effective means of communication in the modern world'? British sport and national prestige," in Roger Levermore and Adrian Budd (eds.), *Sport and International Relations*, Routledge, London , 2004, pp. 76–92.
10 National image making through sport is not new: See Arnd Krüger, "On the origin of the notion that sport serves as a means of national representation," *History of European Ideas*, 16, 4–6, 1993, pp. 863–869.
11 Allen Guttmann, *The Olympics: A History of the Modern Games*, University Of Illinois Press, Urbana, 1992, p. 87.

12 Mika Wickström (ed.), *Helsinki 1952*, Suomen Urheilumuseosäätiö, Helsinki, 2002, p. 159.
13 *Official Report of the Organising Committee for the Games of the XV Olympiad, Helsinki, 1952*, Werner Söderstrom, Porvoo, 1953.
14 Alfred Senn, *Power, Politics and the Olympic Games*, Human Kinetics, Champaign, Ill., 1999, p. 109
15 Barbara Keys, "The 1956 Melbourne Olympic Games and the Postwar International Order," unpublished paper, 2005.
16 *Official Report of the Organizing Committee for the Games of the XVI Olympiad, Melbourne, 1956*, Melbourne, 1956, p. 131. This proximity may have made a contribution to the romance and eventual marriage of the US hammer thrower Harold Connolly to the Czech discus thrower, Olga Fikatova.
17 Ibid, p. 130.
18 It is not known whether the segregation of countries in this way was requested by members of the Eastern bloc or by the Finnish organizers.
19 McWhirter, *Ross*, p. 82.
20 On cultural hegemony during the 1950s and later see David Caute: *The Dancer Defects: the Struggle for Cultural Supremacy During the Cold War*, Oxford University Press, Oxford, 2003.
21 Susan Buck-Morss, *The Dialectics of Seeing*, MIT Press, Cambridge, MA., 1997, p. 326.
22 John Hoberman, *Mortal Engines*, The Free Press, New York, 1992, p. 205.
23 *Athletics World*, 1, 1, 1952, p. 1.
24 Ibid.
25 *Athletics World*, 1, 7, 1952, p. 3.
26 *Athletics World*, 1, 9, 1952, p. 8.
27 *Athletics World*, 1, 1, 1952, p. 9.
28 *Athletics World*, 1, 8, 1952, p. 5.
29 *Athletics World*, 2, 11, 1952, p. 91.
30 *Athletics World*, 3, 4, 1956, p. 60.
31 *Athletics World*, 1, 8, 1952, p. 5.
32 Ibid.
33 *Athletics World*, 2, 11, 1952, p. 91.
34 Ibid.
35 It is still not known how much support, from employees, universities, the military or private benefactors the so-called British "amateurs" received during this period. Gordon Pirie, for one, was adamant that "shamateurism" was rife; Chris Chataway noted that "there are certainly few top-class athletes in this country who would have difficulty in finding a firm to 'carry' them for a few years," and Derek Ibbotson has claimed that at the time "nobody was an amateur" among the elite runners. See Gordon Pirie, *Running Wild*, Stanley Paul, London, 1961, p. 31; Chris Chataway, "The stresses of international competition," in H. A. Meyer (ed.), *Modern Athletics*, Oxford University Press, London, 1964, p. 98; and Jim Denison, *Bannister and Beyond*, Breakaway Books, Halcottsville, NY, 2003, p. 38.
36 James Riordan, *Soviet Sport*, Blackwell, Oxford, 1980.
37 "Sand and Cinders," *Athletics World*, 3, 6, 1956, p. 82.
38 *Athletics World*, 3, 13/14, 1956/7.
39 I am very grateful to Bob Phillips (email communication, 20.11.05) for this information about Milne.
40 Bill Nankeville, *The Miracle of the Mile*, Stanley Paul, London 1956, p. 107.
41 Ibid.
42 Ibid, p. 108
43 Roger Bannister, *First Four Minutes*, Putnam's London, 1955, p. 222.

44   Ibid.
45   Ibid.
46   Senn, *Power, Politics and the Olympic Games*, p. 90.
47   Philip Noel-Baker, "A state subsidy," in H. A. Meyer (ed.), *Modern Athletics*, Oxford University Press, London, 1964, pp. 31–41.
48   Ibid, p. 34.
49   Ibid.
50   Pirie, *Running Wild*, p. 39.
51   Ibid, p. 38.
52   Norris McWhirter, "3 World marks in London," *Athletics World*, 2, 11, 1954, p. 91.
53   Ibid. It is doubtful that Chataway was such a light trainer as McWhirter implied.
54   Ibid.
55   Pirie, *Running Wild*, p. 128.
56   Ibid, p. 130.
57   Ibid, pp. 130–131.
58   Ibid, p. 131. This comment almost certainly alludes to the Nina Ponomereva incident that is dealt with below.
59   p. 31.
60   Dick Booth, *The Impossible Hero: A Life of Gordon Pirie*, Corsica Press, London, 1999, p. 11.
61   Ibid, p. 12.
62   Ibid, p. 154.
63   Ibid, p. 158.
64   Barbara Keys, "The Soviet Union, Global Culture and the 1956 Olympic Games," unpublished paper, 2005.
65   *Athletics Weekly*, 10, 35, p. 3.
66   Peter Beck, "Britain and the Cold War's 'Cultural Olympics': Responding to the political drive of Soviet Sport, 1945–58," *Contemporary British History*, 19, 2, 2005, pp. 169–185.
67   Caute, *The Dancer Defects*, p. 473
68   Ibid.
69   *Athletics Weekly*, 10, 35, p. 3.
70   Ibid.
71   Caute, *The Dancer Defects*, p. 473.
72   Quoted in Beck, "Britain and the Cold War's 'Cultural Olympics,'" p. 180.
73   Quoted in Caute, *The Dancer Defects*, p. 472.
74   Quoted in John McIlroy and Alan Campbell, "'Nina Ponomareva's Hats': The new revisionism, the Communist International, and the Communist Party of Great Britain, 1920–1930," *Labour/Le Travail*, 49, 2 – http://www.historycooperative.org/journals/llt/49/06mcilro.html
75   Ibid.
76   B. Chase, "Letters to the Editor," *Athletics Weekly*, 11, 5, 1957, p. 4.
77   Stanley Jones, "Letters to the Editor," *Athletics Weekly*, 11, 6, 1957, p. 5.
78   "Russians in Hammer Circle Competition," *Athletics Weekly*, 10, 36, 1956, p. 18.
79   Bannister, *First Four Minutes*, pp. 148–52. A less nuanced account of this visit is given by the marathon runner, Jim Peters: see J. H. Peters, *In the Long Run*, Cassell, London, 1955, pp. 115–117.
80   Ibid, p. 150.
81   Ibid, p. 151.
82   McWhirter, *Ross*, p. 154. Tyshkyevich was the gold-medal winner at the 1956 Olympics.
83   Pirie, *Running Wild*, p. 133.

84 *Athletics World*, 3, 10, 1956, p. 151.
85 Booth, *The Impossible Hero*.
86 Caute, *The Dancer Defects*.
87 Keys, "The Soviet Union, Global Culture."
88 Caute ibid, p. 465.
89 Frantisek Kozik, *Zátopek the Marathon Victor* (translated by Jean Layton), Artia, Prague, 1954. Note that Cassell, London, published the autobiography of Hungarian football icon, Ferenc Puskas, *Captain of Hungary*, in Britain also in 1955. Promotional material states that it was especially commissioned by Cassell and translated from his original Hungarian.
90 Kozik, *Zátopek*, p. 208.
91 Ibid, p. 102.
92 Ibid, p. 138.
93 Ibid, pp. 101–102.
94 Ibid, p. 153. This claim of East and West sharing training facilities is not totally implausible. Pirie stated that he trained with Zátopek "on several occasions" though it is not explicitly stated that this was during the Olympics: See Pirie, *Running Wild*, p. 92.
95 Kozik, *Zátopek*, p. 168.
96 Victor Peppard and James Riordan, *Playing Politics: Soviet Sport Diplomacy to 1992*, Jai Press, Greenwich, Conn., 1993, p. 58.
97 Michel Foucault, "Orders of discourse: inaugural lecture delivered at the Collège de France," *Social Science Information*, 10, 2, pp. 7–30.

Chapter 6

"If you want the girl next door ..."

Olympic sport and the popular press in early Cold War Britain

Stephen Wagg

> Great Britain has lost an empire, and not yet found a role
>> (Dean Acheson, former US Secretary of State, 1962)

> If you want the girl next door, go next door
>> (Mae West)

This essay is about changing attitudes to sport and Olympism – the perceived ethos of the Olympic Games – in Britain during the period 1952 to 1972, as reflected in the sports pages of a section of the British press generally designated as "popular." This section of the press is here variously represented by the *Daily Express*, the *Daily Mail*, the *Daily Mirror*, the *Daily Sketch*, and, latterly, *The Sun*. The essay draws on reportage in these newspapers of six successive Olympiads, from 1952, the first Games in which the Soviet Union participated, to 1972, by which time a perceptibly different vocabulary is being used to describe the Olympics. In doing so, it discusses the work of some of Britain's leading popular sport journalists of the post-war era. These men and their newspapers are taken to be important definers of the Olympic spirit in relation to British sport and the British public; their readership is taken to be substantially from the middle, lower-middle and working classes.

The central argument will be that the Cold War, and the concomitant rise of the two superpowers of the United States and the Soviet Union, was an important subtext in the rendering, via these pages, of the Olympics and the lives of Olympic athletes. During the immediate post-Second World War period the coverage of successive Olympic tournaments reveals, ultimately, a loss of the innocence embodied in nineteenth- and early twentieth-century amateurism. By the 1960s, athletics, both in the United States and the USSR had become *work* – as Britons must now accept. Although the press of the time (and, thus, this chapter) also mentions male athletes, this innocence is most typified by the imagery of mythic female athletes conjured up by these newspapers: the girls-next-door who work, perhaps, as typists or clerks or dentists, have families, boyfriends and a balanced life. The girls-next-door are a motif, not only for the Olympic spirit, now credibly reinterpreted for the immediate post-war era, but for Britain itself, as a nation, and perhaps most especially for that fabled strand of British life known as "Middle England." This term I take to refer to a social world composed largely of people of middle income (predominantly Social Classes B and C), who lived in the suburbs, were white, hardworking, modest, middlebrow in their tastes, quietly patriotic, temperate, unpretentious and went quietly about their business (see Barker, 2005 for an interesting recent discussion). By the 1960s, leading commentators are reluctantly beginning to acknowledge that the young, unaffected female athletes who spring briefly from this social world of family, work, church, sport, friendship and honest-to-goodness endeavour, win a medal and then return to their daily round, will soon no longer be viable as Olympians. They are already becoming outmoded in an Olympic culture now largely defined by the Cold War. In the Helsinki summer Games of 1952, the first one contested by both the USA and the USSR, 100 world records were broken. At the following Games, in Melbourne, the USSR took thirty-seven gold medals, five more than the United States. From then until the break-up of the Soviet Union after the Seoul Games of 1988, the battle was joined and Olympic sport, in the process, progressively redefined. That's to say, the tendency, already present in both the United States and the Soviet Union, for sport to become a technocracy – involving experts, tactical preparation, technological assistance and full-time dedication – was accelerated. This is also the period of British imperial decline. The modern Olympics had been forged largely from an imagined Britishness, incorporating the public school ethos, the gentlemanly ethic and the folk ways of villages such as Much Wenlock (MacAloon, 1981; Tomlinson, 1984). By 1970, British-derived modern Olympism had withered, along with British imperial power.

The essay is also, in a subsidiary way, about the depiction of Soviet female athletes in the British popular press of the time. Indeed it was conceived and researched in the expectation that these athletes would be represented in a particular fashion, rendering them, where possible, as masculine, misshapen, sexually unattractive and, thus, as a metaphor for the perversions of communism. I had two reasons to hold this expectation. First, in the suburban world of my childhood in the 1950s – its conversations, its newspapers and general discourse – and among the people I knew in my teenage years in the 1960s, as I remember them, comments such as this about Russian women were commonplace. They were all dumpy and looked like tractor drivers. This, it was clearly implied, was the consequence of a social system that strove unduly to "make people equal": the Soviet Union and its east European dominions were one huge human sausage machine, ran the theory, and women there were encouraged to become engineers, factory workers and the like. One ghastly consequence of this was that, in that bleak little-known vast expanse behind Churchill's "Iron Curtain," all the women looked like men. I have confirmed this remembering with a number of people, male and female, of the appropriate age. Second, though, a good deal of commentary of this kind is already on record. Some of it, for instance, is contemporaneous and is quoted by Rob Beamish and Ian Ritchie and John Bale in this volume. Other examples are retrospective, and usually seek to dignify any disparagement by marrying it to an accusation of malpractice. When the former Soviet athlete Irina Press (Olympic gold medallist in the 80 metres hurdles in 1960 and for the Pentathlon in 1964) died in 2004, an internet obituary remembered her as someone:

> whose gender (and that of her sister Tamara) were questioned by journalists who suspected them of being men taking hormone injections (they were dubbed the 'Press brothers' by journalists), and who withdrew from all further competition after chromosome testing was introduced in 1966 ...
>
> (www.lifeinlegacy.com/2004/WIR20040605.html#DA1)
> (Access: 1 November 2005)

The same year, in the London *Guardian*, beneath the chortling headline "When men were men ... and so were the women," Steven Lynch wrote:

> Rumours that some women were not made entirely of sugar and spice rumbled on through the 1950s. Then came the Ukrainian sisters, Tamara and Irina Press, who won five golds between them in 1960 and 1964, amid whispers that they had been injected with male hormones – or even that they did not need them as they were male to start with. Compulsory sex testing was introduced in the mid-1960s and the Presses stopped. The first athlete to fail a sex test was Poland's Eva Klobukowska, who had won a sprint-relay gold and a 100m in Tokyo in 1964 [...] At one [swimming competition], some British girls became convinced there were men hiding in the changing room, but eventually realised it was deep-voiced East Germans talking tactics.
>
> (http://sport.guardian.co.uk/olympics2004/other
> sports/story/0,14817,1274601,00.html)
> (Access: 2 November 2005)

And, from an American, and a gay, perspective, the writer Patricia Nell Warren has reflected on the impact in the United States of the Soviet performance at the Rome Olympics of 1960. Here the Soviet Union again took the most gold medals, in the first Olympiad to be seen live on TV:

> In their way the Press sisters would be part of the coming changes – human reality arriving to challenge entrenched ideology on both sides. They were big, muscular plain women, complete with Adam's apples. [...] Patriotic Americans had to sit on their sofas and watch helplessly as 'state-supported atheist unfeminine commies' were beating the panties off 'god-fearing American ladies.' Especially those two Amazons, Tamara and Irina Press.

What had the world come to? [...] Though I was staunchly pro-democracy, my heart went out to the Press sisters. They made me remember my high school days, when I was the hulking tomboy who picked fistfights with other students to try to stop the teasing.

(Warren, 2003)

The sex testing, which was introduced by the IOC in 1966 in the wake of Western anxieties about the Presses and lasted until its suspension prior to the Sydney Olympics of 2000, has been called "body McCarthyism" by some writers, mapping it specifically onto the American anti-communist crusade of the late 1940s and early 50s (Hall, 1996, 55). The testing also prompted C.L. Cole to observe that "the properly gendered body has been a means of shoring up Olympic ideals and maintaining the Olympic brand ..." (Cole, 2000, p.332). However, back in the 1950s and 1960s, little trace of the muted moral panic that the Press sisters and athletes like them had apparently inspired in the world of Olympic sport could be found in the mass circulation English newspapers. Instead, these sportspeople are assimilated, where appropriate, to the prevailing British ethos, both of womanhood and of Olympic sport: they, too, become the girls-next-door.

Politik, politik, politik: Helsinki, 1952

"It is difficult," wrote the English historian Robert Colls recently, "to overestimate the impact of a cheap and readable print on national imagining" (Colls, 2002, p.58).

In the 1950s and 1960s, national imagining of sport was mediated to the British suburbs, terraced streets and council estates by a distinctive kind of writing – writing of which the leading football journalist Brian Glanville despaired. "British sports journalism," he wrote in 1965, "is still looking for an idiom ... still waiting for the columnist who can be read by intellectuals without shame and by working men without labour" Glanville, 1965, 84). Outside of the "quality press" in Britain, a popular and populist style had been developed in which "language tends always to be exact and merely emotive"; this style had derived in part from American sports-writing traditions but had been pioneered in Britain by Trevor Wignall and Henry Rose of the *Daily Express* and Peter Wilson of the *Daily Mirror*. This style, like the purported character of the reporter himself, was florid, flamboyant and addressed the senses rather than the intellect, making it "more resolutely low-brow than it was before the war" (ibid., 85); importantly, the style was fashioned with a specific readership in mind and did not stem from the author's own cultural background – Wilson for example, was an Old Harrovian and had, like other sportswriters on the popular press, it seemed, re-invented himself for the purposes of his column (ibid., 86). By the 1950s and 1960s, the main exponents of this form of journalism were Wilson, Desmond Hackett at the *Express* and J. L. Manning and Harry Carpenter of the *Daily Mail*. Their way of writing, however grandiose, could not have been sustained without the daily affirmation of their readers. Indeed, in Glanville's classic disparagement, this kind of writer "is a mimic, a febrile ventriloquist's dummy, using somebody else's eye and ear and experience, and trying pitifully to pass them off as his own" (ibid., 85). Besides, although they wrote emotively, they wrote *specific things* emotively and these things are the concern of this paper.

Three themes, in particular, are noticeable in the coverage by the British popular press of the Olympic Games of 1952.

The first is that the Cold War was being waged with much greater vigour on the front pages than on the back. The Soviet government, along with other similar governments and individuals of a communist affiliation or left-wing sympathy are given the convenient, catch-all label of "Reds." "KOREA – U.S. WARNS REDS" reads the *Daily Express* front page headline on 8 May 1952, a couple of months before the Soviet Union is to make its Olympic debut in Helsinki. Three weeks later (27 May), a similar headline says: "REDS LINE GERMAN BORDER," while during July there are ongoing ruminations in the *Daily Express* about the "RED DEAN" (Dr Hewlett Johnson, the Dean of Canterbury, who had spoken in favour of the Soviet system – see, for example, *Daily Express*, page 1, 16 July 1952). However, while "Reds" haunt the front page, on the sports pages reporter Frank Rostron writes indignantly of the intrusion of politics on the Olympic idyll – an intrusion, he makes clear, that has not begun with the Cold War:

> The favourite international phrase at the last five Olympics in Paris, Amsterdam, Los Angeles, Berlin and London – 'Protest, protest, protest' – has been replaced this time in the merging of East and West by a new one. It is 'Politik, politik, politik'.

Later he suggests:

> The Westerners are such suspicious spy-catchers by now that few take at its surface value the sudden thawing of the Russians in their "for-fellow-travellers-only" Olympic village at Otaneimi where their convenient language barrier is only lifted with finesse by diplomatic interpreters.
>
> (*Daily Express*, 18 July 1952, p.7)

In the *Daily Mail*, an anonymous reporter notes simply and without obvious venom that Finland is on "our" side in the Cold War:

> As for that Iron Curtain, the free 'feel' of Helsinki shows the city is still firmly on the Western side. Newspapers read as free as any in Britain or France. Speech is free too. And, of course, there are no secret police or microphones hidden under the bed.
>
> (*Daily Mail*, 19 July 1952, p.5)

The second theme is that female athletes will be portrayed as pretty and/or grace-ful where possible and that this portrayal will be irrespective of nationality or political connotation. On the 19 July 1952, for example, the *Daily Mail* carries a photograph of three female athletes, dressed for the opening ceremony. The cap-tion reads:

> Cissie Davies, British Olympic gymnast from Wales, wears a beret, not easily caught by the wind, so she can stand with one arm around Carlot Rios, left, and the other round Irma Lozand, who compete for Mexico in diving, while they hold their sombrero-style hats.
>
> *(Daily Mail, 19 July 1952, p.5)*

This is a staple of popular press representation of the Olympics throughout the 1950s and 1960s: pretty British girls waiting to compete in the Olympics, happy meanwhile to pose for photographers, often in the company of athletes from other countries, thus symbolizing the amity of nations. (These nations may, of course, be patronized for wearing funny, impractical hats.)

Three days later, there is a picture of a Soviet female discus thrower, in the act of throwing: "Grace, poise and power, too, are shown by Nina Romaschkova as she throws her discus at Helsinki," *(Daily Mail, 22 July 1952, p.6)*. There is no reference to Romaschkova's physique here and, the "Iron Curtain" notwith-standing, she is freely admitted to the symbolic world of gracefulness historically inhabited by female athletes (Guttmann, 1991).

Third, the athletes are on leave from everyday life: this, and not their ath-letic pursuit, defines them primarily. "Miss Shirley Cawley," reads the caption of a photograph in the *Daily Mail*, "lives in Croydon, Surrey, and works at the Bank of England. Yesterday she was busy at Helsinki on the figures for the Olympic long jump. Gaining third place for Britain Shirley leapt 19 ft 5 ... " *(Daily Mail, 24 July 1952, p.5)*. The following day, Geoffrey Simpson writes in the same paper that "Jean Desforges, the West Ham typist" has only managed fifth place in the 80 metres hurdles final *(Daily Mail, 25 July 1952, p.6)* and, on 28 July, he reflects that, although Britain has "sent our best team of runners" and seen them "surpass their home performances and smash Olympic records ... there is not a single gold medal among them." The best is a silver gained in the high jump by "Sheila Lerwill, secretary housewife of Swanley, Kent" *(Daily Mail, 28 July 1952, p.6)*.

There is, moreover, a place in this rhetoric for the ties that bind the British Empire. Five days earlier, Simpson hails "Marjorie Jackson, the 20 year old Sydney typist ... a well made 9 st[one] with a mop of curly fair hair" who is one of three Australian women to reach the final of the 100 metres. "It was indeed," writes Simpson, "a triumph for the Dominion" *(Daily Mail, 23 July 1952, p.6)*.

Ignore the dismal jimmies: Melbourne, 1956

At the time of the Melbourne Olympiad, the Cold War is more obtrusive than four years previously: the Soviet army has invaded Hungary and its tanks are on the streets of the capital, amid angry condemnation in the British popular press. "THE MURDER OF HUNGARY" is announced on the front page of the *Daily Mail* on 5 November 1956, just as British athletes are about to leave for Australia: "BUDAPEST CRUSHED – Red troops storm into parliament." The decline of British power is also more manifest, British soldiers having been sent in the summer of 1956 to seize the Suez Canal, recently nationalized by Egypt's President Nasser. The mission has been a failure and has been condemned by Britain's key post-war ally, the United States. Both these matters are addressed, obliquely or otherwise, in the popular press discourse of the Games.

The day after the Soviet occupation of Budapest, it is nevertheless business as usual on the sports pages of the *Daily Mail*, where Harry Carpenter reports that each British participant has been weighed by BOAC (British Overseas Airways Corporation), whose aircraft will fly them to Melbourne. They are, he implies, a national family, dissolving class differences: "Cockney boxers lined up for the weighing in alongside elegant, slightly aloof yachtsmen" (*Daily Mail*, 6 November 1956, p.10). Later in the week J.L. Manning confronts the issue of Hungary: the outcome is a (slightly grudging) reaffirmation of the Olympic ethos that sport must transcend politics. He recounts a conversation he has had with K.S. (Sandy) Duncan, Britain's "Chef de Mission" at the Games:

> Duncan told me he had met the Soviet team leader, Konstantin Adrianov, and shaken hands with him. 'Did you think it was the right thing to do', I asked him. 'Of course', said Duncan. 'I am determined that Britain shall show friendship and sportsmanship to all our rivals in the Games. That is what we are here for'.
>
> (*Daily Mail*, 9 November 1956, p.10)

"Politics," therefore, will not be admitted to Olympic sport, although on 12 November 1956, Manning reports that the Hungarian team will march behind "the patriotic Kossuth flag," and not the "hated communist flag," as "a concession from the Soviet masters" (*Daily Mail*, 12 November 1956, p.11). This sense of "Soviet masters" constraining individual freedoms is now becoming more pervasive in commentary on the Games. Beneath the headline "SO DON'T SNARL UP THE GAMES, YOU 'ORRIBLE IVANS" Desmond Hackett in the *Daily Express* pleads with Soviet officials and "cloak-and-dagger men" to "let the boys and girls [of the Soviet party] come out to play and we shall have a jolly good time at Melbourne ..." (*Daily Express*, 7 November 1956, p.14). Five days on, Hackett reports accusations by the English runner Gordon Pirie that the Soviet party has been spying on his training sessions. "You missed a couple of my times," Pirie is reported as saying. "You had better let me give you them." "HE

DID," trumpets Hackett in bold capitals. "– AND THE RUSSIANS TOOK THEM," (*Daily Express*, 12 November 1956, p.14). The Russians should lighten up, argues Hackett, and, as if to demonstrate how they might do so, four days later he is part of a big media contingent that turns out to welcome Soviet discus thrower Nina Ponomareva to Australia. Turned into an ironic celebrity by the British press following her arrest in London earlier in the year on suspicion of stealing from a millinery store, she is now known as "Nina of the Five Hats":

> ... there stood the hefty Russian girl with her head bowed. She looked up uncertainly and then her attractive face eased into a great smile as the crowd applauded and chanted "Nina ... Nina" [...] She looked more than a little untidy in her fawn mackintosh and frilly lace blouse – but no hat.
> (*Daily Express*, 16 November 1956, p.14)

"Russians girls," though "hefty" and "untidy," can still be attractive; they, like their government, just have to let themselves go.

On the matter of Britain's prospects at these Olympics there has been some concern in official circles. Team manager Jack Crump has publicly doubted that Britain will win many medals in Melbourne. "It appears," scorns Hackett, "that only gaunt galloper Gordon Pirie, napped to win the 5,000 metres, and high jump pin-up girl Thelma Hopkins carry Jack Crump's confidence." Hackett rejects this caution: "Ignore the dismal jimmies" reads his headline, "I can see medals" (*Daily Express*, 7 November 1956, p.14). Nevertheless, three weeks later, Crump is still worried, particularly about his female contingent. He tells Harry Carpenter: "I'm dashed if I know what is wrong with our girls. They are so disappointing. It's a mystery." (*Daily Mail*, 28 November 1956, p.11).

As to the Olympic events themselves, English audiences have two gold medals to cheer them. Firstly, on 1 December 1956, the popular press hails fencer Gillian Sheen. Sheen is an unambiguously middle-class figure – a dentist from the affluent north London district of St Johns Wood, but in the *Daily Express* her age (28) and gender are accentuated so that she becomes "dark horse 'Gillie'", "rosy-cheeked Gillian" and "curly-haired, blue-eyed Miss Sheen" (*Daily Express*, 1 December 1956, p.10). In the *Daily Mail*, her emotions are on show to Harry Carpenter: "Laughing and crying alternatively, Gillian said: 'It's all such a shock. I just can't think properly. It's like a beautiful dream. I hope I don't wake up and find it's untrue'" (*Daily Mail*,1 December 1956, p.6). Judy Grinham, who wins the women's 100 metres backstroke for Britain five days later, is from the altogether less glamorous north London suburb of Neasden and, as such, is a readier candidate for the "Britain's sweetheart" treatment. However, in the rendering of Grinham by the popular press, she gives the same sense as Sheen of a young person who steps briefly from "ordinary life," walks in wonderment on the Olympic stage with a gold medal around her neck, but prepares soon to re-embrace the ordinary life that, ultimately, defines her. She is a "happy lass" to have beaten "pretty Carin Cone of America" into second place. Another British swimmer, Margaret Edwards, has taken bronze and there is an honourable mention of "17-year-old tall statuesque Julie Hoyle of Bushey" who has come sixth (*Daily Express*, 6 December 1956, p.12). Back home, proud mothers and wider communities wait their return. In the *Daily Mail*, Pat Besford writes: "The Olympic medal mums, Flora Grinham from Neasden and Ina Edwards, a former mayoress of Heston and Isleworth, toasted their darling daughters over a glass of wine at lunchtime," while on the same page Harry Carpenter reports that Grinham is to be measured for a wedding dress. "But it doesn't mean marriage for this 17-year old London lass. Let Judy explain: 'Before I came away a friend of my mother's said she would make me a wedding dress if I did well in the Olympics. So now I have my wedding gown ... '" (*Daily Mail*, 6 December 1956, p.10). Grinham's win, it is reported, has even tugged an imperial heart string or two. When she has received her medal, *Daily Express* reporter Frank Rostron writes, Australian Prime Minister Robert Menzies "turned to me and said 'Well, Rostron, that's just about made my day'," (*Daily Express*, 6 December 1956, p.12).

But, in amongst the reassuring imagery of home, community, wedding dresses and imperial sentiment, there are glimpses of a less cosy future. For example, the first picture of this Olympiad to be published by the *Daily Express* features Betty Cuthbert winning the women's 100 metres relay for Australia. There is the familiar domestic vocabulary – 18-year-old Cuthbert has "no regular boyfriends" and "in her spare time breeds budgerigars" and a second picture of her putting on her tracksuit "shows more woman, less superwoman." Crucially, though, Cuthbert's power – here unfortunately attributed to "aboriginal energy" – has been too much for the British finisher, "ladylike Heather Armitage" (*Daily Express*, 4 December 1956, p.5). At a separate athletics meeting between the Commonwealth and the United States in Sydney in early December, the US have won 13 events to five. Hackett's reflections on the women's relay team's performance in this tournament are important for two reasons – they show a heightened concern for national pride and they are drenched in a kind of saloon bar sexualization that prefigures the marketing of female athletes in subsequent decades:

> The pin-up pace girls of Britain saved the British Olympic squad from looking the biggest chumps ever to raise a foot on the track in the Commonwealth and United States meeting last night. [...] It looked as though Britain's four fleet and lovelies were about to create a night of national mourning by defeating Australia's idolised 'Hustle Honeys'. Handsomely built Mrs. June Paul shook her pretty head sadly and confessed: 'It was my fault we didn't win. I tried to get away too fast in the takeover. ...'
> (*Daily Express*, 6 December 1956, p.12)

And there is a cautionary word from Carpenter in the *Daily Mail*:

> One athlete, one fencer, one swimmer, and a couple of boxers made us respectable at Melbourne. We may pity poor relations, but they are a bit of an embarrassment to have around. [...] Whether it's the right way to go about financing our lot against the State-aided mobs is not for discussion here, but you'd better think about it ... [...] [British Olympic steeplechase champion Chris] Brasher shook me this week at lunch when he suddenly said: 'I think I shall be the last gold medallist to come out of an English university'.
>
> (Carpenter, 1956)

Carpenter, of course, did not feel the need to specify that the "State-aided mobs" and the universities whence future Olympic gold medal winners were now more likely to come would be found either in the United States or behind the "Iron Curtain."

To us sport is a game: Rome 1960

Most of these elements of representation are present in the popular press coverage of the 1960 Olympics in Rome.

In the *Daily Mirror*, Peter Wilson talks sympathetically about the Soviet Union's preparations for Rome and, in general, about their sports policy. He has talked to Soviet athletics coach Gabriel Korobkov and to the Press sisters – "We were," they tell him, "what you call tomboys":

> 'Tamara and Irina are classic examples of how Russia takes promising young prospects and moulds them through specialised training into outstanding stars'
>
> (Wilson, 1960)

As if to counter this, days later, in the same paper, there is a display of late-imperial hubris. This time it falls to George Harley to rebuke the dismal jimmies and, this time, it is done in an explicitly Cold War paradigm:

> To hear some people talk you would think Britain's Olympic teams are going to Rome just for the ride. I'm tired of hearing hearty types in pubs declaring: 'We shall win nothing. NOTHING' and dismal types in railway trains mumbling: 'We've no chance against the Americans and Russians'. We shall win PLENTY ... and, in some events, the Americans and Russians stand no chance against US. My forecast, and I regard it as a cautious one, is that Britain will win EIGHT individual gold medals.
>
> (*Daily Mirror*, 19 August 1960, p.19)

Britain, in the event, took two golds, against forty-three for the Soviet Union and thirty-four for the United States. In the *Daily Sketch* superpower dominance of the Olympics has begun, in any event, to be questioned. Reporter Laurie Pignon suggests that the accusation made by Mr Ruuska, father of US freestyle swimmer Sylvia Ruuska, "that American swimmers are being pep-pilled spotlights the growing suspicion that some of the 1960 Gold Medals will be won in the chemist shop" (*Daily Sketch*, 9 August 1960, p.1). Two weeks later, on 22 August, with the Games still to begin, the *Daily Sketch* and the *Daily Mirror* both report a claim that a female member of the British Olympic team is turning into a man. This claim, attributed to "officials of two unnamed European nations," is described by Jack Crump, now secretary to the British Amateur Athletic Board, as "sickening ... disgusting ... nauseating" and he offers the nation the reassurance that "of course our girls are our girls" (*Daily Mirror*, 22 August 1960, p.30). Pignon, in the *Daily Sketch* of the same day, writes:

> True or false, the damage has been done. No words of mine can put it right. But, I'm sure of one thing, that the British girls when they arrive next week will behave with a proud feminine dignity that will leave the world in no doubt.
>
> (*Daily Sketch*, 22 August 1960, p.1)

This story, while not necessarily invented, lacks any obvious substance and, with 45 years of hindsight, it reads now like the expression of a fear of changes in the cultural world of the Olympics. In this world, female athletes are now being invited to train and test their bodies in ways which threaten British conventions of femininity. The fear of this upheaval appears here to have been transmuted into an accusation against *British* bodies, so that it can be rebutted with suitably patriotic outrage.

Once again, therefore, where possible, female British competitors are complimented not only for their performances but for their looks – "Blessings ... on the pretty curly head of Liz Ferris who brought us our first medal of the Games by gaining the bronze ... in the springboard diving," writes Harley, (*Daily Mirror*, 29 August 1960, p.19) – or the ordinariness of their lives: "Unheralded Carol [Quinton], a 23-year old Birmingham secretary, ran a terrific race and collected our first athletics medal by finishing second in the 800 metres hurdles to powerful Russian Irina Press," writes Pignon in the *Daily Sketch*, 2 September 1960 p.1.

There are, moreover, further opportunities for the popular press to rehearse the girl-(or boy) next-door story. Don Thompson, a 27-year-old fire insurance clerk who lived with his parents near Heathrow airport in London, won gold in the 50 kilometres walk. The press gleefully reported that, to avoid sunstroke, Thompson had worn a cap with a handkerchief stitched to the back by his mother. Thompson later recalled that the press had exaggerated the primitive nature of his preparation: "They made it seem that I had done all my training in

the bathroom" (Pitt, 2000). And, to set alongside Thompson, is a modest hero-
ine from Huddersfield: Anita Lonsbrough, who attributes her gold medal in the
women's 200 metres breast stroke to the early interest shown in her swimming
ability by the nuns at St Joseph's convent school in Bradford, Yorkshire. She
swims quite a lot but otherwise leads an unremarkable life "making out car
licences in Huddersfield Town Hall" (Carpenter, 1960). In the *Daily Express*,
Hackett reports that Lonsbrough has left her medal in her hut. "If I started to
carry it around they would think I was just a big show-off." This "laughing lovely
lassie" who has "no steady boyfriend" has been promised a week in Scarborough
watching cricket by her father, (*Daily* Express, 29 August 1960, p.10).

The *Daily Sketch* closes the tournament with an angry denunciation of Cold
War threats to British Olympism. The paper's sports editor is rebuked for suggesting, as Fleet Street sports writers have begun to do, that the amateur spirit might
no longer be viable:

> To us sport is a game. That is the glory of it. Let us continue to set the
> Americans and Russians an example, even if we do lose. My dictionary
> defines sport as 'amusement, diversion, fun'. Where's the fun in interna-
> tional sport if success or failure becomes a political matter'.
>
> (*Daily Sketch*, 3 September 1960 p.13)

Love over gold: Tokyo 1964

In the representation of the Tokyo Olympiad by the British popular press, it is
possible to discern a hardening of now-familiar themes: in these depictions, the
Olympics themselves seem more degraded, the Soviet Union more secretive and
British female athletes, as a metaphor for British amateurism, prettier and more
domesticated than ever.

With the tournament still a month away, Mike Grade asserts in the *Daily
Mirror*: "Ann Packer, Mary Hodson and Anne Smith, three of Britain's most
attractive athletes, may beat the Russians even before they get to Tokyo. How?
By having a crack at the world 3×800 metres record, which was beaten by a
Russian trio at the weekend ... ." He finishes: "Go to it girls!," (*Daily Mirror*, 15
September 1964, p.27). A few days later, Pignon employs brittle heterosexual
imagery to decry the passing of Olympic innocence: "Never have so many countries spent so much money – or so many athletes shed so much sweat – as for the
18th Olympiad, which begins in Tokyo on October 10. All figures – even the
36–22–37 variety – frighten me, but this latest quest for phoney gold medals and
sporting immortality makes a Hollywood spectacular look like a penny Punch
and Judy," *Daily Sketch*, 24 September 1964, p.17). Two days later, the same paper
carries a picture of British athlete Mary Rand in her official Tokyo outfit. She
declares it "smart, young and feminine," while team manager Pat Sage is confident "The girls' outfits will hit them for six in Tokyo," (*Daily Sketch*, 26

September 1964, p.1). Further on in the same issue, another member of the British team is rendered straightforwardly as a pin-up. Beneath a photograph and a headline "GOLD MEDAL LOOKS" is the caption:

> If you're pretty, an ex-deb, an old girl of Cheltenham Ladies' College and daddy is lord of the manor at Barton-on-Heath, Warwickshire, you're bound to get your picture in the papers. Janet Bewley Cathie is all this, 24 and an accountant. Southpaw Janet is also in the British fencing team for Tokyo … and there will be plenty of lads willing to carry the Olympic torch for her!
>
> (*Daily Sketch*, 26 September 1964, p.15)

Three days on and Pignon laments:

> Too often we hear the 'Star Spangled Banner' and the rolling Russian anthem. By November 24 Japan will be able to hum these tunes by heart. For the Olympics has become a great battle for international prestige that has long outgrown the ideas of Baron Pierre de Coubertin, who claimed the important thing was taking part and not winning.
>
> (*Daily Sketch*, 29 September 1964, p.21)

Into October – Olympic month but with the Games still not yet opened – the popular press continues to serve from its established menu of pin-ups, innuendo and suspicion. On the first of the month Hackett informs readers that there will be no curfew in the Olympic village "to check an Olympic boy meets girl out-break," (*Daily Express*, 1 October 1964, p.18). Two days later, in the same paper, "KIMONO LINDA WOWS CROWD" heralds a picture of two British athletes:

> TOKYO, Friday. Linda Knowles and Mary Hodson, British girl athletes, became Tokyo traffic stoppers today when they paraded in kimonos. They were surrounded by admiring athletes from 10 countries and a dozen photographers as they walked out in blue and white kimonos – traditional dress of Japanese women. 'Mom will be staggered when I walk in in this', said Linda, 18-year old high jumper from Hornchurch, Essex.
>
> (*Daily Express*, 3 October 1964, p.16)

On 5 October the same young woman, now styled as "leggy Linda Knowles," reportedly *is* subject to curfew, having been seen chatting to a male American athlete after midnight, (*Daily Express*, 5 October 1964, p.1).

Three days later Laurie Pignon claims to have penetrated Soviet defences:

I raid the Russians so-secret hide-out
Today I gate-crashed the best kept secret of the Olympic Games – the hide-out of the Russian 108-strong athletic team and their eleven coaches … 'We chose

this place because we wanted to work undisturbed and wanted to be left alone', [track and field coach Gabriel] Koropkov told me. But back in Tokyo other countries were criticising the Russians for flouting the spirit of the Olympics and [not] joining in the international goodwill of the official training village.

(Daily Sketch, 8 October 1964, p.21)

Again the central thrust is that the Soviets are cheerless and unconvivial, but their chosen seclusion and the pointed references to "work" and to eleven coaches all connote the taking-too-seriously of sport. Nevertheless, if they should soften, the press make clear that there still is a place on the Planet Pretty Girls for Russians with the necessary credentials. The *Daily Express*, for example, on 21 October, refers to "Russian javelin thrower Elvira Ozalina, world record holder, who cropped off her hair after finishing fifth [and] was seen in the village wearing a wig. This loveliest of the Soviet squad was escorted by two giant Russian athletes ... " (*Daily Express*, 21 October 1964, p.24).

On the comment pages, credibility of the Olympic project is now being openly questioned, however. In the *Daily Mirror*, Peter Wilson insists that the Games have become too big (an estimated 97 participant countries, 8,000 competitors and officials), and too influenced both by technology ("Human beings are being overshadowed by the day of the computer") and politics: "And the more the pious platitudes are paid to the hoary old myths of "true amateurism" and "keeping politics out of sport," the more suspect various sports become. And the more obvious are the alliances between the nations representing the world's opposed ideologies." For clinging to now-degraded Olympic ideals, Avery Brundage, 77-year-old president of the International Olympic Committee is denounced as "Brontosaurus Brundage" (Wilson, 1964).

Amid the cultural pessimism and the proliferating pin-ups, the British popular press is gifted with two fresh girls-next-door, apparently as domesticated and as rooted in ordinary life as any of their predecessors. When Mary Rand wins the women's long jump event, she is immediately placed, symbolically, among the small towns and semi-detached houses of Middle England. "It could have been Red Square all over again when the people of the tiny market town of Henly-on-Thames heard about golden girl Mary Rand's fantastic 22ft 2in jump into Tokyo space at the Olympic Games ... [...] Mary, who is 24, was born in a small, semi-detached house in Hervey Road, Wells, Somerset" says the *Daily Sketch* (15 October 1964, pp.6–7). Pignon adds on page 22 that Rand has looked "proud and beautiful as she stood on the winners' rostrum" and, in the *Daily Express*, Rand's husband Sidney says: "The routine of marriage has stabilised her, made her more mature both on and off the track." "And Mary," the paper adds, "has never contradicted her husband's recipe for triumph" (Daily Express, 15 October 1964, p.5). The following week, when Ann Packer wins the women's 800 metres, Peter Wilson notes that Packer, who has run this distance only four times before, will not run again competitively:

Afterwards the 22 year old teacher was besieged with questions. Why wasn't she going to run any more? On December 19 she is going to marry Robbie [Brightwell, a fellow Olympic athlete] and that is why this is a Japanese farewell: 'I couldn't run well – and run a home well', she said. The race? She ran her first half-mile only last May, so ... 'I don't know much about tactics over the distance. I just run. With 150 yards to go, I moved up and found myself boxed in. At that point I thought I had no chance of winning. I just could not believe I had won'

(*Daily Mirror*, 21 October 1964, p.30)

In the *Daily Sketch* Laurie Pignon writes:

A woman's love for a man can be strong enough to conquer the world ... as I saw for myself today when Ann Packer won a gold medal in the 800 metres of these Romeo and Juliet Olympics. Ann, already the proud winner of a sil-ver medal in the 400 metres, made up her mind she'd rather collapse seeking gold than lose after watching fiancé Robbie Brightwell beaten into fourth place in yesterday's 400 metres. 'It was five past three and I promised then that I would run myself into the ground for him'.

(*Daily Sketch*, 21 October 1964, p.17)

Here, then, is the living embodiment of the then-current, but threatened, British Olympic ideal: a young woman, who knows nothing of tactics (unlike the secre-tive Russians) and is unfamiliar even with the event, but will give it a go. She wins, is thrilled and can't believe it, but will walk purposefully away, toward love, home and a simple life – a life in which there are things other than sport.

"I'm terribly sorry. They went much quicker than I thought they would ...": Mexico City 1968

Ann Packer's achievement in Tokyo and its rendition in the British popular press together represent both the high tide and the beginning of the end for girl-next-door Olympism in UK sport culture. Four years later, for the Mexico City Olympiad, the framing of the tournament and its politics is perceptibly and importantly different. While there are still wide-eyed typists from London and shy female teachers from Sheffield, the more powerful rhetorics are of feminism, of professionalism and, thus, of the (more or less) sober acceptance of how the Cold War has changed Olympic sport.

To be sure the British press corps in Mexico is on the look-out for the next Packer and, where a likely candidate presents herself, the same purple prose, stressing modesty, domesticity and another life, is employed. Hackett, for exam-ple, writes:

'Sheila Sherwood, shy, modest, 22 year old Sheffield school teacher, won Britain's first medal in the 1968 Olympics today. She did a wondrous leap of 21 ft 11 ins ... .One of the first to congratulate her was her husband John Sherwood'.

(*Daily Express*, 15 October 1968, p.24)

The most likely heir to Packer's mantle, however, is runner Lillian Board. The following day, Hackett enthuses: "Gorgeous golden girl Lillian Board streaked out the fastest 400 metres time in the world this year as she moved swiftly and with supreme confidence into the final during a thunderstorm" (*Daily Express*, 16 October, 1968 p.24) On 17 October, however, with Board having failed to win gold, he reports that "the 19 year old London typist looked too tensed up at the start to run her best" (p.19). In the newly emergent *The Sun*, beneath the headline "Oh dear! Only a SILVER for Lillian Board," Frank Taylor writes:

As soon as the race was over, Lillian Board threw herself down by the side of the track, overcome with emotion and gasping 'I'm terribly sorry. They went much quicker than I thought they would down the back straight'. I don't know what she was apologising for because, as Mary Rand told me, 'This is not a failure ... '.

(*Sun*, 17 October, 1968, p.13)

In the *Daily Express*, veteran Soviet coach Koropkov tells Hackett that Board should have run in the 800 metres: "I feel sure she does not know how good she can be over the big distance," (*Daily Express*, 18 October 1968, p.24). Two things are important to note about Lillian Board in this representation. Firstly, unlike Grinham, Lonsbrough, Rand or Packer, she carries a weight of national expectation on her shoulders and, thus, now feels the need to apologise for not winning. Secondly, the very things that exalted Ann Packer – her lack either of preparation or of awareness of her own capacities – become the basis for mild regret when judging Board: she was poorly prepared, didn't know the other athletes' likely times and maybe chose the wrong event. While Packer was celebrated for her lack of professionalism, the apparent absence of the same property in Board, by implication saddens her admirers. Part of the affirmation of this comes from a Soviet coach – a former steward, therefore, of the fabled secret training camps and, in tabloid mythology, one of the mean-spirited men who helped turn Olympic sport into work.

This, of course, is not a wholescale transformation. There are still ritual allegations of Soviet chicanery – Pignon accuses the USSR of illegal use of walkie-talkies in the equestrian event (*Daily Sketch*, 23 October 1968, p.22) – and indignation at the intrusion, once again, of "politics" on the tournament. When American athletes Tommie Smith and John Carlos give their famous clenched fist salute after the 200 metres, for example, Pignon writes:

> I have no doubt that many Negroes of the United States have plenty to protest about, but if these two athletes used their brains as well as they use their limbs they would realise that the sort of publicity their action has provoked will do more harm than good to what could be a justifiable cause.
>
> (*Daily Sketch*, 18 October 1968, p.22)

In the *Daily Express* there is, significantly, more interest in the fact that Smith and Carlos are both, effectively, full-time athletes, on scholarships at San Jose University in California, (Morgan, 1968).

Lillian Board is not the only athlete to be fitted for the (now slightly worn) outfit of the girl-next-door. In *The Sun*, Frank Taylor celebrates show-jumper "Marion Coakes, 21 year old farmer's daughter from New Milton, Hampshire" who "did a beautiful job for this country when she steered [her horse] Stroller into second place [...] a marvellous performance from a girl who learned to ride on a donkey at the age of three" (*The Sun*, 24 October 1968, p.13).

In general, two things are notable about the representation of female performers at these Olympics. First, there is the adoption of an explicitly feminist vocabulary. In the *Daily Express*, Anneli Drummond-Hay, herself a rider, wrote from Avandaro:

> Jane Bullen, a pretty 20 year old nurse from London's Middlesex hospital proved beyond all doubt here yesterday that girls can compete in the tough, three-day riding event. For years our Olympic selectors – men, of course – have derided the idea of our best women riders representing Britain in this stern test that takes in dressage, show-jumping and cross-country. 'Girls could never stand up to the rigours', they moaned. But yesterday, up in the hills 90 miles from Mexico City, in the most diabolical conditions of four Olympics, young Jane showed how ridiculous these fears were. My most pleasant memory of this Olympic event is the amazement of the Mexican spectators at the sight of this pretty girl eating up the cross-country fences better than many men. Yesterday Jane struck a major blow for women to compete on equal terms with men in the three-day event. I hope never again to hear that girls are not tough enough to take part.
>
> (*Daily Express*, 23 October 1968, p.18)

Once again, comparison with Packer is striking. The image of a pretty, carefree homemaker, hanging up her spikes and departing to care for house and husband is replaced by one of a determined young woman, still pretty, but in for the long haul and capable of toughing it out with the allegedly stronger sex.

Second, there is a keener sense of female celebrity, transcending national boundaries. A *Daily Sketch* reporter, for instance, covers the wedding of glamorous Olympic gymnast Vera Caslavska of Czechoslovakia (winner of four gold medals at the Games) and reports "a near riot" after an "over enthusiastic crowd of 10,000" has gathered at Mexico City's Roman Catholic cathedral (*Daily Sketch*, 28 October 1968, p.7). Among other things, this near-riot seems to illustrate the growing importance of the Olympics as a television spectacle, this having been the third Olympiad to have been televised. "If you are a slick cyclist or a shapely girl swimmer," wrote Peter Wilson in the *Daily Mirror*, "an Olympic top title can mean you are made for life. Inevitably, with television making Olympic champions as well known as brand name goods, the trend towards more and more commercialism will increase" (*Daily Mirror*, 11 October 1968, p.30).

By far the most important theme of popular press treatment of Mexico, is the acceptance, however reluctant, that in Cold War Olympic culture, British amateurism is no longer feasible. An early contribution here comes in the *Daily Express* from Chapman Pincher, ordinarily a specialist in stories of Cold War espionage. Pincher writes sympathetically about the intervention of science in sport:

> Scores of doctors and scientists are studying Olympic athletes in Mexico City to devise new training methods which will break down the barriers limiting human physical performance. [...] They are certainly convinced from the facts they already have that man as a machine has not reached anything like his full capacity.
>
> (Pincher, 1968)

Five days later, Richard Kilian suggests in the *Daily Express* that the gold medal won in Mexico by Britain's David Hemery in the 400 metres hurdles

> is in fact a pure product of America's unique athletic system. 'It is ironic, in fact, that the honours should go to Britain', says a spokesman for Boston University's athletic department, 'when we developed him from a mediocre runner to the best in the world'
>
> (Kilian, 1968)

Kilian points to the extravagant funding and facilities for elite athletes in the United States, while in *The Sun* Clement Freud praises the dedication of American athletes and their families. He interviews 11-year-old Dallas schoolgirl Leslie Crozier, a talented swimmer, who is already preparing for the next Olympics in Munich. "I guess I've given up pretty much," she tells him;

> – sleeping late in the mornings at weekends. Playing after school. The girl scouts. I gave up going to bed late and going to slumber parties so that I'd be up in the mornings and I took to eating dextrotabs and drinking nutriment ... [...] From now on I'm going to work real hard, four hours every day, so that I can walk round the pool at Munich and have my picture taken.
>
> (*The Sun*, 26 October 1968, p.13)

"Her mother explained," continues Freud, "that in Dallas some of their friends couldn't understand why she and daddy seldom went to week-end parties, but went off to see Leslie compete in some other Texan city … 'but we just love it'" (*The Sun*, 26th October 1968, p.13). The same day, in the *Daily Express*, Brian Park interviews Cheryl Finnegan, whose husband Chris is about to box for the Olympic middleweight title. Her daughter, Cheryl tells Park, has often gone hungry "so that Chris could have the steak and eggs he needed." Their local boxing club in Hayes, west London, has held a dance to raise money for the family and, just prior to leaving for Mexico, a court has ordered Finnegan to pay £70 National Insurance arrears, (*Daily Express*, 26 October 1968, p.11). The implication is clear: to be competitive, Britain must fund her Olympic competitors.

On 30 October, the *Sun* grasps the political nettle of Britain's Olympic future. Much of one page is dedicated to an article entitled "MUNICH WILL PROVE WE'RE NOT FINISHED," written principally by Frank Taylor. It endorses the main finding of the Byers Report on British athletics the previous May: that there should be one governing body, headed by a "professional supremo." "After all, the US, Russia and other nations have sports supremos who really run the sport. One admires the amateur administrator, but his day is over in the bustling 20th century." Sports minister Denis Howell "is to call a series of sports summits to discuss plans for the 1972 Munich Olympics" (*The Sun*, 30 October 1968, p.11).

Thus the polity and the popular press now embrace the Cold War model of Olympic endeavour; American–Soviet style technocracy is the only way forward. The future is science and supremos. There will be no more girls-next-door, stepping out of, and back into, an "ordinary life." Indeed, four years after Ann Packer's definitively amateur triumph in Tokyo, readers of the popular press have glimpsed, in Leslie Crozier, a very different kind of young female athlete – one with, effectively, no "ordinary life" at all.

Conclusion: the agony and the ecstasy – Munich 1972

Not surprisingly, therefore, the tenor of Olympic reportage four years later is largely transformed: there is, variously, an impatience with any lack of preparedness and a lower tolerance of failure. The papers also attend to the rigours and stresses that are entailed in training – sometimes as a means to invoke the more innocent Olympic spirit for which many of their readers will still have hankered. In early August, a *Daily Express* headline announces "OLYMPIC SPLASH AS DOC EATS DOCS" and under it Sydney Hulls writes: "Liz Ferris, who earned diving fame as a 1960 Olympic bronze medallist, has caused a mighty splash with an attack on Britain's Olympic team doctors." In *Sportsworld*, official magazine of the British Olympic Association, Ferris, a qualified doctor – hence the headline, has written:

What of the worthy doctors who accompany our international team abroad …? These doctors, on the whole, are consultants or GPs [General Practitioners] whose normal work is totally unrelated to sports medicine. So consulting them on a sports injury or complaint is like asking an ear, nose and throat specialist to treat a broken leg. It is pathetic that the number of actual sports medicine doctors in this country who can safely treat athletic injuries can be numbered on the fingers on one hand.

(*Sportsworld*, 4 August 1972, p.16)

Ten days later the same paper tells of the stresses that may be generated by the new training regimes. The front page story is headlined "SWIMMER ADMITS: I TOOK POT," beneath which "sacked British Olympic swim star Tyrone 'Tarzan' Tozer admitted last night: "I smoked pot to forget about training"" (*Daily Express*, 14 August 1972, p.1). The following day a further front page headline states "FIVE MORE STARS RAPPED." A group of young British swimmers have been reprimanded, apparently also for smoking cannabis. Their team manager John Verrier reflects on the matter in the language of the new technocracy: "We are here to do a job – to do our best for our country. Thousands of pounds have been spent. It would be a tragedy if it was spoiled." Elsewhere in the same issue, the *Daily Express* carries a photo of the assembled "British swimming team at the centre of the pot-smoking storm." Sydney Hulls' caption, however, offers not reproof but context and, by implication nostalgia for a lost Olympic innocence. The swimmers, he says, have:

been in the pool up to five hours a day, swimming as far as 50 miles a week. Their hair has been bleached close to white by the purifying chemicals in the water. They have been pumped full of antibiotics to combat long-lasting catarrh colds. Other hazards have been costume burns from shoulder straps, ear infections and teeth problems … from almost living in the water for four months.

(*Daily Express*, 14 August 1972, p.7)

Similarly, the following week, the *Daily Express* reports that "David Bedford, Britain's temperamental hope for the Olympics" has "fled from the rigours of training at St. Moritz." Gordon Pirie, now living in New Zealand, tells the paper: "Give Bedford a chance. He needs your support to see him through the tremendous pressures he faces. […] When I started running I was an amateur; I did it for the hell of it," (*Daily Express*, 19 August 1972, p.5). Now, Lynn Davies, British Olympic gold medal winner in Rome, tells Andrew Fyall of the *Daily Express*, it is "an Olympic Frankenstein. People are prepared to lay down their lives for their country and for the honour of winning, no matter how terrible the after effects could be." (*Daily Express*, 14 August 1972, p.6).

On 3 September, Bedford finished well down the field in the 10,000 metres in Munich. On the same day, Mary Peters of Northern Ireland won a gold medal for

Britain in the pentathlon. The *Daily Express*'s front page headline the following day is "The Ecstasy of Mary Peters … The Agony of Dave Bedford," but the first paragraph of Hugh McIlvanney's report is a rebuke for Bedford, rather than praise for Peters:

> David Bedford, the man who invited the nation to watch him win a gold medal in the 10,000 metres, ran from the Olympic stadium in tears here this afternoon after he had failed miserably to put achievement where his mouth had been. He left the stage to Mary Peters, the strapping blonde from Belfast, who had entered the day's pentathlon competition as confident as Bedford claimed to be – but kept quiet about it until she had a golden disc around her neck.
>
> (*Daily Express*, 3 September 1972, front page)

On page 14 of the same issue is a further headline which reads "Bedford … the big flop."

This representation says much about the adaptation of the British popular press to the dominant culture of Olympic sport in the early Cold War period. Bedford is framed by this new culture. For him, and people like him, it is no longer a matter of taking part in the Olympics; it's a matter of winning. He has made the cardinal mistake not only of losing but of having previously raised the expectations of a large national television audience – McIlvanney now rebukes him for "refusing to face the television cameras." This makes him doubly a failure: he has failed both as an athlete and as a television performer. "He began to run again," scorned McIlvanney, "this time through the maze of tunnels that led to the Olympic village. Some are saying cruelly tonight that he should never have left the place" (*Daily Express*, 4 September 1972, p.1). Neither Bedford nor Peters can any longer be defined as having an ordinary life; they are, in effect, full time athletes doing, or failing to do, a job. Most of their time is spent going about this business. Peters is not, and cannot be so easily rendered as, a girl-next-door. Thus she does not receive the same press euphoria that greeted Packer and her other predecessors. As McIlvanney says, she expected to win. Moreover, she is, again, apparently a full-time athlete, with no job to go back to and no proud workmates to be photographed. There is no attendant boyfriend and, besides, with visual judgements growing in importance via television, the "strapping blonde" Peters perhaps cannot compete for newsprint with, say, "Olga … the girl who won more hearts than gold" – the *Daily Express* headline that greeted a gold medal for the "elfin, saucy, self-assured" 17-year-old Russian gymnast Olga Korbut two days earlier (*Daily Express*, 2 September 1972, p.5). Perhaps most importantly it is impossible to think that at Tokyo, only eight years earlier, British reporters would have relegated Ann Packer's gold medal to their second paragraph in order to grumble first about the failure of some other British athlete.

The British Olympic girls-next-door were, as I've argued, a key signifier of the nation in its sport at a particular time in its history. Olympism and Britishness were, after all, historically linked, de Coubertin having been inspired by English folk games and subsequent public school athleticism. These traditions were emphatically not about achievement. By the 1950s and 1960s, British Olympism had been democratized to the point that the British team would routinely include typists from London and Town Hall clerks from Huddersfield. Moreover, until the late 1960s, what they *did* was secondary to what they *were*. And what they were was ordinary members of the national family, springing briefly from local communities and returning to them when the Games were done. In parallel, Britain, in its favoured self-image as an imperial power, was a nation that *was* and not a nation that *did*. Imperial powers, by definition, have an inherent sense of their own superiority – albeit, in the British case, leavened by what Colls calls "those enduring middle-class qualities of self-effacement, understatement, convention and a stifling 'privacy' that characterised Middle England," (Colls,1998: 108). Ideas of achievement and social engineering were thought to belong to other cultures – the brash, market-based USA and the conniving, bureaucratic and secretive Soviet Union. In the 1950s and early 1960s, for Middle England and its favoured writers, the notion of *proving* oneself, as an individual or as a nation or as a social system, was offensive. It belonged to the Cold War, which Middle England insisted should not intrude on sport. The young British women who won Olympic medals and immediately dedicated themselves to marriage and family or disappeared back into the typing pool were, of course, expressing reactionary and restrictive ideas of gender (Hargreaves, 1994). But they were also expressing interconnected notions of sport, amateurism and Britishness: they were unremarkable pieces of the national mosaic – ordinary Britons from Hornchurch, Hendon, Huddersfield ... By the early 1970s, these ideals were redundant. The British press reluctantly embraced the Cold War logic of Olympism: science, preparation, public investment, winners. There would be no more girls-next-door – certainly not in the sense that I have employed that term here – and anyone promising a medal and limping home in 12th place may as well have stayed in the Olympic village.

Acknowledgments

Thanks to Dil Porter, Rob Colls, David L. Andrews, Ron Greenall and Helen Lynott for help in the preparation of this chapter. The project was funded out of a research grant from the School of Human and Life Sciences at Roehampton University.

References

Barker, Paul (2005), "Search for the middle," *Prospect*, No.110, May, pp. 40–44. See also http://www.youngfoundation.org.uk/?p=71, (access: 22 February 2006).

Carpenter, Harry (1956), "Don't let gold medals give us big heads," *Daily Mail*, 8 December, p. 4.

Carpenter, Harry (1960), "The nuns started Anita on her victory road," *Daily Mail*, 29 August, p. 9.

Cole, C.L. (2000), "Testing for Sex or Drugs?" *Journal of Sport and Social Issues* Vol. 24m no.4m November, pp. 331–333.

Colls, Robert (1998), "The Constitution of the English," *History Workshop Journal*, 46, pp. 97–127.

Colls, Robert (2002), *Identity of England*, Oxford: Oxford University Press.

Glanville, Brian (1965), "Press: Looking for an Idiom," *Encounter*, vol. 25, (1), July.

Guttmann, Allen (1991), *Women's Sports: A History*, Oxford: Columbia University Press.

Hall, M. Ann (1996), *Feminism and Sporting Bodies*, Champaign, Ill: Human Kinetics.

Hargreaves, Jennifer (1994), *Sporting Females*, London: Routledge.

Kilian, Richard (1968), "Hemery's gold – was it Britain's or America's?" *Daily Express*, 17 October, p. 10.

MacAloon, John J. (1981), *This Great Symbol: Pierre de Coubertin and the Origins of the Modern Olympic Games*, London: University of Chicago Press.

Morgan, John (1968), "This fuss is all such a sham," *Daily Express*, 24 October, p. 10.

Pitt, Nick (2000), "Great British Olympians: Daley Thompson," http://www.times-olympics.co.uk/historyheroes (access: 1 February 2006).

Pincher, Chapman (1968), "Blueprint for the 'super athlete,'" *Daily Express*, 12 October, p. 7.

Tomlinson, Alan (1984), "De Coubertin and the modern Olympics" in Alan Tomlinson and Garry Whannel (eds.), *Five Ring Circus: Money, Power and Politics at the Olympic Games*, London: Pluto Press pp. 84–97.

Warren, Patricia Nell (2003), "The Rise and Fall of Gender Testing," http://www.out-sports.com/history/gendertesting.htm, (access: 12 January 2006.

Wilson, Peter (1960), "Russia's Golden Gloom!" *Daily Mirror*, 9 August, p. 19.

Wilson, Peter (1964), "The fraud behind the flame," *Daily Mirror*, 8 October p. 29.

Chapter 7

The "muscle gap"

Physical education and US fears of a depleted masculinity, 1954–1963

Jeffrey Montez de Oca

The "muscle gap" was a period of Cold War anxiety projected onto the bodies of young, white males that produced a discourse fixated on their perceived softness and openness to communist penetration. The underlying anxiety was that youth would be unable to uphold the "national heritage" of expansionism built by the hard (white) men of previous generations. Looking at cultural citizenship as a process of subject-formation sheds light on how a racial project can simultaneously be a gender project that (re)produces a racial–gender order in which whiteness and hegemonic masculinity are markers and repositories of superiority, domination, and privilege.

> The vigor of our country is no stronger than the vitality and will of all our countrymen. The level of physical, mental, moral and spiritual fitness of every American citizen must be our constant concern.
>
> (John F. Kennedy, 1961)[1]

This chapter looks at the strategic use of physical education during the 1950s to prepare young (white) men for US citizenship during the Cold War. This is a useful step since it ties Cold War anxiety to "subjectification," or the process of producing productive yet manageable subjects, and it highlights the interconnection of identity (race, class, and gender) and structural relations of power emanating from the "capitalist state." In making this argument, I suggest that we look back to the very old concept of citizenship as a way to conceptualize identity formation within systems of domination. Citizenship is not simply a legal-political categorization that exists external to the individual; it is an identity that must be learned as a part of one's primary socialization or later "naturalization" and practiced in everyday life. The US custom of standing for the national anthem before sporting events is but one example of this. This is why Rosaldo uses cultural citizenship to argue against the legal binary of inclusion/exclusion, preferring to see society as a continuum from full to partial citizenship, where inclusion permits difference in "race, religion, class, gender, or sexual orientation …" (Rosaldo, 1994, p.402). Within this framework, culture is not a soft, unstructured site of symbols in relation to a harder, more real social but a contested terrain where identity and meaning interplay with relations of political, social, and economic power (Hays, 1994). Which makes Ong's discussion of cultural citizenship as a process of subjectification instructive since she sees cultural citizenship as a normative process "of surveillance, discipline, control, and administration" leading individuals to produce themselves as subjects of a state (Ong, 1996, p.737).

Cold War fitness: "muscle gap" and "missile gap"

[I]t may be no coincidence that as our muscles get softer ... our missiles [sic] race becomes harder.[2]

Understanding cultural citizenship as a process of subjectification sheds light on how a "racial project" (see Omi and Winant, 1994, pp.55–6) can simultaneously be a gender project (c.f. Connell, 1987, pp.183–5) that produces a racial–gender order where whiteness and hegemonic masculinity are markers and repositories of superiority, domination, and privilege. This becomes apparent in a period of Cold War cultural anxiety between 1954 and 1963 called the "muscle gap" – a time of concern over white male bodies. "Muscle gap" discourse held that US youths were physically lacking in comparison to European, especially Soviet, youth and older generations of Americans. The rapid rise to Olympic dominance of Soviet athletes in the early 1950s who were seen as successfully waging political warfare by other means only added to this sense of anxiety (see Beamish and Ritchie, 2005; Massaro, 2003; also Domer, 1976; Crawford, 2004; Thomas, 2002). The US response was that Americans needed to step up to the plate to deny the Soviets easy political victories at the Olympics. This, though, should be done in a uniquely "American way," which did not include government programs of mandatory athletic participation. Despite calls for federal athletic training programs, two strategies consistently appeared in the 1950s as means to defeat the Soviets: 1) non-governmental organizations like the United States Olympic Committee, the Amateur Athletic Union, and the National Collegiate Athletic Association would raise funds directly from citizens and businesses to finance US Olympic teams, and 2) US collegiate athletic programs would serve as training grounds for Olympic athletes in sports such as gymnastics and track.[3] John T. McGovern, a US Olympic official, clarified the underlying concern regarding US Olympic performance: "[T]he most important thing of all is to impress on our young people the soundness of constant training and conditioning."[4] The Olympic debates indicate that athletics in the early Cold War was seen as a cultural arena for geopolitical struggle, the condition of US bodies were weapons in that struggle, and that the US invested political and economic resources in the development of athletes.

The problem of the growing softness of post-war (welfare state) youth was that it put the tradition of an expanding American civilization at risk since, it was argued, the current generation of white males did not measure up to previous generations. In a speech to his troops during the Korean War, Col. Lewis "Chesty" Puller (USMC) rested America's destiny on the bodies of its youth in describing the needed preparation for the dirty wars of the Cold War. "I want you to make 'em [your families] understand. Our country won't go on forever, if we stay soft as we are now. There won't be an America. Because some foreign soldiers will invade us and take our women and breed a hardier race" (cited in Slotkin, 1992: 363). While such imagery had not been uncommon in American intellectual life and had been propagated by eugenicist theorists like Lothrop Stoddard in his *The Rising Tide of Color Against White World-Supremacy*, racialized views of the Cold War were not universal. Nevertheless, Col. Puller's quote makes clear how the Cold War's "police actions" were often understood in frontier terms familiar from the US's own history of Manifest Destiny that pitted a white man's burden of spreading democracy and civilization against the threat of racial contamination[5] (Slotkin, 1992; Horne, 1999; Borstelmann, 2001; von Eschen, 1997; Klein, 2003).

The history of the US is a history of expansionism in that state policy follows a performance principle of constantly striving for economic and territorial expansion. The shift from isolationism to post-war internationalism did not change national aspirations so much as broaden the focus from the western hemisphere and parts of Asia to the whole world (Fensterwald, 1958; Klein, 2003). In this sense, as African American critics pointed out in the 1940s (see von Eschen, 1997), the US took over where Britain and France were collapsing, as CIA involvement in the 1953 overthrow of Mosaddeq in Iran (see Kinzer, 2003) and the post-1954 intervention in Indochina suggest. However, US expansionism has historically been constructed in opposition to the "power politics" of European colonialism (c.f. Fensterwald, 1958), which makes Americans uncomfortable with a rhetoric of imperialism regardless of foreign policy practices. We might then term post-war US expansionism as a process of "anti-imperialist empire building" embodied in the two-pronged strategy of containment. Post-war internationalism continued a tradition of white supremacy that took the form of spreading democracy in a free world system of economic exchange and reciprocity that was protected by US military might (see Brands, 1993; Borstelmann, 2001; Horne, 1999; von Eschen, 1997; Klein, 2003).

Fear of a depleted masculinity just as the US was taking leadership of the free world "greatly concerned" President Eisenhower and quickly took on a Cold War coloring. Like its sister gaps, the "missile gap" and the "appliance gap", the "muscle gap" was over-determined by Cold War anxieties (Griswold, 1998). But unlike the other gaps, which largely focused on non-human technologies, the "muscle gap" and the discourse surrounding it was specifically concerned with the human resources of the nation: male bodies. By conflating the nation's human geography with its political geography, the "muscle gap" was not only concerned with the shape of national subjects, it was concerned with the shape of the nation itself. The Cold War led not only to an "arms race" but also to an entire "body race" in that citizens' bodies and the body politic were seen as weapons of geopolitical struggle (c.f. Davis, 1996; also Griswold, 1998).

I suggest two primary frames for understanding the "muscle gap." First, we can understand it within a cyclical pattern of post-war reactions to the rate of wartime draft rejections and a general concern that modern culture feminizes male citizens (c.f. Huyssen, 1986, p.47), which had formed the tenor of "The Strenuous Life," Teddy Roosevelt's famous speech to the Hamilton Club in Chicago (1899). A similar pattern followed the Revolutionary War, the Civil War, and the First and Second World Wars (Dean, 1998, p.35; Welch, 1996, p.175; Lee, 1983, p.228). Dissatisfaction with potential wartime draftees in post-war periods has been a major impetus in the development of physical education in public schools (Weston, 1962; Kirk, 1997). Educational leaders throughout the early twentieth century saw physical education as a felicitous regime of bodily transformation that used popular, recreation activities to "cultivate desirable attitudes and behaviors" in the process of building bodies for citizenship (O'Hanlon, 1980, p.89). The rate of Korean War draft rejects and the performance of US soldiers during the Korean War were the most commonly cited evidence of male softness after the publication of the Kraus–Weber results (see below). For instance, US prisoners of war "brainwashed" in Korea signified mental, in addition to physical, weakness on the part of "our boys" (Mrozek, 1995, p.258). This first frame underscores enduring cultural schemas that defined a hard, aggressive masculinity as central to national security.

If we only employ the first frame – modern culture effeminizing male youth and post–war reactions to deficiencies in wartime draftees – then we would theorize the Cold War reaction as a passive repetition of history structurally indistinguishable from previous or later cycles. However, the specific Cold War coloring of the discourse suggests a need for greater nuance. Therefore, I suggest a second, less passive frame that contextualizes the focus on male bodies within the Cold War. So while US imperialists such as Teddy Roosevelt have historically fetishized on hard white men, Cold War homophobia complicated "muscle gap" discourse by seeing soft white male bodies as open to communist penetration. During this period, gay masculinity became a hidden, subversive other that negatively defined and disciplined a hard masculine norm (see Johnson, 2004; Corber, 1997). Further, this second frame clarifies how government intervention in the social body drew upon familiar cultural schemas to foster a new cultural formation based on the deployment of modern technologies of health and fitness in socializing institutions. Cultural policy deployed technologies of bodily transformation in the arena of health and fitness to produce self-regulating masculine citizens consistent with Cold War imperatives.

The value of the second frame, Cold War subjectification, is not to argue that the State made decisions and the people got in line. Rather, it highlights how an interaction between government and citizens through institutional dynamics led to clear transformations in popular culture. Gorski's (2003) metaphor of state formation as a "top down" and a "bottom up" process is quite useful. On the one hand, Eisenhower created the President's Council on Youth Fitness (PCYF) that Kennedy expanded into the Presidents Council on Physical Fitness (PCPF); both of which extended and professionalized physical education (Weston, 1962). On the other hand, by defining itself as "leader of the free world" in opposition to the "slave world" of the Soviet Union, Cold War logic eschewed policy directives calling for the compliance of citizens, since that would be inconsistent with producing self-regulating, independent subjects. So US cultural policy supported institutions, such as schools, that maximized citizens' self-direction and self-regulation. Furthermore, non-governmental actors, such as fitness experts, helped direct and structure the field of physical education and the habitus (Bourdieu, 1977) which citizens developed in fitness regimes.

Locating "muscle gap" discourse

The bulk of the research for this chapter involved coding 473 articles drawn from a combination of newspapers and popular magazines. In searching for newspaper articles, I used ProQuest's online newspaper archive to search the *New York Times*, the *Los Angeles Times*, and the *Wall Street Journal* from 1945 to 1965.[6] I carried out three full text searches on the key words "physical fitness," "soft American," and "flabby American" that netted a total of 1,936 articles that I narrowed down to 351 by rejecting articles not clearly related to the "muscle gap." I used the *Reader's Guide to Periodical Literature* to search for magazine articles from 1951 to 1963, under a variety of sub-headings such as "physical fitness," and "health-men" or "health-women." After eliminating irrelevant titles, I came up with 121 articles.

I coded the 473 total articles for repeating themes using three basic themes inclusive of most articles.[7] The 231 articles of the first group, "muscle gap," positioned themselves in accordance with government recommendations. The second group of articles, "concern not direct," is consistent with "muscle gap" discourse though not directly participating in it. These 164 articles tend to focus on health and fitness in a less political fashion, such as when physical educators or medical professionals invoked rhetoric of scientific objectivity to discuss businessmen's health. The use of phrases such as "fragile male" and "flabby American" in the 29 "businessmen's health" articles highlights how closely this category parallels "muscle gap" discourse. The 43 articles in the third category, "skeptical," were consistently skeptical of the exercise and fitness craze. Figure 7.1 shows the publication pattern of the three main themes over a 20-year period. We see "muscle gap" discourse emerge at the conclusion of the Korean War and slowly increase in output throughout the fifties before climaxing with Kennedy in the early sixties. "Muscle gap" discourse quickly receded after Kennedy's death and the breakup of the "liberal consensus" of the early Cold War period (1947–1964).

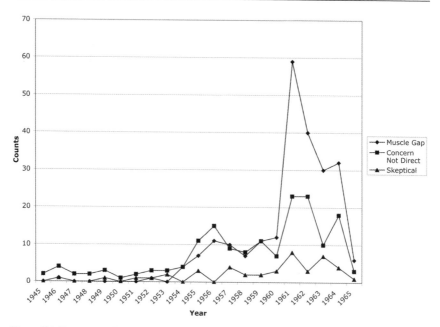

Figure 7.1 Dominant themes in articles

Although the secondary literature on the Cold War is enormous, analysis of the "muscle gap" is scant (see Griswold, 1998; Mrozek, 1995; also Welch, 1996; Lee, 1983; Weston, 1962; Oriard, 2001). Griswold's position that "the concern for physical fitness, at its core, set about redeeming manhood, reenergizing masculinity, and restoring force, dynamism, and control to males in a culture full of doubts and contradictions about men's future" (Griswold, 1998, p.325) is closest to mine. Mrozek makes a similar point in describing "muscle gap" discourse as a ritualization of pain central to the production of masculine Cold War citizens (1995, p.266). However, like much of the literature on masculinities, Griswold and Mrozek's use of terms like "manhood" and "masculinity" to construct men as a universal category obscures much of the racial anxiety coded in the language and the imagery of the "muscle gap." In this sense, the anxieties driving the "muscle gap" did not simply focus on male bodies; they adhered to middle-class white male bodies – the archetypal US citizen (Glenn, 2002) – upon which the purported national heritage was built. In the rest of the chapter, I outline the "muscle gap" as a discursive formation that led to cultural policy concerned with creating self-producing citizens consistent with Cold War imperatives before situating this formation within the US's post-war racial–gender order. For reasons of space and clarity, my analysis draws largely from close textual analysis of the print media that I coded with support from other relevant texts.

The "muscle gap" and cultural policy

The period of national anxiety about white male bodies that I call the "muscle gap" began when a Philadelphia businessman and former national sculling champion John B. Kelly was "horrified" by the results of the Kraus-Weber Minimal Fitness Tests. The crux of the findings was that out of 4,264 US children given the Kraus-Weber tests (six exercises that test strength and flexibility) 57.9 percent failed to meet minimum standards. Out of 2,879 European kids (from Switzerland, Austria, and Italy) of comparable socio-economic background only 8.7 percent failed to meet the minimum standards.[8] Kelly, who had led an underfunded, unsuccessful national fitness campaign in 1947 (Prudden, 1956: 4) passed the report to Sen. James Duff of Pennsylvania who in turn took it to Eisenhower, who reportedly was "shocked."[9] In addition to the Kraus-Weber results, selective service statistics reported that out of 4.7 million draftees called up between 1950 and 1957, 1.6 million or "roughly one-third" were "found unfit for duty" for physical or mental reasons.[10]

Once the "muscle gap" was seen as a "serious problem," cultural policy was created to target and close the perceived gap between US and European youth. Focusing on cultural policy demonstrates that sport is not simply an aspect of a culture but a set of strategies and tactics that create productive yet manageable citizens of a cultural-capitalist state (c.f. Miller, 1993: ix). Enduring cultural schemas of masculinity and race mired in a hard/soft crisis and set in the context of post-war decolonization and confrontation with the Soviet Union gave a Cold War frame to the "muscle gap." Further, these schemas informed the cultural repertoires, or sets of knowledge that direct strategies of action in the material world (Swidler, 2001; Swidler, 1986), that oriented many political leaders' and citizens' perceptions and actions in the early Cold War. Once the post-war period was framed in terms of modern society effeminizing those male citizens responsible for upholding the national heritage of political, economic, and territorial expansion, government enacted cultural policy that disciplined citizens in regimes of bodily transformation.

Following from a series of government-sponsored conferences on national fitness and Eisenhower's creation of the PCYF in 1956, a strategy to "close the 'muscle gap'" began to form. Four themes guiding "muscle gap" discourse and policy emerged in my textual analysis that I call dissemination, surveillance and transformation, development of infrastructure, and social movement building.

Theme one – dissemination

Without a national program of education, citizens would neither be conscious of the "muscle gap" nor have the appropriate cultural repertoires to close it. Media during the "muscle gap" took on the function of teaching the Cold War (c.f. Klein, 2003, p.13). Therefore, the dissemination of the Kraus-Weber results and Korean War draft rejection rates framed by Cold War anxiety defined "muscle gap" discourse. Fear has the political expediency of converting beliefs into pre-scribed actions, and "muscle gap" discourse came with specific recommendations. I coded 139 articles with recommendations on exercise and/or diet and nutrition, 55 articles addressing lifestyle, and 62 articles making practical suggestions for parents and community leaders on hardening "our boys." The primary method of dissemination was print media; though television shows like the *Flabby American*[11] disseminated "muscle gap" knowledge as did community and national level sports festivals and clinics (20 articles covered events).

Additionally, dissemination occurred through scientific, educational, and popular literature channels. An exemplar of scientific discourse is Kraus and Raab's *Hypokinetic Diseases* (1961) that contends a lack of exercise in modern society leads to many of our leading physical ailments; it includes a chapter just on youth. Bonnie Prudden's *Is Your Child Really Fit?* (1956) typifies the popular literature targeting parents and educators by warning despite an appearance of health, our kids are growing soft. At the educational level, the PCPF distributed 250,000 copies of the pamphlet *Youth Physical Fitness* (1961) that was intended to guide primary and secondary schools in adopting "desirable" age- and gender-appropriate workouts in "their own local situations" that students could com-plete in 15-minutes.[12] Additionally, educational films like Encyclopedia Britannica's *Eat For Health* (1954) and Coronet Instructional Films' *Rest and Exercise* (1949) and *Getting Ready Physically* (1951) saw national distribution in public schools. These examples demonstrate multiple levels of knowledge pro-duction that utilized different styles of rhetorical address. These different styles constructed the same "muscle gap" frame of national strength, tied to male bod-ies in need of health interventions, for five different audiences (medical professionals, policy makers, school administrators, parents, and students).

Theme two – surveillance and transformation

The creation of national standards tied to a series of metrics (goals, testing, and recording) designed to measure, rank, and place youth within a national matrix of bodies was seen as central to disaggregating a national mass of bodies so that weak ones could be identified and made subject to bodily regimes of transforma-tion. Kennedy changed the PCYF into the PCPF to target the entire population, not just youth. He appointed the legendary University of Oklahoma football coach Charles "Bud" Wilkinson[13] as its director, and the Council disseminated *Youth Physical Fitness*, national programs of surveillance and transformation were given material form. I coded 50 newspaper and magazine articles that highlighted the importance of testing, most of which included illustrated instructions on exercises and tests for parents to administer at home.

Consistent with the post-war embrace of science and technology, much of the "muscle gap" discourse framed the solution to male softness in medical-scientific discourse. I coded 38 articles as "medico-scientific" however the language and assumptions infused many more. In this discourse, a triage model of fitness testing was seen as the way to diagnose and cure a sick society by creating self-surveilling citizens who take charge of their own health needs. Just as a doctor develops a health profile useful to the patient, the Physical Education instructor would develop a fitness profile useful to the student. As years passed, the student would compare present scores with past scores to measure their successes and failures.[14] In this way, state surveillance becomes self-surveillance, through which the imperatives of a Cold War state were bodily inscribed on the life histories and practices of citizens as they produce themselves (see Figures 7.2 and 7.3). The scientifically built white body provided the surface upon which Cold War masculinity was written into citizenship (c.f. Foucault, 1984, p.83).

SAMPLE RECORD FORM FOR IDENTIFICATION OF PHYSICALLY UNDERDEVELOPED PUPILS

Teacher *Mrs. Boyer*   School Year *Fall 1961*

Period or Section *6th Grade*   Date of 1st Test *9/25/61*

School *Cumberland*

BOYS

Name of Pupil	Pull Ups Ages 10-13; 1 14-15; 2 16-17; 3			Sit Ups Ages 10-17; 14			Squat Thrust Ages 10-17; 4			Remarks*
	1st Test		Retest	1st Test		Retest	1st Test		Retest	
	Pass	Fail	Date Passed	Pass	Fail	Date Passed	Pass	Fail	Date Passed	
Adair, Robert	✓			✓			✓			*Exceptional should exercise at home.*
Bosch, Peter		✓	11/6/61	✓			✓			

*Enter here any conditions, e.g., obesity, posture, etc., that may affect physical performance.

Figure 7.2 Fitness chart that standardizes (President's Council on Physical Fitness, 1961)

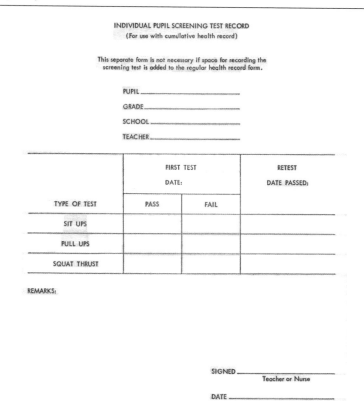

Figure 7.3 Fitness chart that individualizes (President's Council on Physical Fitness, 1961)

Theme three – development of infrastructure

Facilities for training bodies and leaders were necessary to successfully inscribe Cold War ideology on the physical and the human landscape of the nation. This meant surveying existing fitness facilities to determine available resources and inform funding decisions. I coded 55 articles specifically concerned with the quantity, quality, and funding of fitness facilities. It also called for training more physical education teachers as well as increased research to inform policy and decision-making on the use and the development of fitness infrastructure. A 1962 Associated Press article claimed that with Kennedy's emphasis on targeted funding, "fitness programs [have] more than doubled,"[15] which highlights the role of knowledge production in how governments manage a state's complex ensemble of human and non-human resources (Foucault, 1991).

Theme four – social movement building

Citizen leadership was critical to closing the "muscle gap" at a minimal cost to the state and to differentiating the US's liberal approach to social problems from the Soviet's "totalitarian" approach. The primary sites of intervention were schools and homes but recreation centers and YMCAs took on greater importance as did extra-curricular activities such as Little League baseball and the Boy Scouts. Furthermore, participation in government programs by "enlightened businesses," like the Wheaties Sports Federation and Union Oil's 76 Sports Club,[16] acting as responsible corporate citizens, was seen as crucial to hardening the nation. In a 1963 *Recreation* article, "Bud" Wilkinson describes a strategy to increase fitness in a community by organizing an urban regime (a grouping of public workers and/or private citizens that forms to influence local policy) drawn from local government, schools, and businesses where, as chairman, "a real crusader for a cause he deems worthwhile" can coordinate local fitness policy and ensure community buy-in through effective public relations.[17] Actually this describes a local-level version of Wilkinson's position on the PCPF that served to coordinate national fitness policy and engage civic support through dissemination of fitness information.[18]

Part of the logic of the social movement theme was that citizens' obligation to maintain their health and fitness required that they step outside of the family circle to work on community fitness, and thereby increase the health and strength of the nation. As Wilkinson told parents, "[T]he conditions in our country's schools depend on you. They are your schools, and educators will respond to your wishes."[19] In this statement, Wilkinson's direct address takes the reader into a body of engaged-citizens working at the grassroots level to improve the nation's fitness infrastructure. The reader of this article, published in *Parents Magazine*, would likely be a mother interested in ideas about childrearing. Wilkinson's parenting advice suggests a modernized version of "Republican Motherhood" (see Salmon, 2000, p.176) that channels women's political energy into building the nation through domestic concerns such as their children's health. The grassroots strategy of building a fitness movement in a manner consistent with a "free society" shows how women, through caring for others, can participate in reifying an ascendant form of masculinity.

Another outcome of the "muscle gap" was the rise of national and local level fitness events. Beginning in the mid-fifties, sports festivals and clinics were held throughout the country to demonstrate the physical fitness of a local school or a Boy Scout troop and to encourage citizens to take up the disciplined ethic of self on display. In 1959, the American Association for Health, Physical Education and Recreation organized "Operation Fitness – USA." to target youths through schools and community recreation centers for participation in "self-improvement" programs by staging local-national fitness competitions.[20] Also in 1959, *Sports Illustrated* dedicated 12 pages of coverage to Eisenhower's proclamation that the week of 3 May was National Youth Fitness Week with a photo series demonstrating youth from elementary school to college engaging in a variety of activities in diverse sites that included a Boys' Club, a YMCA, a private all-girls' high school, and Purdue University. Consistent with the

notion of citizenship that dissolves difference into universality while simultaneously reifying the very differences it seeks to efface (Warner, 1993, p.239),
out of thirty-two photographs in the article, mostly featuring groups of people,
only one boy playing basketball in a Rhode Island Boys' Club was not visibly
white.[21] Despite the racial homogeneity not actually reflective of post-war
United States, the photo series performs "a narrative of the nation" by representing citizens across geography and class simultaneously participating in a
national narrative of exercise and good health as rights and obligations of citizenship (c.f. Anderson, 1991; Bhabha, 1991).

But, for fitness as local-national "street theater" nothing compares to the
Kennedy era hike craze that later returned in the form of "walkathons" (see King,
2003). In 1963, Kennedy recalled Teddy Roosevelt's requirement that every
Marine be capable of hiking fifty miles in three days without spending more than
twenty hours on their feet.[22] The public responded, as if challenged, by staging
single-day fifty-mile hikes (as well as bike rides) in communities across the
nation throughout 1963 (and in memorial to Kennedy in 1964).[23] Sports sociol-
ogist Michael A. Messner explains how that goal orientation and a desire for
public recognition within his school's "Rah! Rah!" Cold War atmosphere drove
him over the course of a year to be its first student to earn the "JFK 50-Mile Run
Award," despite a personal aversion to running (M. Messner, personal communication, September 2004). Cold War walkathons as theaters of participatory
citizenship mobilized the populace with an ethical fervor to demonstrate commitment to the nation's Cold War mission through personal dedication and
sacrifice.[24]

Militarization of the social body

> Our young people must be physically as well as mentally and spiritually pre-
> pared for American citizenship.
>   (President Gen. Dwight D. Eisenhower, 1962)[25]

The "muscle gap" desire to make our boys hard led logically to constructing the
military as a model for society. The Kennedy–Wilkinson plan for every school in
the nation to subject students to at least 15-minutes a day of calisthenics to train
masses of students and single out weaklings for extra attention clearly follows a
military model of disciplinary efficiency that has a long history in public education (see Foucault, 1979, pp.235–269). To support teacher implementation of
the 15-minute calisthenics program, in 1962 the PCPF produced The Youth
Fitness Song commonly referred to as "The Chickenfat Song" for its chorus: "Give
that chickenfat / back to the chicken / and don't be chicken again."[26] The environment created by classes of children cheerily performing group calisthenics in
unison to the marshal sound of The Youth Fitness Song transforms the social space
of the classroom into a citizen-producing machine where fitness and discipline

become synonymous with health and bravery (c.f. Foucault, 1979: 147). Or as Kennedy expressed in his "Soft American" article, just as the British Empire was built on "the fields of Eton," our American civilization was "won on the playgrounds and corner lots and fields of America" (1960, pp.15–16).[27]

The militarization of public education when following the PCPF recommendations was put on display in a 1962 *Look* magazine article that hailed La Sierra High in Carmichael, CA. The article features nine photos of white male high school students doing physical exercises while wearing nothing but shorts, sneakers, and expressions of pain (see Figure 7.4).[28] The caption reads

> Back bends, which develop lower back and abdomen require flexibility. One boy holds the thighs of his partner, who elevates trunk as high as possible. La Sierra boys can hold this position easily for several seconds but it takes a lot of practice.
>
> (Gordon, 1962)

The article claims that, physical education director and football coach, Stan LeProtti's adaptation of the PCPF's program "popularizes compulsory exercises by giving 'group status' to average, nonathletic youths."[29] The result is a program that uses symbols of hierarchy, like color-coded shorts to signify fitness rankings, and group dynamics to create a hyper-competitive environment where boys gain status from personal achievement in a military-styled regime of bodily transformation. The structural dynamics of the program invests increasing status in boys that reproduce themselves closest to a model of hegemonic masculinity. High status boys are further rewarded, the article explains, by the increased admiration of female students who supported the program. Thus the program actively mobilizes power dynamics of homosocial and heterosexual sexuality to gain male and female participation in a system of domination that inscribes Cold War ideology upon male bodies.

La Sierra blues are required to top Navy plebes on pull-ups

Figure 7.4 Boys at La Sierra High demonstrate strength and flexibility

Imperial modeling – hegemonic masculinity and white supremacy

Jean Mayer in a 1955 *NY Times Magazine* article, "Muscular State of the Union," effectively sums up desired "muscle gap" interventions:

> Perhaps the most effective method [to keep the population active and fit] would be to inculcate all young people with the tenet which has long been an effective lesson of British public schools: if society has brought you up as an educated person, it is your duty to keep fit so that in return for what you have received you may be of some use in an emergency to your neighbors and to your country.[30]

Mayer's quote suggests that the US should take Imperial Britain as a model in building citizens. Membership in national society is based on a system of social relations and mutual obligations stemming back to a socializing process that "inculcates" a disciplined habitus in citizens. Schools as local sites of a national educational field inculcating "enduring, transposable dispositions" in citizens suggests the habitus (Bourdieu, 1977) forms at local, regional, and national scales. In this case, a citizen's habitus forms not simply from their local context but integrates them within larger structural formations of similar acting subjects (Stoddart, 1988). So when cultural policy takes the ethic of British boarding schools (see Mangan, 1986; Morford and McIntosh, 1993) for socializing US cit-izens, cultural repertoires consistent with the structural needs of imperialism are inculcated in the habitus at a local level.

American (un)exceptionalism

"Muscle gap" discourse was rife with the contradictions of Cold War ideology. A central narrative emerges from "muscle gap" discourse that I call "American (un)exceptionalism" that is driven by an Orwellian logic of "success equals fail-ure." This narrative states that our national heritage was built through the vigorous activity of "our forefathers" who wrought civilization from the North American wilderness. This civilization gave rise to such a technologically advanced society that its citizens enjoy the highest standard of living the world has ever seen. This standard of living is apparent in vast arrays of consumer goods and measured in the health of its citizens. However, the greatest measures of our success – children who are bigger, heavier and apparently healthier than previous generations – are also a measure of our failure. Modern technology, the narrative suggests, in producing bigger, healthier kids also takes away the rigors experi-enced in the "strenuous life" of previous generations.[31] In essence, the narrative states that "the national heritage" will lead us to decline in the future unless immediate interventions are made to correct the poor lifestyle choices that US citizens are currently making.

The narrative does not identify the "national heritage" (i.e. manifest destiny) as the problem but the consumer culture of mass society that makes our boys effeminate. Experts warned that the healthy look of our kids could be deceiving because underneath their big glowing exteriors are "sissies" too soft to fulfill the national mission. Dorothy Barclay wrote in the *NY Times Magazine*, "the nation's children this summer present a picture of general health unmatched in previous history … But what about their fitness, measured in terms of muscular power and endurance?"[32] Critics answered that, in the United States, effeminate males were getting softer than Europeans whom we need to lead by example, as one commentator stated of a comparative study between US and British youth, "in some instances British girls were superior to American boys!"[33] And a New York school official concluded, "All I can say is that it's a good thing our boys don't have babies" since their abdominal muscles are so weak.[34]

Hegemonic masculinity: a national heritage

The "muscle gap"'s sexualized language is consistent with a Cold War ideology deeply concerned with containment and penetration (Costigliola, 1997; Cuordileone, 2000; Nadel, 1995). The Cold War itself was framed in sexual language that constructed the USSR as an overly masculine rapist threatening an open, vulnerable West. George Keenan's influential "Long Telegram," sent from the US embassy in Moscow in 1946, that outlined what became the strategy of containment constructs the Soviet leadership as, "engaging in the driving, aggressive behavior conventionally associated with masculinity. Keenan underscored this association in the LT by repeating the word "penetration" five times in reference to the Soviet's insistent, unwanted intrusion" (Costigliola, 1997: 1333). The very discourse of the Cold War was over-determined by cultural schemas that framed issues of international relations within a common sense of hegemonic masculinity that sports philosopher Brian Pronger (1999) would describe as simultaneously homoerotic in its desire to penetrate the other and homophobic in its desire to protect and enclose the space of the self. Which made gay men appear as security threats since their deviant lifestyle made them susceptible to communist penetration through manipulation and blackmail. Furthermore, gay men were constructed as a kind of contagion at the heart of the nation undermining its vigor (c.f. Johnson, 2004).

Arthur Schlesinger, in his 1949 treatise *The Vital Center*, initiated the binary hard/soft discourse on US citizens by framing the problem of masculinity as an excess of luxury in a post-war society that produced men lacking the vitality to carry out the liberal-imperialist tradition of Teddy Roosevelt (Dean, 1998; Cuordileone, 2000). Republicans in the 1950s picked up on Schlesinger's language for a class-based attack on the Democrats' patrician establishment as being too soft on communism, and therefore lacking the masculinity to fight the Soviets (Cuordileone, 2000). Kennedy took back the discourse by framing his candidacy and administration in "muscle gap" discourse that took Teddy Roosevelt's rugged white masculinity as a model of vigorous leadership. Kennedy, who would famously play touch football on the White House lawn, constructed himself as youthful, vigorous, and healthy in opposition to an aging, unhealthy Eisenhower administration that, like the nation, had become flaccid (Walton, 2004; Dean, 1998). Responding to attacks upon his masculinity, vice-president Richard Nixon challenged the senator to a fitness test where both candidates would take medical exams and release their medical histories so the public would see who really was the more physically endowed.[35] At the heart of these cock-fights amongst the political elite, who all made football an important part of their biographies, was an axiomatic belief that the qualities of leadership in a complex, technological world were synonymous with a British boarding school construction of hegemonic masculinity: hard, persistent, and plucky (see Mangan, 1986; Morford and McIntosh, 1993; Stoddart, 1988).

Middle classes in an effeminizing culture

The tension of reinvigorating the empire through submitting citizens to regimes of bodily transformation that instilled the mental and physical discipline necessary to protect our democratic heritage reveals another contradiction in the American (un)exceptionalism narrative. Two objects in the narrative are infused with anxiety: consumer culture and soft boys. Given the causal ordering, it is revealing that only soft boys susceptible to communist penetration were identified as a site for transformation and not the consumer culture that produces softness. As Hans Kraus stated in 1954, "We have no wish in trying to change the standard of living by trying to do away with the automobile and TV. But we must make sure that we make up for this loss of physical activity."[36] So rather than calling for a restructuring of the technology-driven consumer culture that produces deficient citizens, as some critics of the era did – for instance, Marcuse's (1964) repressive desublimation hypothesis – the solution instituted was additive. As Major General Lewis B. Hershey, director of the selective services said, "We've got to learn to stay vigorous and still enjoy luxury."[37] Rather than challenge a culture structured by conspicuous consumption, government intervention would "inculcate" discipline so citizens would work off the pounds, which points to capitalism's need for consuming subjects that remain productive and manageable.

The Cold War call for discipline, unlike earlier periods of concern with unruly populations, was specifically linked to indolence born of post-war affluence. Baseball commissioner Ford Frick claimed, "Today a youngster will back out the car to go a few blocks to the store for five pounds of potatoes, then have them delivered or get an attendant to lift the bag into the car."[38] Frick's concern that modern mechanized society makes young people lazy and soft relative to earlier generations assumes youth have access to expensive consumer goods like cars, televisions, and labor saving appliances more typical of upper-middle class homes

– 54 articles expressed analogous concerns about citizens' lifestyle. The assumption that all youth are affluent and indolent hides the many non-affluent young people economically forced to work throughout the "muscle gap" period without the aid of laborsaving devices. Frick's concern for indolent middle-class kids hides the delivery person and the attendant that make a consumerist way-of-life possible. The exclusive focus on the symptoms of excessive class privilege in "muscle gap" discourse obscures the social relations of domination those privileges are built upon.[39] Although internally contradictory, the additive model of the "muscle gap" (consumerism plus a disciplined habitus) was consistent with US foreign policy that materialized in the strategy of containment. Regimes of bodily transformation would make male citizens hard enough to serve as global cops in third world jungles while still participating in the consumerist culture necessary to demonstrate the economic and cultural supremacy of the United States.

White supremacy: the goal of empire

The very name "muscle gap" makes clear how a traditionally hard and aggressive version of masculinity became ascendant through allied articulations of state, media, and private sector forces during the Cold War but the dynamics of race are less clear. The United States position as "leader of the free world" made its history of racism and white supremacy a liability to its Cold War objectives. The result was the embracing of some civil rights legislation and the whitewashing of racial rhetoric in favor of clearly anti-communist discourse (see Horne, 1999; Dudziak, 2000; Borstelmann, 2001; von Eschen, 1996; Plummer, 1996). Indeed, "muscle gap" discourse makes no explicit reference to race and cloaks difference in abstract references to citizenship and "national heritage." In order to see the white racial formulation within the "muscle gap" discourse, we must look between the imperialist lines.

The anti-communist stance of the US was formally non-racial, having moved away from the racialized language of colonialism. However calling anti-colonial movements "communist" rearticulated the West's imperialist project. As Horne argues, "The tagging of anticolonials as 'red' slowed down the movement against colonialism and – perhaps not coincidently – gave 'white supremacy' a new lease on life" (Horne, 1999: 454). The rearticulation of imperialism necessitates sensitivity to "white supremacy" in understanding Cold War policies (Horne, 1999, p.438). This was a fact unfortunately but understandably overlooked by many African American and labor leaders in the late 1940s when they replaced opposition to colonialism and capitalism with anti-communism (von Eschen, 1997, pp.107–109). This is not to overlook Cold War tensions or contradictions such as the desegregation of the armed forces as a process of expanding civil rights that made possible increasing deployments of racialized soldiers to suppress Third World liberation movements (c.f. Dudziak, 2000, pp.83–88). Few soldiers experienced this contradiction more acutely than American Indians in Vietnam (see

TeCube, 1999), which only points up the fact that civil rights concessions can also serve to re-stabilize white supremacy (c.f. Borstelmann, 2001; Dudziak, 2000). In its invocation of "national heritage" that idealized Teddy Roosevelt's rugged masculinity and the nearly exclusive imagery of young white male and female citizens, the "muscle gap" was clearly concerned with protecting white America's political, economic, and territorial supremacy from the Soviet threat, from Chinese attacks coming out of the Orient and from the rising-tide of youthful nations throughout the Third World (c.f. Dean, 1998, p.46).

The US's "national heritage" can be characterized as a series of violent conquests leading to the establishment of whiteness as the dominant racial category in US social, cultural, and political life (Omi and Winant, 1994, pp.65–6). In situating vigor within the national heritage, Kennedy, in the tradition of Roosevelt narrates the history of the US as vigorous men that "subdued a continent and wrested civilization from the wilderness ... And today, in our own time, in the jungles of Asia and on the borders of Europe, a new group of vigorous Americans help maintain the peace of the world and our security as a nation" (Kennedy, 1962, p.12). The connection of manifest destiny, or the period of American expansionism that saw wholesale slaughter of native peoples, the slave trade, and repeated incursions in Latin America and Asia, to the contemporary context makes his "muscle gap" objectives clear. The Cold War-civil rights project that made racially neutral rhetoric synonymous with non-racist ideology hid the rearticulation of American white supremacy as a leader in global imperialism within a black–white domestic binary (Dudziak, 2000; Horne, 1999; von Eschen, 1996). Tracing the "muscle gap"'s development, a discourse on white masculinity emerged as a crisis in the 1950s from the changing global conditions of the Cold War and domestic conditions of the civil rights movement. Intellectuals like Schlesinger, Eisenhower, and Kennedy, but also Kraus, Prudden, and Wilkinson, addressed the state by enacting cultural policy that created bodily regimes of transformation to stabilize the crisis with a rearticulated formation of whiteness: hard, disciplined, and anti-communist (c.f. Omi and Winant, 1994, pp.83–8). Consistent with Kennedy's "muscle gap" image of cultivating an elite corps of self-sacrificing, rugged white men was his creation of the Green Beret and the Peace Corps that mirrored the military-humanitarian mission of US foreign policy (Dean, 1998, p.56; Weston, 1962, p.103). The "muscle gap" was explicitly about producing young white male citizens that could penetrate and police the Third World while protectively enclosing the nation from similar penetrations.

Cultural policy and the racial–gender order

"Muscle gap" discourse and the cultural policy that flowed from it was simultaneously a racial and a gender project working to rearticulate the United States' racial–gender order. The "muscle gap" emerged from multiple discursive systems, sometimes contradictory and working at cross-purposes, that led to a larger discursive formation and common sense understanding of a citizen's relation to the nation. When looking at the "muscle gap," we see enduring cultural schemas regarding masculinity, race, and national purpose that place bodies in a hierarchy, giving differential access to social resources (c.f. Sewell, 1992). To be certain, all citizens can benefit from increased exercise, improved diet, and abundant recreation facilities. But the "muscle gap" was not a "green wave" where an anti-modernist fitness movement emerges to oppose the alienation of industrial society (see Eichberg, 1998). The 23 articles I coded as concerned with "women's health" were filled with suggestions on de-emphasizing competition to maximize the health benefits of exercise. But the 231 "muscle gap" articles and a majority of the 164 "concern not direct" articles took white males (even when suggesting gender inclusion) as the assumed national subject in need of bodily transformation through highly competitive and regimented athletics. Which meant masculine citizenship, as Connell (1987) suggests, during the "muscle gap" period was constructed in opposition to soft, effeminate masculinities whether intellectual and socialist like Henry Wallace, class privileged like Dean Acheson, or sexually deviant as denounced by Senator Joseph McCarthy in the early 1950s (see Friedman, 2005). The "muscle gap" thus reiterated, in Cold War language, Western Modernity's historical need for aggressive male citizens capable of the economic and military endeavor required to build and maintain empire (c.f. Rotter, 1994, p.526).

Counter-hegemonic movements did emerge vis-à-vis "muscle gap" discourse. The 43 "skeptical" articles took two rhetorical strategies: "satirical" (21 articles) and "scientific" (22 articles). The satirical articles mocked exercise and calls for fitness, like one that held the comedian Jackie Gleason up as a paragon of American athleticism for his unmatched skill as a competitive drinker and pool hustler.[40] One can also imagine children mocking the seriousness of their teachers as they did ten push-ups to the "Chickenfat Song." Skeptical articles invoking a scientific rhetoric were largely written by physical educators and medical professionals who constructed symbolic boundaries to protect their areas of expertise from political and military encroachments by asking epistemological questions like "Fitness for what?" or "How valid are draft rejection rates as a measure of national health?" Providing clarity on un-interrogated assumptions in "muscle gap" discourse allowed skeptics to offer critical perspectives as scientists engaged in social issues. But this strategy also brought social capital for scientists' demanding implementation of their "value neutral" regimes of bodily transformation.[41] So although scientists could "win concessions" and affect the field of physical education, they also provided legitimating objectivity to Cold War cultural policy.[42]

The trajectory of the "muscle gap" suggests that cultural citizenship does not emerge organically but results from cultural policies that rearticulate and reify enduring cultural schemas to socialize self-producing, self-regulating subjects.

Looking at the "muscle gap" through the lens of governmentality indicates how a Cold War racial-gender order became hegemonic. "muscle gap" discourse legitimated cultural policy by drawing on existing notions of hegemonic masculinity and a narrative of manifest destiny and white supremacy framed within the immediacy of the Cold War. Historical concerns about national purpose and racial purity tied to hard white bodies forged in rituals of pain were updated by the incorporation of Cold War homophobia and technologies of bodily transformation. The political use of emotionally charged fears of unwanted penetrations and loss of empire expressed as "national heritage," not to overlook the specter of nuclear annihilation, obscured contradictions that existed in the narrative of American (un)exceptionalism. The result was a reified racial–gender order in a rearticulated Cold War formation where whiteness and hegemonic masculinity framed in terms of anti-communism and pro-democracy are markers and repositories of superiority, domination, and privilege.

References

Anderson, B. (1991) *Imagined Communities: Reflections on the Origins and Spread of Nationalism*, Verso, New York.

Beamish, R. and Ritchie, I. (2005) "The Specter of Steroids: Nazi Propaganda, Cold War Anxiety and Patriarchal Paternalism," *The international journal of the history of sport*, 22, 19.

Bhabha, H.K. (1991) "DissemiNation: Time, Narrative, and the Margins of the Modern Nation," in *Nations and Narration* (Ed, Bhabha, H.K.) Routledge, London, pp.291–322.

Borstelmann, T. (2001) *The Cold War and the Color Line: American Race Relations in the Global Arena*, Harvard University Press, Cambridge, MA.

Bourdieu, P. (1977) *Outline of a Theory of Practice*, Cambridge University Press, New York.

Brands, H.W. (1993) *The Devil We Knew: America and the Cold War*, Oxford University Press, New York.

Connell, R.W. (1987) *Gender & Power: Society, the Person and Sexual Politics*, Stanford University Press, Palo Alto, CA.

Corber, R.J. (1997) *Homosexuality in Cold War America: Resistance and the Crisis of Masculinity*, Duke University Press, Durham.

Costigliola, F. (1997) "'Unceasing Pressure for Penetration': Gender, Pathology, and Emotion in George Keenan's Formation of the Cold War," *The Journal of American History*, 83, pp.1309–1333.

Crawford, R.E. (2004) In *History* University of Nebraska, Lincoln, pp. xvi, 308 leaves.

Cuordileone, K.A. (2000) "Politics in an Age of Anxiety: Cold War Political Culture and the Crisis of American Masculinity," *The Journal of American History*, 87.

Davis, B. (1996) "Reconsidering Habermas, Gender, and the Public Sphere: The Case of Wilhelmine Germany," in *Society, Culture, and the State in Germany, 1870–1930* (Ed, Eley, G.) University of Michigan Press, Ann Arbor, pp. 397–426.

Dean, R.D. (1998) "Masculinity as Ideology: John F. Kennedy and the Domestic Politics of Foreign Policy," *Diplomatic History*, 22, pp.29–62.

Domer, Thomas M. "Sport in Cold War America, 1953–1963: The Diplomatic and Political Use of Sport in the Eisenhower and Kennedy Administration," Doctoral Dissertation, Marquette University, 1976.

Dudziak, M.L. (2000) *Cold War Civil Rights: Race and the Image of American Democracy*, Princeton University Press, Princeton, NJ.

Eichberg, H. (1998) *Body Cultures: Essays on Sport, Space and Identity*, Routledge, London.

Fensterwald, B., Jr. (1958) "The Anatomy of American 'Isolationism' and Expansionism. Part I," *The Journal of Conflict Resolution*, 2, pp.111–139.

Foucault, M. (1979) *Discipline & Punish: The Birth of the Prison*, Vintage Books, New York.

Foucault, M. (1984) "Nietzsche, Genealogy, History," in *The Foucault Reader* (Ed, Rabinow, P.) Pantheon Books, New York, pp.76–100.

Foucault, M. (1991) "Governmentality," in *The Foucault Effect: Studies in Governmentality with Two Lectures by and an Interview with Michel Foucault* (Eds, Burchell, G., Gordon, C. and Miller, P.), The University of Chicago Press, Chicago, pp.87–104.

Friedman, A. (2005) "The Smearing of Joe McCarthy: The Lavender Scare, Gossip, and Cold War Politics," *American Quarterly*, 57, pp.1105–1130.

Glenn, E.N. (2002) *Unequal Freedom: How Race and Gender Shaped American Citizenship and Labor*, Harvard University Press, Cambridge, MA.

Gordon, S. (1962) "LA Sierra high shows how American kids can get physically tough," *Look*, 26, pp.49–52.

Griswold, R.L. (1998) "The 'Flabby American,' the Body, and the Cold War," in *A Shared Experience: Men, Women, and the History of Gender* (Eds, McCall, L. and Yacovone, D.), New York University Press, New York, pp.321–348.

Hays, Sharon (1994) "Structure and Agency and the Sticky Problem of Culture," *Sociological Theory*, 12(1), pp.57–72.

Horne, G. (1999) "Race From Power: US Foreign Policy and the General Crisis of 'White Supremacy'," *Diplomatic History*, 23, pp.437–461.

Huyssen, A. (1986) *After the Great Divide: Modernism, Mass Culture, Postmodernism*, Indiana University Press, Bloomington.

Johnson, D.K. (2004) *The Lavender Scare: The Cold War Persecution of Gays and Lesbians in the Federal Government*, University of Chicago Press, Chicago.

Kennedy, J.F. (1960) "The Soft American," *Sports Illustrated*, pp.14–17.

Kennedy, J.F. (1962) "The Vigor We Need," *Sports Illustrated*, pp.12–15.

King, S.J. (2003) "Doing Good by Running Well: Breast Cancer, the Race for the Cure, and New Technologies of Ethical Citizenship," in *Foucault, Cultural Studies, and Governmentality* (Eds, Bratich, J. Z., Packer, J. and McCarthy, C.) State University of New York Press, Albany, pp. 95–316.

Kinzer, S. (2003) *All the Shah's Men: An American Coup and the Roots of Middle East Terror*, J. Wiley and Sons, Hoboken, N.J.

Kirk, D. (1997) "Schooling Bodies in New Times: The Reform of School Physical Education in High Modernity," in *Critical Postmodernism in Human Movement, Physical Education, and Sport* (Ed, Fernández-Balboa, J.-M.), State University of New York Press, Albany, NY, pp.39–63.

Klein, C. (2003) *Cold War Orientalism: Asia in the Middlebrow Imagination, 1945–1961*, University of California Press, Berkeley.

Kraus, H. and Raab, W. (1961) *Hypokinetic Disease: Diseases Produced by Lack of Exercise*, Thomas, Springfield, IL.

Lee, M. (1983) *A History of Physical Education and Sports in the USA*, John Wiley and Sons, New York.

Mangan, J.A. (1986) *The Games Ethic and Imperialism: Aspects of the Diffusion of an Ideal*, Viking Penguin, Inc., New York.

Marcuse, H. (1964) *One-Dimensional Man: Studies in the Ideology of Advanced Industrial Society*, Beacon Press, Boston.

Massaro, J. (2003) "Press Box Propaganda? The Cold War and Sports Illustrated, 1956," *The Journal of American Culture*, 26, pp.361–370.

Miller, T. (1993) *The Well-Tempered Self: Citizenship, Culture, and the Postmodern Subject*, Johns Hopkins University Press, Baltimore.

Morford, W.R. and McIntosh, M.J. (1993) "Sport and the Victorian Gentleman," in *Sport in Social Development: Traditions, Transitions, and Transformations* (Eds, Ingham, A.G. and Loy, J.W.) Human Kinetics Publishers, Champaign, IL, pp.51–76.

Mrozek, D.J. (1995) "The Cult and Ritual of Toughness in Cold War America," in *Sport in America: From Wicked Amusement to National Obsession* (Ed, Wiggins, D.K.) Human Kinetics, Champaign, IL, pp.257–267.

Nadel, A. (1995) *Containment Culture: American Narratives, Postmodernism, and the Atomic Age*, Duke University Press, Durham, NC.

O'Hanlon, T. (1980) "Interscholastic Athletics, 1900–1940: Shaping Citizens for Unequal Roles in the Modern Industrial State," 30, pp.89–103.

Omi, M. and Winant, H. (1994) *Racial Formations in the United States*, Routledge, New York.

Ong, A. (1996) "Cultural Citizenship as Subject-Making: Immigrants Negotiate Racial and Cultural Boundaries in the United States," 37, pp.732–762.

Oriard, M. (2001) *King Football: Sport and Spectacle in the Golden Age of Radio & Newsreels, Movies & Magazines, the Weekly and the Daily Press*, The University of North Carolina Press, Chapel Hill.

Plummer, B.G. (1996) "'Below the Level of Men': African Americans, Race, and the History of US Foreign Relations," *Diplomatic History*, 20, pp.639–650.

President's Council on Physical Fitness, T. (1961) *Youth Physical Fitness: Suggested elements of a School-Centered Program, Pamphlet*, US Government Printing Office, Washington DC.

Pronger, B. (1999) "Outta My Endzone: Sport and the Territorial Anus," *Journal of Sport and Social Issues*, 23, pp.373–389.

Prudden, B. (1956) *Is Your Child Really Fit?*, Harper and Brothers, Publishers, New York.

Roosevelt, T. (1899) In *History Tools.org: Resources for the Study of American History*, Vol. 2004 (Ed, Voelker, D.).

Rosaldo, R. (1994) "Cultural Citizenship and Educational Democracy," 9, pp.402–411.

Rotter, A.J. (1994) "Gender Relations, Foreign Relations: The United States and South Asia, 1947–1964," *The Journal of American History*, 81, pp.518–542.

Salmon, M. (2000) "The Limits of Independence: 1760–1800," in *No Small Courage: A History of Women in the United States* (Ed, Cott, D.N.F.), Oxford University Press, New York.

Schlesinger, A., Jr. (1949) *The Vital Center: The Politics of Freedom*, Houghton Mifflin Co., Boston.

Sewell, W.H.J. (1992) "A Theory of Structure: Duality, Agency, and Transformation," *American Journal of Sociology*, 98, pp.1–29.

Slotkin, R. (1992) *Gunfighter Nation: The Myth of the Frontier in Twentieth Century America*, Antheum, New York.

Stoddart, B. (1988) "Sport, Cultural Imperialism, and Colonial Response in the British Empire," *Comparative Studies in Society and History*, 30, pp.649–673.

Swidler, A. (1986) "Culture in Action: Symbols and Strategies," *American Sociological Review*, 51, pp.273–286.

Swidler, A. (2001) *Talk of Love: How Culture Matters*, The University of Chicago Press, Chicago.

TeCube, L. (1999) *Year in Nam: A Native American Soldier's Story*, University of Nebraska Press, Lincoln, NE.

Thomas, D.L. (2002) In *History*, University of California, Los Angeles, p.3673.

von Eschen, P.M. (1996) "Changing Cold War Habits: African Americans, Race, and Foreign Policy," *Diplomatic History*, 20, pp.627–638.

von Eschen, P.M. (1997) *Race Against Empire: Black Americans and Anticolonialism, 1937–1957*, Cornell University Press, Ithaca, NY.

Walton, J.L. (2004) In *Doctoral Dissertation, The Ohio State University, Columbus, OH*.

Warner, M. (1993) "The Mass Public and the Mass Subject," in *The Phantom Public Sphere* (Ed, Robbins, B.), University of Minnesota Press, Minneapolis, pp.234–256.

Welch, P.D. (1996) *History of American Physical Education and Sport*, C.C. Thomas, Springfield, IL.

Weston, A. (1962) *The Making of American Physical Education*, Appleton-Century-Crofts, New York.

Notes

1   Kennedy, J.F. (1961) "A Presidential Message to the Schools on the Physical Fitness of Youth," in *Youth Physical Fitness: Suggested Elements of a School-Centered Program*, US Government Printing Office, Washington DC.

2   Public service announcement of the President's Council on Physical Fitness. Cited in Griswold, R.L. (1998) "The 'Flabby American,' the Body, and the Cold War," in *A Shared Experience: Men, Women, and the History of Gender* (Eds, McCall, L. and Yacovone, D.), New York University Press, New York, pp. 321–348.

3   While a thorough review of the Olympic debates is far beyond the scope of this chapter, the following selection of citations provides an outline of the discourse during the period under discussion. Briordy, W.J. (1953) "AAU Launches Drive for $500,000 to Maintain U.S. Olympic Supremacy," *New York Times*, 29; (1953) "AAU Opens Drive for 1956 Olympics," *New York Times*, 20; McGovern, J.T. (1954) "We'll Lose the Next Olympics ..." *Los Angeles Times*, K7 and 16; (1954) "US Olympic Body Seeks $1,000,000," *New York Times*, 37; Canham, D. (1954) "Russia Will Win the 1956 Olympics," *Sports Illustrated*, 1, 11–12, 60–65; Black, R.W. (1954) "Olympic Funds," *Los Angeles Times*, A4; Blunk, F.M. (1956) "US Olympians of Past Hope for Triumph of Amateur Spirit," *New York Times*, 163; Sheehan, J.M. (1957) "Performance of American Gymnasts in the Olympic Games Pleases Coach," *New York Times*, 36; Conklin, W.R. (1959) "Olympic Group Seeks Pennies and Dollars," *New York Times*, 37; Perlmutter, E. (1962) "National Olympics Urged by Ribicoff," *New York Times*, 45; Rondeau, C. (1964) "Physical Fitness of Americans Demonstrated in Olympic Finals," *Los Angeles Times*, A4.

4   In addition to the two cited strategies, McGovern also cited the US armed forces as a resource for preparing Olympic athletes. McGovern, J.T. (1954) "We'll Lose the Next Olympics ..." *Los Angeles Times*, K7 and 16.

5   Although fear of racial contamination has an enduring presence in US history, different racialized groups are seen as posing the threat (i.e. American Indians, Latinos, African Americans, or Asians) depending upon the historical period and region. See Glenn, E.N. (2002) *Unequal Freedom: How Race and Gender Shaped American Citizenship and Labor*, Harvard University Press, Cambridge, MA; Slotkin, R. (1992) *Gunfighter Nation: The Myth of the Frontier in Twentieth Century America*, Antheum,

New York; Horne, G. (1999) "Race From Power: US Foreign Policy and the General Crisis of 'White Supremacy'," *Diplomatic History*, 23, pp. 437–461; Omi, M. and Winant, H. (1994) *Racial Formations in the United States*, Routledge, New York; Gabriel, J. (1998) *Whitewash: Racialized Politics and the Media*, London Routledge.

6   I chose this time period to capture the entire run of the "muscle gap" and to see if there was a similar media pattern following the Second World War – there was not. For an article that anticipated the "muscle gap," see Hershey, L.B. (1946) "'We Must Improve Our Youth'," *New York Times*, 86.

7   Some articles did not clearly fit into any of the three categories, such as the articles I called "women's health" that take a health centered, anti-competitive tact.

8   Anonymous (1957) "Is American youth physically fit?," *US News and World Report*, 43, pp. 66–77. Also, Prudden, B. (1956) *Is Your Child Really Fit?*, Harper and Brothers, Publishers, New York.

9   Boyle, R. (1955) "The Report that Shocked the President," *Sports Illustrated*, pp. 30–33, 72–3.

10   Anonymous (1957) "Is American youth physically fit?," *US News and World Report*, 43, pp. 66–77.

11   Gould, J. (1961) "TV: 'Flabby American'," *New York Times*, 67.

12   Wilkinson, C. B. (1962) "Physical Fitness and Community Recreation: A Pattern for Action," *Recreation*, 55, pp. 343–4. The PCPF also distributed 250,000 copies of *Adult Physical Fitness* that targeted adult citizens (apparently pirated copies were distributed as well). Wolf, A. (1964) "Physical Fitness Programs Claims 'Massive Support'," *Los Angeles Times*, B1.

13   Wilkinson remains one of the most respected coaches in NCAA history, winning national championships in 1950, 1955, and 1956. His teams also had winning streaks of 31 games (1948–51) and 47 (1953–57), which remains the longest streak in NCAA history.

14   Hunsicker, P. (1959) "How fit are our youth?," *National Education Association Journal*, 48, pp. 26–7.

15   Tolchin, M. (1962) "President's Fitness Plan Spurs School Programs," *New York Times*, p. 14.

16   Anonymous (1959b) "Fitness Footnotes," *Sports Illustrated*, p. 41.

17   Wilkinson, C. B. (1962) "Physical Fitness and Community Recreation: A Pattern for Action," *Recreation*, 55, pp. 343–4.

18   Wolf, A. (1964) "Physical Fitness Programs Claims 'Massive Support'," *Los Angeles Times*, B1.

19   Wilkinson, C. B. (1961) "How does your child rate in fitness?," *Parents Magazine*, 36, pp. 78–91.

20   The competitions were held in local contexts but judge against national norms. Anonymous (1959a) "A New Lease on Fitness," *Sports Illustrated*, p. 25.

21   Anonymous Ibid. "1959 National Youth Fitness Week," pp. 39–53.

22   Rusk, H. A. (1963) "Science: Physically fit – But for What?," *New York Times*, 8.

23   Kennedy's hike craze received a combination of praise and ridicule. Much of the criticism was diffracted through praise of Pierre Salinger, the president's, apparently, overweight press secretary who backed out of a scheduled 50-mile hike with reporters. As one article exclaimed, "In a nation suddenly gone berserk, Pierre is a lone voice of reason." Coates, P. (1963) "Hooray for Pierre Salinger – Fuehrer of Fat Freedom Fighters," *Los Angeles Times*, A6. Conklin, W.R. (1961) "4 Tired Collegians End 237-Mile Fitness Hike," *New York Times*, 29; Foster, F.P. (1962) "Trip Lures 300 Cyclists," *New York Times*, 52; Anonymous (1963b) "Bob Kennedy Rests After 50-Mile Hike," *Los Angeles Times*, 23; Smith, J. (1963) "Hiking Plan Puts U.S. on Its Feet," *Los Angeles Times*, A5; Ryskind, M. (1963) "Hiker Out of Step," *Los Angeles Times*, B1;

Buchwald, A. (1963) "'Amis de Pierre' Pursue U.S. Way," *Los Angeles Times*, D3; Anonymous (1963c) "Marathon Walks Defy State Law," *Los Angeles Times*, G1; Rusk, H.A. (1963) "Science: Physically fit - But for What?," *New York Times*, 8; Fox, C. (1963) "A Fitness Walk in the Smog," *Los Angeles Times*, C3; Anonymous (1963a) "Marathon Madness," *Los Angeles Times*, 15; Hoffleit, H.B. (1963) "Traveling on Foot, He Feels Like a Heel," *Los Angeles Times*, A6; Anonymous (1963d) "Substitute for Hike," *Los Angeles Times*, B8; Drezner, P. (1963) "Tour by Bicycle," *New York Times*, 388; Anonymous (1964a) "College Journalists Get in Shape for 50-Mile Memorial Hike Friday," *Los Angeles Times*, G1; Anonymous (1964b) "3 on Cross-Vermont Hike," *New York Times*, 13; Buchwald, A. (1964) "Hike Planned as Memorial to Kennedy," *Los Angeles Times*, CS5. The result of the marathon craze becomes clear in this final article, Anonymous (1965) "Bicycle Makers Rolling Up Record Sales As Adults Discover New Way to Keep Fit," *Wall Street Journal*, 32.

24 Since the 1980's, the walkathon movement has embodied an ethic of volunteerism and personal responsibility for maintaining one's health in participatory sports events linked to charitable causes. Samantha J. King, "Doing Good by Running Well: Breast Cancer, the Race for the Cure, and New Technologies of Ethical Citizenship," in Foucault, *Cultural Studies, and Governmentality*, Eds. Jack Z. Bratich, Jeremy Packer, and Cameron McCarthy (Albany, NY: SUNY Press, 2003), p. 307.

25 Cited in Anonymous (1962) "Your child's health and fitness: symposium," *National Education Association Journal*, 51, pp. 37–40.

26 According to Internet sources, "The Chickenfat Song" experienced wide distribution and is indelibly etched, both positively and negatively, on the minds of people subjected to it in childhood. *The Youth Fitness Song* was written by Meredith Wilson and sung by Robert Preston – the original *Music Man*.

27 In the article "The Soft American" as well as elsewhere, Kennedy's use of "American civilization" works as a euphemism for what could more appropriately be called an empire.

28 When looking at the article, Mrozek concludes that, "the authors had associated good grooming with patriotism and toughness with the citizenship appropriate for good Americans". But given the photo series, the *Look* authors don't only suggest that good Americans are well groomed and tough; they are also racially white. See Mrozek, D.J. (1995) "The Cult and Ritual of Toughness in Cold War America," in *Sport in America: From Wicked Amusement to National Obsession* (Ed, Wiggins, D.K.), Human Kinetics, Champaign, IL, pp. 257–267.

29 Gordon, S. (1962) "LA Sierra high shows how American kids can get physically tough," *Look*, 26, pp. 49–52.

30 Mayer, J. (1955) "Muscular state of the union," *NY Times Magazine*, p. 17.

31 What I am calling the American (un)Exceptionalism narrative re-articulates Teddy Roosevelt's warning in "The Strenuous Life" that our potential to go soft will make the US fall behind other imperialist nations. See Roosevelt, T. (1899) In *History Tools.org: Resources for the Study of American History*, vol. 2004 (Ed, Voelker, D.).

32 Barclay, D. (1958) "Fitness test, a preview," *NY Times Magazine*, p. 25.

33 Eastman, M. (1961) "Let's close the 'muscle gap'," *Reader's Digest*, 79, pp. 122–5.

34 Boyle, R. (1955) "The Report that Shocked the President," *Sports Illustrated*, pp. 30–33, 72–3.

35 Anonymous (1960a) "Nixon Issues Health Test Challenge," *Los Angeles Times*, 5.

36 Anonymous (1960b) "America's youth: fit or unfit?," *Senior Scholastic*, 76, pp. 12–13.

37 Anonymous (1955) "Are we becoming soft?," *Newsweek*, 46, 35–6.

38 Stull, D. (1956) "Conference at Annapolis: First Blow for Fitness," *Sports Illustrated*, pp. 22–4.

39 When issues of class were specifically articulated it was in terms of exercise minimizing deviance.

40 Hopper, H. (1961) "'Soft American' Yet a Remarkable Athlete," *Los Angeles Times*, B5.

41 See Munger, G. (1961) "Challenge to Bud Wilkinson," *Sports Illustrated*, 15, pp. 38–40.

42 Not surprisingly, the issue of American imperialism was not raised as a critique of the "muscle gap" in the articles I read. Although American imperialism was consistently invoked to support "muscle gap" policy, it was euphemized as when Kennedy referred to American civilization.

Chapter 8

Good versus evil?

Drugs, sport and the Cold War

Paul Dimeo

Introduction

The social construction of "good" and "evil," the like of which frequently characterized Western political rhetoric during the Cold War, relies upon stereotypes to feed popular imaginings of sameness and otherness. Such stereotypes must be simplistic, they must be sustained by powerful social institutions, and cannot be undermined by voices from the "other side" that might just provoke basic humanitarian empathy. Phrases like "the evil empire," "closed societies," and "state regimes," constantly reminded Western audiences that "communist" countries were alien and threatening. In the process, "we" were assured of our essential moral superiority, capitalism was reinforced, and the extension of governmental power legitimized on the grounds on national security.

This chapter discusses the ways in which sports doping – the use of banned substances to enhance performance – has been presented through media and official discourses. The underpinning assumption is that doping was more common, systematic, Government sanctioned, and exploitative in the Eastern bloc countries. The "evil" was that athletes were knowingly abused, treated like mere cogs in the chain of the larger enterprise of Marxist–Leninist socialism. Doping in the West has been treated like an aberration – a pimple on the otherwise unblemished face of healthy, meritocratic and democratic elite sports. These "mistakes" are explained away through neat discursive strategies, for instance: accidental use of a medication for another purpose; a rogue doctor who prescribed illegal drugs to an ill-informed athlete; the occasional abuser who like an alcoholic just can't help themselves in their thirst for success. Despite numerous examples of drug-taking in the West and critical exposes of the medical support behind them (such as the Dubin Inquiry in Canada after Ben Johnson's positive test at the 1988 Seoul Olympics), there remains a strongly held view that doping in the West is individualized and the unfortunate result of greed. It is rarely, if ever, interpreted as an endemic problem related to the demands of elite sport. However, as this chapter aims to show, such opportunities for "explaining away" doping are not afforded to those who competed for communist countries. The most sympathy they receive is as unknowing victims of the system. But it is precisely the focus on the "system" that reflects the imbalance of coverage and acceptability, that ultimately serves to reinforce the dichotomy of "good us" and "evil them."

Contemporary narratives

The doping "regimes" of the former GDR and – by implicit association – the USSR, have been re-presented to Western audiences in recent years for two main reasons. The first are the court cases stemming from the doping-related abuse of athletes by the government of the former German Democratic Republic (GDR). The second is the career of coaches and scientists who had worked for the GDR and Soviet sports organizations pre-Glasnost that systematically doped athletes, and the athletes who currently work with them. Both of these have provided opportunities for the Western media to recycle simplistic accusations about cheating, doping regimes, long-term health problems and so on. These are breathlessly reported with little, if any, sense that the West may also have harboured guilty parties. So, for instance, when the British athlete Denise Lewis employed East German Dr Ekkart Arbeit as her coach, she faced "worldwide revulsion at her decision to work with one of the architects of what a German state investigator has described as the 'largest pharmacological programme in history'" (Guardian, 13 August 2003). Two years later, the ongoing compensation claims by former GDR athletes led to such coverage as "Hormone Heidis: Women changed sex, men grew breasts. Now a sensational trial is revealing how the East Germans' ruthless use of drugs in pursuit of Olympic glory destroyed thousands of athletes' lives" (Daily Mail, 25 November 2005). Similarly, reporting of the law suit in Scotland on Sunday led to the emotive description of "East German athletes forcibly drugged by their Communist masters" (30 October, 2005). These are just three examples of a mass of media coverage that forms the public and one-dimensional face of a wider, more complex historical process.

In the wider academic context, it is clear that sports historians' depiction of communist sport has varied over the past 30 years, broadly in line with Western liberal perception of the costs and benefits of communist politics. Writing in 1977, James Riordan concluded in the book Sport in Soviet Society with praise for the state's desire to make sport "culturally uplifting, aesthetically satisfying and morally reputable" with "a tone of altruism and devotion ... in which there is much which cannot but be admired" (p.401). Reflecting on the changes that had occurred in the 1980s, Reet Howell argued in 1993 that: "For the past several decades, the Soviet sport system has been admired and envied by the West"; its "noble aims" contrasted to the "dehumanising and exploitative" capitalist system of sports (1993, p.22, cited in Riordan 1993a, p.247). By the 1990s, though, the situation had significantly changed, in part due to stories of drug misuse and of the general mistreatment of, and pressure placed on, athletes from a very young age. These criticisms of the late 1990s have led to the point where we are now used to blanket condemnation of the USSR and GDR sports systems as being built on doping. In his later publications, Riordan was keen to emphasize the extent of state involvement in sports doping in the USSR. Historians such as Joseph Turrini dismiss the GDR's contribution to international sport by claiming that: "We now know that a large part of the East German athletic success rested on the most sophisticated state-organised drug program in the world of sport" (2001, p.447–8). As such, the involvement of the USSR and GDR in the Olympics is now treated with a mixture of fascination and revulsion: the sense of envy over their success remains, but that is always considered to have been poisoned by the ultra-nationalism, exploitation and drug abuse that lay behind the gold medals.

While this change reflected revelations in the late 1980s and 1990s about various forms of abuse, it fails to take into account two important historical features: first, that while governments in the West may not have actively organized doping in sport, they failed to prevent localized networks of doctors, coaches and athletes from using performance enhancing drugs; second, that the ban on doping did not formally appear until the mid-1960s and adequate testing procedures not until the late 1980s. In other words, taking a historical view, it could be argued that the communist countries did not act in a significantly different way to other countries or in a way always considered unethical or unhealthy. Once these have been recognized, the principal point of contention, as will be discussed, is the role of the state. This chapter will first outline the political and sporting context within which doping began and developed; then it will argue that there are very specific reasons why the former communist countries have come to shoulder almost all of the blame for sports doping.

Sport, drugs and Cold War ideologies: 1945–1988

The Soviet Union did not enter the Olympic Movement after the Second World War partly because of a certain disaffection between the IOC and the Soviet government (see Jenifer Parks' chapter in this book). The former had been irritated by Russia's role in helping organize Worker Games in 1932 and 1936, parallel to the Olympic Games. As a result, the President of the IOC from 1952–1972, Avery Brundage, was ambivalent about suggestions that the USSR could join the first post-war Games in London (Riordan 1993b, p.28). For their part, the Soviet government condemned the IOC after an article published ahead of the 1948 Games in a Soviet magazine claiming that the:

> Olympics were run by capitalists and aristocrats, that workers had little chance of competing, that racial discrimination against Jews and Blacks had occurred in Berlin in 1936 and would be applied against East Europeans who, in any case, might well be corrupted and recruited as spies.
>
> (Riordan, 1993b, p.27)

On top of which Stalin had been strongly opposed to Soviet participation in the Olympics. The dialogue among IOC members highlighted their fundamental suspicion of communist societies just as the USSR's military power, development of nuclear technology, and expansion into eastern Europe proved the catalyst for the intense political and ideological rivalry known as the Cold War. An IOC Executive Committee Member, Colonel P.W. Scharoo, reported in November 1947 that the highly organized system for sport in the USSR was being used for nationalist purposes by the government. His derisive comments reflected an emerging popular stereotype: "In Russia nobody is free and independent. Individuals are only numbers in the state" (cited in Riordan 1993b, p.28). Indeed, the discursive construction of a polarized world of opposing cultures and politics was reinforced in March of that same year in the American President Harry Truman's speech to Congress on the threat of communism that included the following:

> At the present moment in world history nearly every nation must choose between alternative ways of life. The choice is too often not a free one. One way of life is based upon the will of the majority ... The second is based upon the will of a minority forcibly imposed upon the majority. It relies upon terror and oppression, a controlled press and radio, fixed elections and the suppression of personal freedoms.
>
> (Truman, 1955 cited in Saunders 1999, p.25)

Brundage fell in line with this: "According to Communist philosophy, every person and everything is subservient to the State" (cited in Riordan 1993b, p.29). He remained suspicious of Soviet "shamateurism," the puritanical and regimented nature of their sports, and the explicit connection made between sport and national prestige (Hoberman 1992, p.194). Nonetheless, the IOC could not deny the USSR entry because such a decision would contradict their determination to keep politics out of sport. The u-turn among the Soviets was prompted by a number of factors, including the opportunity to assert the success of their political ideology on the most salient of all international stages. In return for his acquiescence, however, Stalin was sent a "special note" to "guarantee victory" by the Chairman of the government Committee on Physical Culture and Sport, Nikolai Romanov (Riordan, 1993b, p.26).

The post-war political context

By the late 1940s in the West, the ideological drive against communism had been heightened, as represented by a range of "information" activities. In Europe and North America, government-funded anti-communist agencies disseminated "bad news" about what went on behind the Iron Curtain. In Britain, the then Labour government set up the Information Research Department (IRD) whose strategies included feeding well-researched stories to the BBC that highlighted Soviet atrocities, poor living conditions, punishment systems and so on (Defty 2004). A parallel initiative in the USA was the CIA-backed Congress for Cultural Freedom (CCF), which assisted selected authors, playwrights and painters whose artistic endeavors represented the values of individualism, capitalism and materialism, while undermining those with even a hint of socialism or communism (Saunders 1999; Aldrich 2001). This propaganda was of course replicated by the Soviets. However, in the West it was linked to the increased fear of nuclear war after the USSR developed the atomic bomb in 1949. By the early-1950s, the balance of power had become increasingly precarious (leading, as we know, to the Cuban Missile Crisis and the apocalyptic concept of Mutually Assured Destruction).

In this context, the arrival of a powerful Soviet team at the Olympics in 1952 spoke to concerns reaching far beyond the track stadia of international athletics. As Turrini argues, 1952 represented "the peak of anti-Communist hysteria" (2001, p.429), exemplified by legislation designed to control the immigration of Soviets to the USA. He further claims that the USA–USSR rivalry fitted neatly into a good versus evil dichotomy already established in other popular television programmes in the USA such as "wrestling and roller derby" (2001, p.431). As such "The USA–USSR track meet series fitted perfectly into this pre-existing model for televised sport. The Cold War environment created the good and evil for the networks within the framework of real athletic competition" (2001, p.431). It seems much more plausible to argue that the events of the 1952 Olympics had much wider symbolic meaning than this, and that in any case the classical good/evil structure was in place long before the television networks cottoned on to pre-fabricated "sport." The events played on this dualism. The Soviet team "won" the 1952 Olympics (on medal count) and went on to dominate in both the Summer and Winter Games until the end of the 1980s. The Americans were no doubt dismayed, given their prominent position in the Games since the turn of the century, both in terms of hosting and medal counts.

This turn of events could not have helped the architects of the wider anti-Soviet propaganda campaign who continued to promote the East–West division through subtle cultural means. In 1953, the CCF worked with the New York Museum for Modern Art (MoMA) to arrange an international tour of modern art that included stops in central Europe. This was framed by an article in the New York Times by MoMA's former president, Alfred H. Barr, arguing: "The modern artist's non-conformity and love of freedom cannot be tolerated within a monolithic tyranny and modern art is useless for the dictator's propaganda" (cited in Aldrich 2001, p.453). Meanwhile in Britain the IRD worked hard to show the public the "cruel, backward and tyrannical aspects of the [Soviet] regime" (Aldrich, 2001, p.455). Given all this (further research on the connection between sport, art and science in this political history is long overdue), it is hardly surprising that American athletes publicly played on the wider significance of their part in the Cold War struggle. In 1959, the high profile 400 meter hurdler Eddie Southern said, "I would rather die than lose ... I wasn't running to a get a point or two, I was running to beat the Russians" (Turrini 2001, p.430). And the Olympic decathlon champion of the late 1950s, Rafer Johnston later said it "was not just man-on-man ... it was Communism vs the Free World" (Turrini 2001, p.430). Many others claimed it was their country and its "system" that they were fighting for on the athletics track.

Drugs in sport

This was a vitally important period for our understanding of sports doping at the international level. It is tempting in retrospect to blame communist countries for taking what ostensibly seems to be "Nazi science" and applying it to the sports environment. We do know that the Nazis gave steroids to soldiers but against that we know that the Allies gave amphetamines to theirs. This mutual culpability did not prevent the drawing of a mythical line that connected Nazi science with the rising profile of communist sports. Rumours of Soviet steroid use "touched upon some of the deepest anxieties of the post-war western psyche – they suggested that the brutal, unprincipled pursuit of global domination had not died with the defeat of the Nazis but lived on in an even more powerful Soviet monolith" (Beamish and Ritchie, 2005, p.784. See also this volume). The later involvement of the GDR has been tacked on to this history in a way that favors the West while offering a simplistic and dangerous opposition of "free societies" and "evil dictatorships":

> Physicians and trainers entrusted with the development of young athletes had been in league with the most ruthless forces of the communist regime. And while that partnership might seem shocking to citizens of a free society, it is not so shocking in the context of the GDR. That government was, after all, the product of two evil dictatorships, the Third Reich and Stalin's Soviet Union, and its history is buried in the deep wounds of the Second World War. The crimes of the STASI police – and their accomplices in the doping programme – were not remotely of the same magnitude as those committed by the Nazis. But the two regimes have a unique relationship, linked as they are by a sinister past.
>
> (Ungerleider, 2001, p.19)

However, the way in which steroids were brought to America complicates the story. Dr Robert Zeigler, a coach with the United States Olympic Committee, realized that the Soviets were using them in the early 1950s. He helped develop a form of the drug that quickly became popular throughout the American sports scene. The fact that Zeigler was able to work with the full knowledge of the US sporting authorities in partnership with a pharmaceutical company called CIBA to develop the anabolic steroid known as Dianabol suggests that the use of such drugs was not widely seen as wrong at this time. As John Hoberman (2005) suggests, many scientists and coaches in the 1950s continued to believe they could use drugs to push the boundaries of human performance as an act of social progress. There were few voices of dissent and the strongest argument against drug use – health – had not been considered since the safety of these drugs had not been questioned. Zeigler has retrospectively admitted he was wrong to help develop and disseminate Dianabol. However, that was a later perspective: at the time it seemed morally unproblematic to use whatever technology was available to enhance athletes' capabilities. As Ivan Waddington points out, "Zeigler's actions should be seen not as those of an idiosyncratic zealot, nor as those of a disreputable cheat, but simply as those of a sports physician whose involvement in the increasingly competitive world of modern sport led him, just as it led other sports physicians, towards the search for performance-enhancing drugs" (2000, p.145–6). These points also weaken the Nazi steroid myth even further: at that time period, these steroids and amphetamines were considered safe and useful.

The question of why the acceptance of drug use gave way relatively suddenly to an ethos of anti-doping is one that has surprisingly been left unanswered in the historiography of modern sport. It is possible that the death of Danish cyclist Knud Enemark Jensen at the Rome Olympics in 1960 was one of the principal moments in turning the tide of opinion against drugs in sport – even though the role of amphetamines in this tragedy was only a rumor and unlikely to have been factually correct (Møller, 2005). This fatality did prompt Avery Brundage to circulate IOC members on the subject and set up a group of medical experts to investigate the problem. On the wider health scene, the thalidomide scandal of 1961 (Nilsson and Sjostrom, 1972) put to rest the notion that all drugs were beneficial; this not long after the American Medical Association's inquiry into the value of amphetamine use for athletes concluded in ambivalent terms with contestable conclusions.

By the early 1960s, the conservative elite, especially in Britain, had begun to react to the nationalism, commercialism, and new internationalism of sport by reasserting the traditional "amateur" fantasy of fair play against which doping became a symbol of all that was corrupting sport in its most idealistic sense. Of course, since the very concept of drugs have become so tied up with countercultural and liberation ideologies, sports anti-doping campaigners drew upon a wider reaction to drug culture amongst the conservative elite. When women appeared who looked like men, the cultural dimension of sexuality, femininity and "lesbophobia" prompted widescale and abusive gender testing (Cole, 2000; Lock, 2003; Ritchie, 2003). This became even more prominent when the GDR arrived on the Olympic scene in 1972 with a coterie of female athletes who had suffered the masculinizing effects of the steroid Oral-Turinabol. The combination of health and gender factors pushed anti-doping forward so that the first testing for steroid abuse was implemented in 1976, though testing procedures were evidently lax from then through to the late 1980s post-Ben Johnson era. This can be seen from several examples: that testing in the 1980 Moscow Games was so poor it has been labelled the "junkie Games"; that the American cycling team used illegal blood doping techniques during the 1984 Los Angeles Games; and that Ben Johnson admitted using steroids for about eight years prior to his public disgrace in 1988.

There is no question that from Zeigler's intervention through to Johnson's positive test of stanazolol, doping products were used in the West as well as in the East (Hoberman, 2005; Waddington, 2005). The list of positive tests and the assumption of widespread usage during the 1970s and 1980s is well documented (Houlihan, 1999). And as Robert Voy, chief medical officer for the United States Olympic Committee 1985–1989 wrote:

> We know the Soviets and East Germans used drugs to aid performance on the playing field for years. We must also remember, however, that the appeal of anabolic-androgenic steroids has always been global. Indeed Western athletes (as exposed in part by the Ben Johnson affair) have always been equally active in the anabolic-androgenic steroid scene. And they still are
>
> (1991, p.11)

However, when the full scale of the doping of GDR and USSR athletes began to surface from the late 1980s onwards, it became a lot easier to shift the blame on to these countries for two reasons: first, the complicity and abuses of the state; second, a combination of primary source evidence and changing political circumstances.

State complicity and abuse

The first trickle of information detailing the extent and nature of drug use in GDR and USSR sports came with the occasional defections to the West of east European athletes through the 1970s and 1980s. While these were sensationalized by the Western media, the message they sent was none too complimentary of the communist management of elite sports men and women. One example is that of Rene Neufeld who defected in 1977. She appeared to be suffering the ill-effects of steroid use, and told the West that her complaints only led to threats of financial penalty and state intervention to ruin her career. When she refused to take more steroids, "at 6am one day in October 1977 she was visited by two plain-clothes men at her quarters in the sports club. They took her to a State security department where she was interrogated for the first of several occasions." (Woodland, 1980, p.145). This led directly to her decision to defect. Which in turn left her family exposed to state punishment: her father lost his job and her sister was expelled from a Berlin sports club.

Neufeld's experience was far from unique since she had become part of "State Plan 14.25," the state organized doping programme that led to thousands of athletes being given regular doses of the steroid Oral Turinabol. The full extent of this programme was not known until Brigitte Berendonk and Werner Franke discovered the Stasi files that held records detailing the implementation of this plan (see Ungerleider, 2001). Thus, it became feasible for writers such as Steven Ungerleider to offer up such broad condemnatory statements as this:

> During the 1970s and 1980s, East Germany's corrupt sports organisation dominated international amateur athletics. In the three decades when the GDR's secret 'State Planning Theme 14.25' was in effect, more than ten thousand unsuspecting young athletes were given massive doses of performance-enhancing anabolic steroids. They achieved near-miraculous success in international competition, including the Olympics. But for most part, their physical and emotional health was permanently shattered.
>
> (2001, p.xv)

Although presented in a much more comprehensive and analytic manner, John Hoberman also offers a similar denunciation: "the unmatched success of East German athletes … was built upon the systematic doping of athletes with anabolic steroids … [as part of] a secret and centrally administered program unlike that of any other society on earth" (1992, p.222).

The USSR does not appear to have had such a well-structured strategy as State Plan 14.25. However, as Riordan has argued convincingly, since the 1950s there had been "long-term *state* production, testing, monitoring, and administering of performance-enhancing drugs in regard to athletes as young as 7–8" (1993a, p.255). There are numerous testimonies to support this, showing that sports federations were complicit in organizing doping, that coaches went to the government for financial support to buy the drugs, and that coaches worked closely with doctors in this "cheating." During the 1976 and 1988 Olympics the USSR had a "hospitality" boat used as a medical centre to ensure that athletes were "clean" before the competitions (Riordan, 1993a, p.256).

It could be argued that the official involvement of qualified experts in doping, the recording of doses, and the monitoring of health – linked to advanced application of sports medicine generally – reduced the risk of long-term health problems. Certainly, a number of critics have argued that the hands-off strategy in the West led to decades of wide-scale self-experimentation with drugs dealt on the streets by criminals. William Taylor (1991) is scathing of the British Association of Sports Medicine and the American College of Sports Medicine for what he calls the "period of false dogma" when they denied that steroids would improve performance and thus no further research or information was required. Whether or not Western athletes have suffered long-term health problems to the scale of the GDR and USSR athletes is an unknown factor. Evidence is episodic but a number of deaths have been attributed to doping, including those of hurdler Dick Howard in 1960, boxer Billy Bello in 1963, British cyclist Tommy Simpson in 1967 and French cyclist Yves Mottin in 1968 (Houlihan, 1999). A number of studies have suggested that anabolic steroid use can cause long-term illness as well as sudden death from heart failure (Dickerman *et al.*, 1995). A research project into the early deaths of Italian professional football players highlighted the use of illegal drugs as one possible contributing factor (Chio *et al.*, 2005). But a lack of research, evidence base of usage, and long-term empirical study of health effects, means that the impact of doping drugs on Western athletes is not known.

Finally, it is possible to argue that, if nothing else, the communist countries were honest about their intentions. Western sports authorities have taken the line of denial: which at best protects the image of sport, and at worst is hypocritical and dangerously deceitful. There have been enough recent cases to suggest that drugs remain a problem in North America and Europe and that taking the moral high ground over former communist states, just because the government admitted knowing about it, is both misleading and a form of self-congratulation.

Evidence and political circumstances

The second important difference between the history of doping in the West and in the East is that the latter can be established to a higher degree. Western authorities have generally taken the position of paying lip service to anti-doping while working hard to avoid any scandals that would tarnish their image and the commercial appeal of sport. It is only recently, in the aftermath of the 1990 Dubin Inquiry in Canada and the 1998 Festina scandal in the Tour de France, that the collective nature of doping has been revealed (Waddington, 2000). However, these tended to involve localized networks established through trust and kept hidden from official organizations, the media and the public. For instance, individual testimonies from elite level Danish cyclists show that a rider can only access the source of doping products by establishing long-term relationships firstly with those on the fringes of the networks who then act as gatekeepers to the source (Christiansen, 2005). Even when the Festina scandal broke after their *soigneur* Willy Voet was caught in the act smuggling doping products over the border, most of the team's management and riders instantly denied any knowledge or involvement thus showing their willingness to let Voet be the scapegoat.

This culture of denial can be seen in numerous cases. When the British tennis player Greg Rusedski tested positive for nandrolone in June 2003, he furiously denied any knowledge of taking the supplement and the following March the blame was found to lie with the Association of Tennis Professionals, who had distributed the tablets that had led to the positive test (Shine, 2004). When the Scottish skier Alan Baxter was found to have methamphetamine in his blood, the source was claimed to be an American version of a cold remedy with different ingredients to the British version he had obtained permission to use.

Making accusations against Western athletes is a delicate business, even for those who competed in earlier times when drug taking was less well controlled.

This is principally for fear of reprisals in the form of legal suits. Linford Christie and Lance Armstrong have both taken out actions against media organizations who accused them of using drugs. Even athletes who competed during the 1970s and early 1980s continue to be granted immunity from accusation. The case of Florence Griffith-Joyner is another: her early death may or may not have been be linked to drug use but it is unlikely we shall ever have a conclusive answer. Moreover, few sports fans wish to see their former heroes hounded by dirt-raking investigators and – if found guilty – stripped of all pride, dignity and honour. Even the authorities have to be excessively careful after the British runner Diane Modahl successfully sued the British Athletic Federation after she was falsely accused of illegal drug-taking when improbable amounts of testosterone were found in her sample, prior to the Commonwealth Games of 1994. By 2000, after lengthy court proceedings (the BAF had an appeal upheld and Modahl lost a subsequent appeal in the House of Lords), the BAF had gone into administration and Modahl and her family were financially ruined.

By stark contrast, the GDR and USSR have left us with a mass of incontrovertible evidence of drug use, state involvement and the long-term legacy of unhealthy victims. The most comprehensive evidence were the files kept by the East German secret police, the STASI, which detailed doses of banned drugs to individuals and the times they were administered. These have led to a number of court cases where the victims, usually former medal winners, accuse the former state officials of forcing them to take steroids thus causing a range of long-term health problems. The sorts of cases brought to light would not prompt any sympathy for the old regime. However, there are structural reasons for this material being allowed a public airing. After the unification of Germany, the new government wished to appear keen to redress some of the abuses that had characterized the communist past. East Germans themselves found themselves struggling to reconcile the attitudes of the past with the ethos of the liberal democracies of western Europe: "Many ... were appalled when they realized how badly they had been treated during the GDR regime. They had been controlled, manipulated, and impoverished by their own leadership" (Ungerleider, 2001, p. 18). Athletes likely felt the same way. They had been told to take pills without any explanation of what they were and the risks posed by their consumption. As such, the politics of the doping accusations are much different than in the West where athletes give their consent. This means that for those former GDR athletes pursuing compensation, they are both the claimant and the primary source of evidence. Moreover, there is no defendant. In Western cases, the athlete and their entourage are the defendants who strenuously deny everything: it becomes much harder for the prosecution to establish a case, and less clear who is likely to prosecute and why.

Therefore, the combination of political expediency, the end of a regime, the collection of records, and the promise of compensation, has continued to keep the doping allegations surrounding the former GDR firmly in the spotlight. This makes it much easier to heap as much blame as possible for drugs in sport on a succession of totalitarian regimes beginning with the Nazis; as if political systems themselves could be blamed for international sports doping.

Even before the USSR was broken up, numerous individuals involved in doping had stepped forward with their tales of how doping was organized from top to bottom (Riordan, 1993a, 1993b). Their testimonies coincided with the revisionist view of the past and an effort to mark out a gulf between the old regime and a new future. As Riordan showed, "to many ordinary Soviet people and the new political leadership, the Olympic Games and Olympism represent all that is bad in the old regime's policies: politics and ideology, hypocrisy and sham, paramilitary coercion, Russian diktat, drug abuse, exploitation of children, and grossly and immorally distorted priorities" (1993b, p.34). For those who had taken part during the communist era, a certain about-turn in attitudes was required. The motivation to confess was linked with the generic desire to establish a break with the past. Once again, the process of accusation, confession, evidence gathering, punishment and eventual reconciliation, has a much different complexion in the former Soviet states than it does in the Western context.

Conclusion

This chapter has emphasized the conditions through which former communist countries, notably the USSR and GDR, have been represented by Western media and academics as having built their successes on doping, been the principal culprits in the history of doping use, and as having an exploitative attitude towards their athletes. The internal political changes of the post-glasnost era, combined with the range of primary source evidence and on-going debates, keep these countries' historical problems in public view. For all that there was wrong-doing, it does seem disingenuous to focus anti-doping rhetoric in this way. First, the lack of ethical parameters, health-related knowledge, and adequate testing, are factors that lay behind drug use in both the East and West. Second, Western governments were culpable in more implicit ways: allowing drug use to continue by not enforcing regulations properly. Third, the discourse around totalitarian regimes from the Nazis onwards forms an ideological background that makes accusations against governments and officials seem reasonable. The totalitarian stereotype disallows individual agency and works because the blanket condemnation of communists is widely accepted.

I would like to end this chapter with reference to an incident in 2001 that suggests a much more ambivalent reading of the doping crisis. During the 2001 Athletics World Championships in Edmonton the Russian 5,000m winner Olga Yegorova was booed by the crowd while British runner Paula Radcliffe held up a placard reading "EPO Cheat." Yegorova had tested positive for EPO but was reinstated on a "technicality." The Romanian Gabi Szabo – who finished eighth and had previously won this event – said that "For me she is not the world champion –

I had no chance of winning against a robot" (BBC online, 11 August 2001). However, the British triple jumper Jonathan Edwards was prepared to criticize his team-mates and realize the process of discrimination that was going on:

> The easiest, and safest, line for me to take would be to fall in step with this vilification of Yegorova, the very personification of evil in sport. But my conscience will not let me do it … She has suffered guilt by association, linked in our minds to the systematic doping by the former Soviet Union.
>
> (BBC online, 14 August 2001)

Edwards shows a rare but reasonable empathy: he allows the authorities to make their judgement, and flags up the cultural prejudices that led to Radcliffe, Szabo and others making personal accusations against Yegorova. It is all the more ironic that Radcliffe has slept in an altitude chamber to boost her red blood cell level (Hoberman 2005, p.275), mimicking the physiological outcome of EPO use. Yegorova was written off as a human robot: the latest in a long history of eastern European athletes denied a voice, agency, personality and individuality. Yet, as this and other incidents show, a simple model of good "us" and evil "them" distorts the past to suit the demands of the present.

Bibliography

Aldrich, R.J. (2001) *The Hidden Hand: Britain, America and the Cold War Secret Intelligence*, London, John Murray.

Beamish, R. and Ritchie, I. (2005) "The Spectre of Steroids: Nazi Propaganda, Cold War Anxiety and Patriarchal Paternalism," *The International Journal of the History of Sport*, vol. 22, no. 5, September, pp. 777–795.

Chio, A., Benzi, G., Dossena, M., Mutani, R., and Mora, G. (2005) "Severely increased risk of amyotrophic lateral sclerosis among Italian professional football players," *Brain*, vol. 128, no. 3, pp. 472–476.

Christiansen, A.V. (2005) "The Legacy of Festina: Patterns of Drug Use in European Cycling Since 1998," *Sport in History*, vol. 25, no. 3, pp. 497–514.

Cole, C.L. (2000) "Testing for Sex or Drugs?" *Journal of Sport and Social Issues*, vol. 24, no. 4, pp. 331–333.

Defty, A. (2004) *Britain, America and Anti-Communist Propaganda 1945–53*, London and New York, Routledge.

Dickerman, R.D., Schaller, F., Prather, I., and McConathy, W.J. (1995) "Sudden cardiac death in a 20 year-old bodybuilder using anabolic steroids," *Cardiology*, vol. 86, no. 2, pp. 172–3.

Hoberman, J. (1992) *Mortal Engines: The Science of Performance and the Dehumanization of Sport*, New York, Free Press.

Hoberman, J. (2005) *Testosterone Dreams: Rejuvenation, Aphrodisia, Doping*, Berkeley and Los Angeles, University of California Press.

Houlihan, B. (1999) *Dying to Win: Doping in Sport and the Development of Anti-Doping Policy*, Council of Europe, Strasbourg.

Howell, R. (1993) "Sport and glasnost: a case study of Estonia" (unpublished paper).

Lock, R.A. (2003) "The Doping Ban: Compulsory Heterosexuality and Lesbophobia," *International Review for the Sociology of Sport*, vol. 38, no. 4, pp. 397–411.

Møller, V. (2005) "Knud Enemark Jensen's Death During the 1960 Rome Olympics: A Search for Truth?" *Sport in History*, vol. 25, no. 3, pp. 452–471.

Nilsson, Robert and Henning Sjostrom (1972) *Thalidomide and the Power of the Drug Companies*, Harmondsworth, Penguin.

Ritchie, I. (2003) "Sex Tested, Gender Verified: Controlling Female Sexuality in the Age of Containment," *Sport History Review*, vol. 34, no. 1, pp. 80–98.

Riordan, J. (1977) *Sport in Soviet Society: Development of Sport and Physical Education in Russia and the USSR*, Cambridge, Cambridge University Press.

Riordan, J. (1993a) "Rewriting Soviet Sports History," *Journal of Sports History*, vol. 20, no. 3, Winter, pp. 247–258.

Riordan, J. (1993b) "The Rise and Fall of Soviet Olympic Champions," *Olympika: The International Journal of Olympic Studies*, vol. 2, pp. 25–44.

Saunders, F.S. (1999) *Who Paid the Piper? The CIA and the Cultural Cold War*, London, Granta.

Shine, O. (2004) "Rusedski findings pose more questions" http://www.rediff.com/sports/2004/mar/11dope.htm 11th March. Access: 17th February 2006.

Taylor, W. (1991) *Macho Medicine: A History of the Anabolic Steroid Epidemic*, Jefferson, North Carolina and London, McFarland.

Truman, H. S. (1955) *Memoirs: Years of Decisions*, New York, Doubleday.

Turrini, J. M. (2001) "'It Was Communism Versus the Free World': The USA–USSR Dual Track Meet Series of the Development of Track and Field in the United States, 1958–1985," *Journal of Sport History*, vol. 28, no. 3, pp. 427–471.

Ungerleider, S. (2001) *Faust's Gold: Inside the East German Doping Machine*, New York, St Martin's Press.

Voy, R. (1991) *Drugs, Sport and Politics*, Champaign, Il, Leisure Press.

Waddington, I. (2000) *Sport, Health and Drugs: A Critical Sociological Perspective*, London and New York, Spon.

Waddington, I. (2005) "Changing Patterns of Drug Use in British Sport from the 1960s," *Sport in History*, vol. 25, no. 3, pp. 472–496.

Chapter 9

The Cold War and the (re)articulation of Canadian national identity

The 1972 Canada–USSR Summit Series[1]

Jay Scherer, Gregory H. Duquette and Daniel S. Mason

It is rare that a Canadian event has made time stand still, even for Canadians … Many older Canadians remember where they were when Hitler invaded Poland, when Pearl Harbour was attacked, when the bomb was dropped on Hiroshima. They remember V-E Day, when the war in Europe came to an end. Everyone … remembers precisely where they were – perhaps even what was said – when John Kennedy was shot on November 22, 1963 … For Canadians, there is only one wholly Canadian event that has left a similar trail of memory: Henderson's goal in Moscow … scored to the soaring, chilling accompaniment of Foster Hewitt. "… Cournoyer has it on that wing! Here's a shot! Henderson made a wild stab for it and fell. Here's another shot! Right in front! THEY SCORE!!! Henderson has scored for Canada!"[2]

If pressed to identify a unifying national experience in the post-Imperial era, many Canadians would likely point to a defining moment in Canadian sporting history: the 1972 Summit Series between Canada and the Union of Soviet Socialist Republics (USSR). Indeed, as Macfarlane noted shortly after the Series' conclusion, for Canadians the eight game hockey series represented "a new adventure in diplomacy. A national identity crisis. A great Canadian happening."[3] According to Gruneau and Whitson, the series "mobilized patriotic interest among Canadians like no other cultural event before or since."[4] While the series itself produced a number of memorable and infamous events, Paul Henderson's goal in the last minute of the final game of the series in Moscow has been heralded by many hockey fans, members of the media, and social commentators alike as the most monumental in Canadian sporting history.

Beyond stimulating intense national interest, the 1972 Summit Series produced an unprecedented level of sporting and cultural contact between Canada and the Soviet Union in the midst of the Cold War – one of the most important events that shaped Canada during the twentieth century. As Whitaker and Hewitt explained, "In a way that succeeding generations will find difficult to comprehend, the Cold War was, for those who grew up and lived within it, an all encompassing experience, the very air that we breathed."[5] The effects of the Cold War, its ideologies, assumptions and propaganda, deeply constituted and structured the lives of generations of Canadians. Thus, the 1972 Summit Series was articulated by citizens, politicians, pundits and Canadian atheletes with substantive Cold War metaphors and broader stereotypes, symbols and practices – it was our way of life against theirs, capitalism versus communism, freedom versus totalitarianism, West versus East. In this sense, the Cold War was also a "time of illusions"[6] related to a broader hegemonic process associated with the politics of socially constructing a unified and apolitical Canadian identity out of difference to the Soviet Union, but also somewhat paradoxically out of difference to Canada's closest Western ally, the United States (US). However, as Ralph Miliband has argued, that while liberal democratic capitalist countries such as Canada and the US differ with respect to their invented traditions, mythologies and national popular cultures, on a broader level they share notable similarities with respect to social structure and class distribution that serve to "attenuate, though not to flatten out, the differences between them."[7] Consequently, on one level Canada and the US are different, but on another level much the same.[8] The 1972 Summit Series was therefore always about the politics of identity construction, "about who We were, and who They – the Other that defined 'Us' – were … ."[9]

Yet, younger generations of Canadians who did not live through the Cold War are also undoubtedly aware of the significance of the 1972 Summit Series in relation to the broader folklore of Canadian hockey and national identity. Since 1972, the televisual images of Paul Henderson's goal accompanied by Foster Hewitt's rousing commentary have been irrevocably etched into the nation's psyche, re-played, re-articulated and re-presented through various media to Canadians of all generations as part of a collective popular memory and the current promotional culture. More specifically, Paul Henderson's goal and the entire 1972 Summit Series have been mythologized as emblematic of a preferred version of Canadian character; an ongoing story Canadians continue to re-invent and tell themselves about themselves, more often than not through the carefully crafted vantage point of nostalgia. Or, as Moore explained, "When Canadians write about hockey they write more about themselves than about the game. It is about identities constructed through the game, the sentimental memories growing up and learning about life and what it is to be Canadian."[10]

Of course, the articulation of a preferred version of Canadianness, one that is so routinely celebrated and normalized by politicians, members of the media, marketers, consumers, and hockey fans, is inherently conservative and firmly entrenched within the dominant national culture as commonsense. This is a version of Canadian identity that is unquestionably hypermasculine, heterosexist, white, and middle class, one that celebrates a tough, passionate individualism that glorifies and normalizes the instances of violence that erupted throughout the 1972 Summit Series.[11] However, beneath the polished surface of popularized and nostalgic narratives of the 1972 Summit Series are historical divisions and cultural tensions that have made the process of socially constructing a unified and apolitical Canadian identity intensely problematic or, as Eva Mackey remarked, "terribly unsuccessful."[12] Beyond the obvious and long-standing tensions between the separatist ambitions of some within Quebec and Canadian nationalism, "there have always been subordinated groups – aboriginal Canadians, people from ethno-cultural groups other than English and French, working-class people, and most women – who have been historically excluded from the process of imaging Canada as a national community."[13] As a result of its continued cultural relevance and ongoing signification as the quintessential Canadian experience, the 1972 Summit Series represents a unique site to explore the articulation(s) of Canadian identity and, in Benedict Anderson's terms, the style in which it is "imagined."[14]

In relation to such issues, this chapter has three interrelated objectives. First, we begin by outlining the broad and tumultuous Canadian Cold War context, paying particular attention to a range of complex Canadian foreign policy objectives that in part spurred the development of the 1972 Summit Series. Second, we examine the emergence and organization of the 1972 Summit Series in relation to a conjunctural crisis in Canadian hockey at the professional and amateur levels. Third, we examine some of the tensions and contradictions associated with the (re)articulation of Canadian identity throughout the 1972 Summit Series to highlight the politics of identity construction and the inherent instability of Canadian identity. In doing so, we pay attention to the turbulent "national" political-economic and socio-cultural context: in particular Canadian Prime Minister Pierre Trudeau's mobilization of the 1972 Summit Series in relation to concerns surrounding national unity and the upcoming federal election.

The Canadian Cold War context

A discussion of the 1972 Summit Series between Canada and the USSR needs to be contextualized in relation to the broader political-economic and socio-cultural climate that dominated international relations and Canadian foreign policy during the Cold War – a period that stretched from the latter half of the 1940s to the end of the 1980s. In the post-Second World War context, Canada emerged from the shadow of Britain and surfaced as an important middle power with a substantive – if somewhat paradoxical – role to play in international relations. On the one hand, Canada emerged as a proponent of a new liberal internationalism associated with the formation of the United Nations in 1945, and a broader foreign policy agenda of maintaining peace through multilateral negotiation and diplomacy.[15] Yet on the other hand, having played an instrumental role in the resolution of the Second World War – at the cost of thousands of Canadian lives – Canadian foreign policy was also guided by a desire to maintain a collective security through strategic alliances with the US and other Western powers in relation to heightened concerns over the perceived nuclear threat associated with the Soviet Union following their deployment of a nuclear bomb in 1949. Indeed, as Washington's North American ally, Canada was inexorably part of the Western Cold War ideological consensus.[16]

In the context of increasing Cold War hostilities following the Second World War, Whitaker and Hewitt identified that the tensions between Canada's dual reputation as an important internationalist and a loyal Western ally were often a difficult balancing act.[17] For example, with respect to military obligations, Canada was a willing participant in the Western military alliance against the Soviet bloc. Canada played an integral role in shaping the North Atlantic Treaty Organization (NATO) which was formed in 1949; this organization emerged as a focal point for Canadian military and diplomatic endeavors during the Cold War. However, it was the Suez crisis of 1956 that constituted an emerging pillar of Canadian post-war identity and foreign policy. Canada had historically sided with Britain with respect to diplomatic disputes; during the Suez crisis, however, Canada sought to engage a uniquely diplomatic initiative spearheaded by Canadian Minister of External Affairs, Lester Pearson. While Canada acted as a bridge between the US and Britain during this crisis, Pearson pioneered the creation of a United Nations peacekeeping force and was awarded the 1957 Nobel Prize for Peace for his efforts. This marked the beginning of the golden age of Canadian foreign policy (what has been referred to as Pearsonian internationalism) and furthered Canada's reputation as an "honest broker or helpful fixer," and an important middle power.[18]

Despite such internationalist ambitions, Canada's Cold War allegiances clearly remained directly tied to the US. For example, with the exacerbation of Cold War tensions following the Soviet suppression of the Hungarian uprising in 1956, Canada and the US formed a North American Air Defence (NORAD) command in 1957: a fear of nuclear attack permeated the nation. However, while the paranoia of "McCarthyism" was arguably more publicly pronounced in the US due to its highly publicized witch-hunting rampage that targeted Hollywood celebrities,[19] it is important to note that a climate of anti-communist paranoia was present in Canada throughout and well before the Cold War. For example, after the Winnipeg General Strike of 1919, corporate and government leaders used "regular" tactics of blacklisting and firings but also employed Red Scare propaganda to discredit union organizing and intimidate left-wing political activity. Moreover, in 1931, Tim Buck, leader of the Communist Party of Canada, was arrested and imprisoned during which time he survived an assassination attempt during a prison riot in 1932.[20] After the Second World War, the Canadian state regularly harassed far left sympathizers most notably in Quebec prior to the Quiet Revolution in the early 1960s.[21] Individuals who engaged in direct protest activities (including those associated with various peace movements) or publicly criticized Canada's anti-communist alignment with its Western allies were cast as enemies of the nation and smeared as communists, communist sympathizers or traitors as they had been since 1917.[22]

During the 1960s, tensions between US and Canadian Cold War policy heightened remarkably. While continental economic and military integration had intensified throughout the 1950s, by the early 1960s "many observers were expressing concerns about the waning influence of Canada in the world and the loss of an independent foreign policy in the face of American power and of the country's economic dependence."[23] Moreover, the Bay of Pigs invasion in 1961 and the Cuban Missile Crisis of 1962 widened an ever visible ideological gap between Washington and Ottawa, while an ongoing continental debate to arm the Canadian military with nuclear weapons further exacerbated diplomatic relations. According to Whitaker, a substantive ideological disjuncture emerged between Canada and the US: "The identity of the enemy was the same, but Canada preferred diplomatic over military means of containment, whereas the United States, having the most powerful military in the world, preferred the latter."[24] Most significantly, the Canadian government failed to support the US invasion of Vietnam and the ongoing Vietnam War. Nevertheless, the Vietnam War "affected Canadians more than any war they did not fight," and "profoundly altered Canada's view of the United States and American goals."[25] This is particularly true with respect to the large number of young American males, often accompanied by their families, who fled north of the border to Canada to avoid being drafted into US military service. In relation to such tensions, a new spirit of radicalism and activism inspired a generation of young Canadians who grew increasingly critical of US imperialism. During the late 1960s the level of activism over a range of social issues including anti-nuclear protests, the rise of feminism, and broader concerns over the Americanization of Canadian society escalated to unprecedented levels.[26] Notably, in 1970 the "Committee for an Independent Canada" movement was formed to promote Canadian cultural and economic independence and demand limits to US investment and ownership; that same year Kari Levitt's book *Silent Surrender* documented Canada's heightened integration and dependence on the US economy.

Around the same time, a broader shift occurred in Canadian foreign policy. According to Macintosh and Hawes, during the late 1960s, Canada sought to maximize its overall international influence through "low-level linkages" with other nations without compromising a commitment to broader Western values and alliances.[27] For example, in a visible departure from US foreign policy, the Canadian and Soviet governments initiated a number of agreements and exchanges that culminated in a formal agreement to increase cultural, scientific and technological exchanges between both nations.[28] Significantly, in 1967, the Department of External Affairs formally proposed that sport exchanges be included in the broader agreement.[29] The election of liberal French-Canadian Prime Minister Pierre Trudeau in 1968 signalled a further expansion of diplomatic relations between Moscow and Ottawa. A youthful and charismatic leader, Trudeau recognized the shifting terrain of international relations and in particular, a mild thaw in Cold War tensions between East and West.[30] Trudeau initiated a Canadian foreign policy review that culminated in the publication of the federal white paper *Foreign Policy for Canadians* on 25 June 1970. The review "cast aspersions on the legacy of Pearsonian internationalism and espoused a new direction in Canadian foreign policy, one that would more directly serve the country's national interest."[31] Such an emergent foreign policy agenda was designed to promote economic growth, social justice and quality of life, and redefined Canada's main national interests as national identity and independence, as opposed to peace and security.[32]

Often, independence meant taking foreign policy stances that ran in stark contrast from those of the US. For example, Trudeau's vision of international relations also included rapprochement with China and the USSR. While Canada had substantially expanded trade with China throughout the 1950s and 1960s, previous Canadian governments had resisted officially recognizing the government in Beijing. Trudeau, campaigning for the leadership of the federal liberal party in 1968, pledged to recognize the People's Republic of China (PRC). In contrast to a pro-Taiwan US foreign policy, Canada officially recognized the PRC in 1970.[33] Trudeau, who adamantly believed that the USSR needed to be brought back into the fold of international relations, visited the USSR in 1971 and met with Soviet Premier Alexei Kosygin, who returned the visit to Canada six months later. Trudeau's journey to Moscow spurred the signing of a Canadian-Soviet Protocol on Consultations which the Canadian leader suggested "had been prompted in part because the Canadian identity was endangered by the 'overwhelming presence' of the United States from a cultural, economic and perhaps even military point of view."[34] Moreover, the visit also offered an opportunity for both leaders to discuss the role of sport and in particular hockey as "a common bond between the two countries, which could be used to strengthen bilateral relations."[35] It is within this context that we now turn to a discussion on the build-up to the 1972 Summit Series and a particular conjunctural crisis in Canadian identity and Canadian hockey.

Build-up to the Series: the declining international influence of Canadian hockey

In relation to these diplomatic initiatives and the broader Cold War context, Canadian hockey was in a simultaneous state of upheaval. On the professional front, the National Hockey League (NHL) added six new US-based franchises in 1967, doubling in size from six to twelve teams. However, to the dismay of Canadian fans, Canadian cities, in particular Vancouver, were completely overlooked. Canadian criticism of the Americanization of the NHL escalated when the financially troubled Oakland Seals franchise was denied permission to relocate to Vancouver by the NHL.[36] While economic ownership of the NHL was clearly dominated by US interests, Canadian cultural "ownership" of hockey was also simultaneously threatened by the rapidly improving Soviet national program. In conjunction with the broader ideological emphasis placed on dominating international sporting competitions, the Soviet Union invested in developing a hockey infrastructure following the Second World War.[37]

During the 1950s and 1960s, Canada's supremacy in international hockey began to erode, primarily at the hands of increasingly talented and skilled teams from the Soviet Union. In 1954, the Soviet Union upset Canada at the World Hockey Championships; at the Winter Olympic Games in 1956 the Soviets defeated a Canadian team that would eventually finish third behind the US. In accordance with the international rules and regulations of the time, the best professional Canadian hockey players who were employed by NHL franchises were unable to represent their country. In response, Canada had sent local amateur club hockey teams to represent the nation in international competitions, and had been able to defeat weaker opponents; however, Canada's success was no longer a certainty following the emergence of the USSR as a hockey power.[38] Given the importance of hockey to the national psyche, these defeats were regarded by Canadians and the press as national disasters.[39]

The crisis in Canadian hockey was not lost on a newly elected Pierre Trudeau, who had publicly deplored Canada's poor showing in international hockey, during his election campaign.[40] Consequently, a national task force on sport in Canada was formed in 1968 to examine the state of hockey specifically, and amateur sport more generally. In addition to recommendations about the relationship between the Canadian amateur hockey system and the NHL, a product of the government's inquiry was the creation of Hockey Canada in February 1969. Despite having two mandates (fostering and developing hockey in Canada, and managing and developing the national team), Hockey Canada focused on exploring the problems associated with achieving its international mandate. Most significantly this included persuading the International Ice Hockey Federation (IIHF) to declare the World Championships an open championship, thereby enabling the use of Canadian professional players.[41] A moderate degree of success was achieved when Hockey Canada negotiated with the IIHF to use nine minor league players and reinstated amateurs. However, in January 1970, this deal collapsed in part because of Soviet concerns that their eligibility for the 1972 Olympics might be jeopardized by playing a Canadian team that consisted of professional players.[42] Following this reversal, Canada withdrew from international competition, refusing to send teams to the world hockey championships in Sweden (1970), Switzerland (1971), and Prague (1972), as well as the Olympic Games in Sapporo (1972).

In relation to these issues, Hockey Canada focused on re-establishing hockey contact/relations directly with the Soviet Union in the hopes of using professional players in international tournaments.[43] Such a concept had been explored by the executive director of the National Hockey League Players' Association (NHLPA), Alan Eagleson, who had traveled to Moscow to discuss the possibility of a world cup in hockey with the Soviet Union in 1969,[44] and would later assure Hockey Canada of the NHLPA's commitment to deliver NHL players for a proposed series with the Soviet Union.[45] In April 1972, a negotiating committee consisting of Joe Kryczka, CAHA President, Lou Lefaive, director of Sport

Canada, and Charles Hay, president of Hockey Canada, went to IIHF meetings in Prague with a proposal to play a series of exhibition games versus the Soviet national team. Indeed, the seeds of the series had been sown in the months leading up to the spring of 1972:

> ... the Canadian government did take an active role in the negotiations that established the series. The Department of External Affairs wanted Canada back in international hockey, in keeping with the Trudeau government's foreign policy objectives. Trudeau and Soviet Premier Aleksei Kosygin had exchanged visits in 1971 and had agreed in a general way that a resumption of hockey competition would contribute to the opening up of relations between the two countries. Hockey Canada was advised that Canadian embassies in Moscow, Prague, and Stockholm were prepared to assist in negotiations aimed at establishing open play between Canadians and Europeans. In fact, the Soviets, who were used to a government presence in all important affairs, insisted that negotiations and arrangements for the series be handled through the two countries' foreign offices. The Canadian government role was therefore significant ... .[46]

Ongoing negotiations between Kryczka, Gordon Juckes, executive director of the CAHA, Hockey Canada board member Douglas Fisher, and the Soviets' chief IIHF delegate, Andrei Starovoitov, led to an agreement, and as a result, in late April, 1972, it was announced that an eight-game series between a select team of Canadian players and the Soviet national team would be played in September.[47] Most importantly, the agreement stipulated that Canada could field an unrestricted team to play in the series.[48]

The 1972 Summit Series:
(re)articulating Canadian identity

The talk all through the summer of 1972 was about the series. And because Canada was the best and sure to win, Canadians couldn't wait for the series to begin. It would be a glorious "coming out" party, a celebration of us ... . For though much may be said about Canada, surrounded as it is historically and geographically by countries that are bigger, richer, more powerful, whose specialness seems more obvious, we cling to every symbol. A game is a game. But a symbol is not. We had to win this series.[49]

The announcement of the 1972 Summit Series ignited immediate interest and fanfare across Canada; within the media it was initially articulated as the remedy for restoring Canadian hockey supremacy in relation to a deeply embedded nationalist agenda. That is, despite the political rhetoric surrounding the importance of the series in strengthening bilateral relations, the 1972 Summit Series was originally articulated by hockey fans, members of the media, and

Canadian players in aggressively nationalistic terms devoid of any spirit of cooperation or cultural understanding. As Ken Dryden and Mark Mulvoy explained, "as far as the vast majority of Canadians are concerned, this series was not conceived in a spirit of brotherhood and understanding but as a means of putting down the Russians and asserting our claim to hockey supremacy."[50]

Indeed, due to the importance of hockey to Canadian identity, it has been argued that Canada had more to lose in competing against the Soviets: "If the Soviets lost this series, they would lose no more than that, a hockey series. But for Canadians, haunted by the knowledge that the world doubted our superiority at the game we called our own, there was more at stake."[51] However, it is also important to note that the Soviet players were also under intense pressure. Consider the following comment from Soviet goaltender Vladislav Tretiak: "Every time our government wanted us to prove that communism was a better system than capitalism. We were programmed to prove this to the world."[52] Intense speculation and debate ensued over which players would be selected to play for Team Canada. While Canada's best player, defenseman Bobby Orr, was unlikely to play due to ongoing knee injuries, the attention of the nation quickly focused on a debate surrounding the availability of celebrated forward Bobby Hull. More specifically, Hull had recently made a well-publicized and lucrative multi-million dollar jump from the NHL's Chicago Blackhawks to the Winnipeg Jets of the emergent World Hockey Association, giving the rival league immediate status, credibility and celebrity. Hull's contentious signing, however, enraged NHL owners to the point that NHL President Clarence Campbell threatened to bar NHL players from competing in the series if any WHA players were selected to play for Team Canada. As an editorial bluntly noted, "In the assembling of Team Canada, the commercialism of North American hockey was made crudely apparent."[53] Campbell's threat undoubtedly fuelled criticism of the Americanization of NHL in Canada; a sentiment that was tangible across much of the nation in light of the NHL's recent expansion into more lucrative markets in the US.[54]

The controversy surrounding the Hull affair engulfed the nation and ultimately prompted Prime Minister Trudeau to send telegrams to the NHL, the NHLPA and Hockey Canada to outline his concerns:

> You are aware of the intense concern, which I share with millions of Canadians in all parts of our country, that Canada should be represented by its best hockey players, including Bobby Hull and all those named by Team Canada, in the forthcoming series with the Soviet Union. On behalf of these Canadians, I urge Hockey Canada, the NHL and the NHL Players Association to take whatever steps may be necessary to make this possible... I would ask you to keep the best interests of Canada in mind and to make sure that they are fully respected and served.[55]

Of course, such a provocative statement was little more than political posturing by Trudeau; the US-dominated NHL had regularly prioritized its economic agenda over Canadian national interest in numerous instances and would continue to do so in the near future. However, Trudeau clearly recognized a politically opportune moment to articulate a populist and nationalist position in relation to broader concerns about national unity in light of an upcoming general election that was soon to be called. Nevertheless, despite such political and popular pressure, the economic interests of the NHL prevailed and, to the despair of Canadians, Team Canada would play without Hull and three other WHA players who were originally selected. In this sense, the original selection controversy signified not only the NHL's continued hold over Canadian hockey, but illuminated a clear disjuncture between the financial interests and ambitions of the NHL and the desire of Canadians to be represented by the best Canadian hockey players regardless of their conditions of employment. From the very beginning, therefore, the selection of Team Canada was neither unifying nor apolitical, and inseparable from the economic logic of the NHL.

Despite the absence of some high profile WHA and injured NHL players, Canadian fans, Canadian players, and members of the media were exceedingly over-confident, treating the Soviet team "with a casualness bordering on contempt."[56] For example, many members of the media arrogantly predicted that the NHL players would easily beat the Soviets in each game. In fact, it has been suggested that the Series was presented to participating NHL players as a friendly exhibition series, "a light-hearted invitation to travel and live it up."[57] Such a lackadaisical approach was entirely consistent with a populist national discourse that heralded Canada as the dominant hockey nation, in spite of their lack of international success. For example, prior to the first game in Montreal, the McGuinness distillery of Ontario ran an advertisement in Toronto newspapers for the "capitalist vodka" that extolled: "If they can play, we can make vodka."[58]

While there were a small number of dissenters within the media, they were generally regarded as unpatriotic. John Robertson of the Montreal Star, for example, was encouraged to write for Pravda after controversially predicting that the Soviets would win the series six games to two.[59] However, in the context of media speculation over the potential outcome of the Series, the opinions of those Canadians who had the most exposure to the Soviet hockey system were conspicuously absent. Notably, Series predictions of Lloyd Percival, Father David Bauer, and former national team players were not sought.

Upon their arrival in Canada, members of the Soviet entourage quickly sought to articulate the hockey series as a diplomatic initiative designed to spur friendly relations between Ottawa and Moscow. Consider the following quote from a Soviet Diplomat:

> We are coming to an era of common cooperation. We have reached an agreement in the scientific field with the Americans by our treaty restricting

the use of nuclear weapons. With Canada we are looking to a mutual design of friendship through hockey. It was boring for us when the Canadians decided to abandon the world tournament two years ago. Now it is pleasant to look forward to playing your strongest players, which we are told, are NHL players. We like to obtain the most use of these games, and we hope the Canadians do too.[60]

The Soviets were, however, thoroughly prepared for the upcoming four games in Canada and motivated to test their skills against the best professionals in North America. As former Soviet coach Anatoli Tarasov commented, "We used to listen to stories about Canadian hockey as if they were fairy tales. That the Canadians were invincible, that the skill of the founders of this game was truly fantastic."[61] In addition to their recent international successes, the Soviets had been training continuously and had been monitoring NHL games for years, producing detailed reports on the style of the professional game and individual Canadian players.[62] Given the timing of the Series, prior to the start of the NHL season, few NHL players trained in advance of the series and arrived at camp in less than peak condition.

The first game of the Series was played on 2 September 1972 in front of 18,818 spectators at the Forum in Montreal. Canadian Prime Minister Pierre Trudeau presided over the traditional pre-game exchange of gifts and dropped the puck for the ceremonial face-off. Also in attendance were former Prime Minister Lester Pearson, and Conservative leader of the opposition, Robert Stanfield. Having recently announced a national election on 1 September Trudeau likely anticipated that a successful Canadian outcome in the Summit Series would create substantial political momentum for the Liberal party anxious for another majority government. Indeed, Trudeau's political platform focused on articulating an inclusive national identity with the hope of easing substantive national divisions. For example, Francophone and Anglophone tensions had heightened drastically following the October Crisis in 1970, when Front de Libération du Québec (FLQ) terrorists kidnapped British trade consul James Cross and Quebec Labour minister Pierre Laporte (later murdered).[63] Moreover, many Anglophone Canadians were critical of the Official Languages Act (1969) which recognized English and French as the official languages of Canada and required all federal services to be offered in English and French. Trudeau clearly recognized the unifying value of the Series as a promotional opportunity to communicate via television with a sizeable audience of Canadian voters, particularly in relation to other national political concerns over rising inflation, increasing taxes, and relatively high unemployment rates.

The Summit Series also provided advertisers with a unique and powerful cultural venue to reach an unprecedented national audience: a reminder that discourses of corporate nationalism are certainly not unique to the current era of globalization. At a cost of $25,000 per minute, the sponsors of the Series were the equivalent of a "bluechip portfolio: Labatts Breweries, 40 minutes over eight games – five minutes per game – at $800,000; Ford of Canada, 32 minutes at $600,000; Toronto-Dominion Bank, 16 minutes at $300,000; CCM, eight minutes at $200,000, Zenith, four minutes at $110,000, Edge shaving cream, $110,000".[64] More specifically, advertisers clearly recognized the substantial currency of the hockey series with respect to reaching a male nation-wide target audience over 18 years of age. As one reporter acknowledged, "And that's right where a beer maker lives".[65] In this sense, the 1972 Summit Series was firmly located within an expanding promotional culture that was being increasingly driven by the language and imperatives of consumerism. Interestingly, the articulation of advertising slogans and brands was not limited to the games that were played in Canada. More specifically, a Swedish advertising agency purchased advertising spaces at the Moscow arena from the Soviet government which were then sold to advertisers for North American goods including Boston-based company, Gillette, whose officials explained: "Every time the players swoop down the ice, line up before the game, or face off in the centre of the rink, the company's advertising is plainly visible to the millions of television viewers."[66]

Canadian hockey supremacy appeared to be confirmed early in the first game, as the Canadian team scored two quick goals to take an early lead. However, it soon became apparent that the Soviets were exceptionally skilled and in superior condition, overwhelming their professional counterparts to produce a one-sided 7–3 victory. During the game, members of Team Canada frequently resorted to violent tactics in a futile attempt to disrupt a disciplined and talented Soviet team, and some Canadian players did not shake hands with the Soviet players after the game. As team leader Phil Esposito blatantly confessed: "I reacted as I would in the National League. I thought there was going to be a full-scale war."[67] The myth of Canadian hockey supremacy and the invincibility of NHL players had been extinguished in one game. The coach of the Canadian team, Harry Sinden, explained the emotional impact of the loss: "A little piece of us died today. I've lost some tough games over the years, but I never thought I could feel as badly about losing a single game as I did about this one."[68] The Canadian press reacted to the loss with disbelief, confusion and embarrassment. An editorial in the *Toronto Star* conceded, "Seldom since Goliath contemptuously looked at David can an opponent have been so grossly underrated as we underrated the Russian nationals. All Canadians concerned shared in this error."[69] Another column despondently highlighted the inherent instability of a Canadian identity predicated on the sport of hockey: "When our national institution crumbles with one Bolshevik bodycheck, what then can preserve the adjacent out-building of our culture? Nothing. Our national inferiority complex, defended only by our hockey, may now become terminal neurosis."[70] Meanwhile, the original McGuinness distillery advertisement continued to run in the papers with one profound change: the word "If" had been crossed out.[71]

The two teams played Game 2 at Maple Leaf Gardens in Toronto in front of 16,485 people. Despite the tumultuous environment that followed the first game, as a political event, the game in Toronto also represented a significant opportunity for federal politicians to receive national visibility; in attendance were Pierre Trudeau, Robert Stanfield as well as New Democratic Party (NDP) leader David Lewis. Indeed, across the nation there had been substantial speculation on the potential impact of the Series on the upcoming federal election campaign: conjecture that intensified following the disastrous first game. For example, the following quote appeared on the front page of the *Toronto Star:* "Will the Canadian inferiority complex increase and thus affect the electorate's thinking on such issues as Canadian-US relations? Will voters, 90 percent of them hockey fans, blame the government? They blame the government for everything else, so who knows?"[72]

Facing intense pressures and media scrutiny, Team Canada won Game 2 at Maple Leaf Gardens in Toronto 4–1, and according to one report "patriotism surged back to the point that a dozen fans pulled the un-Canadian gesture of waving flags."[73] Following the game, many media commentators remarked that some semblance of national pride had been restored, but only after some Canadian players resorted to violence and displays of intimidation. Wayne Cashman was singled out by the Soviets as the main perpetrator. Cashman's actions, however, were for the most part defended in the Canadian media, including one commentator who clearly noted the legitimacy of a contextual morality in such an important and contested sporting series: "Dirty has been a word often used to describe Cashman's style of shinny. But dirty or not, Cashman is a winner and it's a cinch he's one Canadian who won't be going to Russia with love".[74] When asked to describe his actions, Cashman responded: "They'd say a few words and I'd say a few back. I don't know what they were saying but I think they knew what I was talking about."[75] Similarly, assistant coach John Ferguson, himself no stranger to violent acts committed on the ice as a hard-nosed enforcer for the Montreal Canadians, articulated a common-sense understanding that has legitimized, rationalized and normalized the traditional style of play of Canadian hockey. As Ferguson explained, "I don't care how we win, as long as we win. It's been that way for 50 years and it'll be that way for another 50."[76] Ferguson's comments would prove to be foretelling with respect to future deployments of premeditated violence and intimidation by Canadian players. Nevertheless, across Canada the devastating initial loss was re-articulated as a "freak caused by overconfidence"[77] and a more cautious optimism prevailed as the teams traveled to play the third game in Winnipeg.

The tensions and complexity of Canadian identity was further illuminated in Winnipeg, where a distinct anti-NHL sentiment was tangible alongside a palatable sense of regional consternation and cynicism surrounding discrepant regional power relations and Winnipeg's declining urban image and flagging economy. More specifically, there existed a distinct, anti-Eastern Canada animosity towards the federal government which had recently permitted Air Canada to close a large repair depot in Winnipeg, contributing to a perception that Winnipeg was regarded as a "hick town of 'about 200,000' somewhere on the bald Canadian flatlands."[78] Such urban and regional insecurities were further inflamed as a result of Hockey Canada's decision to not participate in international competitions, resulting in Winnipeg losing the rights to host the lucrative 1970 World Championships (and the Canadian national hockey team). Hockey fans and local elites were also dismayed with the NHL's refusal to locate a franchise in Winnipeg; this was considered to be an indictment against local ambitions to be considered a big-league city on par with other significant North American urban centres. As one columnist bitterly explained, many local fans and elites "cringed over the smug innuendos of the National Hockey League, suggesting that Winnipeg is a one-horse town, full of low-salaried workers and the odd old rich man too busy counting his money to know the difference between a hockey stick and a bar stool."[79] Moreover, many hockey fans and members of the local media were outraged over the US-dominated NHL's position regarding the selection of WHA players including Winnipeg's newest adopted favourite son, Bobby Hull. For example, the headline of a column written by reporter Jack Matheson extolled "THE BIG, FAT NHL HAS LOST ITS PATENT ON THE GAME OF HOCKEY," while the column pungently explained: "We have sundry things to be proud about in this country, and the NHL isn't one of them."[80] Thus, in a remarkable instance of disjuncture, in Winnipeg and elsewhere, the team symbolizing a supposedly united Canadian nation, was angrily dubbed "Team US NHL."[81] Here it is also important to note that it is likely that support for the USSR was greater in Winnipeg than elsewhere across Canada. Historically, Winnipeg has been a hub of left-wing political activity ranging from the 1919 General Strike to the regular election of communist civic councillors. For example, Jacob Penner, who was instrumental in organizing the Communist Party of Canada in 1921, was elected to Winnipeg City Council in 1933: a position he held until 1960 when he was succeeded by fellow communist Joseph Zuken who served as a councillor until the 1980s.

On 5 September 1972, the day before the third game, the Munich massacre temporarily displaced the Summit Series from the media spotlight in Canada. Prior to the contest, thirty seconds of silence were observed by the standing crowd (instead of a full minute) to honour the slain Israeli athletes.[82] Game 3 ended in a 4–4 tie. Following the game, assistant coach John Ferguson suggested that the Russians might not only be better hockey players, they might be better coaches. "If I was starting a new expansion team today, I'd go out and buy Anatoli Tarasov's whole collection of books on hockey. Impressed? Harry and I are bloody impressed. We're shocked. The Russians know so much about this game it isn't funny."[83] What is ironic about Ferguson's comment is that Tarasov's system of play had its origins in the work of Canadian Lloyd Percival (*The Hockey Handbook*). Ferguson also highlighted the differences between the

Canadian and Soviet way of life in his new-found admiration of the Soviet system: "Look, we couldn't impose all of their system upon the players in our
society. Our guys will always have a smoke and a drink. But the on-ice techniques, the off-iced training ... man they've got something going. If the NHL
doesn't sit down and analyze what's happened in this series, well, they're really
missing the boat."[84]

The final game in Canada, played in Vancouver, resulted in a 5–3 victory for
the Soviets. After being completely outplayed Team Canada was loudly booed off
of the ice, inciting an impassioned and now famous plea from despondent
Canadian team leader Phil Esposito. During a post-game interview, and again in
later commentary, Esposito passionately defended his team mates from the
onslaught of public criticism: "To give up my summer and a ton of money, and
then to be booed, is beneath my dignity. I'm really disappointed – and every guy
on the team is behind what I said. Although most of us play for United States
teams and are paid by United States teams, we come back to play for Canada
because we love the country. I'm disappointed in the fans in Winnipeg and the
fans here, and the press in general."[85] In a similar vein, Canadian team member
Bill Goldsworthy whined that he was "ashamed of being Canadian"[86] while Peter
Mahavolich angrily indicted the Canadian media: "The whole nation has taken
its lead from the press which has been on us, attacking us since last Saturday
night. In Winnipeg they crucified us in the papers and on the radio stations ...
But here tonight was the worst. They even gave the Russians a bigger cheer than
us before the game started."[87] By the end of the fourth game in Vancouver there
existed a substantial fissure in the national psyche, and without question,
demonstrated the cultural significance that ice hockey plays in the development
of that psyche.

Esposito's public confession arguably spurred yet another re-articulation of
Canadian identity; one that transformed the anger and hostility directed at the
US-based NHL players into unconditional support for an embattled team of
Canadian players about to journey to the ominous and unknown world of the
Cold War enemy. The media then began to champion a Canadian David as he
ventured into the den of the USSR Goliath. Columnist Dick Beddoes bluntly
noted, "I plan to punch the next person who knocks Phil as a money grubber who
was reluctant to play for Canada ... We wanted them to play for their country, and
then we are offended when they tie and lose for their country. If we genuinely care
about hockey, rather than our petty vanities, we should be grateful."[88] Team
Canada members were steadily re-constituted as an extended national family just
as the significance of the 1972 Summit Series was re-framed: "Canadians watching the telecast of 22 September 1972 from Moscow by now were involved in
something deeper than sport. There was an element of heroic daring in the fact of
a middle power contending with the largest national land mass in the world, a
nuclear-armed super-power, for hockey supremacy."[89] Team Canada players
already had collided with the athletic prowess of the Soviet players and the

planned sports system in which they developed their considerable talent. They also came to learn that Canadian Cold War rhetoric had its equivalent in Moscow, where each Soviet win was heralded as a symbolic victory for the communist system. The paradox was obvious. Two teams of highly skilled athletes who self-identified as "hockey players" found themselves painted as political symbols for oppositional economic systems. In this sense, the 1972 Summit Series was anchored to metaphors between disparate systems, communist hockey versus the "hockey capitalism" of Canada's "professionals."[90] With the transfer of the Series to Soviet soil, the great unknown, Esposito's outburst was the catalyst for the re-articulation of the Canadian player, as underdog, a role that was readily embraced. Team Canada coach Harry Sinden noted, "It strikes me that maybe the players relish going to Moscow as the underdog."[91]

In preparation for Game 5 in Moscow, Canada played two exhibition games against the Swedish national team, reinforcing the goon reputation of its hockey teams. According to one Swedish report, "The battle with Canada is over. It left bloodstained ice behind. That is one side of the Canadians. They lose all style and sense when a defeat is threatening. Simply bad losers."[92] In response to the exhibition games, one Canadian columnist went so far as to extol: "I am ashamed to be Canadian."[93]

With respect to the re-articulation of Team Canada, it is telling that three thousand loyal Canadian supporters traveled to Moscow for the remaining games of the Series. Dissention, however, was present within a fractured Canadian team. Vic Hadfield, Rick Martin, Jocelyn Guevremont and Gilbert Perreault demanded to be sent home after receiving minimal playing time. There was little sympathy for the departing players. Cast as selfish deserters and traitors, Assistant Coach John Ferguson voiced the collective opinion of player, coaches and fans alike. "He [Perreault] came to us after the game and complained we hadn't played him enough. He asked for his plane ticket home. So let him go. We've got no room for quitters ... Here's a kid with great ability, but he's not thinking of Canada or anything but Gilbert Perreault."[94] Phil Esposito, rapidly donning the mantle of team spokesman angrily echoed, "If you don't want to play, then get the @#$% home!"[95] The mood among Team Canada players was increasingly volatile and desperate, especially after losing the fifth game 5–4. Referring to the skill level of the Soviet players, even the normally mild-mannered Paul Henderson displayed a growing sense of anger and frustration, remarking that "the bastards should have been in Siberia instead of on the ice after the second period."[96]

Team Canada's desperation and ongoing resort to violence climaxed in Game 6: a penalty-riddled 3–2 and brutally violent victory for Canada. As columnist Jim Taylor noted, "This isn't a hockey series, it's a cold war. They should trade Wayne Cashman for Henry Kissinger."[97] Russian commentators claimed that members of Team Canada actively sought to initiate violent alter-cations: "The chief task for the Canadians was not so much getting the puck through as it was to intimidate their partners with tough and sometimes rude playing."[98] Indeed, Team Canada had literally declared war on the Soviet Union's best player, Valery Kharmalov, whose left ankle was fractured with a vicious slash by Team Canada member Bobby Clarke. The attack was ordered by assistant coach John Ferguson who later recounted the premeditated gesture: "What I told Clarke, I told him, 'Kharlamov's hurting us badly, go over and break his ankle. Put him out of the series.'"[99] When asked about his attack on Kharmalov, Clarke told columnist Dick Beddoes, "Mr. Beddoes, if I hadn't learned to lay on what you call a wicked two-hander, I would never have left Flin Flon, Manitoba."[100] Team Canada would also win the seventh game 4–3. Like the preceding contest, game seven was replete with numerous violent acts including a brawl that was precipitated by an altercation between Gary Bergman and Boris Mikhailov. Soviet players, who did not resort to fisticuffs, chose other methods of aggression. Mikhailov repeatedly kicked at Bergman's shins with his skate blade and after both players were banished to the penalty box, an incensed Bergman exacerbated tensions by pointing to Mikhailov while making a throat-slitting gesture.

The deciding game was unsurprisingly promoted as an event of national significance across Canada. At 12.30 p.m. Eastern Standard Time on Thursday, 28 September 1972, most of Canada was granted (or took) a collective "time out." Ontario's Minister of Education declared that the province's half a million elementary and secondary students could watch or listen to the game. "The game was broadcast on both CBC and CTV. All other programming came to a stop. Canada's population in 1972 was 21.8 million. On this Thursday afternoon, a work day, 7.5 million watched."[101] The significance of the moment was not lost on the Canadian politicians either, with Pierre Trudeau "firing off widely publicized cables of encouragement."[102] The eighth game was also plagued with deplorable incidents. After receiving a penalty for interference and subsequent ten-minute misconduct, Canadian J.P. Parise was thrown out of the game after charging a referee and threatening him with his stick. Coach Harry Sinden exacerbated matters further, angrily throwing a wooden stool onto the ice. His counterpart John Ferguson further attempted to intimidate the referees by making a choking gesture. In another bizarre incident, Alan Eagleson, incensed that the game clock had been allowed to run, charged the official timer, only to be accosted by Soviet soldiers who physically restrained him and attempted to escort him from the rink. Several Canadian players jumped over the boards, and with sticks flailing, rescued Eagleson and guided him to the safety of the Canadian bench. Undiplomatically, Eagleson crossed the ice profanely gesturing at the partisan Soviet crowd. Despite such a surreal disruption, after trailing 5–3, Team Canada eventually tied the game, and, late in the third period completed a seemingly insurmountable comeback when Paul Henderson scored his dramatic game-winning goal.

National reaction

Henderson's feat spurred unprecedented outpouring of nationalism and self-reflection – an "orgy of self-congratulation about the triumph of 'Canadian virtues' – individualism, flair, and most of all, character – over the 'machine-like' Soviet 'system.'"[103] As expected, the national celebration was depicted in sweeping Cold War metaphors, "a triumph not only for 'Canadian virtues' but also for capitalist liberal democracy – a point frequently reinforced by the players themselves."[104] Without question, the Series demonstrated the potential of international hockey to hegemonically unite Canada (at least temporarily) and arguably was an important conduit for the articulation of an emergent Canadian identity. Certainly this was the mindset of columnist Colin McCullough. "For one thing, a lot of Canadians discovered their nationality. Had any of them ever before stood up and loudly sung O Canada, even the high notes, with tears running down their cheeks? They did in the Palace of Sports at Lenin Central Stadium, and it was because of Canada, not hockey." *The Globe and Mail* columnist Jim Vipond concurred, "That they were able to reach their potential, overcome the emotionalism generated by frustration in a foreign country, and stick with it – the majority of them that is – is a tribute to their Canadian heritage."[105] Even the politicians got into the act. In a display of his considerable knowledge of military history Dave Barrett, NDP Premier of BC extolled: "The French couldn't do it, the Germans couldn't do it, now Canada has done it and they better get out of town before it starts snowing."[106] Another journalist remarked, "Napoleon didn't take Moscow, the Nazis got within twenty-one miles in 1943, but in a war of a different kind, Team Canada conquered Moscow."[107] Thus, in many ways, the Series victory produced a distinctly un-Canadian response: an extreme outpouring of nationalism and flag-waving, not different substantively from the overt displays of American patriotism that many Canadians seek to avoid. Nonetheless, as European hockey migration was later to display, the Series' outcome had multiple interpretations. For the die-hard Canadian fan and much of the high performance hockey establishment, however, there was one explanation only. Rather than regarding "the narrow victory as a lucky escape and ominous harbinger, many Canadians regarded the outcome as proof of their inherent sporting and national superiority"[108]

This is not to suggest that there was no alternative explanation provided. An editorial in *The Globe and Mail* heralded the "rough and tough" Series as "superb, winning hockey," while also noting that the games had descended into a "kind of war" from which a united nation had emerged:

> There had been earlier jeering about "Team NHL-USA". The team that won the Series yesterday was a Canadian team – no matter its paymasters back home – and cheering itself hoarse half a world away was a Canada united and proud behind its heroes … It was worth it all, but the lessons of this experience should be carefully considered before anyone organizes another of these bilateral batterings.[109]

Certainly, the boorish behaviour of particular Canadians, on and off the ice, was addressed in political debates. Rhetorically it was asked, did the 1972 Summit Series strengthen and sustain bilateral relations between Canada and the USSR?[110]

The re-articulation of Canadian identity that had occurred as a result of the Series, in some respects, speaks to the instability and ambiguity of national identity. Tellingly, the Premier of Quebec, a young Robert Bourassa sent a congratulatory telegram to Team Canada that simultaneously revealed this fragility of Canadian identity and its inevitable fissures: "your teamwork and your determination to win has earned you the admiration of *Quebeckers* and all Canadians" (Italics added). With an election a little over a month away, Pierre Trudeau strategically leveraged the discourse of unity and spirit of national pride, proudly exclaiming that he was never in doubt of the outcome and noted that he preferred the traditionally aggressive Canadian style of play as compared to the Russian style.[111]

In the end, it must be recognized that hockey remains a game and when more pressing political matters enter the public consciousness, they take precedence. Trudeau's Liberal Party learned this on the 30 October 1972 election day, despite its boastful campaign slogan "The Land is Strong." With Canadian hockey back in its rightful place, the voting public turned its attention to a range of political-economic and socio-cultural issues including the contentious federal program of official bilingualism. While hockey had symbolically united the nation, the regional divisiveness over French language issues expressed the fragility of national identity. Despite the Series outcome and his verbal posturing, Trudeau and his Liberals were only able to form a minority government, with the NDP holding the balance of power.

Conclusion

Despite being played over thirty years ago, the 1972 Summit Series continues to resonate for many Canadians. Indeed, it has been claimed that "perhaps no other single event has produced so much popular writing as the 1972 'Summit Series' with the Soviet Union."[112] The anniversary of the decisive eighth game is nostalgically celebrated within the Canadian media, while consumers can purchase the complete 1972 Summit Series on DVDs to re-visit their experiences, or watch the games for the first time. In 2006, the Canadian Broadcasting Corporation produced a much-hyped 4 hour miniseries on the Summit Series for a national audience.

The continued re-articulation of this historical event as a rare instance of national unity is perhaps not altogether too surprising and speaks to "the celebrated insecurity that many Canadians feel about their national identity."[113] However, as we have argued, the 1972 Summit Series was far from apolitical and, in many ways existed as a contradictory sporting moment that was articulated to a range of contested and contextually specific power relations that illuminated the fissures of Canadian identity. An ongoing nostalgia for the 1972 Summit Series risks glossing over those power relations and inequalities, while simultaneously illuminating the appeal of a dominant form of Canadian identity for many Canadians within an increasingly diverse, complex and multicultural society.[114] As Gruneau and Whitson explained,

> In this chaotic cultural, political, and economic environment, the idea of a single Canadian identity and an all-embracing Canadian nationalism has become more problematic than ever. This has given hockey even greater symbolic currency in recent years, as one of the few "institutions", along with our system of national government, our public health-care system, and the CBC, that we still imagine to be "truly Canadian".[115]

Each of these celebrated "Canadian" institutions are being increasingly questioned, challenged and re-imagined in the context of globalization and the state's adherence to a neo-liberal agenda. Today, even "hockey no longer commands the automatic cultural allegiance it enjoyed in past decades."[116] Others have noted that "the sport of hockey is not the pan-Canadian glue it is often trumpeted to be. Instead, hockey's role as a unifying cultural form is complex and contradictory."[117] A powerful example of the contradictory and multifaceted relationship between Canadians and the game of hockey occurred in 2000 when citizens rejected a federal proposal to publicly fund Canadian NHL franchises. In doing so, Canadians indicted the ravaging effects of the state's adherence to a neo-liberal agenda which, since the 1970s, have exacerbated the disparity between rich and poor in Canada, and dismantled national institutions including the provision of health care and other social services in the name of national interest.[118] Ironically, while the 1972 Summit Series was heralded as a unifying moment for Canadians, it was also popularly articulated as a victory for Western capitalist values: the same "values" that underpin the state's adherence to a neo-liberal governance system that continues to produce such divisive and inequitable power relations.

Notes

1 The authors wish to acknowledge with gratitude a critical reading of an earlier version of this chapter offered by Hart Cantelon.
2 Ken Dryden and Roy MacGregor, *Home Game: Hockey and Life in Canada* (Toronto: McClelland & Stewart Inc.,1994), p. 193.
3 John Macfarlane, *Twenty-Seven Days in September* (Hockey Canada and Prosport Productions, 1973), p. 125.
4 Richard Gruneau and David Whitson, *Hockey Night in Canada* (Toronto: Garamond Press, 1993), p. 249.
5 Reg Whitaker and Steve Hewitt, *Canada and the Cold War* (Toronto: James Lorimer & Company, 2003), p. 6.
6 Robert Bothwell, *The Big Chill: Canada and the Cold War* (Concord: Irwin, 1998), p. xi.
7 Ralph Miliband. *The State in Capitalist Society* (New York: Basic Books, 1969), p. 8.

8 We are grateful to Hart Cantelon for this idea.

9 Reg Whitaker, "'We Know They're There': Canada and its Others, With or Without the Cold War," in *Love, Hate, and Fear in Canada's Cold War*, ed. R. Cavell, (Toronto: University Press, 2004), p. 38.

10 Philip Moore, "Practical nostalgia and the critique of commodification: On the 'Death of Hockey' and the National Hockey League," *The Australian Journal of Anthropology*, 13, (2002), p. 313.

11 Violence in international competition continued after the 1972 Series, including an exhibition game in Philadelphia in January of 1976, when the Soviet Red Army team left the ice and refused to play due to the violent tactics of the NHL's Philadelphia Flyers team. The Soviets were eventually coaxed into returning to the game.

12 Eva Mackey, *House of Difference: Cultural Politics and National Identity in Canada* (Toronto: University of Toronto Press, 2002), p. 9.

13 Gruneau and Whitson, *Hockey Night in Canada*, p. 273.

14 Benedict Anderson, *Imagined Communities* (London: Verso, 1991), p. 6.

15 Whitaker and Hewitt, *Canada and the Cold War*, p. 58.

16 Whitaker, "We Know They're There," p. 37.

17 Whitaker and Hewitt, *Canada and the Cold War*, p. 59.

18 Donald Macintosh and Michael Hawes, *Sport and Canadian Diplomacy* (Montreal and Kingston: McGill-Queen's University Press, 1994), p. 12.

19 Interestingly, a much quieter purge of left wing sympathizers was achieved at the National Film Board of Canada in 1949. See Whitaker and Hewitt, *Canada and the Cold War*, p. 9.

20 Ibid., 32.

21 Ibid., 83.

22 Amid a growing climate of suspicion, the Royal Canadian Mounted Police (RCMP) began secretly building networks of informants and collected information on a broad range of Canadian citizens, including suspected communists. Such acts would later be condemned as excessive by a Royal Commission of inquiry. See Whitaker and Hewitt, *Canada and the Cold War*, p. 66.

23 Tom Keating, *Canada and World Order* (Toronto: Oxford University Press, 2002), p. 117.

24 Whitaker, "We Know They're There," p. 41.

25 John English, "Speaking out on Vietnam, 1965," in *Canadian Foreign Policy: Selected Cases*, eds. Don Munton and John Kirton (Scarborough: Prentice Hall, 1992), p. 135.

26 Whitaker and Hewitt, *Canada and the Cold War*, p. 167.

27 Macintosh and Hawes, *Sport and Canadian Diplomacy*, p. 12.

28 Ibid., 23.

29 Ibid., 23.

30 In one of his first significant acts as Prime Minister, Trudeau reduced Canada's military commitment to NATO in 1969. The decision met fierce criticism from many Canadians who had served in the Second World War and Korea, and disapproval by Western allies.

31 Keating, *Canada and World Order*, p. 117.

32 Bruce Thordarson, "Cutting back on NATO, 1969," in *Canadian Foreign Policy: Selected Cases*, eds. Don Munton and John Kirton (Scarborough: Prentice-Hall, 1992), p. 187.

33 Canada's recognition of the PRC would result in the withdrawal of Taiwan from the 1976 Montreal Summer Olympics.

34 Keaton, *Canada and World Order*, p. 146.

35 Macintosh and Hawes, *Sport and Canadian Diplomacy*, p. 31.
36 Canadian criticism of the NHL continued throughout the eighties and nineties, as the NHL successfully blocked the St Louis Blues' attempt to relocate to Saskatoon in the 1980s, and two Canadian-based franchises – the Quebec Nordiques and Winnipeg Jets – moved to US markets in the mid-1990s.
37 The process first emerged in the 1930s, when the USSR was involved with Red Sport International.
38 It is important to note that other European teams, with developmental structures similar to that of the Soviets, such as Czechoslovakia, were also enjoying success against Canadian teams.
39 Macintosh and Hawes, *Sport and Canadian Diplomacy*, p. 24.
40 Ibid., p. 26.
41 Notably, former Toronto Maple Leaf player Carl Brewer sat out a number of years in order to regain his amateur status and play for the national program.
42 It has been claimed that this decision was forced upon the Soviets by the head of the IIHF, Bunny Ahearne.
43 Roy MacSkimming, *Cold War* (Vancouver: Greystone Books, 1996), p. 8.
44 Macintosh and Hawes, *Sport and Canadian Diplomacy*, p. 29.
45 MacSkimming, *Cold War*, p. 8.
46 Gruneau and Whitson, *Hockey Night in Canada*, p. 264.
47 David Cruise and Alison Griffiths, *Net Worth: Exploding the Myths of Pro Hockey*. (Toronto: Penguin Books, 1991), p. 217.
48 An important condition was that the international "amateur" status of the Soviet players would not be jeopardized by their playing with the Canadian professionals.
49 Dryden and MacGregor, *Home Game: Hockey and Life in Canada*, p. 202.
50 Ken Dryden and Mark Mulvoy, *Face Off at the Summit 1973* (Boston: Sports Illustrated / Little Brown, 1973), p. 65. Canadians widely considered the Soviet players as professionals by virtue of their careers as hockey players in the army. Furthermore, it was held that the Soviets were successful in international play by virtue of their ability to circumvent amateur rules.
51 Macfarlane, *Twenty-Seven Days in September*, 5.
52 As cited in J.J. Wilson, "27 Remarkable Days: The 1972 Summit Series of Ice Hockey between Canada and the Soviet Union," *Totalitarian Movements and Political Religions*, 5(2), (2004), p. 273.
53 "In the end – superb, winning hockey," *The Globe and Mail* (29 September 1972), p. 39.
54 Notably, in 1972, Bruce Kidd and John Macfarlane released *The Death of Hockey*, a passionate indictment of the NHL's American-driven commercialization of hockey and the decline of senior-level hockey across Canada. Kidd and Macfarlane called for a new national hockey league of community-owned teams as part of a broader leftist nationalist political project to counter and indeed reverse the takeover of Canadian hockey by US business interests.
55 Quoted in MacSkimming, *Cold War*, p. 17.
56 Stan Fischler, *Hockey's Great Rivalries* (New York: Random House, 1974), p. 129.
57 Jim Vipond, "Bring on the Europeans," *The Globe and Mail* (29 September 1972), p. 40.
58 Whitaker and Hewitt, *Canada and the Cold War*, p. 195.
59 MacSckimming, *Cold War*, p. 28.
60 Dick Beddoes, "Russians arrive, refuse to predict outcome of hockey's super series," *The Globe and Mail* (31 August 1972), p. 43.
61 Fischler, *Hockey's Great Rivalries*, p. 126–27.
62 Ibid., p. 128.

63 In response, Trudeau invoked the War Measures Act, which placed the nation under a temporary state of martial law.

64 Ian MacDonald, "The simple answer to a ratings problem – show a hockey game," *Montreal Gazette* (2 September 1972), p. 44.

65 Ibid., p. 44.

66 "Esposito remembers every dramatic minute (almost)," *The Globe and Mail* (29 September 1972), p. 40. At the time, it was claimed that the advertising would be the first of its kind to appear in the Luzhniki arena complex.

67 Reyn Davis, untitled, *Winnipeg Free Press* (5 September 1972), p. 1A.

68 Harry Sinden, *Hockey Showdown: The Canada Russia Hockey Series* (New York: Doubleday, 1972), p. 8.

69 Quoted in Fischler, *Hockey's Great Rivalries*, p. 132.

70 Ted Blackman, "A dark day: Sept 2, 1972; when pride turned to trauma," *Montreal Gazette* (4 September 1972), p. 13.

71 MacSkimming, *Cold War*, p. 57.

72 Quoted in MacSkimming, *Cold War*, p. 72.

73 Tim Burke, "Now that's more like it!" *Montreal Gazette* (5 September 1972), p. 37.

74 Reyn Davis, "It isn't to Russia with love," *Winnipeg Free Press* (6 September 1972), p. 49.

75 Tim Burke, "Hey! We're not so red-faced now!" *Montreal Gazette* (5 September 1972), p. 1.

76 Davis, "It isn't to Russia with love," p. 49.

77 Fischler, *Hockey's Great Rivalries*, p. 133.

78 Reyn Davis, "A Hull of a date for Ben," *Winnipeg Free Press* (27 June 1972), p. 49.

79 Reyn Davis, "Now Tuesday is looming as 'H-Day," *Winnipeg Free Press* (23 June 1972), p. 49.

80 Quoted in MacSkimming, *Cold War*, p. 79.

81 Ibid., p. 79.

82 It should also be noted that demonstrations were held outside Canadian arenas to protest the refusal of the Soviet Union to let Jews leave the USSR. See MacSkimming, *Cold War*, p. 85.

83 Ted Blackman, "NHL image already hurt and series isn't over yet," *Montreal Gazette* (8 September 1972), p. 13.

84 Ibid., p. 13.

85 Ted Blackman, "Esposito booed, raps ungrateful fans," *Montreal Gazette* (9 September 1972), p. 25.

86 "Team Canada bitter in defeat," *Montreal Gazette* (9 September 1972), p. 1.

87 Ibid., p. 1.

88 Dick Beddoes, untitled, *The Globe and Mail* (11 September 1972), p. S1.

89 Neil Earle, "Hockey as Canadian popular culture: Team Canada 1972, television, and the Canadian identity," *Journal of Canadian Studies*, 30, (1995), p. 118.

90 Lawrence Martin, *The red machine: The Soviet Quest to Dominate Canada's Game* (Toronto: Random House, 1990), p. 125.

91 "Swedish papers write off Canada," *Winnipeg Free Press* (19 September 1972), p. 24.

92 "European hockey best?" *Vancouver Sun* (18 September 1972), p. 17.

93 Quoted in MacSkimming, *Cold War*, p. 137.

94 Jim Taylor, "Perreault joins Moscow exodus," *Vancouver Sun* (23 September 1972), p. 21.

95 Jim Taylor, untitled, *Vancouver Sun* (18 September 1972). p. 17.

96 Taylor, "Perreault joins Moscow exodus," p. 21.

97 Jim Taylor, untitled, *Vancouver Sun* (25 September 1972), p. 23.

98 "'Rude' Canadians criticized," *Vancouver Sun* (25 September 1972), p. 21.

 99 Quoted in MacSkimming, *Cold War*, p. 186.
100 Quoted in MacSkimming, *Cold War*, p. 244.
101 Dryden and MacGregor, *Home Game: Hockey and Life in Canada*, p. 192.
102 "All of a sudden they're sports nuts," *Winnipeg Free Press* (28 September 1972), p. 56.
103 Gruneau and Whitson, *Hockey Night in Canada*, p. 263.
104 Ibid., p. 253.
105 Vipond, "Bring on Europeans," p. 40.
106 "Barrett Cheers Victory," *Winnipeg Free Press* (29 September 1972), p. 54.
107 As cited in Wilson, *27 Remarkable Days*, p. 278.
108 Toby Miller, Geoffrey Lawrence, Jim McKay and David Rowe, *Globalization and Sport* (Sage: London, 2001), p. 55.
109 "In the end – superb, winning hockey," *The Globe and Mail*, p. 39.
110 Nevertheless, the Summit Series stimulated substantial interest with respect to the usefulness of sport as a diplomatic tool. As Macintosh and Hawes note, the 1972 Summit Series provided the "Department of External Affairs with its first taste of formal involvement with international sport" and "also provided the impetus for the creation of the International Sports Relations desk." Macintosh and Hawes, *Sport and Canadian Diplomacy*, p. 35.
111 Victor Mackie, "PM Cheers," *Winnipeg Free Press* (29 September 1972), p. 1.
112 Philip Moore, "Practical nostalgia and the critique of commodification: On the 'Death of Hockey' and the National Hockey League," *The Australian Journal of Anthropology*, 13, (2002), p. 313.
113 Cynthia Sugars, "Marketing Ambivalence: Molson Breweries Go Postcolonial," in *Canadian Cultural Poesis: Essays on Canadian Culture*, eds. Garry Sherbert, Annie Gerin, and Sheila Petty (Waterloo: Wilfred Laurier University Press, 2006), p. 128.
114 Recently, another outpouring of nationalism occurred with the release of Molson Breweries' infamous beer commercial "The Rant," which ran in 2000 as part of the company's "I am Canadian" advertising campaign. "The Rant" articulated Canadian identity as distinct from the US, but from a dominant, Anglo, white, middle-class, heterosexist, and male perspective.
115 Gruneau and Whitson, *Hockey Night in Canada*, p. 277.
116 Ibid., p. 2.
117 Howard Ramos and Kevin Gosine, "'The Rocket': Newspaper coverage of the death of a Quebec cultural icon, A Canadian hockey player," *Journal of Canadian Studies*, 36(4), (2001), p. 28.
118 Jay Scherer and Steven J. Jackson, "From corporate welfare to national interest: Newspaper analysis of the public subsidization of NHL hockey debate in Canada," *Sociology of Sport Journal*, 21, (2004): pp. 36–60.

Chapter 10

"One day, when the Yankees ..."*

Cuban baseball, the United States and the Cold War

Milton H. Jamail

One day, when the Yankees accept peaceful coexistence with our country, we shall beat them at baseball, too, and the advantages of revolutionary over capitalist sport will become clear to all.

(Fidel Castro, President of the Republic of Cuba, "974)

"You grow up with baseball all around you," Javier Méndez, an outfielder for the hometown Industriales, told me as he was preparing for a game in Havana's Estadio Latinoamericano. "It is part of being Cuban. Baseball is one of the roots of Cuban reality." And as Sigfredo Barros, the baseball beat writer since the mid-1980s for *Granma*, Cuba's official government newspaper, explained, "In Cuba, baseball is more than a sport. It is part of the culture; it is part of our national pride."

It is difficult to find a family in Cuba that does not include a member who loves baseball. Wherever one goes in Cuba, there are young boys playing baseball, and people talk about the game constantly in every corner of the island. Baseball even influences the way the people talk. "When something goes wrong, you might say to a friend, 'They caught you off base,' or to a person who is nervous, 'You've lost control, you need to throw a strike.' And when someone is facing a difficult situation, he is *en 3 y 2* [facing a full count]," explained Miguel Valdés who, until 1997, was technical director of *equipo Cuba* – the Cuban national team.

The Cubans have a great term for a rhubarb. They call it a *cámara húngara*, named after the heated discussions in the Hungarian Parliament during the 1930s. Also, when I asked for the Cuban equivalent of *donnybrook*, I was told it is the common slang word for a brawl, *bronca*. It is, coincidentally, the same word the Cubans use to describe the bizarre relations they've had with the US government over the past forty years.

One hundred and thirty-five Cubans have played in the US major leagues, most between 1947, when the game was integrated, and 1961, when Fidel Castro abolished professional baseball. When the United States severed diplomatic relations

* This chapter was originally published in Milton Jamail's book *Full Count: Inside Cuban Baseball*, pp. 1–12 and 119–30. © 2000 by the Board of Trustees, Southern Illinois University, reprinted by permission.

with Cuba in 1961, the major leagues' main source of foreign players was cut off. With all of its talent now at home, Cuba became a powerhouse in amateur baseball, winning almost every international competition, including Olympic gold medals in Barcelona in 1992 and in Atlanta in 1996 (Cuba took the silver, behind the United States, in 2000 in Sydney and regained the gold in Athens in 2004).

In 1991, a few Cuban players began to defect and play professional baseball in the United States, but it was not until the performance of Florida Marlins pitcher Liván Hernández in the 1997 post-season and the success of Orlando Hernández with the Yankees in 1998 that the US media began to take notice of Cuban players' potential to reinvigorate baseball in the United States. When Liván Hernández struck out fifteen Atlanta Braves batters in the 1997 National League Championship Series, baseball fans in the United States were surprised and when the rookie Cuban defector went on to win the MVP in the World Series, fans wondered whether there were more players like him back in Cuba. When his half-brother, Orlando "El Duque" Hernández, was smuggled off the island in a small boat at the end of 1997, Cuban baseball became front-page news. In 1998, "El Duque" signed a four-year, $6.6-million contract with the New York Yankees in March, made his major league debut in June, and earned a victory in the World Series in October.

Although Cuba has been off-limits to Major League Baseball for almost forty years, all thirty clubs look forward to the possibility of once again having access to Cuban players. For the baseball industry, Cuba represents the most important frontier in the increasingly important global search for players. Cuba will likely soon become the number one source of foreign-born players for the US big leagues.

Baseball was neither imposed on the Cuban people before 1959 nor delivered by the triumph of the Cuban Revolution. For more than 125 years, baseball in the United States and baseball in Cuba have been intertwined. The first Latino in US professional baseball was Cuban Estéban Bellán, who played with the Troy Haymakers in 1872, and US major league teams played exhibition games in Cuba as early as 1890. African Americans played in Cuba at the turn of the century, and Cuban blacks, excluded from Major League Baseball, played in the US Negro Leagues. After Jackie Robinson broke the color barrier in 1947, dark-skinned Cubans such as Orestes "Minnie" Miñoso were actively recruited.

[...] There are still two major hurdles to a full renewal of this relationship. First, the Cuban government clings to an ideology of no professionalism in sport. Because of this prohibition, once a player leaves Cuba, he cannot go back. And second, the US embargo and the Trading with the Enemy Act prohibit US organizations from any dealings with Cuba and keep Cuban ballplayers from taking their salaries home.

So close ...

I could see the lights of Havana directly ahead [and] the lights of the Florida Keys curved like a string of fireflies off to the northeast," recalls former US diplomat Wayne Smith about a flight from Miami. But he notes, "the nearness had been an illusion. Only minutes apart and on a clear night visible to the same eye, the United States and Cuba were nonetheless separated by an immense gulf.[1]

Although Cuba and the United States are only ninety miles apart, the island could just as well be on the other side of the world. Until recently, people in the United States had little or no information about contemporary Cuba. In general, Cubans know a bit more about the United States than their American counterparts know about Cuba. But for the most part, in the absence of formal diplomatic relations between the two countries and in the face of the hostility of the US government toward the regime of Fidel Castro, people in either country during the past forty years have relied on past images of each other or on images constructed by their respective governments.

Even though Cuba has dominated international amateur baseball since the mid-1960s and has done so in the shadow of the United States, Cuba's accomplishments remain obscured. Many reporters visiting Cuba look for exotic traits of the game there, and while Cuba is exotic and foreign, Cuban baseball is not. The rules are the same: nine men on a side, nine innings in a game, and sixty feet six inches from the pitcher's mound to home plate. Cuba used aluminum bats (for economic reasons) and the designated hitter (because the International Baseball Association uses it). While some terms, such as "home club," "double play," "hit" (*jit*), "strike," "hit-and-run," and "squeeze play" (*equiplay*), carry over from English, the positions are most often translated into Spanish. The infield, from first to third, consists of *primera* or *inicialista*. The shortstop is "short" (spelled *siol* in Cuba) or *torpedero*. Outfielders are called *jardineros* (gardeners) and may be referred to in either language: for example, "center fielder" or *jardinero central*. The catcher is the *receptor*, and the pitcher is the *lanzador* or *serpentinero*, named after the streamers thrown at parties.

One difference a US fan would notice while watching baseball in Cuba is that the first time a batter comes to the plate in a game, he will shake hands with the catcher and umpire. Another significant difference is that fans are loyal to teams based on seeing the same players year after year; there is no free agency in Cuba.

Then there are the names. A glance at the rosters of Cuba's development league – taxi squads to the teams in Cuba's main baseball circuit that are composed of players under the age of twenty-three – reveals names such as Yobal, Yuleski, Yosandry, Yohankis, Yoelsis, Yohandris, Yohanet, Yunier, and Yanier. And there are Yoelvis, Orelvis and, of course, Elvis. I asked Raúl Arce who, since the late 1960s, has been a reporter for *Juventud Rebelde*, a weekly newspaper, why there are so many unusual names among Cuban players. Like *Granma*'s Barros, Arce is a baseball beat writer, except that his beat includes all age groups. You might find Arce at the all-star game for the Cuban big leagues or at a tournament for 15 to 16-year-olds. When he travels abroad, it is usually with the younger teams. "It's hard to find any young people named José, Raúl, or Juan in Cuba today," remarked Arce, not really explaining why this phenomenon occurs, "and when you think about the unusual names, you have the famous case of the woman living in Guantánamo in the 1950s who named her son 'Usnavy' after seeing a US plane fly overhead. Another good one is 'Norge,' named after the American freezers. And then there was a time when there were a lot of Russian names like Vladimir, but that period is over."

Many fans in the United States want to know when Cuban players will return to play in professional baseball. Few are pleased with a necessarily imprecise answer, and even fewer are satisfied with an explanation that involves the complex political history of the two countries. However, it is essential to understand some basic facts about the recent political history of Cuba and US-Cuban diplomatic relations of the past forty years to adequately comprehend why US-Cuban baseball relations are so convoluted. Baseball also provides a window to view both the current economic crisis and the difficult transition to a new economy and, eventually, a new political order and a new relationship with the United States.

The "dollarization" of Cuba

Traveling to Cuba is not easy, is rarely predictable, and is always exciting. Because of the Trading with the Enemy Act, US citizens – with the exception of Cuban Americans on family visits, full-time journalists, and academics who request a special license from the US Department of the Treasury – are not allowed to travel to the island. Those persons travelling to Cuba who don't fall into the aforementioned categories are subject to steep fines and prison terms. Most trips to Cuba begin in Havana, and going to the Cuban capital is like going back in time. Even in its current state of disrepair, Havana is one of the most beautiful and romantic cities in the world. Unlike most other Caribbean destinations, there are no tour ships arriving daily.

Since the early 1990s, Cuba is a society in disintegration, and few, if any, of its residents have the slightest idea of where it is going. But the Cuban people, even in the midst of an economic crisis, are outgoing and cordial. Most are genuinely interested in discussing the United States and are extremely courteous to the few Americans they encounter.

On my first visit in 1979 as a tourist (permitted by a relaxation of travel restrictions during the Carter administration), I saw a country that was justifiably proud of its accomplishments – particularly in education and health care – and whose citizens, compared to other countries in Latin America, were relatively well-off. Aid from the Soviet Union, while not compensating for the losses caused by the US embargo, did cushion the shock and enabled Cubans to maintain a vision of better days ahead.

When I returned in July 1992 with the US Olympic baseball team, I was appalled. I saw a Cuba that had come to a standstill. In the wake of the Soviet Union's collapse, Cuba was struggling to survive. Cuba was in the *período especial* (special period), which was the excuse used for broken machinery and lack of goods and services. On that trip I went to Holguín, a city of 250,000 residents situated 500 miles to the east of Havana, for a US–Cuba baseball series. I cannot recall seeing a passenger car on the street during my three-day stay there. In Havana, there was also very little traffic on the streets and nothing to buy in the stores. There were frequent electrical black-outs, and there was aggressive prostitution – unlike anything I had seen in thirty years of travel in Latin America. Why, I asked, did the government object to selling the contract of baseball players, while it seemed to have no problem letting young Cubans sell their bodies?

As the Cuban economy entered a free fall, the government latched on to whatever it could for national pride and prestige. Baseball was its main asset. Whatever else, at least Cuba had the best amateur baseball team in the world.

When I returned in 1997, I expected to find a slightly different Cuba than the one I left four-and-a-half years earlier, but I was not prepared for the drastic changes I encountered. In 1993, the Cuban government began to allow the circulation of US dollars. Now there was wonderful Cuban food available in restaurants and in *paladares* (small family eateries). Almost anything was available for US dollars, but the only Cubans with access to dollars were people who worked in the tourist industry, sold handicrafts in street markets, or received dollars from family and friends overseas.

In 1998 and 1999, I saw a society even more divided between those with access to dollars and those who had to struggle to obtain the basic elements necessary for survival. Even medications prescribed by physicians in Cuba's highly touted health-care system had to be purchased in dollars. The "dollarization" was necessary to stop the economic free fall of the Cuban economy, but it also introduced a dynamic that is difficult for the Cuban government to control. By 1997, US dollars brought to the island either by tourists or through remittances – money sent to Cuba by family members living off the island – had far surpassed sugar as the number one source of foreign exchange for Cuba. Much of the dollar economy is controlled by hustlers who offer tourists everything from black-market cigars to prostitutes, while those citizens who remain loyal to the decaying socialist system and continue to support the Revolution are left out in the cold. While in the recent past the Cuban economy might have been ailing, the difficulties were, for the most part, shared collectively. Today, there are sharp cleavages in Cuban society, and those with access to dollars suffer less than those without access. More important, there is a growing sense in Cuba that the collective advances of the Cuban people have broken down into an individual struggle for survival. The sign on the left field wall in the Estadio Latinamericano – Havana's main ballpark – proclaiming *Somos de la misma casa* (We are all from the same house) clearly was wishful thinking.

How does this situation relate to Cuban baseball? The bottom line is that since Cuba legalized dollars in 1993, the position of baseball players in Cuban society has gone from privileged to underprivileged. Cuban players receive only a small salary, less than the equivalent of $30 a month, but it takes at least $120 a month to sustain a basic level of comfort in Havana. Cuban musicians and artists are allowed to come and go – and to bring dollars back into the country. University professors and medical doctors can become waiters in tourist hotels, hawk wares to tourists on the street, or bake cookies to sell to neighbors – and earn dollars. Baseball players are effectively excluded from this sector of the economy, and if they receive money from the United States, they become suspect for fear they are planning to defect. They must remain poor to be above suspicion.

When *equipo Cuba* lost the title game at the Intercontinental Cup in Barcelona in 1997, breaking a ten-year undefeated streak in official international competitions, some observers in the United States attributed the decline in Cuban baseball to the defections that began when pitcher René Arocha left in 1991. But the two main problems facing Cuban baseball are, ironically, Cuba's abundance of players with little possibility of advancement and the unwillingness of the Cuban government to provide the necessary economic stimulus for players to remain in the country. When the government allowed some players to "retire," play in amateur leagues overseas, and bring home a portion of their earnings, it recognized the nature of the problem. But Cuba's very discerning and demanding fans missed some of their star players and quickly noticed the decline in play in the Serie Nacional, and they stayed away in droves.

The problems the government encounters in baseball are linked to every other aspect of the crisis facing Cuban society and cannot be solved through a quick fix. The situation poses a challenge for the Cuban government that is not easily surmounted. If Cuba is to remain a world baseball power, Cuban teams must travel outside of the country. And when they do, the government runs the risk of players not returning. The temptation is, of course, to select players not likely to defect, but the result is a national team not selected entirely on athletic ability. As one Cuban fan told the *New York Times*, "It's not enough to be a good guy and a good comrade. You've got to perform, too."[2]

One logical but currently impossible solution would be to allow the players to go to the United States. The best baseball in the world is played in the heart of the island's principal enemy. And even if the Cuban government encouraged its players to go to the United States, because of the blockade they could do so only as defectors. Baseball also has become *parte de la bronca*.

The revolution of 1959

Although many in the United States think of Cuba as a small island ruled by Fidel Castro that produces exquisite cigars and magnificent baseball players – neither of which has free access to the US market – the reality is more complex. In fact, Cuba is not small. Although its widest section is only about 75 miles, the island stretches in length some 750 miles – about the same distance as between New York City and Chicago. Its almost 12 million people are a blend of European- and African-origin populations. They live both in large cities such as Havana, with a population of 2.5 million, and spread out across the beautiful countryside, which is dotted by palm trees. While tobacco is the crop many Americans would like to freely savor, sugar dominates the island's history.

Cuba became one of Spain's first colonies in the New World in the early 1500s. In 1902, it was also the last country to receive its independence from Spain. Cuba was dominated by the United States, first with the occupying forces during the Spanish–American War (of 1898), then by the 1903 Platt Amendment, which allowed the United States to intervene directly in the internal affairs of the island's government. Significantly, in 1959, Cuba became the first country in Latin America to define the interests of its own people ahead of the interests of foreign investors.

Although the revolutionary forces led by Fidel Castro did not take control of the Cuban government until 2 January 1959, the struggle to overthrow the dictatorship of Fulgencio Batista began almost six years earlier. On 26 July 1953, Fidel and a group of 165 revolutionaries attacked the Moncada military barracks in the eastern city of Santiago de Cuba. Historians have described the attack as daring and spectacular. Although it was a failure, it propelled Fidel Castro into the leadership of the armed opposition.[3] "The nation was horrified by the governmental repression and moved by the daring, if reckless, action of the young Cubans," notes historian Marifeli Pérez-Stable. "Fidel Castro especially captured the popular imagination."[4]

After the overthrow of Batista on 1 January 1959, Fidel's revolutionary agenda soon brought Cuba into a collision course with the United States. By January 1961, the United States broke diplomatic relations with Cuba, and they have not been reestablished. Soon after, in April 1961, the United States sponsored an attempt to overthrow the Castro government. The Bay of Pigs debacle was based on the faulty premise that Cubans on the island would rally around an invading force. Although the invasion failed, the Cuban government's understanding that the United States would continue to undermine the gains made by the new government brought about a closer relationship between Cuba and the Soviet Union. This relationship led to the Cuban Missile Crisis of October 1962, which brought the world to the edge of nuclear war.

The focus of the antagonistic relationship between the United States and Cuba is Fidel Castro. By 1999 in his fortieth year in power, Fidel, who turned 80 in August 2006, has outlasted nine US presidents – Eisenhower, Kennedy, Johnson, Nixon, Ford, Carter, Reagan, Bush Snr. and Clinton – and may still be in charge when George W. Bush leaves office. In addition to the Bay of Pigs attempt, the US government has been involved in efforts to destroy sectors of Cuban agricultural and livestock production and has hatched several plots to embarrass and even assassinate Fidel. "Castro's continuing interest in baseball was noted by the CIA and became the basis for some of the agency's assassination plans," wrote former US Senator Eugene McCarthy. "Our operative tried first to get him to play catch with a baseball loaded with explosives" [5] Another plot had the CIA spraying LSD in a Havana television studio to make it appear that Fidel had gone mad while addressing the Cuban people. Yet another effort involved the CIA's contamination of a box of Fidel's favorite cigars in 1960 "with a botulinum toxin so potent that a person would die after putting one in his mouth."[6] The cigars were never delivered.

In addition, the United States has maintained an embargo on Cuba for almost forty years, even though at the end of the century, the United States is the one now isolated. While most nations of the world – including our two closest neighbors, Canada and Mexico – openly trade with Cuba, in 1997 the United States began to tighten the embargo with the passing of the Helms-Burton law.

Why does major league baseball need to import players?

The baseball industry, like most other multinational enterprises, does not confine itself within the borders of one country. While some US major league teams go into Latin America, Asia, Australia, and Europe as a cost-cutting measure, the baseball industry also must recruit talent overseas because it suffers from a shortage of quality players at home. Some analysts believe that sports talent in the United States is spread too thin, with US youngsters playing basketball, football, volleyball and increasingly, soccer, in addition to baseball. Others see kids in the United States as too pampered, unwilling to put in the long hours and hard work necessary for success in baseball and choosing instead to spend their afternoons playing video games or watching television. Whatever the reasons, the talent pool for baseball in the United States clearly is shrinking, thus making it necessary to look elsewhere for players. To be competitive today, almost all major league organizations consider active participation in the Latin market – basically, the Dominican Republic, Venezuela, Mexico, and Panama – essential, and many scouts believe Cuba will be the cornerstone of that market.

Strip away the forty-year-old political impasse between the United States and Cuba and two facts about baseball emerge: Cuba produces a surplus of players, and the United States does not produce enough quality players to fill out the rosters of thirty major league teams. The solution to both problems? Cuban players reentering US professional baseball. When relations between the two countries improve, Cuba will become the number one source of foreign-born talent in US professional baseball. The world's largest producer of baseball players outside of the United States will be reunited with the world's largest consumer of baseball.

Statistics provided by the baseball industry show that almost 35 percent of players in professional baseball at all levels, from rookie to big league, were born outside of the United States. (Puerto Rico is included in this figure.) Baseball clearly is no longer just a US sport; it is an international one that is played at its highest level in the United States.

But why Cuba?

Although Cubans really only had access to the major leagues between 1947 and 1960, 135 Cubans have played in the big leagues. Before 1947, only light-skinned Cubans were allowed to play; after 1960, only defectors. One can only imagine how many players from this baseball-crazy island would have reached the pinnacle of baseball had barriers not been in place.

Cuba's best athletes still choose baseball, and the Cuban people's deep love and understanding of the game permeate the island and ensure that baseball will continue with succeeding generations. These facts, coupled with Cuba's creation of a very effective system for identifying and developing young players, guarantees that Major League Baseball will keep its attention focused on the island. For all its defects, the Cuban political system after 1959 greatly expanded educational opportunities and availability of health care. The result is a more literate and healthier population that that of the Dominican Republic, which is currently the leading foreign supplier of players to the baseball industry in the United States.

"Cuban baseball today is at a crossroads – está en 3 y 2. It is facing a full count," Gilberto Dihigo, a Cuban baseball journalist whose father, Martín Dihigo, is enshrined at Cooperstown (the National Baseball Hall of Fame and Museum in New York state), told me. "Baseball will never die in Cuba, but it needs to be renovated." What is it about Cuba's baseball system that needs to be overhauled? Dihigo remembers an interview in the early 1980s with Carlos Rafael Rodríguez, the third-highest-ranking Cuban government official and clearly the Cuban leader who best understood the United States. Rodríguez, who died in late 1997, told Dihigo, "If you want to learn about technological development in baseball and the latest strategy, you have to talk with people in the United States. You have to give credit where credit is due." Cuban baseball officials understand this fact, even if the country's top political leaders are unwilling or unable to deal with it. Es parte de la bronca.

The image of Liván Hernández standing on the mound before the opening game of the 1997 World Series and the fact that it was seen, even if only on video-tape, in Cuba ensure that young Cuban players will continue to dream about going to the United States. And the $312,042 share earned by Orlando "El Duque" Hernández for playing in the 1998 World Series means that winning the gold medal in the Olympics may no longer be as satisfactory a reward – especially given the economic hardship players must endure in Cuba.

Even so, there is something less tangible and more romantic about baseball in Cuba. One evening, I went to the Estadio Latinoamericano at 6.00 p.m. for a 7.30 p.m. game. Most of the Industriales players were standing around in the parking lot just outside the entrance to the ballpark. Dressed in their uniform pants and T-shirts, they were intently watching a serious game of street baseball being played by men between the ages of eighteen and thirty-five. There was no field or base-lines, and there were only pieces of cardboard to mark the bases. No one hounded the Industriales players for autographs, and everyone was focused on the batter. With the sun setting on a beautiful winter afternoon in Havana, with Cuba's best players mingling with pick-up players, it was baseball at its best, harking back to images of the game long past in the United States.

"Bring on the gold rush": major league baseball and Cuba

In the 1950s, one scout – Joe Cambria – and one team – the Washington Senators – focused on one country – Cuba. There were so many Cubans play-ing for the Senators that, on 23 July 1960, the team was able to record the big leagues' only all-Cuban triple play. In the third inning with no one out and runners at first and second, Kansas City outfielder Whitey Herzog hit a line drive to pitcher Pedro Ramos, who tossed the ball to first baseman Julio Becquer, who relayed the throw to shortstop José Valdivielso covering at sec-ond.[7]

"I was the first to hit into an all-Cuban triple play," Herzog told me when I asked him about the event almost thirty years later, adding, "and the last." But maybe not. Although Cuba has been off-limits to Major League Baseball for over forty years, all organizations look forward to the prospect of again having access to the island's players.

Cuba was a major supplier of players to US professional baseball prior to 1959. Although a few players, such as Tony Oliva, Tony Pérez, Luis Tiant, Jr., and Cookie Rojas, were in the minor league pipeline and made their major league debuts after Fidel came to power, and although Bert Campaneris and Tito Fuentes left in 1962, for the past forty years Cuban baseball talent generally has remained on the island.

Fred Claire, who until 1998 was the general manager and executive vice pres-ident of the Los Angeles Dodgers, the leading team in signing Latin American players, believes Cuba will be a major source of players for US baseball. "If the talent was available in Cuba, and all clubs could go in and scout, and sign or draft, I can only envision a gold rush."

To get an idea of how much talent there is in Cuba, one need only look at Puerto Rico and the Dominican Republic. If Puerto Rico, with only one-third of Cuba's population, had only amateur ball, Juan González, Bernie Williams,

Sandy and Roberto Alomar, Edgar Martínez, Iván Rodríguez, and Carlos Baerga would not be playing in the major leagues. The Dominican Republic, with three million fewer residents than Cuba, has 1500 players signed to US professional baseball contracts. How many players would Cuba, with a much more highly developed baseball system, produce? One US scout told me he thought each US organization could sign at least twenty Cuban players – from young prospects through major league talent.

Although the US baseball commissioner's office has a ban on talking with Cuban players, this doesn't keep scouts from pulling out their radar guns and stopwatches whenever they have an opportunity to see Cuban teams in international competition. Cuba's junior team, composed of 17- and 18-year-olds, also has players abroad in international competitions, and major league scouts are always in attendance. There were sixty scouts at a tournament in Monterrey, Mexico, in 1992, where 17-year-old Liván Hernández threw a no-hitter.

But the only players fans in the United States know anything about are the defectors – principally Liván and Orlando Hernández, Rolando Arrojo, and Rey Ordóñez – and a very small core of the stars of Cuban baseball, the players who have been the backbone of *equipo Cuba* for the past decade – Omar Linares, Orestes Kindelán, Antonio Pacheco, and Germán Mesa.

Major League Baseball is more interested in the young Cuban players who are unknown in the United States. More than 800 players participate in the Serie Nacional and Serie de Desarrollo, and US teams have scouting reports on only a handful of them. Virtually nothing is known about Cuban players between the ages of fifteen and eighteen, the prime ages for signing professional contracts.

What sets the Cuban players apart from other players coming out of Latin America? "Physically, they are faster and they have tremendous reflexes. Mentally, they are very quick, and they have an intuition to play baseball," says Andrés Reiner, assistant to the general manager of the Houston Astros, and the scout who established the Astros' highly successful Venezuelan baseball academy. Reiner, who has had the opportunity to watch Cuban players for the past decade, is also impressed with the educational level of the Cuban players and the fact that they come from a disciplined system. He believes this would give them an advantage in making the difficult adjustment to playing in the United States.

But like Cuban cigars in the United States, the few Cuban players who have defected have often been overpriced. Why are Cuban players so overvalued? Because they are exotic, writes columnist Tracy Ringolsby: "Put the word Cuban in front a player's name, and the teams are ready to add zeroes behind the dollar sign on their contracts."[8]

Most scouts agree it is difficult to get an accurate reading on just how good Cuban players are because they use aluminum bats, face poor competition, and lack state-of-the-art instruction. But they know the raw talent is there. "Who does

Cuba face in its international competitions? The US team is mainly composed of university students with little international experience," said René Arocha. "On the other hand, the Cuban team has played together for a long time and has players who would have been in the big leagues."

"Cuban baseball needs to go to the next level. It is better than you see played on the field at international competitions," *Deportivamente* producer Pedro Cruz González told me, echoing a sentiment heard throughout the island. "When you realize that you are going to win, you don't play as hard."

One Cuban fan complained that baseball on the island was *estancado* (stagnant). While he thought Germán Mesa was a better shortstop than Rey Ordóñez, he felt Ordóñez's three years of experience in the major leagues had allowed him to bypass Mesa. Tito, an elderly member of the Peña, explained it in a more colourful manner. "Germán Mesa has finished at a very good prep school," said Tito, "while Rey Ordóñez has already completed his university degree."

"In 2000, we will have a good team. I believe our team could stay in the game with anybody," said Miguel Valdés. "The Olympics are a short event, and we are specialists at playing short events. But playing against major leaguers is something we have never had to do." The ultimate test would be to play against a US major league team, and that had never happened until the Baltimore Orioles visited Havana in March 1999. But efforts to have a big league team visit Cuba began as early as 1960.

Torrential rains in Florida in March 1959 forced the cancellation of so many spring training games that Cincinnati Reds general manager Gabe Paul called Bobby Maduro, president of the Cuban Sugar Kings of the Triple A International League, to ask whether he could take his Cincinnati team to Cuba for the weekend. Madura was thrilled, and with only one day's notice, arranged a three-game series in Havana at the Gran Stadium, now the Estadio Latinoamericano, between Cincinnati and the Los Angeles Dodgers. Rain delayed the Reds' arrival, and eventually only two games were played.

In the first game, Don Drysdale pitched seven innings and "cha-cha-cha-ed through the ranks of the Reds with virtual disdain," reported the *Los Angeles Times*[9] The Dodgers won 3–2. The next day, Sandy Koufax pitched five innings, and Carl Erskine got the victory in the Dodgers' 4–3 win.

Havana fans were delighted to see Duke Snider, Jim Gilliam, and John Roseboro. And the *Times*'s game story featured gems such as "several score of pistol packin' rebels were in the stadium today." The games were played less than three months after Fidel Castro had ousted Batista.

Since the Reds and Dodgers left Havana on 21 March 1959, no US teams had played on the island, notwithstanding numerous efforts to send major league teams to Cuba, until the Orioles' visit in 1999. "I believe it was 1960 when Baltimore was going to play Cincinnati here in Havana," recalled Marcelo Sánchez in early 1999. "It was called off because the proceeds from the game were going to be used for the agrarian reform movement in Cuba and there was some disagreement over that."

Marcelo promised to check on the details, and within a few weeks had sent a packet of newspaper clips on the Baltimore–Cincinnati series that did not happen.

In November 1959, it was announced that the two teams would play a three-game series in Havana beginning 28 March 1960. Baltimore general manager Lee MacPhail canceled the games at the last minute, stating that some of the Baltimore players refused to participate due to the unsafe conditions in the country. [10] Bobby Maduro fired off a telegram to Cincinnati general manager Gabe Paul thanking him for his efforts, and another to MacPhail castigating him for calling off the games and thus spoiling the opportunity to help alleviate the tension between the two countries. It was not the last time Maduro would be upset by US professional baseball during the year.

In July 1960, Maduro's Cuban Sugar Kings franchise was relocated to Jersey City, New Jersey. US Secretary of State Christian Herter asked Commissioner of Baseball Ford Frick to take the step, ostensibly to protect US players from possible anti-American aggression in Cuba. The decision was made only a few days after President Eisenhower eliminated the sugar quota (the above-market price paid for sugar holdings on the island.[11] It is indeed ironic that the United States took the Sugar Kings from Cuba at the same time that Cuba took back sugar production on the island.

Later in 1960, Herter pressured Frick to prohibit US players from competing in the Cuban winter league. In 1960–61, Habana, Almendares, Marianao, and Cienfuegos played with only Cuban players for the first time since 1905. It was the last professional season in Cuba.

There were no attempts by US professional teams to go to Cuba during the rest of the 1960s as conflict between the two countries deepened. In 1971, Preston Gómez, then manager of the San Diego Padres, announced plans to take a major league all-star team, including Cubans Tony Pérez, Tony Taylor, Tony Oliva, and Leo Cárdenas, to Havana. The tour would have "good will value for the United States similar to the recent table tennis team's trip to Red China," said Gómez.[12] While Gómez received the approval of Commissioner Bowie Kuhn, he was denied permission by the US government.

Pedro Gómez was born on a sugar plantation – Central Preston – in eastern Cuba and, because everybody called him Preston, officially adopted that name when he became a US citizen. Gómez was signed by Joe Cambria and, in 1944, played eight games for the Washington Senators. He later managed the Padres, the Houston Astros, and the Chicago Cubs. He has made regular visits to Cuba for the past four decades and, in 1999, supplied the Cubans with dozens of wooden bats as they prepared both for the new changes in international baseball and to face professional teams.

In early 1975, Gómez met with Cuban baseball officials who expressed interest in having a US professional team play a series in Cuba that March. The US government was also very interested, and a State Department official noted that "US major league baseball has a magic value in projecting a positive image of the US wherever the sport is played."[13]

Commissioner Kuhn met with Cuban baseball officials in Mexico City in February. In addition to the series in question, Kuhn got the impression that "the Cubans are thinking about their relationship with US professional baseball. They have done their best to develop their talents, but being shut out of professional ball here hurts. They would now like Cuban players to be able to look forward to the opportunity to play some day in our major leagues."[14]

Secretary of State Henry Kissinger made it clear that he opposed a US team going to Cuba but nevertheless asked the State Department to send their arguments as to why it should happen. "The Chinese ping-pong players were accepted by the US public as a good way to break the ice between two nations separated by decades of hostility. Baseball with Cuba would serve a similar purpose in bridging the gap between the Bay of Pigs and a new relationship with Castro," read a secret memorandum prepared for Kissinger. [15]

On 24 February 1975, the game was called off by Kissinger, and Kuhn transmitted this decision to Cuban baseball officials. Over the next year, Kuhn persisted in his efforts for a series with the Cubans. "The purpose of the trip would be to engender cordial relations between baseball in Cuba and in the United States. There would be no political aspect or purpose," [16] wrote Kuhn. A game scheduled for March 1976, which was to have been televised by ABC, was canceled when Kissinger was angered by Cuba's military involvement in the Angolan civil war. [17]

Chicago White Sox owner Bill Veeck made a quick trip to Cuba to evaluate talent in 1977. Although he returned convinced that Cuban players were not going to be available to the major leagues, he was optimistic about the possibilities of an exhibition game.

When President Jimmy Carter took office in January 1977, US–Cuba relations encountered a four-year period of semi-thawing, and the travel ban was lifted for a brief period. In March 1977, newly appointed Secretary of State Cyrus Vance said he thought visits by US athletes to Cuba would be constructive and promised a prompt decision regarding a proposed visit by the New York Yankees to Cuba in April. [18] If Fidel had had his way, the *New York Times* headline might have read, "Yankees Land in Havana as Mr. Castro Awaits with Open Arms."

"Before the Carter opening Castro had mentioned, several times in fact, that he really would like to have the Yankees come down and play against the Cuban national team," recalled Wayne Smith who, as the head of the US Interests Section in Havana at the time, was the United States' top diplomat in Cuba. Smith was first assigned to the US embassy in Havana in 1958 and was also there when the embassy boarded its windows and closed in 1961. "With the Carter opening, having an American major league team go to Cuba seemed natural. But Bowie Kuhn put the skids to the Yankees going down, saying it would not be fair in that it would give the Yankees an advantage in recruiting. He thought it would be better to put together an all-star team," Smith told me.[19]

"If our government is in favor of it, I don't see how he [Kuhn] could stop a team from going," said Yankees owner George Steinbrenner who, in 1977, made a trip to Cuba to meet with sports officials. "If no players are going to come out, then no team can get a jump on the talent there." And New York Yankees president Gabe Paul, the man responsible for the last major league game in Cuba in 1959, was miffed because it was obvious the Cubans wanted to face the Yankees, not an all-star team. [20]

When the Cubans stated that no team would have an advantage in recruiting because they were not interested in selling their players, Kuhn responded by stating that there would be no games if Cuban players were not free to negotiate contracts to play in the United States. Clearly Kuhn was receiving pressure from others, especially Los Angeles Dodgers owner Walter O'Malley, to prevent the Yankees from going. [21]

The idea of a game against a Cuban team was resuscitated in 1978. Gabe Paul, now Cleveland Indians team president, had proposed to play three exhibition games against a Cuban team in Tucson, Arizona, during the first week of April. Kuhn referred the decision to Major League Baseball's executive council. By the end of March, the commissioner's office had taken no action on the request, Kuhn had offered no comment, and the games were not played. [22] Smith remembers that Kuhn had received mixed signals from the Carter administration, with the State Department favoring the games, while the national Security Council was opposed.

In May 1978, it was announced in Cuba that *equipo Cuba* would play against the Montreal Expos in Montreal that August, but the game was canceled in July reportedly over a failure to reach agreement over television rights. In 1982, the Seattle Mariners canceled a spring exhibition game against a Cuban team. Mariners president Dan O'Brien, Sr, said it was pressure from Cuban Americans and not Kuhn that caused the game to be called off. "They just brought up the usual things about the placement of missiles in Cuba aimed at American cities and wondering how we could be part of it. We felt it was in the best interest not to stir that situation up," said O'Brien. [23]

Cuban fans mention Milwaukee, Texas, and California as other teams that made attempts to play in Cuba. [24] In 1997 and 1998, the Baltimore Orioles requested permission to go to the island and were denied on both occasions by the Treasury Department. In February 1999, the Anaheim Angels put their hat in the ring once again, asking the US Treasury Department for a license that would allow club officials to travel to Cuba to negotiate a game. Preston Gómez is a special assistant to the general manager of the Angels.

Disagreements between the US government agencies, disputes among the owners of major league teams, and protest from Cuban Americans had thwarted any efforts at baseball diplomacy. The central figure for many of these efforts was commissioner Bowie Kuhn, who would have the last word in the form of a 1977 directive: "No discussion or negotiation with anyone in Cuba regarding the signing of any player to a professional contract is permitted. When and if Cuban players become available, an orderly system will be created for the allocation of player talent."[25]

The Kuhn Directive is still in effect in the early twenty-first century.

Astros 1977 Havana trip

While no US team had played a game in Cuba since 1959, the Houston Astros did go to Cuba in late 1977 for a series of clinics in Havana. Astros president Tal Smith, then the club's general manager, remembers being in the office of a Cuban sports official who asked, "Do you want to say hello to Fidel?" The official handed the phone to Smith, who was greeted by the *comandante en jefe*. Castro expressed his hopes that the trip was going well and apologized for not meeting with the Astro delegation, but he assured Smith that he would see that all their needs were met.[26]

Smith's interest in Cuba dates back to 1958 when he worked in minor league development for the Cincinnati Reds, who had a working agreement with Bobby Maduro and the Cuban Sugar Kings.

The 1977 trip was arranged by Dave LeFevre, who later was part of the ownership group led by John McMullin that bought the Houston team in 1979. LeFevre was also the person who told the New York Yankees in 1977 that Fidel was interested in having them play in Cuba.[27] "Dave and I had established a relationship when I was with the Yankees," said Smith. "He was a lawyer in New York and his maternal grandfather was Cyrus Eaton, and Cyrus Eaton had an association with Castro. We were able to do this through Dave's contacts at the State Department and in Cuba."

The Astros contingent included manager Bill Virdon, coaches Mel Wright, Deacon Jones, and Bob Lillis, and players Bob Watson, Ken Forsch, and Enos Cabel. Virdon played in the Cuban winter league in 1955, and Lillis was on the Dodger team that played in Havana in 1959. The players and coaches spent a week in Cuba conducting clinics, working with the Cuban national team, and watching games at the Estadio Latinoamericano. Many Cuban fans recall seeing those clinics. One of those fans is Asdrubal Baró, who played in the US minor leagues in the 1940s and 1950s, including a stint with the Double A Houston Buffs in 1956.

Tal Smith did not tell Commissioner Kuhn that the Astros were going to Cuba because he didn't want to get turned down. "It was quite an experience. It was done on the spur of the moment because I felt that if we made a lot of noise about this before we went down, there would be somebody who would find a reason for us not to do it."

"Our interest was, of course, in getting a firsthand look at the Cuban talent, try to establish a relationship, and to foster that relationship in the event that the situation would open up in the future," said Smith.

Real baseball diplomacy

Wayne Smith, then chief of the US diplomatic mission in Havana, recalls a small but telling event at a 1979 international baseball tournament during a particularly tense moment in US–Cuba relations. "When the American team came on to the field, the 'Star-Spangled Banner' was played, and the Cuban crowd stood in silent respect." A Cuban fan leaned over and whispered to Smith: "You can't raise your flag over us by force, but you can through baseball."[28]

Cuban fans have great respect for US players who outduel their own heroes, and none more than for Jim Abbott, who defeated the Cuban team in Havana in 1987. "Jim Abbott is so popular," one fan told me, "that if the Cuban government had any money, it would erect a statue to him."

In 1991, "Welcome Home Desert Storm" signs were raised next to the "Welcome Cuban Baseball Team" banners in the motel where *equipo Cuba* was housed in Millington, Tennessee, just north of Memphis. This small town opened its arms and hearts to *equipo Cuba*, the pride and joy of the United States' number one enemy. The fans stood silently while the Cuban national anthem played and a Cuban flag, shipped express from the Cuban Interests Section in Washington, flew above the Olympic training site.

The people of Millington, many of whom were stationed or worked at the Memphis Naval Air Station at the time, were genuinely interested in becoming acquainted with their guests. A journalist pressed into service as a translator strained to comprehend the visitors' rapid Cuban Spanish and the hosts' Southern drawl. But there was no need to translate the smiles on both sides. I remember Cuban second baseman Antonio Pacheco, in the on-deck circle, motioning to the young US batboy (the two did not speak each other's language) to share with him a folding chair reserved for players.

The reality is that while the two governments are at loggerheads, Cubans and US citizens like each other – in part because of baseball. The tournament in Millington was baseball diplomacy at its best. "We need to stop the Cold War with Cuba. We need to break that barrier down, and we can start with baseball," said Dick Case, then executive director of the United States Baseball Federation, the national body representing all amateur baseball, told me. Case was the mastermind behind the annual USA–Cuba baseball series that was held each summer between 1986 and 1996. Mr Case would make a fine diplomat.

"Several years ago we decided that to beat Cuba in baseball we had to play them head to head on a regular basis," explained Case. "I called Mr. Morales of the Cuban Baseball Federation. He said they wanted to set up an exchange to share ideas. It was in the best interest of both countries. They know that we are not after their players," said Case.

The Cuban team was set to make an eight-game tour in July 1997 but canceled the day they were supposed to arrive. Although there was much speculation that the Cubans were concerned about defections, the cancellation came on the same day that two bombs exploded in Havana hotels. And when the Cuban team turned down an invitation to go to Tucson, Arizona – the new USA baseball headquarters – to play a five-game series against Team USA in the summer of 1998, it appeared unlikely that this form of baseball diplomacy would continue.

"I think baseball can be very useful. It is a passion we share, and that the Cubans don't share with any other major country," observed Wayne Smith. "Obviously, without the will on both sides to move in the direction of a better relationship, baseball can't do much to bridge the gap. But given some will, baseball can help because it is something we have in common." But no matter how much goodwill exists on both sides, the US embargo of Cuba remains a structural impediment to improved relations between the two countries.

The embargo

Few baseball fans know or care much about the embargo, but it is the fundamental barrier impeding improved baseball relations between Cuba and the United States. Imposed unilaterally in 1962 in an attempt to pressure Fidel Castro out of government, it would appear that is has been a failure. Ten US presidents and over forty years later, Castro is still in power, and almost every country in the world trades with Cuba – except the United States.

On 8 July 1963, the US government issued the Cuban Assets Control Regulations under the Trading with the Enemy Act. The regulations are administered by the US Treasury Department's Office of Foreign Assets Control. "The basic goal of the sanctions is to isolate Cuba economically and deprive it of US dollars," reads an overview of the regulations published by the Treasury Department. [29] In practical terms, this means no US baseball organization is allowed to engage in any transactions with Cuba unless it requests a specific license. No club may enter into contractual relations with Cuba or Cuban nationals. And if a Cuban ballplayer signed a multimillion-dollar contract with a US team, he would be prohibited from sending money home to Cuba without a Treasury Department license. The maximum penalties for ignoring US government rules are ten years in prison and a $250,000 fine.

With the passage of the Helms-Burton legislation in 1996, President Clinton gave up his authority to change policy on Cuba without the approval of both houses of Congress. No representative or senator wants to be known as having given in to Castro – a charge they would surely face in a reelection bid.

The Cuban government's position of not allowing baseball players to sign professional contracts also presents a problem for renewed contact between Cuba and Major League Baseball. "Until Fidel dies, I don't see any way that would allow Cuban players to become professional," said Dihigo. "And now with Helms-Burton, *menos* [less]! *Menos!* During all these years, the Helms-Burton law and the embargo have served to strengthen the Cuban Revolution. It has not weakened it because the people have united behind nationalism, the same theme that Cubans rallied around against the Spanish over one hundred years ago," added Dihigo.

While there has been a great deal of discussion regarding "baseball diplomacy," especially in the wake of "ping-pong diplomacy" with China during the Nixon administration, there has really never been any serious effort at using baseball to ease the tension between the United States and Cuba. Both countries have attempted to use baseball as a weapon to gain some advantage over the other. Fidel has long harboured the idea that he can defeat his principal enemy at their own game. US administrations from Eisenhower to Clinton have utilized baseball as a political tool, never as a move toward a real thawing of relations.

I recalled the words of sports talk radio producer Pedro Cruz González when I asked why major league baseball could not be discussed on his show. "*Es parte de la bronca* [It is part of the donnybrook]," he answered. *La bronca* is the best way to describe the impasse between the two countries. In both countries, any interest in or close relations with the other are viewed with suspicion. *La bronca* explains why US Customs agents at the Miami airport harangue and hassle legal travellers to Cuba, and why Cuban academics who study the United States are not allowed to communicate with the US Interests Section in Havana. *La bronca* simply reflects more than forty years of hostile relations between the United States and Cuba during which the two governments have used their hatred of each other to define the relationship. Baseball is, indeed, *parte de la bronca*.

Notes

Fidel Castro's remark at the start of the chapter can be found at:
http://www.telegraph.co.uk/sport/main.jhtml?xml=/sport/2004/07/30/sobren30.xml
Thanks to Sean Mendez for help in the preparation of this chapter.

1 Wayne Smith, *The Closest of Enemies* (New York: W.W. Norton, 1987), pp. 13–14.
2 Larry Rohter, "No Joy in Cuba, as Baseball Team Strikes Out," 3 November 1997, p. A.4 of the print edition of the *New York Times*.
3 Louis A. Pérez, Jr., *Between Revolution and Reform*, 2d ed. (New York: Oxford University Press, 1995), pp. 290, 313.
4 Marifeli Pérez-Stable, *The Cuban Revolution: Origins, Course, and Legacy* (New York: Oxford University Press, 1993), p. 53.
5 Eugene McCarthy, "Diamond Diplomacy," *New Republic*, 28 April 1982, p. 12.
6 US Senate Select Committee to Study Governmental Operations with Respect to Intelligence Activities, *Alleged Assassination Plots Involving Foreign Leaders* (Washington, D.C.: US Government Printing Office, 1975), p. 73.
7 "Nats Execute Triple Play, Win by 8–3," *Washington Post*, 24 July 1960; and Tom Miller, "Little Havana's Triple Play," *Hemispheres*, April 1993, pp. 68–71. For details on Joe Cambria, see González Echevarría, *Pride of Havana*, pp. 268–70.
8 Tracy Ringolsby, "Cubans Didn't Cross Water on Foot," *Baseball America*, 8 January 1996, 11; see also Tracy Ringolsby, "Mystique Makes Teams Ignore Questions of Talent," *Baseball America*, 31 May 1999, p. 15.
9 Frank Finch, "Drysdale Hurls as L.A. Beats Reds in Havana," *Los Angeles Times*, 21 March 1959.
10 Marcelo Sánchez sent me several clips from unidentified Havana newspapers, which were undated, describing the proposed Baltimore–Cincinnati series. See González Echevarría, *Pride of Havana*, 345, for more on the canceled Baltimore–Cincinnati

series. Marcelo also sent a 7 January 1957 clip from an unidentified Havana newspaper that described the efforts of Cincinnati Reds owner Powell Crosley, Jr, and the club's general manager, Gabe Paul, to open a training camp on the Isle of Pines (now Isla de la Juventud). The plan was to have the Cincinnati team train there and play exhibition games against Cuban teams before they returned to Florida for spring training exhibition games.

11 Edward Boorstein, *The Economic Transformation of Cuba* (New York: Monthly Review Press, 1968), pp. 28–29.
12 "Ball Stars' Tour of Cuba Is Sought," *New York Times*, 2 May 1971.
13 Memo William Rogers to Henry Kissinger, 13 February 1975. This is one of eighteen secret documents that were made public by the national Security Archive in early 1999 and are posted on their website (www.seas.gwu.edu/nsarchive/).
14 Memo from William Rogers to Henry Kissinger, 13 February 1975.
15 Department of State, Secret/NODIS Memorandum, 19 February 1975. Cited in Peter Kornbluh, "Here's the Windup: Scouting a Lefty Named Castro," *Washington Post*, 17 January 1999.
16 Memo, "Outline of Cuban Exhibition Game Proposal," 13 June 1975. This is also one of the secret documents that were made public by the National Security Archive.
17 Les Brown, "US Cancels Cuban Baseball Telecast," *New York Times*, 7 January 1976.
18 "State Department Not Opposed to Yanks Visiting Cuba," *New York Times*, 5 March 1977.
19 Personal interview with Wayne Smith, 28 October 1988.
20 Murray Chass, "Behind the Kuhn-Cuba Tangle," *New York Times*, 12 March 1977.
21 Chass, "Behind the Kuhn-Cuba Tangle."
22 "Indians Seeking to Play Cubans," *New York Times*, 2 March 1978; and "Indians vs. Cuba Series Snagged," *New York Times* 24 March 1978.
23 "Mariners Absolve Kuhn," *New York Times*, 22 January 1982.
24 After meetings with LULAC (League of United Latin American Citizens) in Havana in 1974, the Cuban government announced that it was willing to play an exhibition series against any major league team. Mario Obledo, "It's Time for Baseball Diplomacy," *Latino* (LULAC) 56, no. 1 (Winter 1984–85): p. 6.
25 In 1999, two Cuban players, Juan Díaz and Josué Pérez who had been signed by the Los Angeles Dodgers in 1995, were declared free agents by Major League Baseball, which ruled that the two players were signed in violation of the Kuhn Directive.
26 Houston Astros president Tal Smith has had an ongoing interest in Cuba since the late 1950s. He began his baseball career with the Cincinnati Reds in 1958. At the time, the Reds had a working agreement with Marianao in the Cuban League and the Cuban Sugar Kings of the Triple A International League.
27 Murray Chass, "Yanks Upset as Kuhn Vetoes Their Cuba Trip," *New York Times*, 9 March 1977.
28 Smith, *The Closest of Enemies*, p. 191.
29 US Department of the Treasury, Office of Foreign Assets Control, *What You Need to Know about the US Embargo: An Overview of the Cuban Assets Control Regulations. Title 31 Part 514 of the US Code of Federal Regulations* (Washington, D.C.: US Government Printing Office, 1996).
    The May/June 1999 issue of *Cigar Aficionado* is devoted almost entirely to Cuba. Included in the coverage are articles by US Senators Christopher Dodd (D-CT) and Jesse Helms (R-NC), as well as an article by Ricardo Alarcón, president of Cuba's National Assembly, examining the effects of the embargo.

Chapter 11

Playing the "race card"
US foreign policy and the integration of sports

Damion Thomas

Traditional narratives that examine the integration of team sports tend to connect integration with the opportunities that emerged out of the Second World War or with the subsequent Civil Rights movement. Both are appropriate and useful. However, this chapter attempts to show the intimate connection between the integration of sports and Cold War repression. Thus, this work considers the political imperatives, costs, and consequences associated with the opening of opportunities for African Americans in team sports.

Jackie Robinson and the meaning of black athletic success

Jackie Robinson made his first appearance as a member of the Brooklyn Dodgers on April 15, 1947, before a home crowd at Ebbets Field. As the first African American Major League Baseball player in the twentieth century, Jackie Robinson assumed the oft-passed mantle as "a savior, a Moses leading his people out of the wilderness." After a successful rookie campaign in which he batted .297, while finishing first in the league in stolen bases, second in runs scored and leading his team in home runs, he was named Rookie of the Year. Robinson's success made him the game's biggest drawing card since Babe Ruth, and like Ruth, his success had ramifications that transcended the world of sports. As historian Jules Tygiel suggested, "Robinson's entry into organized baseball ... created a national drama, emotionally involving millions of Americans, both black and white."[1]

Ever since Branch Rickey signed Jackie Robinson in 1946, historians and sportswriters have attempted to grasp the gravity of the development. Baz O'Meara, a reporter for the Montreal-based newspaper, *Daily Star* argued that Robinson's first game as a member of the Dodger organization was in a way "another Emancipation Day for the Negro." African American sportswriter, Sam Lacy, wrote that by himself Robinson "represents a weapon far more potent than the combined forces of all our liberal legislation." The implication of Lacy's claim was that Jackie Robinson had the hopes, aspirations and ambitions of thirteen million black Americans upon his shoulders. In essence, Robinson was viewed as a "one man civil rights movement."[2]

Before 1947, baseball reflected the values of American segregation. However, after the emergence of Jackie Robinson, African Americans and White Americans suggested that the successful integration of professional baseball symbolized the movement toward a society devoid of racial prejudice: a major concern during the early days of the Cold War. The notion that America was moving toward a social order where African Americans would be fully accepted in the United States was strengthened when one poll labeled Robinson the second most popular man in the United States behind only Bing Crosby, the great entertainer. As one of the first and most visible institutions to accept African Americans on relative terms of equality, the symbolic significance of Jackie Robinson meant that baseball became viewed as a model for the nation and would help provide a blueprint for future, widespread integration.

At social functions of all types – church services, horse races, and community picnics – people wanted to know, "How'd Jackie make out today?" Many African Americans thought that Robinson's success proved that if given a fair chance, African Americans would be productive, responsible, and exhibit a strong work ethic. Perhaps, all-time home run champion and Hall of Famer, Hank Aaron, best captured the sentiments of black America when he said, "[Jackie Robinson] gave us our dreams."[3]

One month before Jackie Robinson integrated Major League Baseball, President Harry S. Truman, the first Cold War president, articulated what has become known as "the Truman Doctrine," before a joint session of Congress on 12 March 1947. The Truman Doctrine warned the nation of the communist threat and it pledged United States support for nations struggling for freedom in a speech that became the dominant reference point for United States foreign policy for the next twenty-five years. "At the present moment in world history every nation must choose between alternative ways of life," Truman said. He characterized the "American way of life" by his reference to "free institutions, representative government, free elections, guarantees of individual liberty, freedom of speech and religion, and freedom from political oppression," while the "Soviet way of life" was depicted as relying upon "terror and oppression, a controlled press and radio, fixed elections, and the suppression of personal freedoms." The Truman Doctrine linked America's vision of itself as a nation with a purpose and destiny with the post-war battle against communism for worldwide supremacy. The anticommunist sentiments of Americans were fused with Henry Luce's notion of the American Century to assert a vision of global responsibility. As John Fousek has argued, the Truman Doctrine did not create a new world view, but it "encapsulated and reified ideological beliefs that were already widely shared, and it used them to mobilize support for the Truman administration's major foreign policy objectives."[4]

Certainly, the Second World War had positioned the Soviet Union as a superpower, and a threat to the "American Way of Life." Russian domination of

Eastern Europe, the communist upsurge in Turkey and Greece, coupled with the trials of United States government officials on espionage charges, emboldened American anti-communists. In 1947, lawmakers proposed legislation that would have outlawed the Communist party, forced the party and affiliated organizations to register with the Attorney General, and compelled labor union officials to file non-communist affidavits. Concurrently, President Truman established a federal loyalty program that was used to dismiss employees for being affiliated with any group "designated by the Attorney General as totalitarian, fascist, communist, or subversive."[5]

The "subversive" charge would be most frequently used to intimidate African American protest organizations, which were challenging the racist status quo. An increasingly repressive atmosphere led to a fundamental shift among black organizations, which had previously argued that African American struggles to end segregation were linked to anti-imperialist struggles throughout the world. Increasing Cold War consensus meant that organizations such as the NAACP had to affirm their commitment to the democratic capitalist system in the Untied States by embracing the messianic vision of the Truman Doctrine. Hence, Walter White and other NAACP leaders began to assert that the United States was the legitimate leader of the "Free World." As part of their reshaping of African American political and rhetorical strategies, White ceased his criticism of the United States foreign policy. As Penny Von Eschen has argued, the subsequent privileging of African Americans as American citizens first "left no room for the claim of commonality with Africans and other oppressed peoples. Consequently, the promise of advancement for African Americans "came at the expense of muting their belief in the international character of white racial domination in the early Cold War." Thereafter, White attempted to convince the president that domestic discrimination had to be eradicated because international condemnation of American domestic racism was a hindrance to United States Foreign policy.[6]

The repressive tactics of the Truman administration were a major facet of the shifting politics among many African Americans. As Walter White realized, criticism of United States foreign policy was becoming untenable; yet, conformity helped open new opportunities to promote civil rights within the administration. Thus, White and others gambled that they could achieve their goals through an alliance with the president, rather than through working to create linkages between the domestic civil rights agenda and the global, anti-colonial movement. This is an important shift because the NAACP's engagement with global anti-colonial movements had led to unprecedented growth. Between 1940–1946, the NAACP grew from 50,556 members in 1940 to over 450,000 members by 1946.

A major thrust of the political compromise between Truman and Walter White was the creation of President Truman's Committee on Civil Rights in 1946. *To Secure These Rights* was the title of the report that the President's

Committee on Civil Rights released the following year. The report recommended that the federal government take responsibility for ensuring that the civil rights of African Americans were not violated. The committee advocated for anti-lynching legislation, an anti-poll tax measure, and an end to segregation in the military. When the President publicly embraced the report, Carl Rowan, an African American journalist stated that Truman affirmed "unequivocally that the federal government has the primary responsibility to secure the basic civil rights of minority group citizens." *To Secure These Rights* established a national agenda that the Civil Rights movement mainstream pursued for the next twenty years.[7]

The Democratic Party regained control of key congressional committees after the 1948 midterm elections. This development was significant because it placed many southern, segregationist Dixiecrats in positions of power as chairmen of committees that reviewed proposed civil rights legislation. Dixiecrat Congressman favored the doctrine of state's rights, and were adamantly opposed to an increased role of the federal government in the arena of civil rights. Consequently, many of the recommendations that Truman's Committee on Civil Rights proposed were blocked and stalled in committees. [8]

Failure to pass adequate civil rights legislation was important because between 1945–1968 over 40 nations in Africa and Asia gained their independence, and the US and USSR were fighting for the allegiance of nations of color worldwide. In the late 1940s, State Department officials estimated that almost one-half of Soviet anti-American propaganda focused on American racial discrimination.[9] Only South Africa, an American ally, received greater criticism than the United States for its policies of racial discrimination in the immediate years after the Second World War. Furthermore, prominent American figures such as Walter White, Richard Nixon, A. Philip Randolph, Paul Robeson, Eleanor Roosevelt, and Secretary of State Dean Rusk publicly stated that the biggest single burden that the United States carried in its foreign policy was its domestic policy of racial discrimination. United States Ambassador to the United Nations Henry Cabot Lodge accurately described American race relations as its "international Achilles heel" because nations of color saw the treatment of African Americans as reflective of the nation's attitude toward all people of color.[10]

Dean Rusk, an Assistant Secretary of State, received two letters from the President's Committee on Civil Rights concerning the impact of race relations on United States foreign policy. More specifically, the Committee wanted to know: "Do you feel that the formulation and conduct of a sound and desirable foreign policy is handicapped by our bad domestic record in the civil rights area? If the answer is in any sense in the affirmative, does this mean that American security is in fact endangered by this condition?" Rusk responded: "There is no question … the moral influence of the United States is weakened to the extent that the civil rights proclaimed by our Constitution are not fully observed in practice." "Our failure," Rusk continued, "to maintain the highest standards of performance in this field creates embarrassment out of proportion to the actual instances of violation." Rusk was willing to acknowledge that "on a small scale" African Americans were affected by racial discrimination, but his judgement that foreign press coverage of racial oppression was more important than the prevalence of racial discrimination in the United States was crucial. Although Rusk's suggestion was contrary to the recommendations of the President's Committee, his strategy became the primary response to dealing with international condemnation of American racism during the Truman and Eisenhower administrations. Because Southern segregationist congressmen were unwilling to support civil rights legislation, President Truman, used Rusk's analysis to begin a campaign that focused on altering international perceptions of the nation's race relations, rather than removing the legal impediments to African American advancement.[11]

President Truman and his successor, President Eisenhower, began to define the protests of African Americans, rather than segregation, as the threat to the nation's security. As the Cold War intensified, the United States government began a campaign of silencing dissenting Black voices. W.E.B. Du Bois and Paul Robeson, both harsh critics of American racism, had their passports revoked because of their ability to attract large international audiences. Silencing Du Bois, Robeson and other dissenting voices was crucial to the State Department's attempt to manipulate foreign perceptions of race relations in the United States.[12] Consequently, rather than providing immediate, substantive changes to the social landscape, the United States government moved to re-define and re-contextualize the slow and unsteady advancement of African Americans into the American mainstream as a narrative of progress and as an example of American democracy.

Paul Robeson was a leading activist in the African American community who refused to curtail his critiques of the American democratic-capitalist system. In 1949, the House Un-American Activities Committee (HUAC) held hearings to denounce Paul Robeson and to investigate the loyalty of African Americans. Jackie Robinson was the star witness at the hearings. Robinson made national headlines when he re-affirmed his faith in the United States democratic system by asserting that "we're going to fight [racial discrimination] all the harder because our stake in the future [of the nation] is so big. We can win our fight without the Communists and we don't want their help." [13]

After working to marginalize prominent African Americans critical of American race relations, the State Department recruited prosperous African Americans who projected middle-class American values to participate in goodwill tours abroad. With this goal in mind, African American athletes, along with jazz musicians, and other artists were sent abroad as cultural ambassadors and "rebuttal witnesses."[14] By overemphasizing the extent to which social mobility was achievable for African Americans, the State Department sought to influence Diasporic political alignments during the Cold War. The US government tried to show that American policies were supportive of the liberation and rise of all people of color worldwide, and the touring athletes were depicted as symbols of America's commitment. Over 500 athletic goodwill tours were sent abroad between 1945–1968: basketball and track and field were the preferred sports.

Exploring the nature of the State Department athletic goodwill tours

In the summer 1956, the State Department sent the University of San Francisco Dons on a tour of Latin America. At the time of the tour, the Dons had won fifty-five consecutive games, and had amassed an incredible 57–1 record on the way to back-to-back NCAA championships. The team was led by their All-American center, Bill Russell, a 6'10" African American, whose shotblocking and defensive skills were the cornerstone of the team's domination. At the time, conventional wisdom held that defense was a time to rest until your team had the ball again, so most players did not expend energy jumping. Even when the occasional shot was blocked, the ball typically went out of bounds, which allowed the offensive team to maintain possession. However, Russell became adept at tipping the blocked shot to a teammate and initiating a fast break.[15]

Even as Russell's dominance propelled the Dons towards their first national championship, his coach Phil Woolpert, perhaps too fixated on tradition, kept telling Russell that by jumping to block shots he was "fundamentally unsound." Eventually, Woolpert came to appreciate and encourage Russell's innovation, which helped transfer the sports' emphasis from "offensive flash to defensive tenacity."[16] Two championships later, Woolpert, Russell and the rest of the Dons were rewarded with a State Department-funded trip throughout Latin America.

The Dons' first stop was in Guatemala where they spent a hectic three days, winning their two games by an average of thirty-four points. Although the games were lopsided, the contests were "two of the best games of basketball ever played in this country," according to the American Embassy's report. The highlight of the tour was the team's invitation to visit Guatemalan President Castillo Armas, an avid sports fan and recreational basketball player. After their visit with President Armas, the Dons appeared on the government-sponsored television station where a USIS film "Foreign Sports in the United States" aired before the station broadcast interviews with Guatemalan players and the Dons. Acting Public Affairs Officer in Guatemala, Maurice J. Broderick, described the players' maturity, level of commitment to their tasks, and basketball skills as "noticeably outstanding."[17]

Throughout their tour, the effort of the Dons was lauded. Harry S. Casler, the Public Affairs Officer in Panama said that the Dons "exemplified true democratic principles applied to the field of sports." The team conducted a well-attended clinic the day before it beat a tough Panamanian all-star team, 57–49, after the score had been tied at intermission. Similarly, the team's visit was labeled the most successful venture arranged by the State Department's exchange program in El Salvador. Gene Karst, the Public Affairs Officer in San Salvador, said that he had never come across a group of athletes who conducted themselves "in such a fine manner as the Dons," who made "great quantities of friends for the United States."[18]

In other tours of Latin America, close contests had engendered hostility towards the United States, as quibbles over officiating and player conduct had led some to leave the games with their negative thoughts and perspectives about the United States reinforced. However, on one occasion the Dons had to come from behind to eke out a 43–41 victory in Asuncion, Paraguay, against Club Olympia, the ten-time defending Asuncion champions. Ten thousand fans watched as the Dons beat the stiffest competition that they faced on their tour. In Paraguay, basketball was a major sport played throughout the year. Rather than becoming hostile as the close game came to an end, the Paraguayans were ecstatic over the competitiveness of the home team.[19]

In additional to his team's defensive philosophy, Woolpert's racial philosophy also went against conventional wisdom. He started three African Americans on his championship team: Russell, K.C. Jones and Hal Perry. The coach whom Russell referred to as "a fine and decent man" received hate mail and was called "Saperstein," a derogatory comparison to the founder of the Harlem Globetrotters because of his extensive use of African American basketball players. The talented African American star from UCLA, Willie Naulls, accompanied the Dons on their tour. Thus, Woolpert was able to put four African Americans on the floor at the same time. The State Department was well aware of the potential political implications of Woolpert's bravery.

In Guayaquil, Henry B. Lee, the Public Affairs Officer reported that every effort was exploited to "picture the racial mixture of the Dons," because a majority of the city's citizenry had black blood. The public display of camaraderie between the black and white players made the Dons tours "worth more than hundreds of thousands of printed words" on American race relations.[20] Apparently, the racial harmony that the Dons displayed was genuine. Russell later wrote in his autobiography, *Second Wind: The Memoirs of an Opinionated Man* that one of the reasons that the Dons had amassed a mediocre 14–7 record the season before they won their first national championship, was because of racial strife on the team. The Jesuits who ran the University of San Francisco had progressive racial attitudes, but as Russell volunteered: "not all of the students took them to heart, especially on the basketball team." However, according to Russell, all of the "jerks" graduated before the 1955 season and the team began to gel after the divisive racial issues were solved.[21]

The purpose of this tour and similar goodwill exchanges was to promote basketball internationally, while showcasing African Americans as the preeminent citizens of the African Diaspora, rather than as victims of racism. The State Department hoped that the material prosperity of the African American athletes, their expression of free speech, and, support for the American democractic capitalist system would refute reports regarding racial discrimination. The basic idea was to stress "progress." The State Department did not ask tour participants to not criticize the United States. Indeed many of the touring athletes were critical, but the athletes were asked to express faith in the American democratic, capitalistic system to solve the US racial problems.

The Sprague Committee, which investigated American propaganda campaigns abroad, clearly expressed the purpose of goodwill tours involving African Americans: "to *define* and *influence* the African Diaspora."[22] The tours were a crucial aspect of the State Department's three-pronged approach to transforming international understandings of American racial dynamics. The effort included: (1) subversion of the rhetoric and organizational affiliations established in the pre-war period that linked the African American struggle for equal rights with African and Asian struggles against colonialism, (2) re-configuration and re-interpretation of the battle to end American racial segregation within the contours of the American democratic tradition of progress, rather than as a facet of the global anti-colonial movement, and (3) portrayal of the "advancement" of African Americans as evidence of American commitment to creating a world where race was not a basis for oppression.

The State Department was often able to hide its involvement in the tours by partnering with the organizations that had international jurisdiction over their sports to send integrated sports teams abroad. For example, in the case of basketball and track and field, the two most popular sports in the State Department program, the government agency worked in collaboration with the Amateur Athletic Union (AAU). Typically, when the State Department decided to send a sports team abroad, it developed the team's itinerary, but let the sports governing organization choose the specific players that would be involved. Hence, many of the touring athletes were unaware of the State Department's sponsorship of their tours, and the non-athletic aims of their goodwill tours abroad.

Among the varied reasons sport was prominently featured in the complex State Department efforts were: 1) after Jackie Robinson integrated baseball, the swiftness with which sports integrated far outdistanced all other American institutions, thus giving sports a privileged space in the discussion of US race relations; 2) foreign audiences were less likely to see sport tours as politically motivated. Consequently, the mistaken, yet widespread notion that sport was non-ideological minimized athletics' vulnerability to the charge of cultural imperialism that plagued other American propaganda efforts; 3) the Cold War contest between the United States and the Soviet Union elevated the significance of sport in the international arena because it was one of the few places where the two nations competed head-to-head after the Soviet Union re-entered the Olympic Games in 1952; 4) and sport appealed to children, teenagers, and other "high-value" audiences that officials hoped to reach before they developed hostile, anti-American attitudes.

Sports: playing from a different deck of cards

Given the rising international significance of United States race relations in the post-Second World War period, when Jackie Robinson integrated baseball, he was taking part in shaping the political and social destiny of this country. For an African American man to play in the national pastime had ramifications that extended far beyond the playing field. It is not too strong to assert that Jackie Robinson became a symbol of the Cold War; in particular, Robinson symbolized the accessibility of the "American Dream" for African Americans. As the symbol of Cold War integration, Robinson's success helped characterize integrated sports as proof that a world with the United States as the "leader of the free world" held forth a realistic change that all people of the world would experience progress and be able to live "the good life."

When Robinson integrated Major League Baseball, the National Football League (NFL) had just re-integrated the year before, and the National Basketball Association (NBA) integrated three years later. However, by 1968, one fourth of the professional baseball league, one third of the NFL, and one half of the players in the NBA were African American. Given the growth of the popularity of all of the leagues in the post-war period due to television, an improved travel infrastructure, and post war prosperity, this development was astonishing. The rapidity of the advancement of the black athlete served as a reference point for those who were calling for widespread integration. For a generation of African Americans the exploits of Robinson, Joe Louis, and other athletes confirmed their belief that if provided a fair chance, African Americans would show that they were capable of performing at the highest levels in all professions.

Initially, most African Americans were supportive of the tours because integration of the athletic arena was thought to be a foreshadowing of widespread integration. However, the symbol of the black athlete became contested terrain during the mid-1960s. As athletics became more inclusive, the athletic arena lost its symbolism as part of the vanguard of racial progress within Black America and instead became "part of the status quo, the expected, the taken for granted." The articulation of African American athletic success as a positive, progressive racial force became contestable because the success of Black Athletes did not translate into widespread access to better housing, education, or other high-prestige employment.

One of the unintended consequences of the State Department goodwill tours was that they helped politicize athletes and former athletes such as Tommie Smith, John Carlos, and Harry Edwards. Edwards, the organizer of the Olympic Project for Human Rights that helped produce the lasting symbols of the athletic revolution[23] – the raised fists of John Carlos and Tommie Smith at the 1968 Mexico City Olympics – became determined to produce a counter narrative to the State Department's story of progress. "The United States government has taught us well," Edwards observed. "In the ideological wars with other world powers, the US State Department has time and time again used athletes – both professional and amateur – as political adjuncts."[24] Rather than celebrating the suggestion that sports were at the forefront of racial advance, the athletes increasingly came to assert that sports were tied to a racist, oppressive system.

The emergence of a new, defiant approach to athletics – as expressed by the defiance of Tommie Smith and John Carlos in Mexico City – did not cause the State Department to stop sending African Americans abroad. However, it did mean that the American government was more likely to send dissenting voices as representatives of the African American community. No longer were African Americans as willing to assert a belief in the inevitability of progress in American race relations. The touring athletes were increasingly willing to stand in opposition to American policy, thus altering the political nature of their trips abroad. Coupled with the escalation of the Vietnam War, the altered political landscape after decolonization, the militancy of the Black Athletes helped severely hinder the aims of the program.

For example, on Thursday, 3 June 1971, The Bureau of Educational and Cultural Affairs, which organized many of the tours abroad, presented Oscar Robertson and Kareem Abdul Jabbar, the two stars of the World Champion Milwaukee Bucks, along with their coach, Larry Costello to the media. The three men were at the State Department to answer questions about their impending goodwill trip to Algeria, Senegal, Mali, Nigeria, Tanzania, and Somali. The genesis of the Robertson-Jabbar-Costello Tour was the success of the Arthur Ashe and Stan Smith tour to Africa in 1970. When he returned to the United States, Arthur Ashe confirmed the Bureau's beliefs concerning the growth of basketball and the popularity of the sport in Africa. Consequently, Mark Lewis, the Bureau's Director of Cultural Affairs, went to a Milwaukee Bucks–Washington Bullets game held in Baltimore and asked the three key forces on the Bucks if they would be interested in going to Africa. All happily agreed and the tour was organized.[25]

At the press conference, Kareem Abdul Jabbar was asked if he had any regrets about not playing on the gold-medal-winning Olympic basketball team at the 1968 Games. Avoiding the implied reference to the contentious atmosphere surrounding the 1968 Games, Jabbar answered simply: "I have no regrets on that. The team did very well. I am glad that they did well, and I accomplished what I wanted to accomplish by not going, so I don't feel that I have any regrets about it." Dissatisfied with Jabbar's uncharacteristically timid and conservative response, the follow-up question, "Did you ever get any ill-will from your colleagues in pro ball who have competed in the Olympics," pushed for greater specificity. "No I got none of that from them," Jabbar responded. "They all understand, or they all say they understand, and I haven't found there to be any ill-will from anybody. I got a few bad letters, you know, but I am always getting bad letters." The assembled reporters knowingly laughed.[26]

After news stories about Jabbar participating in a State Department-sponsored venture began to appear, the State Department received letters from private American citizens who complained about the Department sponsoring a tour involving Kareem Abdul Jabbar because of his decision not to compete for the 1968 United States Olympic Basketball Team. When asked about the 1968 Games, Jabbar and Larry Costello informed Mark Lewis that he did not refuse to compete, rather the Games scheduled for October conflicted with his class schedule at UCLA. Jabbar maintained that he simply skipped the Games in order to pursue his studies.[27]

At the State Department briefing, Jabbar did not address the ways in which the treatment of African Americans had factored into his decision to boycott the Games. However, Jabbar spoke at the 22 November 1967, workshop sponsored by the Los Angeles Black Youth Conference and organized by Harry Edwards, at Second Baptist Church in Los Angeles. The theme of the conference was "Liberation is Coming from a Black Thing."

Four of the five world class athletes present at the meeting – Tommie Smith, Lee Evans, Otis Burrell, and Lew Alcindor (later known as Kareem Abdul Jabbar) – spoke in support of the boycott. Alcindor addressed the 200 assembled athletes to discuss the possibility of a black boycott of the 1968 Olympic Games. "Everyone knows me," Alcindor began. "I'm the big basketball star, weekend hero, everybody's all-American. Well, last summer I was almost killed by a racist cop shooting at a Black [man] in Harlem. He was shooting on the street – where masses of Black people were standing around or just taking a walk." The crowd was mesmerized as he continued, "But [the police officer] didn't care … I found out last summer that we don't catch hell because we aren't basketball stars or because we don't have money. We catch hell because we are Black. Somewhere each of us has to make a stand against this kind of thing. This is how I take my stand – using what I have. And I take my stand here." Harry Edwards maintained that Alcindor's statements were "the most moving and dynamic … [and] memorable" words spoken on behalf of the boycott idea. That the most powerful statement supporting the boycott idea came from the most celebrated athlete at the meeting, caused the assembled athletes to give Alcindor a five-minute standing ovation.[28]

Along with other African American collegiate All-Americans Elvin Hayes, Neal Walk, Bob Lanier, Wes Unseld, Larry Miller, and Don May, Jabbar's withdrawal from the Olympic Basketball trials caused an uproar. On an appearance at the *Today* show shortly after he announced his decision not to attend the 1968 Games, Jabbar told Joe Garagiola that the United States was "not really my country." Responding to the resentment and bewilderment that his comment unleashed, he tried to explain his stance: "What I was trying to get across was that until things are in an equitable basis this is not my country. We have been a racist nation with first-class citizens and my decision not to go to the Olympics is my way of getting the message across." A myriad of events had caused Jabbar to withdraw from White America: the bombing of an African American church in Birmingham resulting in the death of four little girls had a chilling effect on him; the "Whites Only" signs that he saw on a trip to North Carolina were difficult for him to handle; the white media's preoccupation with property damage, rather than racial injustice during the Harlem riots in 1964; and the publication of Malcolm X's autobiography helped shape his view of race relations and his role as an African American athlete. Frustrated with "the silly, routine questions" reporters asked him, Jabbar developed a reputation as being ill-mannered and inconsiderate because he wanted to talk about racism and injustice, instead of basketball strategy and defensive rebounding.[29]

The State Department trip came at a crucial point in Jabbar's maturation. He had just been married and publicly changed his name from Lew Alcindor after becoming a Sunni Muslim. Additionally, he was searching for a way to "fulfill his obligations to the black community." Shortly, before Jabbar's departure, his father Ferdinand Alcindor commented that, "[Jabbar] had matured and found direction in his thinking ... He wants to do things for the betterment of black people. One of the things he is doing is this tour. He feels strongly about it." In response to a letter lambasting the State Department's selection of Jabbar as a goodwill ambassador, the Department said, "The fact that Mr. Jabbar is making this tour on behalf of the Department of State speaks for itself."[30] Defying traditional State Department logic that African Americans would not embarrass the United States on an international tour, Jabbar's rising black consciousness led him to make sure that he was not portrayed as an advocate for American policies.

When asked directly, "Are you here as [an ambassador] of America's foreign policy?" at a press conference in Tanzania, Jabbar proclaimed that his tour of Africa should not be as interpreted as support for the claim that he supported American policies. He specifically singled out America's policies in Indochina and American race relations as points of disagreement. He asserted that the purpose of his trip was not to politick on America's behalf, but to "meet some of my brothers from the other side of the Atlantic."[31] His decision to accept the tour was not based upon a commitment to American values or American foreign policy concerns, but his duty to help uplift African Americans. Thus his reasoning is reflective of the shifting thinking of African American athletes during the late 1960s, after the end of the McCarthy-era repression.

Factoring in Jabbar's hesitancy to blindly champion American State Department policy, it is not surprising that the tour was judged to be of limited value. The American Embassy in Lagos, Nigeria, reported that the June 16–19 visit by Costello, Robertson, and Jabbar was successful but fell short of expectations because of the players' unwillingness to adhere to the plans and policies of the Cultural Exchange Program. Indeed, the ingredients for a great tour were present: the "most famous one-two basketball combination in the United States and their very successful White coach." However, Robertson and Jabbar refused to participate in the full schedule that was planned for them. Understandably more comfortable on the basketball court than being gawked at during the cocktail receptions, Jabbar missed one-fourth the activities they were supposed to attend.

Additionally, he expressed disdain for the standard receptions hosted by the American Embassy and indigenous sports agencies where he was supposed to serve as a representative of American Democracy and improved American race relations.[32]

Described as "mercurial and moody," Jabbar's personality and his infrequent gestures to connect with the host nations were detrimental to the American effort. A memo from the Nairobi American Embassy written to the head of the Cultural Presentations Program, Mark Lewis, said, "It was probably a mistake to include Alcindor. Dramatic looking as he is, he is also too moody … for people-to-people activity." The comments were expressed after Jabbar refused to take part in an ill-planned early morning reception and basketball clinic.[33]

Jabbar's unwillingness to be used by the American government suggests the shift of black athletes from the model set up by an earlier generation including Rafer Johnson, Jesse Owens, and Joe Louis. Now African American athletes were determined to make sure that they were not being used by a racist sports system, but rather using all available means to help improve the lives of African American people by challenging American racism on all fronts and taking control of their own symbolism.

The raised fists of Tommie Smith and John Carlos are the enduring symbols of the co-optation of the symbolic meaning of African American athletes. The notion that docility and acquiescence in the face of racial discrimination would be a benefit to the struggle for equal rights became associated with "Uncle Tomism." Coupled with political protests by Muhammad Ali, economic ventures by Jim Brown and the Negro Economic Industrial Union, the massive protests on college campuses involving African American athletes, the Mexico City games were the highpoint of the struggle to place the athletic world at the center of efforts to fight racial oppression, under terms set by African Americans.

Notes

1   Jules Tygiel, *Baseball's Great Experiment: Jackie Robinson and His Legacy*, (New York: Vintage Books, 1984), p. viii; Wendell Smith, "Dodgers Have Drawn 95,000 Fans in Four Exhibition Contests," *Pittsburgh Courier*, 26 April 1947.

2   *Baseball's Great Experiment*, pp. 4, 75; Jules Tygiel, ed. *The Jackie Robinson Reader*, (New York: Dutton Books, 1997), pp. 6, 9.

3   Peter Golenbock, "Men of Conscience," in Joseph Dorinson and Joram Warmund, eds. *Jackie Robinson: Race, Sports, and the American Dream*, (New York: M.E. Sharpe, 1998), p. 20; Peter Levine, "Father and Son at Ebbets Field," in Joseph Dorinson and Joram Warmund, eds. *Jackie Robinson: Race, Sports, and the American Dream*, (New York: M.E. Sharpe, 1998), p. 64.

4   Paul Gordon Lauren, *Power and Prejudice: The Politics and Diplomacy of Racial Discrimination*. (Boulder, Colo.: Westview Press, 1988), p. 187; Mary Dudziak, *Cold War Civil Rights: Race and the Image of American Democracy*, (Princeton: Princeton University Press, 2000), p. 27; Laura Ann Belmonte, "Defending a Way of Life: American Propaganda and the Cold War, 1945–1959," (PhD diss: University of Virginia, 1996), p. 270; John Fousek, *To Lead the Free World: American Nationalism*

and the Cultural Roots of the Cold War, (Raleigh: University of North Carolina Press, 2000), pp. 126–129.

5   Jeff Woods, *Black Struggle, Red Scare: Segregation and Anti-Communism in the South, 1948–1968*, (Baton Rouge: Louisiana State University Press, 2004), p. 27; Gerald Horne, *Black and Red: W.E.B. Du Bois and the Afro-American Response to the Cold War, 1944–1963*, (Albany: State University of New York Press, 1986), p. 62.

6   Penny Von Eschen, *Race Against Empire: Black Americans and Anti-Colonialism, 1937–1957*, (Ithaca, N.Y.: Cornell University Press, 1997), pp. 97, 109, 112; Borstelmann, *Apartheid's Reluctant Uncle*, (New York: Oxford University Press, 1993,) p. 56; Horne, p. 92.

7   Borstelmann, p. 66; Michael R. Gardner, *Harry Truman and Civil Rights: Moral Courage and Political Risks*, (Carbondale: Southern Illinois University Press, 2002), p. 61; Azza Salama Layton, *International Politics and Civil Rights Policies in the United States, 1941–1960*, (New York: Cambridge University Press, 2000), pp. 3, 79.

8   Carol Anderson, *Eyes Off the Prize: The United Nations and the African American Struggle for Human Rights, 1944–1955*, (New York: Cambridge University Press, 2003), p. 213.

9   Michael Krenn, *Black Diplomacy: African Americans and the State Department, 1945–1969*, (London: M.E. Sharpe, 1999), p. 76; Walter L. Hixson, *Parting the Curtain: Propaganda, Culture, and the Cold War, 1945–1961*, (New York: St. Martin's Press, 1997), p. 121; David Southern, *Gunnar Myrdal and Black-White Relations: The Use and Abuse of "An American Dilemma," 1944–1969*, (Baton Rouge: Louisiana State University Press, 1987), pp. 102.

10 Lauren, p. 190, 192–3, 228; Thomas Borstelmann, *Apartheid's Reluctant Uncle*, (New York: Oxford University Press, 1993,) p. 142.

11 Letter from Mr Rusk to The Secretary of State, National Archives (NA), RG 59, 800/ 432.213.

12 Von Eschen, pp. 126, 3.

13 Herb Heft, "Jackie Robinson Chides Robeson," *Washington Post*, 19 July 1949; HUAC Hearings, pp. 480–82.

14 Nikhil Pal Singh, *Black is a Country: Race and the Unfinished Struggle for Democracy*, (Cambridge: Harvard University Press, 2004), p. 178.

15 "US Specialist Program," 11 April 1956, NA, 032 San Francisco Basketball Team/4–1156; Frank Deford, "The Ring Leader: The Greatest Team Player of All Time, Bill Russell was the Hub of a Celtics Dynasty that Ruled Its Sport As No Other Team Ever Has. (The 20th Century)," *Sports Illustrated*, v90, n19 (10 May 1999), pp. 96–97.

16 Bill Russell and Taylor Branch, *Second Wind: the Memoirs of an Opinionated Man*, (New York: Random House, 1974), pp. 79–80; Deford, p. 96.

17 "Visit of US Specialists San Francisco Dons Basketball Team," American Embassy Guatemala, 26 July 1956, NA, 032 San Francisco Basketball Team/7–2056.

18 "Appearance in Panama of San Francisco Dons Basketball Team," American Embassy Panama, 16 August 1956, NA, 032 San Francisco Basketball Team/8–1656; "US Specialists Program – President's emergency Fund for San Francisco Basketball Team Project," American Embassy San Salvador, 25 June 1956, NA, 032 San Francisco Basketball Team/6–2556.

19 US Specialists: Report on Visit of San Francisco Dons to Asuncion," American Embassy Asuncion, 28 August 1956, NA, 032 San Francisco Basketball Team/8–2856.

20 "US Specialist Program: Visit of the University of San Francisco 'Dons' Basketball Team," American Embassy Caracas, 26 July 1956, NA, 032 San Francisco Basketball Team/7–2696; "US Specialist Program Visit of San Francisco Basketball

Team – President's Emergency Fund," USIS Sao Paulo, 13 August 1956, CU, 92, Folder 14; "Visit of the San Francisco 'Dons' to Guayaquil," USIS Guayaqui, 22 August 1956, NA, 032 San Francisco "Dons"/8–2256; "US Specialists Program – President's Emergency Fund for San Francisco Basketball Team Project," American Embassy San Salvador, 25 June 1956, 032 San Francisco Basketball Team/6–2556."

21 Russell, pp. 119–121.

22 "The President's Committee on Information Activities Abroad: Africa, PCIAA no. 31," Dwight D. Eisenhower Presidential Library, US President's Committee on Information Activities Abroad (Sprague Committee), Box 21, folder PCIAA # 31.

23 For a detailed examination of the athletic revolution, see Jack Scott's *The Athletic Revolution* published by The Free Press in 1971.

24 Harry Edwards, *The Revolt of the Black Athlete*, (New York: The Free Press, 1969), pp. 115–16.

25 "Transcript of Press, Radio and Television News Briefing," 3 June 1971, Bureau of Educational and Cultural Affairs Papers (CU), University of Arkansas-Fayetteville, Box 89, Folder 28.

26 "Transcript of Press, Radio and Television News Briefing," 3 June 1971, Bureau of Educational and Cultural Affairs Papers (CU), University of Arkansas-Fayetteville, Box 89, Folder 28.

27 Frank A. Scott to Mark B. Lewis, 14 May 1971, CU, Box 91, Folder 20.

28 *The Revolt of the Black Athlete*, pp. 52–53.

29 *The Struggle That Must Be*, pp. 177–80; *Santa Barbara News-Press*, 24 November 1967; *The Revolt of the Black Athlete*, pp. 52–53; Bass, p. 256; Kareem Abdul Jabbar, *Giant Steps*, (New York: Bantam Books, 1985), pp. 46, 60–63, 72, 157.

30 "Alcindor's Trip To Africa To Be 'Like Going Home'" *Washington Post*, 7 May 1971.

31 Lester O. Geppert to Mark B. Lewis, 6 July 1971, CU, Box 89, Folder 29;

32 "Cultural Presentations: Milwaukee Bucks," June 30, 1971, CU, Box 89, Folder 28.

33 Nairobi Embassy to Mark B. Lewis, 1 July 1971, CU, Box 89, Folder 29; "Alcindor-Robertson-Costello Basketball Tour," 26 June 1971, CU, Box 89, Folder 28.

ous" masculinity
ilitarization

:he 1980 USSR–US men's Olympic
match and Cold War politics

Mary G. McDonald

As the 1980 Winter Olympic men's ice hockey semi-final game between the Soviet Union and the United States concluded with an unanticipated 4–3 US upset victory, television announcer Al Michaels excitedly asked his viewing audience, "Do You Believe in Miracles?" Michaels then answered his own question with a resounding "YES," further encouraging viewers (of a taped-delayed primetime US telecast) to share this enthusiastic support of the upset win. Two days later the team would go on to defeat Finland 4–2 to capture the gold medal in Lake Placid, New York. This unexpected victory over a powerhouse, highly favoured Soviet squad and an unanticipated gold medal performance against Finland were subsequently narrated as the "miracle on ice."

One need only point toward two more recent events to understand how this victory has been seared into US public consciousness. Indeed, the entire 1980 US Olympic team helped to light the Olympic torch during the opening ceremonies of the 2002 Winter Olympic Games in Salt Lake City, Utah. More recently, a 2004 Disney film, *Miracle*, has served to rearticulate and, in many ways, sanitize Cold War fears and US imperial power (see this text, Chapter 16 by Silk, Bracey and Falcous for a thoughtful analysis of the meanings of *Miracle* in this contemporary moment). And yet a central storyline of *Miracle* still reproduces the notion of an overmatched US team defying the odds in securing the gold medal.

In some respects this re-occurring framing is not surprising. It would be hard to dispute the claim that the US victory over the Soviet Union was an unexpected defeat of a highly favoured squad. After all, the Soviet Union had won every Olympic hockey gold medal since 1960, had lost only one Olympic match since 1968, "had crushed the NHL's best only a year earlier, had beaten the Americans by seven goals in an exhibition they had no reason to win and had outscored their opponents in these games by 51–11" (Powers and Kaminsky, 1984, p. 199). As one account suggested, "Who would imagine an American victory over the Soviets? The Soviets are their nation's pride. They have challenged the world and won" (Kindred 1980, February 23, p. A1). And yet, prevailing nationalistic Cold War sentiments meant that the subsequent US gold medal performance represented more than a victory on ice. Much as with previous Cold War "battles" between teams representing the US and Soviet Union, this game was broadly narrated as a contest between the world's two superpowers competing – not just for sport supremacy – but, by extension, for political, economic, ideological, and military supremacy as well.

Read from the dominant US perspective, the state-sponsored "Russian hockey world was planned, subsidized and continuous" (Powers and Kaminsky, 1984, p. 3). And the US team – largely subsidized by a less formal apparatus of collegiate and amateur hockey – had toppled this juggernaut. That the United States was able to defeat such an established powerhouse at its own game helped bolster narratives promoting a jingoistic version of American exceptionalism and rugged individualism both within and outside the realm of US Olympic sport. Sport and political commentators suggested this victory helped to revive US popular confidence following a number of Cold War setbacks such as the Soviet invasion of Afghanistan in December of 1979, the American hostage crisis in Tehran, and increasing economic "stagflation." In short, conservative and neoliberal forces also mobilized the "miracle on ice" storyline as an antidote in troubling times and to suggest the "righteousness" of a whole way of life.

Against the romantic visions promoting American ingenuity, resolve and freedom, several critics have noted that Cold War fears actually served to escalate military build-ups, to extend militaristic values deeper into the realm of everyday life and to expand the imperial reach of both the Soviet Union and the United States. Prior to the Second World War "both counties had built empires – the United States in Latin America and the Pacific, the Russians in the Caucasus and Central Asia – and both acquired new territories in fighting that war" (Johnson, 2004, p. 32). During the Cold War new tactics emerged within the respective policies of containment whereby each nation justified their military and international diplomatic actions as necessary to stop either "Soviet expansion" or "American aggression." During this period "both countries adopted the idea that they were in mortal danger from each other, even though they had been allies during World War II" (Johnson, 2004, p. 32).

Early in the Cold War and until around 1980, the so called "Third-World" nations that chose not to belong to either the communist or capitalist camps did have a measure of autonomy in playing one of these two powerful nations against the other, as each superpower was hesitant to exert control over contested nations lest one bolt into the other camp (Johnson, 2004, p. 258). This state of affairs did shift in the mid-1980s as the threat of a war between the Soviet Union and the United States receded. In the meantime, the philosophy of containment ushered in a new form of imperialism as each nation sought to establish their military presences in all corners of the globe under the guise of trying to "forestall a superpower war" (Johnson, 2004, p. 32). The United States, for example, used Cold War fears to establish a military presence, not via the annexation of territory, nor via the colonization of "weaker" nations, but via the establishment of "permanent naval bases, military airfields, army garrisons, espionage listening posts, and strategic enclaves on every continent of the globe" (Johnson, 2004, p. 23). The conflict in Central Europe helped to legitimate the presence of approximately 1,700 US military installations in nearly 100 countries (Johnson, 2004). Even with the subsequent break-up of the Soviet Union, many of these bases remain and thus continue to bolster both American and multinational corporate hegemony.

As well as promoting an ideology of the superiority of either capitalism or communism, then, both countries used Cold War rhetoric also to advance their own national, strategic interests. Sporting contests such as the USSR–US Olympic ice hockey game thus proved to be important symbolic sites where competing worldviews and national interests were represented, challenged and rearticulated. In this chapter, I explore key US narratives surrounding the 1980 US–Soviet Union Olympic hockey match as an entry point toward thinking critically about "the constitutive meanings and power relations" of Cold War discourses, including those connected to sport (McDonald and Birrell, 1999, p. 283). I offer evidence to suggest that the dominant US representations of the "miracle on ice" were imagined symbolically to reverse an alleged loss of American self-confidence and global political influence. These narratives of masculine solidarity and resolve, which worked as antidotes to Cold War anxieties, additionally served to legitimate the increasing encroachment of military metaphors on everyday life and helped to justify the deployment of American military power and presence around the globe. Far from being limited to the Olympic Games, these narratives also anticipated similar regressive discourses eventually deployed by President Ronald Reagan throughout the 1980s to justify and intensify the processes of American militarization and global capitalist expansion.

This analysis, then, is committed to the central tenets of cultural criticism in exploring the ideological stakes of US representations of 1980 Olympic ice hockey. In that spirit, this chapter must be seen as a counter-narrative designed to offer an alternative way of understanding what has been "decentered, obscured, and dismissed by hegemonic forces" (McDonald and Birrell, 1999, p. 295). While dominant narratives matter as they do political work in seeking to legitimate a particular version of events, counter-narratives are important as they are infused with resistant political possibilities. Counter-narratives make visible the competing interests at play, thus disrupting the historically created "matrices of social inequalities" that helped to constitute the Cold War processes of national imagining, and which continue to impact on everyday life (McDonald and Birrell, 1999, p. 295).

We need a hero: masculinity and militarization

On the surface, Cold War Olympic narratives easily lend themselves to binary formulations, an "us" versus "them" or capitalism versus communism mentality where the athletes stand symbolically for an imagined unified nation. Here the focus is on the ideological salience of particular ways of life. Olympic hockey accounts frequently followed this sensibility with one story suggesting that the "grim air of [Soviet] professionalism was in severe contrast to a U.S. team playful and outgoing throughout its practice, a team that has endured all manner of inconveniences for months for just this chance" (Denlinger, 22 February 1980, p. E3).

Similar popular pre-match accounts helped to support an image of a youthful and inexperienced but exuberant US team as determined to battle the odds and optimistically challenge the veteran Soviet team and its domination of the ice. According to US defenseman, Mike Ramsey, "No team is invincible ... The Russians are close. But any team can be beaten. If we catch them on a bad day, who knows? We've got a shot" (cited in Shapiro, 21 February 1980, p. F1). "Might be history in the making ... If anybody's gonna beat 'em, it might as well be us", goalie Jim Craig was quoted as saying (cited in Denlinger, 1980, p. E3).

Similar Cold War Olympic storylines also frequently reflected what Hall (1992) has termed the narratives of nation. These narratives of nation include sets "of stories, images, landscapes, scenarios, historical events, national symbols and rituals which stand for or represent the shared experiences, sorrows, and triumphs and disasters which give meaning to the nation" (Hall, 1992, p. 293). That Olympic hockey could easily assist in the construction of such narratives of nation is not surprising given that "sport has become arguably the most emotive – peacetime – vehicle for harnessing and expressing bonds of national cultural affiliation" (Silk, Andrews, and Cole, 2005, p. 6). A particularly salient narrative of nation – and indeed of imagined belonging and national superiority – was evident in US Coach Herb Brooks' comments during a telephone conversation with US President Jimmy Carter immediately following the team's gold medal victory. During this conversation, Brooks asserted that this "was a great win for everybody in sport and the American people in general. From the things we had to overcome, to the different beliefs, ways of life. It just proves our life is the proper way to continue" (cited in Powers and Kaminsky, 1984, p. 228). In recounting the President's response, Brooks would tell reporters that "President Carter said we made the American people very proud, ... He invited us to the White House for a couple cases of Coke on Monday" (cited in Kindred, 1980, p. A1).

Media discourses promoting an imagined sense of belonging meant that the victorious squad became "billed as America's Team, screw the Dallas Cowboys" (Powers and Kaminsky, 1984, p. 198). The team also "found themselves carrying the load for the President, the State Department, the Pentagon, the hostages, General Motors, Dow Jones, the Saturday Evening Post and the Four Freedoms." Of course, as with all national imaginings, this process of trying to make the team stand for the various constituencies of a larger collective is a problematic one. This procedure serves to create a deceptive sense of national unity thus erasing important global interconnections and internal national differences and inequalities including those related to race, class, gender and sexuality.

In actuality, the vision most often connected to the nation in Olympic hockey narratives was a highly selective image of white masculinity. There are important historical reasons for this state of affairs. Ice hockey – with its emphasis on bone-crushing body checks and physical punishment – exists as one of many sports that have influenced a broader sense of idealized masculinity wherein aggression, strength and dominance are culturally rewarded. The result is that "throughout history, dominant groups have successfully persuaded many Americans to believe that sport" – including contact sports like hockey – "builds manly character, develops physical fitness, realizes order, promotes justice and even prepares young men for war" (Trujillo, 2000, p. 17).

Numerous Olympic accounts celebrated the efforts of the "US Pluckies" (Delinger, 24 February 1980, p. F1) as Herculean. For example, US Goalie Jim Craig's semi-final performance in stopping 36 of the Soviet Union's 39 shots on goal was mediated as an act of skill, dedication and dominance. Indeed, Head Coach Brooks lauded Craig suggesting he "was a tower of strength for us, no question … For an American team to be successful, the catalyst has to be the goalkeeper. Craig told me yesterday, 'You wait, till tomorrow, Coach. You haven't seen it. Tonight the Soviets saw it.' (cited in Shapiro, 1980, p. D1). And Mike Eruzione ("the tough kid from Massachusetts"), who scored the winning goal against the USSR, was immediately represented as possessing a sense of manly purpose and fortitude and reporters were reminded that the victory over the Soviets had not secured the gold medal and thus the team "can't forget we've got one game left. I'll be dammed if I'll let them get lazy now. We've one more day away from a dream" (Shapiro, 1980, February 23, p. D1). In another interview after the victory over the USSR, Eruzione sought to put his comments into a broader context, suggesting his dream was open to all those with similar strengths: the US team had come to "typify the American people, … We put on our hard hats, pick up our lunch pails and come to work" (cited in Delinger, 24 February 1980, p. F1).

Frequently both teams were discussed not just in relation to masculinity, but also via militarized themes thus providing an ideologically salient case where "competitions, rivalries, strategies, and plays" were described "in the language of military force" generating "many of the same emotions and investments as war" (King, forthcoming, p. 4). One sports writer captured the parallel emotional sensibilities between Olympic ice hockey and war in this way:

> On Friday night, the U.S. beat Russia, 4–3, in a game of ice hockey that some in attendance said was the most stirring athletic event of their lifetimes.
> The difficult problem, of course, is to analyze exactly which deep recesses of the spirit that game aroused. And to ask whether that is an emotional cal-dron which needs stirring. The US – vs. – USSR game duplicated, in miniature, many of the emotions and motivations that have fed the fires of every war in history.

It was an athletic contest of the highest order. And it was, in the deepest sense, contrary to the Olympic spirit. If these are the last Olympics, no one need ask why.

(Boswell, 1980, p. F 5)

Few of the militarized metaphors and analogies associated with the Olympic hockey tournament were as reflective about the human investment in war as the above quotation. More frequently the descriptions appeared as naturalized accounts that helped delineate or celebrate a particular aspect of the two teams. Therefore the Soviet squad was often referenced as the veteran team "drawn chiefly from officer-players of the Central Army Sports Club in Moscow" (Klose, 1980, p. F4). The US players "play like hell. They play the way Americans did in lots of big games, including that memorable one against the redcoats at Bunker Hill" (Kindred, 25 February 1980, p. A1).

Samantha King (forthcoming) has argued that sport discourses play a key ideological role in helping to legitimate the language, practices and aims of the military, thus simultaneously indicating the "militarization of everyday life … and the 'sportification' of political life in the US." Cynthia Enloe (2000) suggests "that militarization is a step-by-step process by which a person or a thing [such as sport] gradually comes to be controlled by the military or comes to depend on its well-being on militaristic ideas" (Enloe, p. 2). This is an important point to consider when discussing the narrative significance of Olympic ice hockey for the "more militarization transforms an individual or a society, the more that individual or society comes imagining military needs and militaristic presumptions to be not only valuable but also normal" (Enloe, 2000, p. 2). The result is that people also become "militarized in their thinking, in how they live their daily lives, in what they aspire to for their children or their society, without ever wielding a rifle or donning a helmet" (Enloe, p. 2).

The ritualized and ceremonial structures of the Olympic Games lend themselves to displays of both nationalism and patriotism, which help support a highly uncritical form of militarism. The US hockey team was constantly cheered by an enthusiastic hometown crowd dressed in red, white and blue while chanting "U-S-A, U-S-A." The victorious US team was honored with the playing of the Star Spangled Banner, an anthem that glorifies militarism and war. This Olympics also featured a special lakeside outdoor evening medal ceremony set against a background of darkness. A particularly powerful emotional effect was achieved as,

Lasers and spotlights crease the sky; a hang glider spitting fire flies through a sky lit up by spectacular fireworks that put many a Fourth of July show on the Washington Monument grounds to shame. "The Fantasy of the Lake" is the extravaganza's name as disco boogie accompanies the bombs bursting in air.

> It is all harmless, but it is also moving. The bomb bursts of celebration resemble the bomb bursts of war.
>
> (Boswell, 1980, p. F5)

Similar expressions suggest that military sensibilities occupied a significant affective prominence – not only in foreign and defense policy matters – but on the level of everyday popular practice such as sport.

The stories about the USSR–US contest carried considerable intensity given that the Winter Olympics were played just a few months after the Soviets invaded Afghanistan in order to halt the revolt of anti-Soviet Muslim fundamentalists. Claiming that this defensive action served as a logical extension of the "Brezhnev Doctrine,"[1] the Soviets argued that their movement into Afghanistan was vital to the interests of keeping a secure boarder. President Jimmy Carter fearing for US and anti-communist interests in the area, responded with harsh language and diplomatic sanctions claiming that this military action represented a "quantum jump in the nature of Soviet behavior" and that it posed "the most serious threat to peace since the second World War" (cited in Grogin, 2001, p. 307). He issued an embargo on grain exports, limited Soviet access to fishing waters and computer technology, and called for a boycott of the Summer Olympic Games to be held later that year in Moscow (Grogin, 2001).

This series of events left the Soviets considering whether or not to boycott the Lake Placid games before finally sending their delegation to the US in February, 1980. On 9 February, US Secretary of State Cyrus Vance addressed the International Olympic Committee (IOC) suggesting that Soviet aggression violated the peaceful, cooperative principles of the Olympic movement (Coffey, 2005). Some critics within the United States and abroad suggested that Carter had seized the boycott issue in an election year in which his poll approval ratings were abysmally low. Given the administration's initial goals of improving human rights and international cooperation while slowing nuclear proliferation, other critics suggested that the boycott proposal represented one example of Carter's increasingly hard-line stance toward the Soviet Union (Grogin, 2001). In his State of the Union address of January 1980, Carter declared the oil rich Persian Gulf region was vital to US interests; thus "an attempt by any outside force to gain control of the Persian Gulf region" would "be repelled by any means necessary, including military force" (cited in Grogin, 2001, p. 308). The US sent medical and military aid to the Afghan rebels and helped form a coalition with Pakistan, China, Saudi Arabia, Egypt and Britain "on behalf of the Afghan resistance" (Grogin, 2001, 308).

Given this history, it is safe to say that "an ebb tide under these games" (Boswell, 1980, p. F5) related to this conflict and the question of an impending US boycott of the Moscow Summer Olympic Games. And the increasing diplomatic and military tensions between the two governments provided yet another context in which to understand these militarized sport constructions. US goalie

Jim Craig's words reflected these anxieties and the consequences of the intensifying diplomatic conflict between the two superpowers in stating: "I might have to fight in a war against these guys ... But now I'm playing hockey. I hate them. I don't hate their hockey players specifically, but I hate what they stand for." Later, Craig would use militarized references in clarifying his original remarks: "What I'm trying to bring out is that these guys are great athletes ... Of course, if they weren't playing hockey, they'd be in uniforms marching somewhere." Craig's crass expressions of hatred and resolve further support the contention that militarized rhetoric is far from innocent.

Mobilizing the "Miracle": anticipating Reaganism

Within the US national political context, the team's victory was mobilized by a variety of actors across the political spectrum to support competing interpretations of the state of the nation and what would best serve broader US interests. President Carter's congratulatory attitude toward the Olympic hockey team and other Winter Olympic athletes was meant to harness the excitement that had greeted US Olympic victories in order to enhance public support for his administration's policies. A day prior to a White House ceremony honoring Winter Olympic athletes, Carter again stated his opposition to the 1980 Moscow Olympics and called for a permanent Olympic site to lessen the game's nationalistic sentiments. For Carter, Soviet military aggression in Afghanistan meant that holding the Olympics in Moscow "would violate those very principles of peace, of brotherhood and of the non-political alignment of those participating in the Games – exactly the kind of defect that would be corrected with a permanent site" (Kornheiser and John Feinstein, 1980, p. A1). Months later in April, 1980 when the United States Olympic Committee did vote to support the US boycott,[2] Presidential Press Secretary Jody Powell responded in a similar vein suggesting that "the US was confident that other leading nations of the free world will join in this demonstration that no nation is entitled to serve as host for an Olympic festival of peace while it persists in invading and subjugating another nation" (Lorge, 1980, p. A1).

Later, in a White House ceremony, Carter greeted 1980 Winter Olympians proclaiming that as "president of the United States of America this is one of the proudest moments I have ever experienced. I am deeply grateful for your tremendous achievements" (cited in Kornheiser and John Feinstein, 1980, p. A1). In particular, Carter praised the hockey team noting that their gold medal performance "was one of the most breathtaking upsets, not only in the Olympics, but in the entire history of sports" (cited in Kornheiser and John Feinstein, 1980, p. A1). House Speaker and Democrat Thomas "Tip" O'Neill proclaimed that the victory offered "a great lift to the American people, and it goes beyond that. There is nothing the Soviets appreciate more than sports – it is their one area of freedom – and their biggest sport is hockey. And now with the United States boycott you can believe me, heads will eventually roll in Russia" (cited in Kornheiser and Feinstein, 1980, p. A1).

And yet, liberal Democrats were not the only politicians attempting to rally public sentiment around the "miracle on ice." Years later while reflecting upon the untimely 2003 death of Head Coach Brooks, Oliver North[3] – himself a key Cold War figure through the Iran-Contra affair – also argued that the 1980 US Olympic champions served an important role in bolstering the nation during troubled times. North's New Right position proposed that the 1980 Olympic victory occurred, not at the height of US political dominance, but at a time when American international hegemony was faltering. Other popular accounts of the day also reflected this interpretation suggesting that "the national mood was malaise: the citizenry was gloomy, frustrated, angry, helpless" due in part to the economic restructuring accompanying deindustrialization and globalization (Powers and Kaminsky, 1984, p. 198).

According to Oliver North, this temporary American "malaise" was not due to the failure of the American people but due to the loss of the Vietnam war, increasing communist expansion and President Carter's ineffectual and demoralizing leadership around key issues related to US interests in domestic, foreign and economic policy realms. Conservative voices suggested that "failed" liberal policies had contributed to the Soviet invasion of Afghanistan, and the taking of 52 Americans hostages in Tehran in the fall of 1979.

For former President Richard Nixon, the Carter years had not only weakened the nation but the absence of a determined national "will" had enabled the spread of communism around the globe and possibly turned the United States into a minor power. The "hard-headed détente" he had practised during his presidency had spiralled downward to the "soft-headed détente" and failed policies of Carter's presidency with disastrous consequences that needed immediate attention (Jeffords, 1994). In Nixon's words, "thus reduced we will not survive – nor will freedom or Western values survive" (cited in Jeffords, 1994, p. 8). Immediate corrective attention was needed as ineffectual leadership and ill-conceived policies had left the nation "drifting," "floundering," "uncertain," and "irresolute" (Jeffords, 1994, p. 8).

Suggesting that Carter had unfairly berated the American public for a "'crisis of confidence' and a state of 'paralysis, stagnation and drift ... being too greedy, keeping their thermostats too high and taking vacations'," North lauded Coach Brooks and the US hockey team for not taking a similar defeatist position in battling adversity (North, 2003). For "Brooks could have easily followed Carter's lead and made excuses for his team – there were plenty. But Brooks knew they had at least one thing in their favor – they were Americans" (North, 2003).

According to Oliver North, US hegemony could only be restored with heroic, decisive and masculine figures like Brooks, the US hockey team and with a shift in national leadership, direction and ideology. Thus the

"Miracle on Ice" could be seen as a turning point for the nation. Less than a year later, Ronald Reagan would be in the White House and, under his leadership, the hostages came home, Soviet expansion was turned back in Afghanistan and Central America, and the malaise was lifted. It was Morning Again in America.

(North, 2003)

Again drawing upon ethnocentric narratives of American exceptionalism that "ignored the expansionist and militarized foreign policies which have helped to create and bolster American hegemony," North further argues that

Brooks and his players illustrated a belief shared by Ronald Reagan: Leadership is the courage to defy the fatalism of the quitters and so-called "experts." From Plymouth Rock to the Moon, we are an intrepid people not made for defeat. The Soviet skaters learned that lesson on a rink in Lake Placid. Their political leaders learned it years later in a cottage in Reykjavik.[4]

(North, 2003)

For North the hard-bodied masculine resolve of the victorious US hockey team eventually would also be successfully embodied by President Ronald Reagan in drawing upon "good old fashioned" American ingenuity and tough talk to restore the United States as a leader in world affairs. In this way then, the conservative, masculine and militarized narratives surrounding the 1980 US Olympic hockey team offered "staying power" and, in so doing, played a very similar role to other popular cultural forms of the day. According to Susan Jeffords (1994) some of the era's most popular Hollywood films also offered militaristic themes and determined masculine characters and these representations ultimately helped reinforce the domestic and foreign policies of President Ronald Reagan throughout the 1980s. In the late 1970s, Hollywood films began to shift away from previous plots focusing on the US losses suffered in Vietnam toward those that celebrated masculine foreign policy and military heroes (think, for example, of Sylvester Stallone's muscular Rambo). Reagan was eventually able to capitalize upon, build upon and reinforce a similar change in the cultural Zeitgeist in portraying himself – and by extension the nation – as strong, determined and assertive in battling the "evil empire" of the Soviet Union, the Sandinista government and the Columbian drug cartels. Much like the masculine action heroes of the era, Reagan used a similar hard-bodied individualistic sensibility to justify capital expansion and military initiatives while severely demonizing and limiting domestic social welfare spending. Read from this perspective, the puckish resolve of the victorious US hockey team was narrated in such a way that both anticipated and helped promote the broader sentiment, which eventually became know as the "Reagan Revolution."

The series of policies that popular representations – including Olympic hockey narratives – helped to legitimate greatly impacted upon people living within the US and across the globe. The cornerstone of the conservative policies enacted by Reagan depended upon cutting taxes for the most wealthy Americans, promoting multinational capital expansion throughout the world, while Reagan set about "initiating the most expensive peacetime military build-up in US history" including the Strategic Defence Initiative (Powaski, 1998, p. 262). While Reagan's willingness to accept Mikhail Gorbachev's internal work toward change that would eventually lead to the disintegration of the Soviet Union, in sum Reagan's policies more often had damaging consequences (Powaski, 1998). These militarized and anti-collectivist strategies severely compromised the national infrastructure as demonstrated by an increase in crime and educational inequalities, greatly elevated the national debt and noticeably widened the gap between the poorest and richest Americans. Furthermore, the escalating military build-up and crusade against communism, perhaps most famously embodied by the Iran-Contra fiasco, helped escalate conflict that adversely affected the lives of people in the postcolonial world.

Future imaginings

To paraphrase Cynthia Enloe (2000) charting and then intervening in the spread of militarization, requires a diverse array of skills – not the least of which are an ability to piece together fragmented, but often intersecting histories, an understanding of the dynamics of national memory and imagining, a working knowledge of economic rationales and an awareness of how hero worship intersects with gender and other manifestations of social difference.

In this chapter, I have applied these concepts in order to make visible the practices, which support the logic and aims of national military aggression and to make clear that militarization can be present in diverse sporting form – including narratives about the "miracle on ice." Thus, this chapter argues against those who proclaim that athletic battles between nations including those waged throughout the Cold War between the USSR and the US served as important cathartic substitutes for war. This incomplete line of reasoning suggests that symbolic sport battles are preferable to "real" wars and battles between nations where the stakes potentially include the massive loss of life. This analysis carves out another position that suggests that highly charged nationalistic athletic contests must be taken seriously as they often serve as an important site for the articulation and normalization of military world views. This understanding of the role that sport has played and continues to play in legitimating militarization is an important component of producing counter-narratives so that demilitarized sensibilities might be more widely valued and practiced.

Notes

1   The Brezhnev Doctrine is named for Leonid Brezhnev, the leader of the Soviet Union from 1964–1982 and is based upon information from a speech Brezhnev gave in 1968. This doctrine suggested that the Soviet Union could protect itself against (capitalistic) forces hostile to socialism. The doctrine was also used to justify the invasion of Czechoslovakia.

2   The United States would be eventually joined in the boycott by 55 nations including China, Germany and Japan.

3   Oliver North ran a covert government operation, which illegally sold weapons to Iran in order to free US hostages in Lebanon. The profit from those sales was then directed to the Contra rebel army in Nicaragua. North's felony convictions for this illegal activity were eventually overturned.

4   In 1986, Ronald Reagan met with Soviet leader Mikhail Gorbachev in Reykjavik, Iceland to discuss eliminating nuclear weapons. Reagan would not agree to stop work on the ballistic missile defense system.

Bibliography

Boswell, T. (24 February 1980). "Bittersweet memories of Lake Placid will endure." *The Washington Post*, F5.

Coffey, W. (2003) *The boys of winter: The untold story of a coach, a dream, and the 1980 US Olympic team*. New York: Crown.

Denlinger, K. (22 February 1980). "Only two to go for US Skaters, but watch that first step." *The Washington Post*, E3.

Delinger, K. (24 February 1980). "America finds a team to love." *The Washington Post*, F1.

Enloe, C. (2000) *Maneuvers: The international politics of militarizing women's lives*. Berkeley: University of California.

Grogin, R. (2001). *Natural enemies: The United States and the Soviet Union in the Cold War, 1917–1991*. Latham: Lexington Books.

Hall, S. (1992). "The question of cultural identity." In S. Hall, D. Held, and T. McGrew (Eds.). *Modernity and its Futures* (pp. 273–326). Cambridge, MA: Polity.

Jeffords, S. (1994). *Hard bodies: Hollywood masculinity in the Reagan era*. New Brunswick: Rutgers.

Johnson, C. (2004) *The sorrows of empire: Militarism, secrecy and the end of the Republic*. New York: Holt Henry.

Kindred, D. (23 February 1980). "Born to be players, born in the moment." *The Washington Post*, A1.

Kindred, D. (25 February 1980). "Joy on ice." *The Washington Post*, A1.

King, S. (forthcoming). "Offensive lines: Sport-state synergy in an era of perpetual war." *Cultural Studies–Critical Methodologies*

Klose, K. (24 February 1980). "Soviet fans seek reasons for loss." *The Washington Post*, F4.

Lorge, (13 February 1980). "A major victory for Carter." *The Washington Post*, A1

McDonald, M. and Birrell, S. (1999). "Reading sport critically: A methodology for interrogating power." *Sociology of Sport Journal*, 16, pp. 283–300.

Powaski, R. (1998) *The Cold War: The United States and the Soviet Union, 1917–1991*. New York: Oxford University.

Powers, J. and Kaminsky, A. (1984). *One goal: A chronicle of the 1980 US Olympic hockey team*. New York: Harper and Row.

Shapiro, L. (1980). "US hockey hopes start with Sweden." *The Washington Post.* D3.

Shapiro, L (21 February 1980). "US will meet Soviets Friday." *The Washington Post.* F1.

Shapiro, L. (23 February 1980). "US shocks Soviets in ice hockey." *The Washington Post,* D1.

Silk, M. Andrews, D. L. Cole, C. L. (2005) "Corporate nationalisms? The spatial dimensions of sporting capital," in M. Silk, D.L. Andrews and C.L. Cole (eds.). *Sport and Corporate Nationalisms* (pp. 1–12). Oxford: Berg.

Trujillo, N. (2000) "Hegemonic masculinity on the mound: Media representations of Nolan Ryan and American sport culture," in S. Birrell and M. McDonald (eds.) *Reading Sport: Critical essays on power and representation.* Boston: Northeastern (pp. 14–39).

Chapter 13

The Soviet Union and the Olympic Games of 1980 and 1984

Explaining the boycotts to their own people

Evelyn Mertin

Introduction

The increasing political tension between the two super powers – the USA and the USSR – in the late 1970s and early 1980s turned the Olympic Games of 1980 in Moscow and 1984 in Los Angeles into victims of the Cold War. The development of global politics not only prevented the athletes of these two direct ideological opponents from visiting each others' countries, but the boycott movement also influenced other nations within the two political blocs. Both of these Olympic Games suffered from the absence of the most important and interesting sporting opponents.

On each side of the "Iron Curtain" political campaigners, sport officials and journalists were involved in PR campaigns explaining decisions, shaping public opinion and trying to influence foreign decision makers and opinion leaders.

In this situation, the Soviet side found itself in a difficult position. On the one hand, they could not openly discuss the American-initiated boycott approach without referring to the Red Army's invasion of Afghanistan in December 1979. So this connection was never publicly confirmed. Nevertheless the Soviet public had to be prepared for a US American boycott of the Moscow Games and a reasonable explanation had to be created. On the other hand, the diametrically opposed situation four years later, when the socialist athletes did not compete in Los Angeles, had to be just as soundly justified without breaking the consistent Soviet propaganda line. This chapter will take a closer look at the way the Soviets explained their position, as morally correct and in full accordance with the Olympic ideal. The study is based mainly on Soviet sources (archive material, publications and newspapers) in order to examine the exclusive Soviet point of view at first hand.[1] After taking a brief look at the Soviet interpretation of their position within the Olympic movement, the socialist view of the events surrounding the Games 1980 and 1984 will be analysed separately. Finally some of the main features of both campaigns will be looked at comparatively.

The Soviet Union and the Olympic movement

In order to explain the Soviet line of argumentation concerning both Olympic boycotts, it is necessary to take a look at their interests within the Olympic movement. The young Soviet state was not (actively) part of the international Olympic movement for a number of reasons. Even though the *International Olympic Committee* (IOC) recognised the tsarist Russian *National Olympic Committee* (NOC) and its IOC members until 1932, the USSR was not invited to the Olympic Games in the Interwar period[2] as part of the "so called 'sanitary cordon', when a political and economic blockade covered Soviet Russia and its sporting contacts."[3] At this time, the socialist state tried to establish its own international workers' sports movement and was therefore not interested in competing in the "bourgeois" Olympic Games.[4]

A number of Russian authors see the "Soviet authority," clearly demonstrated in the victory over Hitler's Germany, as a crucial moment in the IOC's changing position towards the USSR,[5] preventing socialist sport from being further ignored internationally. But it was, more importantly, the Soviet side that developed an increasing interest in the Olympic movement. After the Second World War, the USSR adjusted their foreign policy strategies according to the newly emerged global political situation. Competing successfully in international sports was now recognised as a worthy and effective instrument against the ideological opponent within the "Cold War." Soviet athletes were to demonstrate socialist achievements to a global audience and represent the ideal "stereotype of a 'harmonically developed, ideologically convinced, plain and modest Soviet sportsman'."[6]

Because of the Olympic Games' particular importance as a sporting climax within an internationally approved and socially highly appreciated sports movement with its own ideals and values,[7] Soviet officials developed a special interest in Olympic sport. In addition to the publicity generated by gold medals and world records, the participation in the Olympic Games in particular opened up a completely new field of action for socialist propaganda. Consciously selecting the Olympic goals of peace, friendship and international understanding, the propaganda machine effectively succeeded in turning the Soviet Union from a former position of total rejection into a fully accepted, model participant in the modern Olympic movement from 1952 on.[8] The Soviet Union's participation was proclaimed as "in quality a new phase in the history of the Olympic movement and Olympic Games"[9] and was used to justify the political acceptability of the Soviet Union at international level.

Even though the Soviet side stretched the rules of the Olympic Charter with their interpretation of, for example, the amateur status of Olympic athletes or the demanded political independence of a nation's *National Olympic Committee* (NOC), they were never seriously sanctioned by the IOC. Soviet propaganda enthusiastically used the successful results of their athletes and the active participation of their sport officials within the Olympic movement to demonstrate the socialist commitment to fulfilling Olympic ideals and values, not only to their own public but also to a worldwide audience. They described their entry as a:

> terrific change in the existing powers [within the Olympic movement], supported by the developing worldwide socialist system [...] helping the growth of the idea of peace and democracy. The entry of the socialist countries' sports organisations into the wide Olympic arena not only demolished the Olympic movement's class restrictions but also defined a new distribution of sporting power within it.[10]

While Soviet publications related to the Olympic movement and socialist participation in international sports constantly criticized "the reactionary policy of the imperialistic West"[11] exploiting international sports for their political means and goals, they at the same time mocked the bourgeois slogan "sport without politics."[12] The irony in this criticism becomes comprehensible when the Soviet side points out the close relationship between sport and politics in the socialist system.[13] This ambivalent line of argumentation is interesting when it comes to the campaign surrounding the two major Olympic boycotts of the 1980s.

Selecting the Olympic venues for 1980 and 1984

Just as the Soviets had carefully planned their – guaranteed – successful entry into the Olympic arena at the Helsinki Games in 1952, their steps and activities within this global movement were also cautiously selected and determined in advance. In order to coordinate their interests and to attempt to influence decisions in the international sports organizations, the leading sport officials of the socialist countries met on a regular basis.[14]

After entering the Olympic Games as a sporting super power and actively pursuing a goal of establishing the socialist influence to "further democratise" the Olympic movement and prevent it "being used for class exploitation, the goals of commerce and business, propaganda for a bourgeois lifestyle and the capitalist system and its ideology [...]"[15] the Soviets now felt prepared for a further step. Not expecting any "political, economic, or sporting reasons why Moscow should not be chosen"[16] they were disappointed when their first bid to host the Olympic Games in 1976 was not successful. This defeat at the IOC session of 1970 in Amsterdam is scarcely mentioned in Soviet literature. Only a few months later, the Soviet NOC announced Moscow's second proposal to host the Games in 1980. In order to avoid another defeat and the mistakes made in the first bid, a strategic campaign was staged to present the Soviet Union's capital as a "perfect host" and more effort was applied in communicating with IOC members.[17] The city of Los Angeles, which had not campaigned as full-heartedly as Moscow, was the only other candidate at the IOC session in Vienna in 1974.[18] After Moscow was chosen to organize the Olympic Summer Games in 1980 in a secret ballot, the Soviets saw this choice as a logical consequence of their achievements within the Olympic movement:

> Alone the fact of carrying out the Olympic Games in Moscow was a clear device for the success of the progressive powers within the persistent and long battle for more democracy in international sports and the Olympic movement. At the same time it was an unconditional acknowledgement of the Soviet athletes' leading performances and their great authority. By awarding the organisation of the Games to Moscow the world sports leaders basically approved the peace loving foreign political course of the Soviet government.[19]

Due to the endlessly increasing costs of organizing Olympic Games and athletes' security, the IOC did not have to "vote" for the host of the 1984 Games, as Los Angeles was the only candidate. And it was due to the lack of other opportunities that the IOC agreed that the organization of these Games should be funded by private enterprise.[20]

Not only were the Summer Games of 1980 and 1984 to be organized in ideologically opposed countries, but the Olympic Winter Games of 1980 were to be held in the American Lake Placid while the white Olympics of 1984 would be staged in the Yugoslavian city of Sarajevo. Even without any political interference, the choice of Olympic cities for the early 1980s would have promised interesting comparisons and offered ideological campaigners in East and West a variety of approaches for their work.

However, the increasing political tension between the two superpowers did directly influence the Olympic Games in just these countries. And the information campaigns surrounding these major sport events had to be adjusted to combat the threat of any loss of authority over public opinion.[21]

Hosting the first Olympic Games in a socialist country

The Olympic Games in Moscow in 1980 were the most significant international event to be organized in a socialist country.[22] Hosting the Games was seen as an opportunity to invite the world to the Soviet capital and present the socialist way of life in perfection. As the head of the organizing committee for the Moscow Games 1980 (OC "Olimpiada-80"), Novikov stated in a letter to the Central Committee of the CPSU in January 1976:

> For the first time in all their history the Olympic Games will be staged in a socialist state – in the capital of our mother country – Moscow. They are a great international event, arousing the interest of a worldwide public, they are an important means of strengthening contacts between people of different countries and developing mutual understanding and friendship. [...]

> Thousands of athletes, officials from international organisations, representatives of the press, radio and television and also large numbers of foreign tourists will have the opportunity to get acquainted with the achievements and life of the Soviet nation, with their culture and arts, and the historic memories of our mother country for the duration of the Olympic Games.[23]

In addition to the "usual" work of the OC "Olimpiada-80," the Soviet Union increased their international sporting contacts in preparation for the Games. Soviet embassies abroad were instructed not only to communicate regularly with the heads of the Olympic and sports movements of each country, but also to report on the foreign press activities concerning the Olympic preparations in Moscow. This way the Soviet propagandists could monitor foreign reactions and create a suitable "contra propaganda" campaign, if necessary.

The Soviets had high expectations of the Games as a unique opportunity not only to demonstrate the power and strength of socialism to their own people but also to non-socialist countries. The Soviet media played an important role in this plan. A large publicity campaign was designed and staged in preparation of the Olympic Games, not just within the socialist bloc but also with special emphasis internationally.[24]

The Moscow Games were depicted in the Soviet media, commentaries and publications just as they were planned to be – regardless of the boycott. The coverage and later discussion of the first Games staged in a socialist country pursued lofty aims. The successful organization and preparation of the world's greatest sports festival was considered to be a collective achievement.[25] Including the whole nation consequently meant that the success was not only due to Moscow and its inhabitants but to the whole Soviet people. This strategy had a cunning effect: as a result, every positive reaction towards the Moscow Games was construed as a socialist achievement.

Connecting the success of a sports meet to the achievements of the socialist system was possible because the Olympic idea underwent selective exposure. At any time, Soviet officials and press releases would stress that the Moscow Games contributed to what they called "enhancing cultural understanding, friendship, and peace."[26] These so-called "noble ideals of the Olympic Movement" were "close and coherent for the Soviet people"[27] and furthermore they concurred with what the Soviet Union referred to as their "peace loving and progressive policy."[28] All this would have happened and been the tenor of Soviet propaganda – even if there had not been a boycott. Gold medals and the leading position in the medals table were just one way of demonstrating socialist achievements. Much more valuable, however, was the international acknowledgement of the successful organization and accomplishment of the Games in Moscow which their own propaganda used as proof of the Soviet achievements.

Working hard to keep it a success

Even before the boycott, discussion provoked by the Soviet invasion of Afghanistan in December 1979 threatened the perfect Games and the Soviets had therefore kept a close eye on critical remarks in the Western press. Up to this point the Soviet propaganda had spread positive reports on the Olympic preparations to serve the interests of a good PR campaign. But the new political situation called for a more concrete reply.

A vital reaction was to intensify all means of communication with IOC members, other NOCs and sport officials in order to avoid as much damage as possible. At the IOC session in Lake Placid, where the Winter Olympics of 1980 were to take place, the IOC confirmed Moscow as host of the Summer Games once again, rejecting any suggestions of rescheduling or moving these Games to a different venue. In Novikov's report on the participation of the Soviet delegation at this session, he stated that Lord Killanin had regarded a letter from Leonid Brezhnev, General Secretary of the Soviet Communist Party, as an official document guaranteeing official support of the Moscow Games. "In this situation Killanin, just as many of the IOC members, characterised the Soviet situation, expressed in comrade L.I. Brezhnev's letter, as an act of political wisdom."[29] This exaggerated version of the situation is characteristic for the Soviet interpretation and official line of argument regarding the position of the IOC and the Moscow Games. After almost three decades of presenting the Olympic movement as socially acceptable and morally sacrosanct – and describing themselves as the ideal participants – it only took a minor effort to portray the IOC as *the* neutral court, guiding opinion and making decisions that were final. The IOC's verification of Moscow as Olympic host therefore also confirmed the Soviet position as "untouchable," correct and acknowledged by a "superior authority." Any criticism or anti-Moscow comment could now be warded off with reference to the IOC's statement, a handy instrument for ideological campaigners.

Only a few days after the first public calls for a boycott of the Moscow Games, following the invasion of Afghanistan, the head of the news agency *Novosti*, Tolkunov, sent the Central Committee of the CPSU a briefing. Entitled "A few features of the anti-Soviet propaganda connected to the Olympiad-80 and recommendations for contra propaganda" he commented that: "In the last couple of days the west has again activated the campaign for a boycott of the Olympiad-80 in connection with the events in the Middle East."[30] In addition to the new topic "Afghanistan" the Western commentaries criticized "human rights in the USSR" and the bottleneck situation in customer service and accommodation issues in the Olympic host city. The briefing goes on to recommend a special line of argumentation for press releases in the Soviet Union and abroad and for Soviet sport officials communicating in this issue. "Determinedly repulse the attempts by bourgeois reactionary elements to exploit the Olympiad-80 for interfering with the home affairs of the USSR and conducting political and ideological diversion."[31] *Novosti* offers a number of quotations of Olympic figures, ranging from

IOC president Lord Killanin to the president of the NOC for [West] Germany, Willi Daume, to underline this and attest that this line of argument is "general" and internationally approved. Further suggestions for contra propagandistic approaches are, for example, to emphasise that the Games will take place at a high technical and organizational level, that more than 600 restaurants, cafés and dining halls are waiting for Olympic tourists, and that the Soviet people do not have a negative feeling about the Olympic Games. This last point will be exploited *vice versa* four years later, when one of the often repeated points of criticism will be the lack of Olympic enthusiasm among the Los Angeles inhabitants or the Americans in general.[32]

The Soviet press and the threatening boycott

While contra propaganda material was mainly directed at foreign recipients, the Soviet public also had to be "taken care of" in this emerging situation. It is obvious when studying the press coverage of these months that neither the organizers of the Games nor the planners in the propaganda unit anticipated a boycott of Moscow-80.[33] In the first days of January 1980, the Soviet press almost ignored the growing discussion in Western countries. But the policy makers soon noticed that they might well end up with an even greater problem if they totally concealed this issue. If the global political situation was to end in a boycott of the 1980 Games, it would be even more difficult for Soviet propaganda to explain the absence of the American athletes, in particular, to the Soviet people. Coverage of this topic early on allowed for the preparation of the Soviet public for this occasion, developing their own (Soviet) line of argumentation – one which consciously created a carefully selected picture in the public's awareness.

So the responsible editors were to blend the means and goals of Soviet propaganda into the boycott discussion. The account was selective: unpleasant topics such as the reasons why a boycott was being demanded were played down, described at a distance from the original context or just left out. These methods were applied, for example, when it came to the invasion of Afghanistan, which was not once named as the "real" reason for the boycott campaign[34], nor therefore as the reason for the ultimatum which US President Carter gave the Soviets in the first months of 1980. Nor was there reference to any of the other arguments presented in support of the boycott.

The Soviet press emphasized the intense political debates surrounding the Olympic participation within the Western democracies and thereby questioned the "real" freedom and human rights of these countries. Socialist propaganda took advantage of this situation and documented their anti-American approach with vivid examples. The picture of the betrayed athlete as a victim of political intrigues grew within the coverage of the boycott discussion. The reader's attention was mainly directed to the USA, but the description of the situation in other Western democracies was very similar. Time and again the Soviet press underlined that the Kremlin had guaranteed in writing to the IOC that the Games would be staged according to the Olympic Charter. This given promise functioned as proof that they had done everything possible and thus pushed the entire blame onto foreign – mainly US – politicians for failing to keep international agreements. Regardless of the very close connection between politics, party and sports in the USSR, Soviet propaganda accused the Western governments of "rudely" and "wrongly" interfering in sports affairs.

The Soviet public received an explanation for the absence of some of the world's best athletes, but its attention was directed to the great number of participating countries, the cheerful and colourful festival in the Soviet capital and the great sports competitions that proved the authentic character of Olympic Games. The polarization between the questionable activities of the boycott initiators and the pure intentions of the organizers of the Games supported the familiar Soviet propaganda. The boycott was criticized in such a way as to make it look ineffective and ridiculous and to show that the Games had not lost any power, brightness or importance:

> The failure of the boycott around the Moscow Olympiad and its generally acknowledged major success confirm just what the bourgeois politicians feared: The Olympic Games in Moscow have become an impressive new demonstration of the socialist athletes' successes, an enormous support for propagating the achievements of the workers' USSR in the fields of economy, politics, society and culture, socialist democracy as well as the Soviet way of life. The Games have proven our nation's devotion to peace and outstanding hospitality.[35]

Shifting gears: heading for Los Angeles 1984

After the Soviets had presented their "perfect" Games to a worldwide audience, they had little time to rest from their efforts. The "brightness" and "joyfulness" of the Moscow Games was to be promoted at any occasion that came up: meetings of international sports organizations, IOC sessions, the official viewing of the Moscow film, and so on. Preparations for participating in the 11th Olympic Congress in Baden-Baden in 1981, and in the upcoming Summer Games in Los Angeles, required sport officials and propaganda campaigners to continue their work at full speed. The Soviet participation in the Olympic Congress was carefully planned and coordinated with other socialist countries, who weren't pleased at all with the private enterprise surrounding the next Olympic location. But they also felt pressured by attempts to change the amateur status within the Olympic movement.[36]

Still a long way away from deciding not to send their athletes to Los Angeles, the Soviet sport committee discussed "Measures of preparing Soviet sportsmen for the Olympic Games of 1984" at their regular meeting. They decided on increasing the number of so-called "Olympic reserves" and called for a plan to "morally, politically and psychologically prepare athletes, trainers and judges and educate them to a high political culture." With a skeptical look at the next Olympic venue in America, they demanded "a careful watch on the preparations" development for the Games of the XXIII Olympiad and [to ensure] that the organisers give a guarantee and follow all IOC rules and requirements."[37] The political situation was also taken into consideration:

> The clear anti-Soviet position of the present US government [...] has already damaged international sports cooperation and can darken the atmosphere of the Games of the XXIII Olympiad. Therefore it is necessary to carefully watch the developing situation in and around Los Angeles and take compulsory steps to oppose ideological diversion.[38]

Looking at the Soviet activities in between the Olympic Games in Moscow and Los Angeles, it becomes obvious that no "revenge" for the Moscow boycott had been immediately planned. The archive records clearly show how much money and effort was expended on the preparation of the Soviet athletes and sport delegations. Great attention was paid to the impression their representatives would make while competing in capitalist countries. Ideological lectures were intensified to secure the delegations "exemplary behaviour" and prevent them being influenced by ideological opponents "under the circumstances of the aggravating international situation."[39] Soviet officials repeatedly denied any kind of sanctions against the Los Angeles Games, and were not eager to diminish any of Moscow's glory by upsetting the IOC. In an interview in summer 1982, Pavlov, the Soviet NOC president at that time, brought the discussion to the following conclusion:

> We do not intend to boycott the Olympic Games. The USSR is not planning any kind of revenge action for the American boycott in 1980. On the contrary, we vehemently support every strengthening of the Olympic Movement. However, the participation of Soviet athletes [...] is only possible, if the American government guarantees to obey the Olympic Charter.[40]

The final part of this statement already shows the common line of Soviet argumentation in this period: The rules and requirements of the Olympic Charter – the codification of the fundamental principles, rules and bye-laws adopted by the IOC – were rendered as neutral and "untouchable." Any kind of disrespect or neglect of this charter was considered to be not-Olympic or even anti-Olympic.

Keeping the public informed

Soviet publications and the press show a very similar approach for the time in between the Moscow and LA Games. The glory of the Moscow Games is always kept in mind while regular criticism of the Olympic preparations in Los Angeles makes this past success shine even brighter. After the "Olympiad-80" had brought a flood of Olympic literature, the number of new publications was drastically lower in the following years. A small number of booklets such as "The Olympiad-80 in the eyes of the Americans"[41] or "US sports after the Olympic Games in Moscow"[42] took a closer look at the next Olympic hosts and the "deficits" of sports in capitalist countries. They can be considered as propaganda material against the ideological opponent, but they are not comparable to the increasing number of Soviet publications on this topic in 1984, when decision-making came nearer and had to be explained in detail.[43]

An analysis of the Soviet newspapers shows that there was no decisive or clearly set outline of approach from the propaganda unit.[44] In 1980 and 1981 the few articles and reports on the preparations for the Los Angeles Games carefully criticised the American organisers – it was as if the Soviets were waiting for the outcome of the US elections early in 1981. This critical undertone increased the following year and was mainly resumed in a column headed "Focussing on Olympic Problems." The problems troubling the Soviets were commercialism[45], racism in the US and environmental questions. In October 1981, daily sport newspaper *Sovetskij Sport* wrote: "Problems, problems, problems ... The Olympic City of Los Angeles has already, [...] overtaken all other host cities when it comes to problems that have occurred."[46]

From May 1982, a new topic was included in Soviet scolding of the upcoming Olympics: the correct maintenance of the Olympic Charter during the preparations. The Soviet sport officials demanded official guarantees to ensure their rights within the Olympic movement. They already feared being discriminated against by American authorities and anti-Communist groups in the US. Examples of hostile movements and plans against Soviet athletes in America were described in the press.

For the time being, the Central Committee of the CPSU delayed the final verdict of participation and decided to approach this issue again in May 1984 according to the political situation.[47]

Dramatizing the build up to Los Angeles

The press coverage on the preparations of the 1984 Games changed after Brezhnev died in November 1982. His successor Andropov obviously viewed Soviet participation in the Los Angeles Olympics with much more optimism. In his fairly short time in power, his comments on the Olympic preparations were – in the first instance – more friendly. Critique was even supplemented by suggestions for solving problems.

However, this pleasant tone changed radically following developments in American–Soviet diplomacy after the shooting down of a South Korean plane in September 1983. The increasing tension in global politics after this event clearly influenced the decision of whether or not still to come to Los Angeles. Two further facts that played an important role were changes in the leading positions of Soviet sport and politics. In late 1983, the long time official head of Soviet sport Pavlov was succeeded by M.V. Gramov, who came directly from the propaganda department of the Central Committee. And political differences between Reagan's America and the Soviet Union were not resolved when Tshernenko, a representative of the "Brezhnev guard,"[48] became head of the Soviet state in February 1984.

Los Angeles was portrayed more and more critically, with references to anything from smog and ecological problems to facts such as that Los Angeles boasted the world record holder in "competitive smoking"[49] or that a murder was committed there every 24 minutes. The atmosphere was also soured as Los Angeles was reported to be a "chauvinist city" and centre of anti-Soviet organizations[50] which would support the "US politics of enhancing anti-Soviet hysteria."[51] It was reported that the Californian Congress had adopted a resolution directed to the US administration in mid-September 1983 that demanded the exclusion of Soviet athletes at the Games in Los Angeles. Further, the Soviet sporting press reported on the founding of the anti-communist group called "Ban the Soviets" in Los Angeles and their plans of anti-Soviet activities.[52]

The other fact massively influencing the atmosphere surrounding the Games was commercialism. The Soviets could not get accustomed to the idea of financing the Games commercially and feared that this would cause less interest among the public. "In this sense, the Olympiad in Los Angeles has turned into its own form of a psychological vacuum. It is probably the first Olympic city to express such an amazing indifference towards their 'own' Games."[53] In the Soviet interpretation, commercialism filled the existing "psychological vacuum" and could therefore be seen as the connection between the Olympic Games and the Americans, "translating" the Olympic ideals into an advertising language that was understandable to them. "This language, however, doesn't suit the expression of the Olympic Games' humanistic meaning at all."[54]

Attention also focussed on the "helpful" topic of the Olympic Charter and the claim that the US government had not fulfilled all the necessary requirements – even that it had violated the Charter by not sticking to the specification that only one Olympic village should be built, for all athletes. Although all this criticism was leveled at the Olympic hosts, the Soviets were willing to show that they were well prepared for competing in Los Angeles:

> [...] the participants of the Olympiad-84 must be convinced that this competitive inspection doesn't only reveal their sport mastery but [...] their ideological firmness, moral maturity and political preparedness for this difficult test which the Soviet Olympic athletes must leave as winners and only as winners.[55]

Examples like this quotation from a brochure containing an ideological lecture scheduled for April/May 1984 demonstrate that even just before the Central

Committee made its decision at the beginning of May, the internal signs and hints indicated that Soviet athletes would participate. On 29 April 1984, the head of the Soviet sport committee, Gramov, sent the Central Committee a paper[56] informing in detail about the "aggravating situation" in Los Angeles. All relevant points of criticism and problems were summarized and the atmosphere of threat and hostility against the Soviets was particularly stressed. Gramov suggested continuing the athletes' preparation and, thus, increasing the pressure on the Americans to issue a guarantee for the Soviets' safety. Only if such a written document was provided "could a decision be made in favour of the participation of the Soviet athletes." Already trying to find ways to place the Soviet Union in "for us a favourable worldwide public opinion" by implying particular propaganda strategies, he goes on also to recommend that the Soviet Union "look at the question of organising a number of sport events [...] to compensate for the blow to morale that will inevitably hit the athletes" in case of the USSR's not competing in Los Angeles. So even though Gramov proposes to continue the athletes' preparations, his further comments already head in a different direction.

The Soviets played a double game in these last months before the opening of the Games. On the one hand, they maintained the version that no one was planning a boycott.[57] On the other hand, the American hosts were constantly being attacked by Soviet propaganda, leaving little space for hope. "It is obvious that the top of the Soviet state either left the question of participating in the Olympiad-84 open until the last minute, or that only a very small circle of people already knew of the formed 'collective opinion'."[58] Even the archive material that is accessible today does not answer this question unequivocally.

On 9 May 1984, the Soviet boycott declaration was published – although it has to be stated at this point that the Soviets themselves never spoke of or applied the term "boycott." In the following days, a propaganda campaign was extended to underline the rightfulness of this decision. Declarations by all other boycotting countries were also printed. Selected interviews and press clippings from abroad were used to suggest that the international community had reacted positively to this resolution. The main factors used in explaining the boycott and blaming the Americans were: missing guarantees for Soviet security, the threat of anti-Soviet and anti-Communist actions endangering the Soviet athletes and finally the claim of disregarding the Olympic Charter.[59]

Comparing the strategies of 1980 and 1984: festival of youth and peace versus psychological vacuum of Los Angeles

The propaganda campaigns surrounding both Olympics had to be adjusted to the increasing political tension of the Cold War. In 1980, Soviet officials' public reactions and comments developed according to the growing boycott discussion in the West and, up to 1984, the political undertone of these reactions was dependent on the particular head of the Soviet state. Both events were blamed mainly on American politics. While the 1980 boycott was rendered as a political motivated campaign initiated by Washington, the Soviets did not see any interference of their own politics in the discussion of 1984: "When we made the decision [not to compete in Los Angeles], we did not demand any kind of political concession from the Americans, for example the military retreat from Grenada, and we did not threaten any sanctions."[60] The "wrongful" intrusion of politics on the Olympic Games in America was again portrayed as an act of the US government. Interestingly enough, the socialist criticism in the build-up to 1984 mainly targeted the organizing city of Los Angeles and the state of California. Even if there were lines of argument constantly aimed at the political heads in Washington, the main and most frequent accusations were directed at the "local" organizers. This "correspondence" with the Olympic Charter, clearly declaring the city and not the country to be host of the Games, not only supported one of the most important Soviet allegations in this campaign but also clearly displays the American boycott campaign in 1980, that targeted Soviet politics in general, as unacceptable. In both campaigns, the Soviet version dissolves the expected diametrically opposed positions by declaring and "proving" their own total compliance with the Olympic Charter as clear evidence for the rightfulness of their position. This is achieved by accurately displaying every disregard of the Olympic movement's official legislation committed by the Americans.

> For the government of the USA the noble Olympic ideals are no more than empty words, and the Olympic Charter is nothing but meaningless paper. [...] Today we can be sure to say: nothing that is connected to the USA brings anything good to the Olympic world.[61]

By exposing the American activities as politically motivated threats against the Soviet Union in 1980 and against the socialist and especially Soviet athletes in 1984, anti-Soviet and anti-socialist intentions were selectively underlined instead of anti-Olympic purposes. In the case of 1980, this strategy made sense, as it prevented the Soviet Union's own absence in Los Angeles four years later being interpreted as anti-Olympic. In the discussion of 1984, this characteristic helped to explain why only socialist countries withdrew from the Games.

A further feature helping to compare the Moscow Olympic Games favourably with the LA event was a look at the consequences: in 1980, the American athletes were portrayed as victims of their government's politics as they were deprived from competing in the "world festival of friendship and peace." The American nation and especially the organizers were again seen as victims in 1984 as they were prevented from hosting a real "festival of friendship and peace." To prove this point, both Soviet press and literature used foreign press clippings and quotes, for example referring to foreign journalists who were of the opinion that: "[…] Games without the athletes from the USSR and other socialist countries just could neither be a worldwide festival of friendship nor an interesting sports event."[62] While the Soviets always underlined the authenticity of the Moscow Games by recalling the sheer number of world and Olympic records, they used the number of world championship titles in Olympic sports won in 1983 as proof of their superiority even without competing in Los Angeles.[63] Myths about the Soviet athletes having to stay home as officials feared they might be defeated by either the East German athletes or the American hosts are – of course – never mentioned and specific arguments are given to oppose any such kind of suggestion. They even turn this idea around and use it for their own purposes, describing how determined the Americans were to win the Olympic Games in their own country that they were only left with finding a way to "[…] not let the Soviet athletes come to the Games in Los Angeles […] [as] 'when everything else is forgotten – the medals will remain'."[64]

Finally, both Olympic Games were summarized and compared: while the Moscow Games were viewed as a "worldwide festival of friendship, peace and understanding" the Los Angeles Games were described as a commercial event staged in an "atmosphere of psychosis, hate and hostility"[65] and with too much patriotic symbolism – and, to obliterate any claim to authenticity, the description "Americaniada-84"[66] is used.

In the three decades leading up to the 1980 and 1984 Summer Games, the athletes of the two opposing superpowers had raced, fought and competed to prove social, political and cultural superiority. But the combination of time and place in Moscow and in Los Angeles prevented the athletes from even entering these substitute battlefields of the "Cold War." Politics had already determined supposed winners and losers before the Olympic flame had reached the host city – depriving athletes from both blocs of competing in maybe their most important competition and fulfilling their greatest dream.

Notes

1   Most of the material used from the Soviet period must be classified as socialist propaganda. All Russian texts were translated by the author herself. To facilitate easy reading, the author mainly refers to "America" and "American" instead of using the term US American, but all events and comments relate to the United States of America.

2   Cf. Riordan J. (1980) *Sportmacht Sowjetunion* Bensheim: päd.-extra Buchverlag, p. 83.

3   Prozumenshtshikov M.J. (2004) *Bol'shoj sport i bol'shaja politika* (Series: Kul'tura i vlast' ot Stalina do Gobertsheva Issledovanija) Moscow: Rosspen, p. 168.

4   Cf. ibid. and Riordan (1980) *Sportmacht*, pp. 83–85.

5   For example: Demeter G.S. (2005) *Otsherki po istorii otetshestvennoj fizitsheskoj kul'turj i olimpijskogo dvijenija* Moscow: Sovetskij Sport, p. 261 or Shtejnbach V.L. (2002) *Vek olimpijskij. Kniga I* Moscow: Terra-Sport, Olimpija Press, p. 247.

6   Prozumenshtshikov (2004) *Bol'shoj sport*, p. 14.

7   Cf. Lenk H. (1980) "Auf dem Weg zur Erneuerung der olympischen Idee," in: *Olympisches Feuer* 30(1), p. 10.

8   Cf. Bernett H. (1990) "Olympismus in der DDR: Als die Ideologie mit der Idee verwechselt wurde," in: *Olympisches Feuer* 40(5), pp. 17–18.

9   Pavlov S. (1980) *Olimpijskaja Enziklopedija* Moscow: Sovetskaja Enziklopedija, p. 252.

10   Stolbov V.V. and Filatov J.I. (1981) *Novaja rasstanovka cil v olimpijskom dvijenii posle vtoroj mirovoj vojnj* (Lekzija dlja studentov-saotshnikov) Moscow: [no publisher], p. 7.

11   Ibid., p. 16 just as one example.

12   Cf. Potshinkin V.M. (1985) *Sport i ideologitsheskaja bor'ba v sovremennom mire* Moscow: Fizkul'tura i Sport, p. 31; Dolgopolov N. (1988) *Po tu storonu sporta* Moscow: Molodaja Gvardija, p. 266; Romanov A.O. (1973) *Mejdunarodnoe sportivnoe dvijenie* Moscow: Fizkul'tura i Sport, pp. 9–10.

13   "The two opinions in this matter, whether there is a connection of sport with politics or not, do not exist for Soviet researchers and Marxist researchers abroad. The answer, clearly, is positive, as sport, an important phenomenon of social life, is controlled by the state and political parties in one way or the other in every country, [...]." Potshinkin (1985) *Sport i ideologitsheskaja bor'ba*, p. 31 or cf. Kozlovskij A.A. (1999) *Sozial'no-pedagogitsheskie aspektj preodolenija krizisa mirogo olimpijskogo dvijenija v period podgotovki i provedenija igr XXII Olimpiadj v g. Moskve* Moscow: [unpublished dissertation], p. 39 or Luk'jynov V. (2004) *Rossija i olimpijskoe dvijenie: vtshera – segodnja – zavtra* Moscow: Terra-Sport, p. 143.

14   A "Commission of the socialist countries' sport organisations for the cooperation in the field of preparing and carrying out the Olympic Games 1980 in Moscow" was specially founded to coordinate the efforts of all socialist countries contributing to this "greatest event in international sport life." In his welcoming speech to the commission's meeting in Moscow on 16 March 1976, the head of the organizing committee Novikov went on to say: "And here I may openly say yet something else, that this is not only a distinguished sporting, but also social-political event." State Archive of the Russian Federation (GARF), fond 9610, opis' 1, delo 82, list 8 (from here on: GARF, f. 9610, o. 1, d. 82, l. 8).

15   Stolbov and Filatov (1981) *Novaja rasstanovka cil*, p. 5.

16   Soviet IOC member Andrianov cited in Senn A. (1999) *Power, Politics, and the Olympic Games* Champaign: Human Kinetics, p. 145.

17   Cf. Hazan B. (1982) Olympic *Sports and Propaganda Games. Moscow 1980* New Brunswick: Transaction Books, p. 74.

18   For more details on the campaigns see: Knecht W. (1980) *Der Boykott. Moskaus mißbrauchte Olympiade* Cologne: Verlag Wissenschaft und Politik, pp. 34ff.

19   Committee for Physical Culture and Sport of the USSR [Department for educational work] (eds.) (1984) *Voprosj ideologitsheskoj bor'bj na mirovoj arene. Ideologitsheskaja bor'ba i mejdunarodnoe sportivnoe dvijenie. Tema XII* [Metoditsheskie rekomendazii v pomosh' propagandistam, rukovoditeljam polititsheskoj podgotovki tshlenov sbornjch komand SSSR, DSO i vedomstv sportivnjch shkol] Moscow, p. 32.

20   Cf. Shaikin B. (1988) *Sport and Politics. The Olympics and the Los Angeles Games* New York: Praeger Publishers, pp. 39–40.

21   The Soviet term "propaganda" does not have a critical or negative connotation, it is often found in a context where it can be replaced by "promote" or "advertise." "In our understanding, propaganda is the spreading of truth about the Soviet Union, our foreign and home policies, the life of our nation as well as their cultural and sport achievements." Gus'kov C.I. (1982) *Olimpiada-80 glasami Amerikanzev* Moscow: Fizkul'tura i Sport, p. 33.

22   Cf. Hazan (1982) *Olympic Sports*, p. 85.

23   Novikov to Central Committee of CPSU, [7.01.1976], in: Russian State Archive for New History, fond 5, opis' 69, delo 423, list 2 (from here on: RGANI, f. 5, o. 69, d. 423, l. 2).

24   Cf. Hazan (1982) *Olympic Sports*, p. 106. Three main issues were highlighted in the presswork, in special Olympic publications and by members of the Moscow Organizing Committee: "(1) progress of the construction of Olympic facilites [sic] and other preparations for the Moscow Olympics; (2) the Moscow Olympics as the greatest sports event ever to take place; (3) the special contribution of the Moscow Olympics to peace, friendship, détente, and international cooperation."

25   This was a general aim of propaganda and implemented in sporting commentary. In the Soviet Union, successful sport results were not considered the achievement of an individual but were always interpreted as acknowledgement of the socialist collective.

26   For example: "World Festival of Sports," in: *Izvestija*, 20 July 1980, p. 1.

27   "Opening of the IOC Session," in: *Izvestija*, 15 July 1980, p. 3. The Deputy Chairman of the Supreme Soviet, Kusnezov, said in his speech at the opening of the IOC Session in Moscow 1980: "The modern Olympic movement, capable of creating an atmosphere of confidence, good will and peace among nations, has become an important factor in the social life of our world. The noble Olympic ideals are very close and coherent for the Soviet people."

28   For example: "Peace and Olympism are inseparable," in: *Sovetskij Sport*, 20 January 1980, p. 4.

29   RGANI, f. 5, o. 77, d. 130, l. 12.

30   RGANI, f. 5, o. 77, d. 133, l. 2.

31   Ibid., l. 5.

32   Gel'perin for example criticizes the lack of interest in amateur sports and therefore Olympic sports in the USA; Gel'perin J.M. (1982) *Sport [USA] posle olimpijskix igr v Moskve* [Moscow: booklet printed at VNIIFK], p. 5.

33   For more details on the Soviet press coverage of the boycott of the 1980 Games in Moscow see: Mertin E. (2003) "Der Boykott der Olympischen Spiele 1980 in Moskau in der sowjetischen Presse," in: *Stadion. International Journal of the History of Sport* 29, pp. 251–261.

34   Soviet literature, especially concerned with the questions surrounding the Olympic Games 1984 in Los Angeles, generally mentions the "connection to the events in Afghanistan" but does not refer to it as the main reason for the boycott movement.

35   Booklet "Collected material for the ideological and informative-propagandistic preparation of sport delegations going abroad" [Moscow 1982] in: GARF, f. 7576, o. 31, d. 8432, l. 16.

36   The 11th Olympic Congress in Baden-Baden is also an interesting subject when looking at the Soviet activities and interests of the time. However, this chapter concentrates on the two Olympic boycotts and can therefore not take this matter into consideration.

37   GARF, f. 7576, o. 31,d. 6421, l. 5.

38   Gel'perin (1982) *Sport [USA]*, p. 21.

39   Ibid., p. 154.

40   "From Spartakiads to Olympic Games," in: *Sovetskij Sport*, 18 June 1982, p. 4.

41   Gus'kov C.I. (1982) *Olimpiada-80 glasami Amerikanzev* Moscow: Fizkul'tura i Sport.

42   Gel'perin (1982) *Sport [USA]*.

43   For example: "Games on sale": Bezrukavnikov I.B. and Kukushkin V.V. (1984) *Igrj na progazhu* Moscow: Fizkul'tura i Sport; "Who is undermining the Olympic ideals": Popov S. and Srenizkij A. (eds.) (1984) *Kto podrjvaet olimpijskie idealj* Moscow: Agenstvo petshati novosti; "Olympic Games: incomparable in comparison":

Kolodnij A.G. and Spasskij O.D. (1985) *Olimpijskie igrj: sopostavlenie nesopostavimogo* Moscow: Sovetskaja Rossija; "Sport and ideological battle in today's world": Potshinkin V.M. (1985) *Sport i ideologitsheskaja bor'ba v sovremennom mire* Moscow: Fizkul'tura i Sport.

44   For a more detailed analysis of the Soviet press coverage leading up to the Olympic Games 1984 in Los Angeles see: Martens A. (2005) *Der Boykott der Olympischen Spiele 1984 aus Sicht der sowjetischen Presse* Cologne: [unpublished diploma thesis at the German Sport University Cologne].

45   The daily sports newspaper *Sovetskij Sport* introduced a specific column focussing on the "critical point" commercialism. "The problem of commercialism can only be seen in the broad and true Olympic context and in consideration of the social and ethical aspects of the Olympic movement. Experience shows that growing commercialism, its penetration into all areas of international and national sporting life objectively and inescapably leads to undermining the humanistic principals of Olympic sport, to forgetting the noble Olympic ideals and in the end to a transition to professionalism." in: "Under the sign of the golden calf," in: *Sovetskij Sport*, 12 February 1982, p. 4.

46   "Thousand and one problems," in: *Sovetskij Sport*, 28 October 1980, p. 4.

47   Cf. Prozumenshtshikov (2004) *Bol'shoj sport*, p. 213.

48   Prozumenshtshikov (2004) *Bol'shoj sport*, p. 220.

49   Committee for Physical Culture and Sport of the USSR (1984) *Voprosj ideologitsheskoj bor'bj*, p. 5.

50   Ibid., p. 47.

51   "[…] The Reagan administration is fuelling anti-Soviet hysteria. The provoking affair surrounding the South Korean airplane is used as a pretence. The reactionary groups in the USA demand a breakdown of connections between our countries. The 'Falcons' are collecting signatures in order to hinder the Soviet athletes from performing at the Olympic Games in Los Angeles.[…]" in: "Nothing was learned", in: *Sovetskij Sport*, 22 October 1983, p. 4.

52   "The failure of an affair," in: *Sovetskij Sport*, 23 November 1983, p. 4.

53   Kolodnij and Spasskij (1985) *Olimpijskie igrj*, pp. 45–46.

54   VNIIFK [All Soviet Scientific Research Institute for Physical Culture] (1983) *Nekotorje polititsheskie i organisazionnje voprosj podgotovki Los-Anzhelesa k igram XXIII Olimpiadj. Obzor* Moscow: booklet printed at VNIIFK, p. 15.

55   Committee for Physical Culture and Sport of the USSR (1984) *Voprosj ideologitsheskoj bor'bj*, p. 59.

56   RGANI, f. 5, o. 90, d. 144, l. 39–43.

57   On 16 April 1984, the president of the Soviet NOC and head of the Sports Committee of the USSR, Gramov, spoke at a press conference. Being asked about foreign press speculating about a possible boycott Gramov answered: "We are not aiming at a boycott of the 1984 Summer Games. […] Soviet sports organisations have always advocated the development and maintenance of the Olympic Movement. Concerning a boycott it must be said that this term and not lastly its meaning and consequence in action are totally unacceptable to us" in: "For the maintenance of the Olympic Charter," in: *Sovetskij Sport*, 17 April 1984, p. 1.

58   Prozumenshtshikov (2004) *Bol'shoj sport*, p. 220. Prozumenshtshikov, who is vice director with the archive of the Central Committee's documents, describes the actions of April and May 1984 in great detail from page 212 onwards.

59   "'No!' to the attacks on the ideals of peace," in: *Sovetskij Sport*, 16 May 1984, p. 4.

60   Kolodnij and Spasskij (1985) *Olimpijskie igrj*, p. 6.

61   Ibid., pp. 36–37.

62   Ibid., p. 15.

63   "Soviet athletes gained a total of 62 gold medals in championships and world championships in 1983 in sports that are on the Olympic programme, the GDR – 44, the USA – 29." in Gramov's (secret) letter to the Central Committee of the CPSU entitled "About the aggravating situation concerning the Olympic Games in Los Angeles (USA)." RGANI, f. 5, o. 90, d. 144, l. 39–43.

64   Popov and Srenizkij (1984) *Kto podrjvaet*, pp. 23–24.

65   Ibid., p. 30.

66   Ljubomirov N.I. (1985) *Sovetskij Sport na olimpijskich arenach* Moscow: Znanie, p. 49.

Chapter 14

"Sport and politics don't mix"
China's relationship with the IOC during the Cold War[1]

Susan Brownell

> I believe that we have it in our power to lead the world in showing that we're the only non-political, international, independent, non-governmental organization in the world.
>
> (Lance Cross, IOC member in New Zealand, in the Executive Board meeting in Montevideo, Uruguay, April 5–7, 1979, during discussion of the China problem)

One of the legacies of the Cold War is the aphorism "sport and politics don't mix." It is a common misperception that this is an official policy of the International Olympic Committee (IOC), and it is often accompanied by the belief that because the aphorism is clearly false, the IOC must be hypocritical.

Probably the main forum in which this aphorism was employed was in the rhetoric surrounding the China question. Nowhere is the dilemma of the IOC's position as a non-governmental organization in a governmental world more evident than in the China question, which was on the agenda of almost every Executive Board meeting and IOC Session from 1952 to the 1980s, and which bedeviled four IOC presidencies – Sigfrid Edström (1942–1952), Avery Brundage (1952–1972), Lord Killanin (1972–1980), and Juan Antonio Samaranch (1980–2002). Although the prohibition against "talking politics" often prevented constructive discussion, ultimately it was the stubborn insistence of key IOC members that "sport and politics don't mix" that enabled them to carve out enough space in which to act. And thus, it was within the partially independent world of sports that "ping-pong diplomacy" initiated the restoration of diplomatic relations with China worldwide in the 1970s. The "Olympic formula", developed in 1979, made possible the co-participation of Taiwan and China in international events and organizations in various realms, even while their governments remained officially hostile.

"Athletic geography": Coubertin's enduring legacy

Pierre de Coubertin (1863–1937), who led the establishment of the IOC in 1894, felt strongly that the IOC should be independent from any government. In Allen

Guttmann's analysis, Coubertin's aristocratic conception was that IOC members should be a circle of like-minded gentlemen who shared a liberal consensus based on the nineteenth-century Western distinction between private and governmental spheres. Guttmann argues that the liberal consensus made it possible for IOC members to believe that they were not engaging in politics even while the Olympic stadium was ringed with a hundred flags (Guttmann, 1984, pp. 170–71, 134–35, 138). The unique characteristic of the IOC is that it elects its own members in a process called "cooptation," considering them to be trustees of Olympism and ambassadors of the Olympic Movement to their respective countries. Near the end of his life, Coubertin maintained, "I continue to believe that the constitution of the IOC is excellent, based as it is on the principle that I will call 'reverse delegation'. This means that the mandate comes from the idea, which then attracts followers" (Coubertin, 2000, p. 743).[2]

While the IOC was to be independent of national politics, the task of organizing Olympic Games and Olympic teams was, over time, delegated to national Olympic committees (NOCs). Only one NOC could represent a country, and only citizens of a country could represent it in the Olympic Games. National Olympic committees were conceived in like fashion to the IOC: they must be politically independent of national governments, but unlike the IOC, they were representatives of territorial units over whose sports they had jurisdiction. From Coubertin's time to today, the political units with which the IOC constructs its relationships have been called "countries" in English (*pays* in French, the official legal language of the IOC). In practice, most of these territorial units were sovereign nations, but many of them were not, since their numbers included colonies, dependent territories, countries of contested independence, and various other anomalies. "Country" (or "nation") assumes a homogeneous ideal that does not exist in the real world. The meaning of "country" or "nation" was frequently discussed in the IOC debates about the German, Korean, and Chinese problems during the Cold War, and their meaning was first clarified in a footnote in the Olympic Charter in 1960. "Country" was not formally defined in the Olympic Charter until 1997, in the wake of the dissolution of the Soviet Union and the ongoing conflict between China and Taiwan (*Olympic Charter*, Rule 31.1).

Almost from its inception, the IOC began to arbitrate its own decisions about what constituted a country. Coubertin distinguished "political geography" from "athletic" or "sports geography," and wrote,

> The fundamental rule of the modern Olympiads is summarized in these terms: "All games, all nations." It is not even within the power of the International Olympic Committee, the highest authority in this matter, to change this. I must add that a nation is not an independent State. There is an athletic geography that may differ at times from political geography.
>
> (Coubertin, 2000, p. 590, see also p. 266)

It is important to remember that Coubertin was the product of a time before "nationalism" and "politics" took the form that would characterize them at the time of the Second World War and the Cold War; his understanding of these terms was different from the understanding with which we now read his works. In his time, the major perceived threat to the purity of sport was the rise of the working class; nationalist politics were not conceived as the major threat until the Cold War. Thus, Coubertin could extol the appeal of national flags in a way that was not possible after history had shown to what horrors extreme nationalism could lead.

Even in the context of the tremendous political pressures surrounding the "Nazi" Olympics of 1936, Coubertin argued that the "ravages" that politics can cause were only superficial; Olympism was the "soul" of the Olympic Movement, and would not change according to the whims of fashion, but would evolve slowly and healthily, in conformity with the laws of humanity itself (Coubertin, 2000, p. 584). Coubertin was simply not overly concerned about the influence of politics on Olympism because he had ultimate faith that Olympism was permanent while politics were ephemeral. He died in 1937.

Origins of the China question

The People's Republic of China (PRC) was established on 1 October 1949. The defeated Nationalists (Kuomintang) headed by General Chiang Kai-Shek fled to the island of Taiwan, also known in the West as Formosa, taking with them the name of their defeated regime, the Republic of China (ROC). The two governments each claimed to be the legitimate government of all of China and remained in a state of mutual hostility. Direct contacts were forbidden. At first, most nations retained diplomatic relations with the regime on Taiwan, which held a seat in the United Nations until the PRC's admission in 1971. Both the PRC and Taiwan adhered to the "one China principle," which stated that no expression either of Taiwanese separatism or of the existence of "two Chinas" could be tolerated. For the PRC, this meant that in international organizations, the "Chiang clique" must first be expelled before the mainland could consider entering because the simultaneous membership of both Taiwan and the PRC would be an expression of "two Chinas."

There were three IOC members in the Republic of China. C.T. Wang[3] had held important posts in the new government of the Republic of China (established in 1912) and was active in sports due to his connection with the YMCA. He was co-opted by the IOC in 1922 and settled in Hong Kong after the Revolution (Sun, 2000, p. 23). At his recommendation, H.H. Kung had been co-opted in 1939 when he was Minister of Finance in a vain attempt to secure more government financial support for sports (Tan and Dong, 1993, p. 96). Kung was not interested in sports, never attended an IOC meeting, and moved to New York in 1948 (Sun, 2000, p. 23). Up to three IOC members were allowed in a country, so in order to maximize China's influence in the IOC, Wang recommended Shou-yi Tung (Dong Shouyi), with whom he had worked closely. Dong had spent two years at Springfield College in Massachusetts, where he had played basketball, baseball, and football. He was co-opted in 1947 when he was the General Secretary of the China National Amateur Athletic Federation (CNAAF). Dong remained in China after the revolution despite the urging of friends to leave. Thus, after 1949, the IOC was confronted with an unusual situation in which two members were linked to a state that had lost its nation. Wang and Kung were generally not involved in Olympic affairs and neither of them settled in Taiwan. Kung submitted his resignation from the IOC in 1955 and Wang in 1956.

When the Soviet Union was recognized by the IOC in 1951, the IOC itself became politicized as never before. The USSR led a socialist bloc within the IOC, which met before IOC Sessions in order to develop a unified strategy dictated by the USSR. Hoping to strengthen the socialist contingent at its first Olympics, the USSR drew China's attention to the upcoming 1952 Helsinki Olympic Games. The All-China Athletic Federation sent a telegram to the IOC Secretariat, which stated that it intended to participate in the Helsinki Olympics in that year.[4]

Early in 1952, Dong Shouyi read the text of the 5 February telegram in a newspaper. From the text he realized that the All-China Athletic Federation did not understand the nature of IOC membership, so he wrote them a letter explaining that membership was determined by the IOC and was permanent, and that he was the sole IOC member remaining in China; after reflection, he added that he had not yet received the approval of the Chinese people (Tan and Dong, 1993, p. 113).

In the new China, Dong's political background was "complicated." He was not a Communist Party member and had never paid much attention to politics, but he had associated with high-ranking officials in the Nationalist regime. It is unlikely that he would have been allowed to continue as the IOC member in China but for a lucky coincidence that had occurred 32 years previously. In 1919, while Dong was coaching and refereeing basketball for the YMCA in Tianjin, he came to know a Nankai University student who often came to the YMCA to play basketball (Tan and Dong, 1993, pp. 21–23). That student was Zhou Enlai, who would later become the Premier of the new government and China's most beloved revolutionary leader. Zhou was interested in sports and personally oversaw China's relationship with the IOC until his death in 1976. Thus, it was he who received the report on China's communications with the IOC followed by a mention of Dong's letter with the assessment that his "past politics are not good." The report suggested that whether or not to "utilize" him should be decided after questioning him. Zhou requested that Dong be brought to Beijing for further questioning and supported allowing him to continue. The Soviet embassy also argued that he could be useful because of his international connections (Tan and Dong, 1993, pp. 123–124).

Sigfrid Edstrøm

In 1952, at the 46th IOC Session in Oslo, Sheng Zhibai, attaché at the Chinese embassy in Stockholm, requested recognition of the All-China Athletic Federation as the National Olympic Committee of China (Speech submitted by Sheng Chih-pai, Appendix to the Minutes of the 46th IOC Session in Oslo). It does not appear from the minutes that Taiwan was represented there. Edstrøm told Sheng that the national Olympic committee must be politically independent, and when Sheng was unresponsive, he struck the table with his cane and left the room, "leaving Otto Mayer to explain the difference between sport and politics" (Guttmann, 1984, p. 143). From their very first encounters, Edstrøm and the IOC members seemed antagonistic to the "mixing of sport and politics" by the Chinese.

At the 47th Session in Helsinki on 17 July 1952, two days before the opening ceremonies of the Helsinki Olympics, the IOC received Gunsun Hoh from Taiwan and Sheng from mainland China. In 1948, Gunsun Hoh had been bitterly disappointed when C.T. Wang recommended Dong Shouyi to the IOC instead of himself, and from that time on was an enemy of Dong and Wang (Tan and Dong, 1993, pp. 93–98). In 1952, he reemerged as the President of the self-styled "Chinese Olympic Committee" in Taiwan and was a key figure in Taiwan's interventions with the IOC until Henry Hsu became an IOC member in 1970. Hoh began by declaring himself a lover of sport and loyal defender of sporting ideals, but when he arrived at the topic of sport on mainland China, he stated that they had information that Dong Shouyi had been sent to a concentration camp behind the "iron wall" and was perhaps dead. Dong's signature on the telegram to the IOC did not match the one on his identity card for the 1948 London Olympics and the Communists were deceiving the IOC (Annex 4 to the Minutes of the 47th IOC Session in Helsinki).

In an even less diplomatic presentation than that of Hoh, Sheng presented two demands to the IOC: 1) the immediate expulsion of the reactionary Kuomintang clique along with H.H. Kung and C.T. Wang, 2) the continued recognition of the All-China Athletic Federation and an invitation to participate in the XV Olympic Games. Edstrøm responded by informing Sheng that he was not in a position to impose conditions, nor to give advice or instructions to the IOC, and that the IOC made its decisions in complete independence. The Session reacted with applause (Minutes of the 47th Session, p. 9).

A long discussion ensued, after which a compromise proposal was approved in which neither national Olympic committee was recognized, but each was allowed to compete in the sports in which its national governing body was recognized by the respective international federation (Minutes of the 47th Session, p. 10). Erik von Frenckell of Finland stated that the Helsinki organizing committee had studied the problem and decided to invite both, and that the IOC should ignore "racial, religious and political questions, and apply the ideal which inspires us, which is that of the union of the youth of the world" (Minutes of the 47th Session, p. 8).

In the end, the Taiwanese boycotted the Olympic Games and the mainland delegation only arrived just before the closing ceremony because of the difficulty in traveling imposed by the fact that most countries did not have diplomatic relations with the PRC. Dong had not been sent to the Session because his political status was still under assessment, but he was finally included in the official delegation (Tan and Dong, pp. 119–124).

Although he had missed the IOC Session, he arrived in time to attend an Executive Board meeting. When he entered the room Edstrøm, who suspected an imposter, asked, "Have we met?" Dong suppressed his annoyance and, through his interpreter, listed the times that they had met in 1947 and 1948, and asked how Edstrøm could have forgotten. Edstrøm then questioned why he needed an interpreter. Dong replied that he had not used his English for many years. Edstrøm demanded that the interpreter leave, and Dong stood up and left with his interpreter. Mayer rushed to his side and said in a low voice, "Dong, please stay and speak with us for a few moments." Dong left angrily. It was not until later that Dong understood that the IOC members had believed that the interpreter had been sent by the Communist Party to control him. Edstrøm's behavior had been a ploy to get rid of the interpreter so that they could speak with Dong alone.

Since he was not a Party member, Dong had no confidence in his ability to correctly interpret policy. IOC members apparently did not understand that if Dong had met with them alone, he could have exposed himself to criticism upon his return to China. The interpreter, in other words, was a safeguard and a backup, not a warden. The issue of the interpreters used by socialist nations in the IOC remained contentious, for the USSR and others as well as for China.

Avery Brundage

At the Helsinki Session, Avery Brundage was elected president of the IOC. Brundage had earned his spot on the IOC by opposing a US boycott of the Berlin Games. In Allen Guttmann's portrayal, the heated debates leading up to the Berlin Games solidified Brundage's belief that sport should be kept separate from politics (Guttmann, 1984, pp. 68–81). Guttmann argues that Brundage shared Coubertin's vision of the Olympic Games as non-political and was never able to understand that calling for freedom from government interference was *ipso facto* a political position (personal communication, March 10, 2006). I would add that, given their difference in background, Coubertin's understanding of politics was not the same as Brundage's, but what they both shared was a belief that the Olympic Movement could only thrive if utilized in the service of its own self-defined mission, and not in the service of national governments, commercial interests, or other interests.

Brundage was one of the world's foremost collectors of Asian art. In 1939, he had spent several weeks in Japan and had visited Shanghai and Hong Kong, where the war between Japan and China was already underway (Guttmann, 1984, p. 203). Although his art collecting took him to Taiwan frequently after that, he never returned to China. In a meeting with Brundage before the 51st Session in 1956, Dong presented him with an art book and sports postcards and showed Brundage a letter to the IOC members that outlined the history of the China–Taiwan problem. Brundage took out a pencil and crossed out sections of the letter, forbidding him to discuss politics, stating "you can talk about this," "you can't talk about this." Then he pointed to the art book and the photos and said, "We are interested in those, we don't discuss politics" (Tan and Dong, 1993, p. 142). It seems likely that Brundage's involvement in the Taiwan art market reinforced his impression that the Nationalists appreciated culture while the Communists only cared about politics. Brundage once said that he "had not yet met a sportsman from Red China with whom I could discuss athletic matters, but only diplomatic representatives" (Espy, 1979, p. 44).

The accusation of "talking politics" as a way of silencing discussion

In 1954, the Athens Session recognized the "Olympic Committee of Democratic China" (that is, the PRC, but mistakenly called by a different name) by a vote of 23 to 21, with Kung and Wang absent (Minutes of the 49th Session, p. 24). The IOC was left with two national Olympic committees in what was claimed to be one national territory – a point that was used for the next twenty-five years to argue that the IOC had violated its own Olympic Charter.

Before the 50th IOC Session in Paris in 1955, the Chinese delegation engaged in extensive preparations to present the case for recognizing only the PRC and expelling Taiwan. Against protocol, Dong was allowed to have an interpreter, 26-year-old He Zhenliang. At the meeting of socialist nations before the Session, the Chinese proposed to discuss their opposition to the "two Chinas," but were discouraged by the Soviet representative Constantin Andrianov, who felt the language was too "political."

During the next day's meeting of the Executive Board with the National Olympic Committees, Rong Gaotang, the Chinese Olympic Committee representative, started to explain the Chinese position that Taiwan was a province of China. Brundage impatiently silenced him by stating that it was a political discussion that did not concern the IOC, to which Rong replied that Brundage himself was engaging in politics and that the dividing of the Chinese Olympic Committee into two was precisely a political question (Tan and Dong, 1993, p. 133; Minutes of the Executive Board Meeting, 12 January 1956).

Before the Session, Andrianov again cautioned the Chinese that they could be expelled if they were not careful. Dong twice wanted to take the floor to speak, but each time when he and He Zhenliang sought the advice of Andrianov, they were told that if they spoke again they risked expulsion (Liang, 2005, p. 29).

When Dong finally resolved to ignore Andrianov and began to stand up, he felt a large hand press down on his left thigh, and Andrianov said to him, "We socialist nations occupy a very small minority, if you provoke something it will be bad for us" (Tan and Dong, 1993, p. 135). After the Session, Andrianov presided over a meeting of the socialist nations, at which Rong Gaotang protested that the Bulgarian, Stoytchev, had stated that there were "two Chinas." Andrianov retorted that what Stoytchev had said was true and an argument ensued. Finally Andrianov said angrily, "In the past the Soviet Union had no status in the IOC and international sports. Our position only improved because of our achievements in sports. I hope China can also do this!" (Tan and Dong, 1993, p. 135).

In January 1956, Dong Shouyi and He Zhenliang attended the 51st IOC Session at the Winter Olympic Games in Cortina d'Ampezzo. He Zhenliang's biography recounts,

> Dong Shouyi's speech was not granted a discussion and was shelved by Brundage in the name of "not talking politics." … [T]he meeting gave one the feeling that it was tightly controlled by the West in all respects, while the Soviet Union and Eastern European countries each had their own plans and were not prepared to stand up for what was right, and there was no room for reason. Zhenliang had attended two IOC meetings in one year, and both times he felt very oppressed.
>
> (Liang, 2005, p. 31)

Thus, a situation evolved in which the China and Taiwan sides were not able to discuss their situation because anything they said was labeled "talking politics." The "Soviet Elder Brother" silenced them with the same admonition. The lack of support from the Eastern bloc stemmed from the problem of divided Germany. West Germany was recognized by the IOC in 1951 and an agreement to field a joint West–East German team was signed. The unified German team, which had always been beset by tensions and ill will, was hailed by Brundage as a triumph of sport over politics. It was constantly held up as a model for the Chinese, despite the very important difference that, unlike the German regimes, the governments on Taiwan and the mainland had just engaged in a bloody civil war. The USSR and the other socialist nations supported East Germany's desire for independent recognition, but it was not granted until 1965. China's request that the IOC recognize only one China ran counter to the request to recognize two Germanies and thus was not welcomed by the Eastern bloc nations.

When China's advance group arrived at the Melbourne Olympic Games in 1956, it discovered that the Taiwan side had already entered the Olympic Village, registered under the name "Formosa, China," and the "illegitimate national flag" of the Republic of China had been raised. Since the presence of a PRC team would have "created the appearance of 'two Chinas,'" the Chinese declared that they were pulling out of the Games. Facing the Melbourne Session,

Dong discussed strategy with his colleague Huang Zhong, but they could see no way out. As Huang put it, "You have two sets of household rules. One is the IOC, one is the Chinese Olympic Committee, and it is not easy to please two grand-mas!" (Tan and Dong, 1993, p. 160). Huang and Dong met privately with Brundage, but the conversation followed the usual tack: When they tried to state their position, Brundage said, "This is a political problem, sports are not concerned with politics, the IOC cannot solve this problem." Huang got up and left. Brundage asked Dong, "Who is he?," and after being assured that he was a sportsman, left for a meeting (p. 160).

The Melbourne Session decided that a letter should be sent to the Peking Chinese Committee expressing "displeasure [at its] repeatedly raising political questions which have no place in IOC discussions." Dong objected and made a long speech, stating that he could not understand why Brundage said he was engaging in politics, and accusing some people within the IOC itself of engaging in "dirty politics" (Tan and Dong, 1993, p.162).

In December of 1957, Dong wrote a letter to Brundage contesting the representation of their exchange in the minutes of the Melbourne Session, stating:

> I cannot agree when people with certain intentions call these remarks "of a political character." In Melbourne Session [sic], I simply explained that we should recognize only one Olympic Committee in China and that should be the All-China Athletic Federation …
>
> (Letter from Dong to Brundage, 20 December 1957)

Brundage replied on 8 January 1958,

> We cannot approve that your contention and remarks at Melbourne and at Sofia were not political. Even the third paragraph in your letter [which included the excerpt just quoted] is political. You know, and as a matter of fact, everyone knows that there is a separate Government in Taiwan. We did not create this situation. As for Taiwan, it was last part of Japan and not of China. As a matter of fact, the natives are neither Chinese nor Japanese … one of the fundamental principles [of the Olympic code] is that there shall be no politics in sport. That's why we are not pleased to have representatives of your country continually introducing political questions into our meetings.
>
> (Letter from Brundage to Tung, 8 January 1958)

As Dong later recounted it, this letter outraged him.

> He not only completely denied our protests of these many years, but he completely tore open that veil which had already been so thin, and revealed his true face … without the slightest bit of knowledge he distorted

history, confused black and white, and offered a typical bad example of 'not talking politics' while obviously engaging in politics.

(Tan and Dong, 1993, p. 173)

One of the interesting points in Brundage's letter is his interpretation of the Fundamental Principles of the Olympic Charter, which had been revised in 1949: they did not state that there shall be no politics in sport, but only that there shall be no discrimination on the grounds of color, religion, or politics (Lennartz, 1995, p. 40).

Although Dong's account makes it sound as if his letters represented his individual reaction, they were drafted by He Zhenliang and doubtless underwent careful review by the All-China Athletic Federation and ultimately Premier Zhou himself. And yet, one could also understand if something in Dong snapped at that moment. He was then caught in the middle of the anti-Rightist campaign. Like many intellectuals, he had responded to the Party's calls for corrective suggestions and had published an article analyzing China's sports system at the end of 1957. The request for advice was immediately followed by a backlash in which those who had offered the solicited advice were labeled "counter-revolutionaries" and "rightists" and denounced. Dong's 22-year old son, Dong Erzhi, had already been labeled a "rightist" while Dong was at the Sofia Session.[5] Demonstrating the opposing ideologies of the IOC and the Chinese Communist Party, while Dong had been criticized within the IOC for putting politics above sport, he would be criticized and denounced in China for the next twenty years for "only caring about sport, not about politics" (Tan and Dong, 1993, p. 194). This was the beginning of a disastrous quarter century for intellectuals. The rise of "extreme leftist ideology" was reflected in the tone of the letters exchanged with Brundage. On 23 April 1958, Dong wrote a fierce reply to Brundage that included the paragraph:

As for your remark "There is a seperate [sic] Government in Taiwan", Mr. President, you must not forget how this situation is brought about. ... That these traitors are able to survive in Taiwan until today is due to the political, economic and military aid openly given by the US Government and open interference in the internal affairs of our country by the US Government.

In March, Dong was assigned to a year of thought reform in a so-called "socialist academy" and was only able to return home once a week (Tan and Dong, 1993, pp. 183–184).

Brundage's reply on 1 June stated:

... The I.O.C. has nothing to do with politics. It does not recognize nor deal with governments. ... Despite your obligations as a member of the International Olympic Committee, on every occasion you have attempted to introduce political questions and if you continue to violate both the letter and the spirit of our rules the only remedy will be to request your resignation.

On 19 August 1958, Dong replied:

> Mr. President,
> I am most indignant at your letter dated June 1. Evading the questions I raised in my letter of April 23, you continued your mean practice of reversing right and wrong, wantonly slendered [sic] and threatened the Chinese Olympic Committee (All-China Athletic Federation) and myself, and shamelessly [sic] tried to justify your reactionary acts. This fully reveals that you are a faithful menial of the US imperialists bent on serving their plot of creating "two Chinas."
> [...]
> I have been a colleague to other members of the I.O.C. for many years. We have jointly made contributions to the international Olympic Movement and built up a good friendship among us. I feel painful [sic], however, that the I.O.C. is today controlled by such an imperialist like you and consequently the Olympic spirit has been grossly trampled upon. To uphold the Olympic spirit and tradition, I hereby declare that I will no longer cooperate with you or have any connections with the I.O.C. while it is under your domination.
>
> Tung Shou-yi

In 1958, China also withdrew from eleven international sports federations and thus began its long exclusion from the Olympic Movement, along with internal chaos. The economically disastrous Great Leap Forward began in 1958.

Despite the absence of any IOC members in China or Taiwan, the China question continued to receive attention within the IOC. At Soviet instigation in 1959, Taiwan's Olympic committee was required to change its name. Brundage bypassed ratification of the new name by the Session and entered Republic of China Olympic Committee onto the list of recognized Olympic committees, an act that was later deplored by the Chinese and Lord Killanin.

In 1960, the Rome Session voted to add a footnote in the Charter clarifying the terms "country" and "nation":

> Since the Olympic Movement is non-political, the words "country" or "nations" in these rules are intended to apply also to a geographical area, district or territory ...
>
> (Minutes of the 57th Session 1960: 3)

Nineteen years later, this clarification would allow China to accept Taiwan's membership in the IOC on the basis that Taiwan is a territory of China.

Ping-pong diplomacy

Meanwhile, after China's withdrawal from the IOC its diplomatic efforts turned toward Asia, Africa, and Latin America. The 1962 Asian Games were held in Indonesia, with which the PRC had established diplomatic relations. The Indonesians privately assured the mainland Chinese that Taiwan would not compete, but they were unwilling to take a public stance. In the end, the identity cards posted by the Indonesian organizers to Taiwan mysteriously disappeared in the mail, and the team was unable to enter Indonesia. Gunsun Hoh tried to enter with the team from Thailand and was seized and deported. The Asian Games Federation withdrew recognition of the Games, according to the mainland Chinese view, "on the pretext of opposing political interference in sport." The mainland Chinese further felt that Avery Brundage "insistently used the excuse that politics should not interfere with sports to practice his politics against the people" (Liang, 2005, pp. 55–56). The IOC withdrew its patronage of the Asian Games and threatened sanctions, which angered Indonesia's President Sukarno. He responded by leading the establishment of the Games of the New Emerging Forces (GANEFO) with the declaration, "Let us declare frankly that sport has something to do with politics. And Indonesia now proposes to mix sport with politics" (Espy, 1979, p. 81). While Western observers might not have understood the bitterness expressed in this remark, clearly Sukarno was directly attacking the IOC ideology that had effectively silenced Asia's voice in the world of international sport. A coup d'etat in Indonesia and the Cultural Revolution in China put an end to GANEFO after the first installation in 1963 and the Asian GANEFO in 1966, but they had sent shockwaves through international sport.

During this period, Brundage's attitude toward the China problem remained so rigid that IOC members began secret contacts with mainland China behind his back. In 1970, Brundage was approached by Taiwan's Henry Hsu about standing for election to the IOC, and responded by designing a strategy to bypass the unanimous opposition of the Executive Board by collecting the signatures of a majority of IOC members on a petition to the President (Hsu, 1998, p. 63). With respect to this affair, Killanin later accused Brundage of the kind of behavior about which Brundage himself was most self-righteous: of not being politically independent, of mirroring the views of the US State Department, and of violating the rules and spirit of the IOC (Killanin, 1983, p. 11).

Due to the Cultural Revolution, China had stopped taking part in international sporting events until a personal entreaty from the head of the Japanese Table Tennis Federation persuaded Chairman Mao to send a team to the 31st World Cup in Table Tennis in Japan in March 1971, where they had friendly contacts with the US team. In April, Mao decided to accept the request of the US to send a table-tennis delegation to China. "Ping-pong diplomacy" paved the way for China's admission into the UN in October, 1971.

In 1972, the Asian Games Federation passed a motion recognizing the PRC and revoking Taiwan's membership. This was the first time since 1959 that

China had succeeded in being admitted to a major international sport organization and having Taiwan expelled from it.

Lord Killanin and China's re-admission to the IOC

Lord Killanin followed Brundage as IOC president in 1972. He had always been interested in China since his days in China as a young reporter during the Sino–Japanese War in 1937. "It was, I felt, a curious anomaly that the country with the world's largest population did not take part in the Games" (1983, p. 108).

The biography of He Zhenliang recounts that from their first contact with him in 1973,

> we understood that Killanin was very different from his predecessor Brundage … He was sympathetic toward China because Ireland had a long and bitter history of domination by England … He was not as arrogant as Brundage and enjoyed listening to our stories …
>
> (Liang, 2005, pp. 90–91)

By contrast, Henry Hsu's first meeting with Killanin left a bad impression. When he ran into him on a train after the 1965 Madrid Session,

> he asked if I came from Taiwan and I answered, "I come from Taiwan's Republic of China." I never expected that he would cock his head and say, "In Rome in 1960 your entering the stadium 'under protest' was an insult to the entire IOC." … He was very agitated during the whole conversation, and his prejudice toward our Chinese Olympic Committee was also very deep.
>
> (Hsu, 1998, p. 67)

The China problem heated up before the 1976 Montreal Olympics. Canada had recently formed diplomatic relations with the PRC and Prime Minister Pierre Trudeau declared that Taiwan could only compete under the name "Taiwan." The US supported Taiwan. Taiwan did not accept Trudeau's conditions and withdrew at the last moment.

The Cultural Revolution officially ended in 1976, Premier Zhou and Chairman Mao died, Deng Xiaoping rose to power, and in 1978 the Era of Reform and Opening-up began. On 1 January 1979, China and the US announced the establishment of diplomatic relations and the US acknowledged the PRC as the sole legitimate government of China. Taiwan was left with official diplomatic relations with only a handful of nations in the world. China also changed its official diplomatic policy toward Taiwan's membership in international organizations, no longer insisting on the expulsion of Taiwan, but allowing Taiwan to maintain its membership so long as it was indicated as a province of China and did not use the name "Republic of China."

At the 80th Athens Session in 1978, Killanin had established a three-member committee to visit China and Taiwan and submit a report. The committee was constituted of New Zealand's Lance Cross, Romania's Alexandru Siperco, and Jamaica's Roy Anthony Bridge. Killanin had assumed that Siperco would favor mainland China, Bridge would favor Taiwan, and Cross would be neutral; thus the committee would be balanced. However, Lance Cross came out strongly in support of Taiwan (Killanin, 1983, p. 113). Cross, a quick-talking radio announcer, had become an IOC member in 1969, and his stance against mixing sport and politics was no doubt strengthened by the African boycott of the 1976 Montreal Olympic Games over the visit of a New Zealand rugby team to South Africa. He had argued that the boycott was unjustified as rugby was not an Olympic sport and was not under the control either of the New Zealand government or the IOC (Dictionary of New Zealand Biography). He had been identified by the Taiwanese as a friend as early as 1970 (Hsu, 1998, p. 62). At the Executive Board meeting in Lausanne on 10 March 1979, Cross argued vigorously for an arrangement under which both the PRC and the ROC changed their names, claiming that "geographic" designations would sidestep the "political" problem: "That's why I tried to avoid political determinations because the IOC cannot be involved in a political decision. Let the political people make those decisions" (audiotapes of Executive Board Meeting, March 10,1979).

The Executive Board received a Chinese delegation at this meeting.[6] He Zhenliang answered the discussion questions through an interpreter. He had begun his career as a French interpreter for top Chinese leaders and spoke fluent French, and could have dispensed with using Chinese altogether, but this was a tactic to allow him time to collect his thoughts before speaking. He bested Cross at his own game when Cross raised the only hostile question: "It is a fact that there are two regimes existing, both claiming control of respective areas and this has been existent for 26 years without the respective governments reaching a solution. Why is it felt that the IOC should solve it?" Having mastered the IOC logic that had been used against China for two decades, He replied in Chinese, and Lou Dapeng translated into English, "This is an interesting question. The IOC is a non-political body that considers questions from the interest of sports" (audiotapes of Executive Board Meeting, 10 March).

At the 81st Session of the IOC in Montevideo in April 1979, the mainland Chinese conceded that after their "rightful place" was restored, they could allow Taiwan to remain in the IOC as a local Chinese organization. This was in accord with the change in the Taiwan policy that had occurred after the restoration of Sino–US relations. The "one China principle" was still in effect, however. The prerequisite would be that Taiwan could not use the written words "Republic of China," nor the word "Taiwan" alone, nor could it use the flag, anthem, nor any other symbol representing the "Republic of China." This was the first time in an IOC meeting that the Chinese Olympic Committee had made such a concession (Liang, 2005, p. 119).

After the Session, the Executive Board continued meeting into early morning. It was during this meeting that Lance Cross made the statement about the political independence of the IOC that opened this chapter. While maintaining some degree of neutrality, Killanin felt that they had already established that the PRC would not change its name, flag or anthem, and that if they were asked to, it would end the negotiations. Cross and Killanin both used the "sport and politics don't mix" argument to support their position:

> *Killanin:* There's no doubt at all that the Chinese Olympic Committee is based in Peking. That, to my mind, is a fact of life.
> *Cross:* How do you come to that conclusion?
> *Killanin:* Well, I'm an ordinary human being and I know what's going on in the world. China, in your country, in my country, is Peking.
> *Cross:* But that's not the Chinese Olympic Committee, that's the Chinese government.
> *Killanin:* Yes, I know, but we're dealing all the time with these things which are basically names of countries.
> *Cross:* Well, but we made it clear today that we're dealing with national Olympic committees, not with countries, not governments.
> *Killanin:* [speechless for a moment] But I don't think you can refer to the mainland as anything other than what they want to call themselves. China Olympic Committee.
> (Audiotapes of the 1979 Executive Board Meeting in Montevideo)

The Montevideo Session produced a resolution requiring both sides to change their names, which was unacceptable to the mainland Chinese. After a further series of twists and turns, in October 1979, the Executive Board Meeting in Nagoya, Japan, approved a resolution requiring only Taiwan to change its name. Then by means of a postal vote it was passed by the membership by a vote of 62 to 17, with one abstention (Minutes of the Executive Board meeting, Nagoya, Japan, 23–25 October 1979, p. 103). Afterwards the "Olympic formula" was used to settle the question of the use of national symbols in other organizations and international settings. China is known as the "Olympic Committee of the People's Republic of China" and competes under the national anthem and flag of the PRC. Taiwan is known as the "Olympic Committee of Chinese Taipei" and competes under the anthem and flag of its Olympic committee.

Dong Shouyi died in 1978 at the age of 83, one year short of seeing China readmitted to the IOC (Tan and Dong, 1993, p. 208).

Killanin summed it all up by noting,

> The dispute was a political one between the two Chinese governments and, as such, required a political solution. Sport and the Olympic Movement should not have been involved.
> (Killanin, 1983, p. 116)

Summary: "dreadful ignorance"

The Western-dominated IOC was generally quite ignorant about East Asia but the ban on "talking politics" made it difficult to fill in this void. The most striking indication is that, despite the fact that the names used to designate the different Olympic committees were at the centre of the China question for 30 years, the IOC rarely managed to get the names right. In the minutes of the 1952 through 1955 Sessions, the People's Republic of China was called Democratic China, and in 1956 it was called the Democratic People's Republic of China. Dong Shouyi protested this misnaming at the 1956 Session, but the Session minutes did not reflect it, so he wrote a letter asking that the minutes be corrected to reflect the official name of his country. Brundage finally approved the correction in the letter written to Dong in 1958, but Chancellor Mayer did not seem to get it right until around 1964. While it was under Killanin's leadership that the name question was resolved in 1979, in his 1983 book he misnames the PRC as the People's Democratic Republic of China. The ROC was often designated with the label Formosa, a Portuguese word first applied to the island by Portuguese sailors in the sixteenth century. It is not a Chinese word and is not used by Chinese-speakers. The Nationalist Chinese themselves rejected it because it was associated with the native Taiwanese independence movement; in 1959 ethnic Taiwanese wrote to Brundage in the name of the Formosan Olympic Committee, requesting him to recognize them as representing the people of Formosa, and not the Nationalist Chinese (letter from Frank Lim to Avery Brundage, 8 July 1959).

Personal names were also consistently misspelled. Dong Shouyi (Shou-yi Tung) was almost never spelled accurately in the minutes, and in his book, Killanin misspelled it as Shou Yi-tung (pp. 109–110).

The mistakes in names were symptomatic of larger misconceptions. With the exception of the Japanese members, the major figures in the IOC did not understand the history of China and Taiwan. Avery Brundage thought that he did, but a collector's knowledge of art and a dilettante's love of Far Eastern culture do not constitute a profound understanding of national identity. Dong once won some sympathy from France's Comte de Beaumont by asking him, "If you were Chinese, how would you feel seeing two different Chinese flags flying over the Olympic gatherings?" (Tan and Dong, 1993, p. 58). If the aphorism "sport and politics don't mix" had not been used on so many occasions to cut off what might have been constructive discussions, perhaps a solution could have been reached sooner.

However, the problem was still bigger than this. IOC members were intellectually ill-equipped to understand the larger philosophical matters in which they were entangled. These included the rise of a new kind of increasingly legally-defined nationalism after the Second World War that demanded an increasingly homogeneous definition of the nation even though actual nations never conformed to it. The lawsuits brought by Taiwan against the IAAF, the Lake Placid

Organizing Committee, and the IOC forced the IOC toward more legally-defensible – that is, more inflexible – criteria for membership. However, the IOC was fundamentally structured in such a way as to mitigate against its following this legalistic trend in international politics, because Coubertin had built checks against rigid nationalism into the fabric of the organization in the form of the cooptation process and the separation of powers between the IOC, NOCs, and organizing committees.

Entangled in the irresolvable nationalist politics of the Cold War and lacking understanding of the historical and cultural issues involved in the China question, the key IOC members instinctively realized that no forward movement was easily achieved and they shut off debate with the simplistic mantra that "sport and politics don't mix." Neither Brundage nor Killanin were sophisticated enough thinkers to think their way out of this impasse. Thus, Killanin ultimately saw the problem as one of rules, noting,

> There would not be so much heart-searching and agonizing over problems of the China type if the IOC had undergone an internal restructuring of its rules so that most became principles and the remainder bye-laws and guidelines ... I will admit to having aided and abetted some of the many breaches of rules to give governments their way, for it was not they who suffered but always the competitors.
>
> (1983, pp. 116–17)

Killanin thus in practice, if not in theory, continued Coubertin's original vision: "The Games must embrace the life of the world and not remain prisoners of utterly arbitrary regulations" (Coubertin, 2000, p. 521).

Heading into the Beijing 2008 Olympic Games, which China critics have likened to the 1936 Berlin Olympics, we might recall Coubertin's assessment of the 1936 Games as a "wonderful success" because of his faith that

> The choices and struggles of history will carry on, but gradually understanding will replace dreadful ignorance; mutual understanding will sooth impulsive hatreds. In this way, what I have worked toward for half a century will be strengthened.
>
> (p. 520)

In order to realize Coubertin's vision, we must first acknowledge that Olympic sport is inextricably intertwined with politics, and that is what makes it interesting and important. This relationship has become so complex that simplistic conceptions cannot express it. A more complex understanding will require, among other things, the involvement of intellectuals. We should work harder to communicate a more complex understanding of the relationship between sport and politics to a wider audience – and hopefully this volume will do so.

References

Coubertin, Pierre de (2000), *Olympism: Selected Writings*. Lausanne: International Olympic Committee

Dictionary of New Zealand Biography (2005), "Cross, Cecil Lancelot Stewart." http://www.dnzb.govt.nz.

Espy, Richard (1979), *The Politics of the Olympic Games*. Berkeley: The University of California Press.

Fan Hong and Xiong Xiaozheng (2002), "Communist China: Sport, Politics and Diplomacy." *International Journal of Sport History*: pp. 319–342.

Guttmann, Allen (1984), *The Games Must Go On: Avery Brundage and the Olympic Movement*. New York: Columbia University Press.

Hsu Heng [Henry Hsu] (1998), *Xu Heng Xiansheng fangtanlu [Conversations with Henry Hsu]*. Taipei: National Historical Archives.

Killanin, Lord (1983), *My Olympic Years*. London: Secker and Warburg.

Lennartz, Karl (1994), "The Presidency of Sigfrid Edstrøm (1942–1952)." *The International Olympic Committee: One Hundred Years, The Idea – The Presidents – The Achievements* (Lausanne: International Olympic Committee), pp. 13–76.

Liang Lijuan (2005), *He Zhenliang, wu huan zhi lu [He Zhenliang and the Road of the Five Rings]*. Beijing: World Knowledge Publishing House.

MacAloon, John (1981), *This Great Symbol: Pierre de Coubertin and the Origins of the Modern Olympic Games*. Chicago: The University of Chicago Press.

Sun Baoli (2000), *Aolinpike yundong yu Zhongguo [The Olympic Movement and China]*. Beijing: Popular Literature and Art Publishing House.

Tan Hua and Dong Erzhi (1993), *Suyuan – Dong Shouyi Zhuan [Long-cherished wish – the story of Dong Shouyi]*. Beijing: People's Sports Publishing House.

Notes

1 Funding for the research upon which this project is based was provided by a Research Award from the University of Missouri-St. Louis. For their help in various aspects of the research I am grateful to Ren Hai, Director of the Olympic Studies Center at the Beijing University of Physical Education, who provided facilities and help; Xu Guoqi, who gave me Henry Hsu's book; Philippe Blanchard, Director of the Information Management Department of the IOC, who approved access for my research in the Olympic Studies Centre; and Nuria Puig and Ruth Beck-Perrenoud of the Olympic Studies Centre, who made the concrete arrangements.

2 See John MacAloon's discussions of the IOC's principle of cooptation (1981, p. 160, p. 172, p. 181) and of Coubertin's awareness of the irony of this process in a "democratic" organization (p. 180).

3 During the time in question, the system used to transliterate Chinese was the Wade-Giles spelling system, which is still used in Taiwan. It was replaced in mainland China in the 1970s by the Pinyin system. Further, while the Chinese custom is to place the family name first and personal name second, this order was reversed to suit the Western custom. In this article I have transliterated Taiwanese and mainland Chinese names in the way that is now their custom. When they managed to get his name right, the IOC knew the Chinese member as Shou-yi Tung, but I will call him Dong Shouyi in this article.

4   This telegram is a bit of an enigma. While a copy of it exists in the Chinese National Sports Administration archives (Fan, 2002, p. 339, n. 16), it no longer seems to be present in the IOC archives. It is not clear to this researcher whether the PRC or ROC contacted the IOC first to announce the change of address of the Chinese Olympic Committee. The June 1951 *Olympic Bulletin* did list an address in Taipei (Lennartz, 1995, p. 59), but Killanin noted no trace had been found of notification of the change of address of the Chinese Olympic Committee in 1951 from Nanjing (former capital of the ROC) to Taipei (Killanin, 1983, p. 109).

5   Dong Erzhi was sentenced to labor reform that involved gathering stones on a mountainside and carrying them on his back to be crushed into gravel. He ended up doing twenty years of labor reform and developed lung disease from breathing the stone dust. He found me in 1996, when he was very insistent. He died of lung disease half a year later. It was only in writing this chapter that I came to understand his urgent insistence. I acquired the book about Dong Shouyi (Tan and Dong, 1993) by chance in a bookstore in 1995 but did not read it until doing the research for this chapter. I then realized that the second author of the book was Dong Erzhi, and that he had become dedicated to writing his father's story in 1985 after finally being rehabilitated in the mid-1970s. In turn, he was carrying on his father's desire to record this history, which he had been enjoined to do by Premier Zhou after the premier had arranged his transfer back to Beijing in 1972 following two years of labor reform at a cadre school in the countryside (Tan and Dong, 1993, pp. 193–198). He was prolific until his death in 1978. Dong Erzhi knew that I was one of the few persons in the world who was in a position to write his father's story in English. I am also in the process of translating the biography of Dong's successor in the IOC, He Zhenliang, to fill out the second half of the story (Liang 2005). Through several chance events, this history found me and called me to write it.

6   A question that remains to be explored is the degree to which corporate interests in the "China market" contributed to pressure on the IOC to admit the PRC. Horst Dassler, son of the founder of Adidas, had first become a "friend" of the mainland Chinese in the early 1970s. His father died at the beginning of September 1978, and in that same month Horst visited Beijing and engaged in long discussions of strategy concerning China's admission into the IAAF, other international federations, and the IOC. It appears that he was present in Lausanne during the March 1979 Executive Board meeting and acted as a liaison with the Chinese delegation (Liang, 2005, pp. 108, 115). He Zhenliang's biography states, "Some people said he was more interested in influencing international sports organizations behind the scenes than he was in developing the sports industry. Even more people said that he was the 'king-maker' in many international sports organizations. His influence in resolving our rightful place in some international federations was irreplaceable. He also had a powerful network inside the IOC" (Liang, 2005, p. 92). Thanks to Stephen Wagg for bringing this question to my attention.

Chapter 15

Sport after the Cold War

Implications for Russia and Eastern Europe

James Riordan

Introduction

One of the major legacies of the European communist era (1917–91) is fragmented governments that have provided a context for entrenched Mafioso power, and the consolidation of corrupt elites in nearly all the erstwhile Soviet Union (now fifteen independent states within some of which civil wars are in progress for further secession – for example, Chechnya in Russia, Ossetia in Georgia) as well as some of communist eastern and central Europe. This situation signifies a transition not to democracy, but to what has been called post-Marxist kleptocracy.

Immediately after the demise of the Soviet Union in 1991, Russia underwent a brief period of illusory freedom before robber-baron capitalism took over for some seven to eight years. Various mafia gangs, often run on ethnic lines – Chechen, Caucasian, native Russian, Jewish – filled the market vacuum left by defunct state enterprises. With the connivance of Boris Yeltsin, Russia's first post-Soviet president (1991–1999), they bought up Russia's key strategic assets – its natural resources such as oil, gas and metals – at risibly rock-bottom prices. After a series of gang wars to reduce the ranks, establish "turf" boundaries, financial control and domination of essential industries, the survivors made a truce and sought quasi-respectability within the law at the end of the 1990s.

When Vladimir Putin succeeded Yeltsin as Russian president (on the recommendation of leading oligarchs, such as Boris Berezovsky), some of the illegal Mafiosi reconstituted themselves as "legal" oligarchs operating within boundaries set by the regime. The oligarchs were those tolerated and supported by the Russian president who operates not exactly as a "godfather," more as a neo-authoritarian dictator over Russia. As long as the oligarchs do not threaten his power, they may coexist with the regime. If, on the other hand, they overstep the mark (like Boris Berezovsky, based in Britain, or Badri Patarkatsishvili based in Georgia) they have to seek political asylum abroad. If they remain and challenge the president's power, as Yukos chief and oil billionaire Khodorkovsky did, they can find themselves incarcerated (for nine years in Khodorkovsky's case – on fraud and tax evasion charges).

President Putin's objective is *state capitalism*, whereby "Kremlin Inc.," as it is known, becomes the major shareholder in newly privatized society. Besides being fabulously wealthy chiefs of state firms, the oligarchs in Russia therefore also act as servants of the Kremlin and have to toe the political line. That is Russia. But it would be misleading to lump together the one-time nine European communist nations, now 35 independent states. Each marches under its own banner, following its own traditions and geo-political situation. Bosnia, Kosovo, Chechnya, Nagorno-Karabakh are all engaged in sanguinary inter-ethnic struggles that are not the lot of Poland, Hungary or the Czech Republic (now that it has divided from Slovakia). Albania, Romania and Bulgaria are desperately trying to deal with poverty and "primitive capitalism." At the same time, the five nations that emerged from Yugoslavia are going their separate ways, while having constantly to look over their shoulders. For each, sport has its own meaning and priorities. Developments in post-communist sport have to be seen against this background. The oligarchs of Russia in particular see sport, especially potentially lucrative spectator sports like football, basketball, boxing, tennis and ice hockey, as a veil/shroud to cover their less sporting activities, as well as a means to launder their vast wealth.

Yet sport is not simply a plaything of the unimaginably rich oligarchs, it plays a role among the public of considerable social significance. In a society of cataclysmic change and authoritarian dictatorship, sport has acquired a unique meaning for ordinary people in terms of "escape" (from politics and economic hardship), and the Platonic "empathy and catharsis." Nikolai Starostin, one-time Soviet football captain and Gulag victim came close to explaining this role when he talked of Soviet football in the 1920s and 1930s:

> I think that the prewar social role and significance of football grew out of the special relationship the public had with it. People seemed to separate it from all that was going on around them. It was like the utterly unreasoned worship by sinners desperate to seek oblivion in their blind appeal to divinity. For most people, football was the only, and sometimes the very last, chance and hope of retaining in their souls a tiny island of sincere feelings and human relations.[1]

Russia will be our focal point for most of this chapter; some of its post-Cold War sporting developments mirror those elsewhere in former communist Europe, some do not.

Beginning of the end: the Moscow Olympics of 1980

In searching for clues to the start of the demise of communism, it might be instructive to go back to the Summer Olympic Games held in Moscow in 1980. At the time, this seemed to many to be the pinnacle of sporting glory for the

Soviet Union – the first communist state to host the summer Olympics. And yet, to others, it was seen as the beginning of the end.

The IOC selected Moscow as the 1980 host at its 75th Session on 23 October 1974 in Vienna. Moscow won the vote comfortably over its sole rival, Los Angeles. At the time, many felt the USSR worthy of the honour: not only was it the most successful and versatile nation in Olympic history in terms of sporting performance, but it was considered to have done much in Olympic forums to enhance the pre-eminent role of sport and the Olympic movement. It was a popular choice with both east European states (but not all communist nations – China and Albania turned down their invitations to Moscow) and many Third World countries whose political and sporting causes had gained Soviet support in such matters as, for example, the banning of racist South Africa from the Olympic movement, the training of coaches, construction of sports facilities and free attendance of athletes at Soviet sports institutes.

As for Western governments, despite their distaste for communism and the Soviet human rights record, it was generally thought that the appointment of Moscow as Olympic host might somehow make a contribution to the process of *détente* then underway. At the very least, it might encourage some liberalization within the country or, at worst, expose it to the world as a cynical violator of the Helsinki Accords on human rights.

Despite the subsequent US-led boycott (ostensibly in retaliation for the Soviet invasion of Afghanistan in December 1979 – ignoring the hosting of the Winter Olympics in the USA after the US invasion of Vietnam), the IOC announced on 27 May 1980 that eighty-five countries had accepted invitations to compete in Moscow. Of the twenty-two nations that had won two or more gold medals in the 1972 and 1976 Olympics, only five had decided not to compete: the USA, West Germany, Norway, Kenya and Japan.

The Games went off without a hitch and represented one of the most successful and eye-catching sporting spectacles of our time.

And yet ... at the very moment of reaching the pinnacle of sporting glory, the Soviet Union precipitously (and, to most Westerners, unexpectedly) began to fall apart at the seams. Two years after the Games, the Soviet President, Leonid Brezhnev, died; three years later, Mikhail Gorbachov came to power with radically new policies of *perestroika* (restructuring) and *glasnost* (openness). Four years later, the communist edifice crumbled throughout the eight nations of eastern and central Europe. The Soviet Union followed suit and ceased to exist as a unitary state in late 1991.

It would be a mite extravagant to blame the Moscow Olympics for the demise of communism. Yet for many citizens of communist states, the 1980 Olympics brought tensions to a head, especially as the public was able to see those tensions in its own backyard. It is noteworthy that when the revolutions swept across eastern Europe in late 1989, there was an intense debate about sport. Far from being at the periphery of politics, sport was right at the core.

The events of 1989 and subsequently in the one-time communist states demonstrated to many people that sport, and particularly elite Olympic sport, was identified in the popular consciousness with privilege, paramilitary coercion (the two largest and best-endowed sports clubs in all communist states were the armed forces clubs and the security forces club – *Dinamo*), hypocrisy (having to pretend that communist athletes were amateur when they were being paid by the state and given either army officer sinecures or fictitious employment) and distorted priorities (the huge sums of money that were lavished on sports stars and the Moscow Olympics, while sports facilities for the masses – not to mention hospitals, schools, housing and consumer goods for the public generally – were poor and minimal). In the case of the non-Soviet nations (and non-Slav Soviet republics, such as Latvia, Lithuania and Estonia), the Soviet sports structure was regarded as an alien, Communist Party-imposed institution.

The principal reason for the Soviet targeting of the Olympics to achieve world supremacy in sport was seen by the public as an attempt to gain recognition and prestige for the communist states and the Soviet brand of communism – and thereby to advertise that brand, especially in Africa, Asia and Latin America, as being superior to the capitalist system. It should be noted that, apart from the early years of space exploration, sport was *the only area* in which the Soviet Union could demonstrate superiority over the leading capitalist states – in the full glare of the world's media.

To many people in eastern and central Europe and the USSR, however, the Olympic attainments and the Moscow Olympics diverted attention from the realities of living under communism. The Olympics illuminated the gap between elite sport and the rest of society, the manipulation of sport for political ends and the profligacy of pouring funds into a sporting spectacle for propaganda purposes when the economy had run out of steam and, in the case of the Soviet Union, was teetering on the brink of bankruptcy (partly as a result of US President Reagan's policy of "squeezing till the pips squeak" in terms of the arms race).

The Moscow Olympics confirmed that there are moments in history when sport, instead of simply reflecting the economic and political superstructure of society, may significantly contribute to changing it. A parallel might be drawn to some extent with the holding of the Olympic Games in Seoul, South Korea, in 1988, and the effects on Korean society. Prior to South Korea's appointment as host of the 1988 Summer Games, it had been a totalitarian state whose external policy was dictated by the American military. With the world's gaze focussed on the imminent Olympic host, the need to show a more human face not only encouraged dissident movements and trade unionists to demonstrate for democratic change (without the danger of being brutally crushed, as previously), it also constrained the authorities in their reaction to protests, as well as prompting them to open up relations with communist countries, such as China and eastern Europe, and loosen the US hold on the country's external politics. This salutary role for sport is especially likely in relatively closed societies that make sport an appendage of politics. What is more, it is precisely when totalitarian constraints are loosened and the populace is exposed to other values and cultures that pressure for change is at its most irresistible.

In a reference to the *ancien regime*, the French historian Alexis de Tocqueville made this apposite comment: "It is not only by going from bad to worse that a society falls into revolution ... experience shows that the most dangerous moment for a bad government is generally that in which it sets about reform."[2]

Russian history is littered with such disruptive, revolutionary or near-revolutionary moments. The "enlightened despot" Catherine the Great (1729–1796) clamped down on political dissent following the "shock" of the French Revolution of 1789. Napoleon's abortive invasion of Russia in 1812 and the trek of Russian troops all the way to Paris led to the unsuccessful conspiracy of Russian army officers (known as the Decembrists from the month of the uprising to remove the Tsar from the throne, 14 December 1825) who had picked up doctrines of European liberalism. Similarly, the First World War brought down the tsarist regime in a country ripe for social revolution.

Some three score and ten years later, as the British historian Eric Hobsbawm comments,

> The assent to communism of 'the masses' depended not on their ideological or other convictions, but on how they judged what life under communist regimes did for them, and how they compared their situation with others. Once it ceased to be possible to insulate populations from contact with, or even knowledge about, other countries, these judgements were sceptical.[3]

As never before, the Moscow Olympics opened up the country (through television, and football and yachting events in Kiev, Minsk, Leningrad and Tallinn) to other countries and their cultures. But it also brought to a head the tensions surrounding Soviet sport, and especially the Soviet Olympic priority, themselves. By a fortuitous circumstance, therefore, the Olympic Games of 1980 occurred at one of those junctures in history that presaged and precipitated monumental change, not only in the Soviet Union and across the east European plain, but throughout the world.

Immediate changes to communist sport: 1985–92

In 1985, Party chief Mikhail Gorbachov had the task of saving a political system whose centre was experiencing dissolution, inevitably strengthening the centrifugal forces and making the system's break-up inevitable – and with it the last remaining major world empire (the old Russian empire, with the cardinal exceptions of Poland and Finland, came under the rubric of the USSR after the 1917 Russian Revolution).

It was particularly in the field of sport, more rapidly than anywhere else – perhaps because of its popular nature – that the new era of *glasnost* (from 1985) exposed to public scrutiny the realities of the old system. Victims of repression began to publish their memoirs. Not just any old victims, but former sports stars whom the public had idolised. To take just one example, Nikolai Starostin had captained his country at both football and ice hockey, helped to found the Spartak Sports Society in the late 1930s, and managed the Soviet national football team.

He also spent ten years in Stalin's labour camps. In his memoirs, published in the late 1980s, he revealed his punishment for playing abroad (against communist worker teams, like the Parisian team *l'Etoile rouge*). The charge read:

> Nikolai Petrovich Starostin publicly praised bourgeois sport and tried to instil into our sport the mores of the capitalist world.[4]

His real crime was captaining the Spartak team that had the temerity to beat Moscow Dinamo in league and cup in 1938 and 1939, so incurring the wrath of the Dinamo President and brutal secret police chief, Lavrenty Beria.

In a way, Nikolai and his three brothers, also Spartak players sent to camps beyond the Arctic Circle, was lucky. Attempts to purge Soviet sport of foreign influence resulted in a crime unprecedented in history. No one knows the exact number of victims; but the Terror carried off five sports ministers, Olympic Committee members for the Baltic states, heads of the principal physical education colleges, eminent sports scientists and medics, and probably thousands of leading athletes.[5]

Repression was not the only dark corner to have light shed on it during the Gorbachov era. Another was the extraordinary lengths to which the authorities went to ensure victory over capitalist states. As the immediate postwar Chairman of the Committee on Physical Culture and Sport, Nikolai Romanov, revealed in his memoirs (published in 1987):

> Once we decided to take part in foreign competitions, we were forced to guarantee victory, otherwise the 'free' bourgeois press would fling mud at the whole nation as well as our athletes … To gain permission to go to international tournaments I had to send a special note to Stalin guaranteeing victory.[6]

While the Soviet Union dominated the summer and winter Olympic Games from its Helsinki debut in 1952 (as well as some non-Olympic sports, such as chess), with outstanding performances from some other communist states – for example, the German Democratic Republic, it never seriously challenged the world's leading football teams. Despite the amazing performance of Moscow Dinamo in its four-match unbeaten tour of Britain in 1945, Soviet football failed to gain a place among the world's leading nations or clubs. The same might be said of professional basketball and cycling, though *not* ice hockey where the Soviet national team took on and beat the leading NHL clubs in the 1980s.

During the 1980s, radical changes began to appear in Soviet sport, breaking the mould of its functionalizzed and bureaucratic (plan-fulfilment) structure. Until then, not only had the state-controlled, utilitarian system hampered a true appraisal of realities that lay beneath the "universal" statistics and "idealised" veneer, it had prevented concessions to particular groups in the population – the "we know what's best for you" syndrome whereby the fit tell the disabled that sport is not for them; men tell women what sports they should play; the old tell the young that they can play only on (old) terms, in their clubs, using their facilities; the leaders, mindful of international prestige, decided that competitive Olympic sports were the only civilized forms of culture. It also entailed Moscow (via the Warsaw Pact organization) telling other European communist countries that they were to boycott the Los Angeles Olympics of 1984 (Romania and Yugoslavia demurred).

What no one could say openly before, including during the 1980 Olympics, owing to strict censorship, was that *Dinamo* was the sports club sponsored and financed by the security forces, that athletes (Master of Sport ranking and above) devoted themselves full-time to sport and were paid accordingly, that athletes received bonuses for winning (including scarce dollars), that the Soviet NOC was a government-run institution and that its chairman had to be a member of the Communist Party, that the Soviet state manufactured, tested and administered performance-enhancing drugs to its athletes (while condemning bourgeois states for encouraging drug-taking).

Down the years, the Soviet leadership had produced regiments of statistics to show that millions were regular, active participants in sport; that the vast majority of school- and college-students gained a national fitness badge (the GTO – *Gotov k trudu i oborone* – Prepared for Labour and Defence, originally based on Baden-Powell's athlete's badge); that rising millions (a third of the population!) took part in the quadrennial spartakiads; and that the bulk of workers did their daily dozen – "production gymnastics" – at the workplace.

Just a few years after the Moscow Olympics, however, the new leaders declared that these figures were fraudulent, a show to impress people above and below, and to meet preset targets. It was now admitted that no more than eight percent of men and two percent of women engaged in sport regularly.[7]

Once people started to see journalists writing about the past (under the slogan: "a nation that does not know its past has no future!") and exposing the realities of elite sport, they started to question the very morality of sport, the price that society should pay for talent. Many expressed their unhappiness at what they saw as a race for false glory, the cultivation of irrational loyalties, the unreasonable prominence given to the winning of victories, the setting of records and the collecting of trophies – an obsessive fetishism of sport. This was, incidentally, the very criticism made of "sport" by strong opposition groups in the 1920s, particularly the "Hygienists" and the "Proletarian Culture" group.[8]

This is, of course, an issue not unknown in other societies, especially those of scarcity. But for a population who had been waiting years for housing, phones and cars, who saw their economy collapsing, and who felt that sporting victories were being attained for political values they did not share – that is, that sports "heroes" were not *their* heroes – they were somehow accomplices in gilding the lily of the Communist Party – the vast sums being lavished on ensuring a Grand Olympic Show represented the straw that broke the camel's back.

To many the worst aspect of the old system was misplaced priorities, the gap between living standards and ordinary sports and recreation facilities, on the one hand, and the money spent on elite sport and stars, on the other. As a sports commentator put it a year after the Berlin Wall came down and a year before the Soviet edifice tumbled, we won Olympic medals while being "a land of clapped-out motor cars, evergreen tomatoes and totalitarian mendacity."[9] Valuable resources were used to buy foreign sports equipment and pay dollar bonuses to athletes who won Olympic medals. For a gold medal at the Seoul Olympics of 1988, for example, Soviet recipients gained as much as 12,000 rubles (6,000 for silver and 4,000 for bronze medals). Since the Soviet team won 55 gold and 132 medals overall, it cost the Sports Committee about a million rubles (almost half paid in dollars) in bonuses alone.[10]

Some journalists suggested that alongside Olympic medal tables, Soviet newspapers ought to publish sports amenity comparisons: the 2,500 Soviet swimming pools by contrast with the million plus in the USA, the 102 Soviet indoor skating rinks by contrast with Canada's 10,000.[11] To give another example, before 1988 the USSR had never held sports competitions for any category of handicapped person; it sent a team of invalid athletes (thirteen blind men, mostly Afghan veterans) to the Paralympics for the first time in Seoul. Unlike their able-bodied compatriots in the Olympic Games, who won 132 medals, the blind athletes won no medals at all. But at least a start was made.

As the Soviet Union began to crumble, it was pointed out that the country supported an elite system on an extremely weak and ramshackle base. For the first time it was admitted that the nation was fifty-third in per capita GNP in the world, that as many as 100 million people, over a third of the population, lived below the official poverty line, that while scarce foreign currency was being spent on expensive foreign sports equipment and paying dollar bonuses, children were dying for want of basic medicines, food and disposable instruments (more Soviet children than adults had died of AIDs by the late 1980s because of unhygienic conditions and the backward state of the health service). To one sports commentator, the sporting achievements diverted attention from conditions that "reinforce the most anti-human and anti-sport system in the world."[12]

Having allowed the nation to bare its soul, the leaders in the post-Gorbachov era radically changed their scale of priorities. They no longer saw the need to demonstrate the advantages of socialism in so far as they were trying to distance themselves from the command economy that had failed so badly and the totalitarian political system that had accompanied the imposition of communism from above.

Such a radical shift of policy was bound to cause a twinge of sadness to those who had admired aspects of Soviet and east European sport down the years – and not only because it provided good competition with the USA. The old system, it merits saying, was generally open to the talents in all sports, probably more so than in the West. It provided opportunities for women to play and succeed, if not on equal terms with men, at least on a higher plane than Western women. It gave an opportunity to the many ethnic minorities and relatively small states within the USSR and eastern Europe to do well internationally and help promote that pride and dignity that sports success in the glare of world publicity can bring. Nowhere in the world was there, since the early 1950s, such reverence for Olympism, for Coubertin, for Olympic ritual and decorum. One practical embodiment of this was the contribution to Olympic solidarity with developing nations. Much of the sporting aid given was free. None of it was disinterested, it went to those states whose governments looked to socialism rather than to capitalism for their future. Further, no nation outside the Third World did more than the USSR to oppose apartheid in sport and to have South Africa banned from world sports forums and arenas.

Once the curtain came down on communism (in 1989 in central and eastern Europe, 1991 in the Soviet Union), the international challenge was diluted through lack of state support; the free trade union sports societies, as well as the ubiquitous *Dinamo* and armed forces clubs, mostly gave way to private sports, health and recreation clubs; women's wrestling and boxing extracted more profit than women's chess and volleyball (just as former ballet dancers found they could earn far more money, with perhaps less effort, in foreign or domestic strip bars and brothels); the various nationalities preferred their own independent teams to combined effort and success. So Dinamo Kiev opted to compete in a Ukrainian league, Tbilisi Dinamo in a Georgian league, and Russian clubs in the Russian Football League, set up in 1991.

Right across the central and eastern European plain, as far as the Ural Mountains, sports and every other aid and subsidy came to an end. The Third World students (in medicine and engineering as well as in sport) all went home as their support grants ran out. The ex-communist states became competitors with other poor nations for development aid from the West. And such aid, as the International Monetary Fund dictates, comes at a cost. As A. DeSwan has pointed out,

> Aid is forthcoming with the liberalisation of prices, rapid privatisation, removal of food and housing subsidies, and the wholesale dismantling of the social welfare system.[13]

The failed communist coup of 19–21 August 1991 accelerated the shift from state control of and support for sport towards private, commercial sport, and a massive "brain" and "muscle" drain of top athletes, coaches, sports medics and scientists to the richest overseas "buyer." The international market for sports talent enabled stars from one-time communist states to offer themselves for sale to promoters around the world. Basketball and hockey players and coaches found a home in the USA and Canada, soccer stars and cyclists in Europe, boxers and weightlifters in Japan. Others, as in tennis and track and field, became international entrepreneurs attached to top, mainly US, coaches/agents, virtually stateless and part of a world jetsetting circuit.

This affected not only athletes. At the 1988 Seoul Olympics, as many as 32 top Polish coaches were employed by non-Polish national teams. The former Polish Olympic athlete, Wojciech Liponski, estimated that in 1993 (four years after the end of Polish communism), some 180 Polish coaches, formerly employed at national team level in Poland, worked abroad, as did over a thousand sports instructors.[14] The emigration of East German sports medical experts (particularly in doping) was well documented and on the same dangerous footing as the exodus of Soviet nuclear scientists prepared to sell their services (and sometimes their hardware) to the highest bidder. Communist incentives, then, were steadily replaced by market incentives that promoted elite sport as effectively as state apparatchiks once did.

By 1995, more than 300 soccer, 700 hockey and 100 Russian basketball players were working in North America, Asia, and western and eastern Europe.[15] As in Latin America and Africa, post-Soviet domestic clubs and leagues rapidly became "farm teams" for capitalist sport.[16] This new and much-resented subordinate status made it difficult for Russians (and other east Europeans) to assemble their players for international games, collect transfer fees, and get their clubs into lucrative European tournaments.[17]

All these developments weakened Russian interest in the Olympic movement, and led to the removal of the sinecures of an army commission and "eternal" studenthood for all top athletes, and to the dismantling of the forty-two sports boarding schools.[18] The Army Sports Society held out under the Russian Defence Ministry until 1997 when it became a joint stock company, with the ministry retaining a controlling stake; nominal ownership of its leading football team, TsSKA, went to Roman Abramovich's company Sibneft.

During the Gorbachov era, up to 1990, there had arisen a multiplicity of grass roots sports organizations: disabled sports people, women (playing rugby, boxing and wrestling, as well as football), small-scale private swimming and tennis clubs, and senior fitness associations. They were soon to be steamrollered by a "revolution" as far-reaching as anything in the past: exposure to the "free" market and selling out to the global economy. At least in the fifteen years of its operation, those advocates of such capitalistic "blessings" should bear in mind that post-Soviet market capitalism, in the words of J. McMurtry,

> has been by every measure far more destructive of people's daily and long-term security and well-being than any Communist Party policy since the Second World War.[19]

The uncertainty and destruction of people's living standards that accompanied the break-up of the Soviet Union had two disastrous consequences. The first was that life expectancy drastically fell, especially for Russian men: to fifty-eight years, lower than in Bangladesh and six years less than it was in 1965. The second was that from a Soviet population of nearly 300 million, overnight the Russian population became 149 million in 1991. With the swiftly declining birth rate, the Russian population might even be half as much, 75 million, by the year 2050. This has resulted in the government being forced to encourage large-scale immigration (initially of manual workers from China and India). In some ways, this policy has been matched in sport, with the mass importation of foreign players, as we shall see below.

Longer-term results of the free market: 1993 onwards

In the wake of the crumbling of the communist edifice came a tough, even deadly, struggle for control of sport. Seeing the inevitable end to their political power, a number of communist officials quickly turned themselves into business people and, using their influence and contacts, purchased state firms at very low prices (about 20 percent of their real market value) under the cover of privatization. These became known as "nomenklatura" companies, such as the huge outfits like Sibneft (Siberian Oil), Lukoil, Yukos and Rosneft (Russian Oil), as well as Russia's largest company, Gazprom (Gas Industry). They were soon joined by similar companies formed by members of the new political elite, the embourgeoisified "New Russians" (Novye russkie) or, now, the "Newest Russians" (Noveishie russkie) who are immensely wealthy – like Roman Abramovich, one-time master of Sibneft and owner of the London football club Chelsea, and whose company also owns TsSKA (the Army football team based in Moscow).

People like Abramovich have brought a radical break with the past in world football. In so doing, they are also bringing about a major shift in football's balance of power – from west Europeans to Russians. For the first time, the clubs they own can buy players from all over the world, no matter what the price or wages demanded. Money does not matter in seeking success. Chelsea's wage bill alone in the 2003–04 season was £115m, and is estimated to be some £170m in 2004–05, by far the highest in the world. For the moment, the Russian football club owners are permitted more or less free rein both by their own government and by the football authorities in the countries where their clubs play. The former make no insistence that money taken from the Russian people should be reinvested at home; the latter, along with the fans, turn a blind eye to the origins of such an evidently Fortunatus Purse – with all its moral implications.

Both sets of the new elite soon accumulated excess wealth and, wishing to put a "healthy gloss" on their public image, turned to sports sponsorship. As these ostentatiously rich "New Russians" went about acquiring the symbols of wealth, sport became a convenient place to invest their money. Like the primitive capitalism that underlies their power, the methods used to promote commercial sport are often primitive in the extreme, including the fixing of results, bribing of referees and even "hit" killings of those who stand in their way or expose their nefarious operations.

One of the rare public admissions about "dirty" or "criminal" money being involved in Russian sport was made by Nikolai Tolstykh on Russian State Television on 1 March 1996.[20] Tolstykh should know: he was concurrently head of the Russian soccer league and president of Moscow Dinamo. He freely admitted that he had threatened referees who gave "controversial" decisions against his team (in one case allegedly beating up a referee), while at the same time running the league that controlled the careers of those who refereed the matches. Tolstykh's assumption, like that of many others, was that everything and everyone was up for sale.[21] As an aside, at the "derby" match I witnessed in the Olympic (once "Lenin") Stadium between Spartak and TsSKA, on Sunday 29 May 2005, the three officials were from Germany, for the first time in a domestic Premier match, owing to the fear of corruption of Russian referees in such a vital encounter (notwithstanding the recent bribery scandal surrounding referees in Germany!).

In regard to "sports murders," after Russia's most popular soccer team, Spartak Moscow, had refused repeated offers of "assistance" from Moscow's politically powerful mayor, Yuri Luzhkov. In the autumn of 1997, the club's President, Larissa Nechayeva, was assassinated at her dacha outside Moscow in what was rumoured to be a dispute over television rights.[22] In the same year, Valentin Sych, head of the Russian hockey league since 1995, was assassinated in what appeared to be an organised crime dispute over the importing of tobacco, an activity that sports federations had been permitted to engage in tax free. Unusually for Russia, someone was actually accused of Sych's murder. One of the members of the conspiracy was Robert Cherenko, the first head of the post-Soviet international hockey league whom Sych had forced out of power. The case is still in progress without an end in sight.[23] This certainly isn't cricket or fighting according to Queensbury rules.

As Liponski writes of Polish sport,

> The severe economic crisis, added to clashes between the old and new power elite, keep Polish (and, I think, East European as well) sport much below the level of commercialisation which in the West is commonly recognised as harmful to sports morality.[24]

In modern-day Russia it has to be remembered that, lurking behind business activity, is organized crime whose precise role is hard to specify but is certainly as widespread as it is in any other sphere of business. The situation has been exacerbated by what the US scholar Robert Edelman calls "capitalist talent hunters of widely varying degrees of scrupulousness ... regardless of the consequences for the individuals involved or for the future of sport." [25] These "talent scouts" are often accompanied by other "Big Game hunters" from the increasingly globalized entertainment market. Their ideology was spelled out in 1996 by Alexander Weinstein, chief of the US-based International Management Group's Moscow Office:

> We think that now it's really the right time to start a civilised sports market here in Russia because as it was before … it was financed by the government. Now … it's really time for a big commercial structure of some kind of independent company to be involved. [26]

Such developments undoubtedly leave Russians with mixed emotions. To some, participation in the global market for sports talent is seen as part of living in a "normal" and "civilized" world. Yet the process of sports globalization confirms Russia's subordinate status in the world. This is deeply resented by some people. Post-Soviet television has fostered the same kind of globalization and homogenisation ("dumbing down") in all forms of popular culture. Russian nationalism is wounded by the international sports and pop culture developments that underscore Russia's decline as a world power and emphasize its subordinate place in the global sports market.

No wonder some (mostly the older generation) hark back to the "good old days" of educational Soviet "entertainment." Among the youth, however, contemporary films, TV, radio, music and video games, largely but not entirely foreign, are more popular than a great deal of late Soviet fare ever was. But, to the detriment of Russian sport, young men, the largest group of spectator sport consumers, have developed other interests. As Robert Edelman writes,

> there are lots of ways to have a good time. Sport has become but one segment of a post-Soviet entertainment industry in which the specifically Russian finds it difficult to resist the impact of an increasingly homogenised global popular culture. [27]

As elsewhere in the world, the sporting diaspora has stimulated among Russians the same kind of nationalistic ire against such multinational juggernauts based mainly in the USA. It has also had the effect of forcing sports fans to turn away from sport altogether. Football is the most popular spectator sport during Russia's summer months (ice hockey is the winter sport). Some thirty years ago, in Soviet times, stadiums were packed to capacity, with an average of 35,000 fans at Premiership matches. Today, the six top-flight Moscow clubs (Spartak, TsSKA, Dinamo, Lokomotiv, Torpedo and the newly-formed Moskva) average just over 7,000 fans a game between them – a pitiful figure on any European comparison. [28] Part of the reason is given by Vladimir Rodionov, General Secretary of the Russian Football Federation,

People can watch three or four live Russian games (on TV) every week. And they can watch English, Spanish, Italian, German football, all live. So why spend money to go to the ground when it's cheaper and more enjoyable to sit at home or in a bar with a beer?[29]

Another reason for the decline in attendance at sporting events is lack of nationalistic interest in contests against other Russian teams, rather than teams from other ethnic regions. There was always added "spice" to watching a Russian team take on the Georgians or test themselves against the top Soviet football team, Dinamo Kiev, from the Ukraine. Another reason for drastically falling attendances is that, today, many young people have access to computers, cars and other leisure facilities that were unavailable in Soviet times.

However, money is certainly a problem for many sports enthusiasts. What is visible to Westerners is the apex of the new Russian pyramid: the fabulously wealthy oligarchs. What they don't see is the widespread poverty and destitution.

The cumulative impact of the "free market" on post-Soviet sport had also resulted in little success for Russian teams in international competition. The latter part of the 1990s and early 2000s witnessed some spectacular failures. Russia's performance at the 1994, 1998 and 2002 (soccer) World Cup were, to say the least, mediocre (failing to make the Finals of the 1998 and 2002 tournament). The once-dominant hockey team was eliminated in the semi-finals of the sport's inaugural World Cup in 1996 , while the basketball team finished only seventh in the 1995 World Basketball Championship, failing to qualify for the Atlanta Olympics. To some extent, the problem is that nowadays athletes are part of an international monoculture of wealthy and privileged elite performers, many of whom have no patriotic loyalty to their country of birth and refuse to play for Russia (for example, in cycling, boxing, weightlifting) or change nationality (for example, in athletics). Success in international sports today, as Edelman succinctly puts it, "follows the world-wide 'golden rule' (the one with the gold makes the rules)."[30]

In Soviet times, there was undeniably a different attitude by sportsmen and women (who in any case were banned from playing for non-Soviet teams). Rodionov again, harking back to the "good old days": "We were proud, we were patriotic, we played for love of our sport and our country. Now it's all about money. It affects everything."[31]. Robert Edelman, makes a similar point in regard to sports consumers:

Soviet citizens created an arena of popular culture that was human and genuine, spontaneous and playful. In the vortex of globalised sport, that difference has been lost.[32]

While some fans might look to the national teams as representing a new Russian nationhood, the players often regard themselves, as one recently told me, as "gypsies" who roam the world looking for a hook on which to hang their clobber: "One year Bordeaux, the next Chelsea, on to Portsmouth, back to Chelsea, then Charlton. God knows where I'll be next year."[33]

However, a radical shift is taking place in football that could soon affect other sports. Leading European and South American footballers, whom the Russians dub "legionnaires," are heading eastwards at an ever-increasing rate, helping to bring unprecedented international success to their Russian teams. In the 2005 season, the Russian Premiership had an astonishing average of 11–12 foreign players on the books of each club – more than any English, French, German, Spanish or Italian club.[34]

Moscow Dinamo was even contemplating the appointment of the first-ever west European coach; the Portuguese Vitor Pontes and Antonio Oliveira were two names mentioned. Already Dinamo has a core (nine in mid-2005) of Portuguese-speaking players, including top-class names like Tiago, Derlei, Cicero, Maniche and Costinha – the latter pair being purchased in early May 2005 for between £15 and £16 million. Dinamo President, Alexei Fedorychev, favours a single culture and language that help knit the team together. More significantly, what entices players to Moscow is that "our wages are much higher than the players could expect in Portugal."[35]. No work permit problems stand in the way in so far as Fedorychev's co-President is Yuri Zavarzin, coincidentally President of the Russian League.

TsSKA, with whom Abramovich's company Sibneft signed a £29m three-year sponsorship deal in 2004, beat off competition from a host of European clubs to sign Vagner Love, one of the most highly rated Brazilian strikers, for £5.5m, while Croatia international Ivica Olic opted to join the Club instead of moving to western Europe. Small wonder that TsSKA won the UEFA Cup in 2005, beating Sporting Lisbon on its own soil – the first Russian football team to reach or win a European final since Moscow Dinamo in 1972.

The current (mid-2005) most successful football team is the once unfashionable railway trade union club Lokomotiv, today sponsored by the Russian state railways, a vast network of 1.2m employees headed by deputy prime minister Alexander Zhukov. It therefore differs in ownership from other Moscow clubs in having direct state, rather than oligarch, control.

It was when Lukoil-sponsored Moscow Spartak signed up arguably the hottest talent in Argentine football, Fernando Cavenaghi, for £8million that southern European clubs especially began to worry. Young South American stars had previously been hand-picked by clubs in Spain, Portugal and Italy; now they were being outbid by the nouveau riche of European football.

As with Abramovich's Chelsea, money seems to be no object. Moscow Dinamo president Alexei Fedorychev admits to investing some £40million in the Club. A former Dinamo player, he acquired 51 percent of Dinamo shares in September 2004, having made his fortune in agrochemicals. His company, Fedcominvest, is registered in Monaco, where Fedorychev lives. In 2002, his attempt to buy the Monaco club, which was facing bankruptcy, was blocked because of allegations of money-laundering and criminal connections. Like Abramovich, however, he now owns one club and sponsors another – the Fedcominvest logo embellishes the Monaco shirt.

Fedorychev admits that at the moment Russian clubs are unprofitable, with attendance receipts, sales of merchandise and TV money being insufficient for them to break-even. In may not come as a surprise in the intricate and incestuous business of Russian football that Fedorychev also owns the TV rights for the entire Premier League!

The Russian oligarchs are men with huge personal wealth who are stealthily, and often covertly, taking over debt-ridden Western clubs, from Holland to Spain, Brazil to England, Monaco to Moscow. Exactly where the funds come from to finance their activities is a well-kept secret. Russian clubs and their investors are unwilling to reveal their financial accounts and the law does not oblige them to do so. What also makes them attractive to investors/money launderers is that they pay less tax than other businesses and experience less government control. No one will admit openly to having links with the mafia or laundering money through transfers. However, like all business, it is a precarious situation that could change at any moment, with the oligarchs walking out of the clubs they presently sponsor (perhaps through state – President Putin – fiat), leaving behind chaos and enormous debts.

Fixing the economy, cleaning up corruption, stopping the outflow of Russia's wealth and restoring a sense of pride and community, would certainly contribute to a healthier society and sports system in both Russia – and the rest of the world. But in a land where more money is spent on bribing officials – $30billion by one estimate – than on paying income tax[36], you won't find many Russians betting on it happening.

Notes

1   Nikolai Starostin, *Futbol skvoz gody* (Sovetskaya Rossiya, Moscow, 1989, p. 83.
2   Alexis de Tocqueville, *L'Ancien Regime* (1856), ed J. P. Mayer (Paris 1951), p. 223.
3   Eric Hobsbawm, *Age of Extremes. The Short Twentieth Century 1914–1991* (Michael Joseph, London, 1994), p. 496.
4   Nikolai Starostin, *Futbol skvoz gody*, p. 73.
5   For full details, see Jim Riordan, "The Strange Story of Nikolai Starostin, football and Lavrentiy Beria," in *Europe-Asia Studies*, vol. 46, no. 4, 1994, pp. 681 and 689.
6   N Romanov, *Trudnye dorogi k Olimpu* (Fizkultura i sport, Moscow, 1987), p. 57.
7   Olga Dmitrieva, "Bokal protiv detstva," *Komsomolskaya pravda*, 24 October 1987, p. 14.
8   See James Riordan, *Sport in Soviet Society* (Cambridge University Press, London, 1977).
9   Vladimir Maslachenko, "Ya po-prezhnemu v igre," Sobesednik, 1990, no. 46, p. 15.
10 D. Rennick, "Soviet Olympians compete for pre-set quota of medals," *The Korea Herald*, 27 September 1988, p. 9.
11 Vladimir Salnikov, "Vremya nadyozhd," *Argumenty i fakty*, 1989, no. 1, p. 3.
12 Maslachenko, p. 16.

13 DeSwan, ed, *Social Policy Beyond Borders: The Social Question in Transnational Perspective* (Amsterdam, Amsterdam University Press, 1994), p. 68.
14 Wojciech Liponski, "Will East Meet West?" *GAA Coaching News*, no 3, 1993, p. 29.
15 *Sportexpress* (Moscow), 27 December 1995, quoted in Robert Edelman, "There are no rules on planet Russia: Post-Soviet spectator sport," in Adele Barker, ed., *Consuming Russia: Popular Culture, Sex and Society Since* Gorbachov (Duke University Press, 1999), p. 221.
16 *Sportexpress*, 8 February 1996.
17 *Komsomolskaya pravda,*17 March 1992; 8 April 1992; 30 May 1992.
18 See James Riordan and Hart Cantelon, "The Soviet Union and Eastern Europe," in James Riordan and Arnd Kruger, eds, *European Cultures in Sport: Examining the Nations and Regions* (Bristol, Intellect, 2003), p. 101.
19 J McMurtry, *Unequal Freedoms: the Global Market as an Ethical System* (Toronto, Garamond, 1998), p. 208.
20 Nikolai Tolstykh, interview on Russian State Television, ORT, 1 March 1996. Quoted in Edelman, "There are no rules on planet Russia," p. 226.
21 See Edelman, p. 240.
22 See Edelman, p. 227; *Sportexpress*, 18 December 1995.
23 See Edelman, p. 226.
24 Liponski, p. 30.
25 Edelman, p. 222.
26 Alexander Weinstein, interview with US cable sports network, ESPN, Moscow, 26 June 1996.
27 Edelman, p. 219. See also Robert Edelman, *Serious Fun: A History of Spectator Sport in the USSR* (Oxford, Oxford University Press, 1993).
28 Quoted in Gabriele Marcotti, "Russia's flawed foreign policy," in *The Times*, 15 November 2004, p. 22 (of "The Game").
29 Rodionov, quoted in Marcotti.
30 In Edelman, p. 238.
31 In Marcotti, p. 23.
32 Edelman.
33 Interview with Alexei Smertin, Moscow, 31 May 2005.
34 *Novye izvestiya*, no. 88, 23 May 2005, p. 8, no. 88, 17–23 May 2005, p. 6.
35 *Futbol*, no. 88, 17–23 May 2005, p. 6.
36 Nick Paton Walsh, "Putin's Russia," in 6 July 2005, G2, p. 4.

Chapter 16

Performing America's past

Cold War fantasies in a perpetual state of war

Michael Silk, Bryan Bracey and Mark Falcous

At the Salt Lake City Winter Olympic Games in 2002, the US broadcaster, NBC, opened their coverage with a sweeping panoramic vista of the Uinita and Wasatch mountain ranges in Utah; not surprising, given the sporting events scheduled to take place over the next two weeks. Yet, these images were overlaid with a narrative far removed from the Olympic rhetoric of peace, harmony and universalism. Rather, and as part of the broader (sporting) response[1] to the events of 11 September 2001[2], the narratives that accompanied this first night of coverage, and which set the scene for the remaining two weeks, domesticated (see Hogan, 2002) the Games. Specifically, they offered a carefully construed rhetoric centred on the peculiar construction of the juridical or the concept of "right", of absolute certainty about "goodness" and a "caring" way of living, and, of a "power that can legitimately intervene anywhere where American security is involved, and, perhaps, well beyond this too" (Johnson, 2002, p. 219; also Baudrillard, 2001; McClaren, 2002). As the coverage continued, and following an interview with President George W. Bush, presenter Bob Costas narrated:

> The Opening Ceremony will *not* convene with a simple ceremony, [rather, it will be] a ceremony of resonance, where nations have come together to *imagine a world as we wish it could be*, where flags fly with pride, where men and women are not judged by the circumstances of their birth or beliefs but only by the depth of their character and imagination (emphasis added).

Centred on "a landscape of utter tranquillity" and the world as it *ought* to be – a vision that firmly placed, at the centre, *the* legitimate American response to terror – NBC's 2002 Winter Olympics became a space in which the "heart of darkness came to live with the souls of heroes … [lived through the] tides of history" (Jim McKay, NBC Commentator). The culmination of this night focussed, as ever, on the lighting of the Olympic flame. Bound within the narrative already espoused by NBC[3], the *world as it ought to be* was dramatized as Mike Eruzione and other members of the "heroic" United States 1980 gold-medal-winning Olympic Ice Hockey team – who famously overcame adversity in beating the USSR at

Lake Placid in 1980 – acted as emblematic subjectivities that conjured up the spectre of Cold War triumphs (see Hogan, 2003, for a more detailed account on the lighting of the flame). Bound within the material relations of the world after 11 September 2001, and evoking the Cold War past, this moment in Olympic history was part of a discursive reconstitution of the nation. The lighting of the torch should be read within the wider moment, a time of ontological disruption in which US nationalism was facing a challenge to its self-referentiality and its existentialism, and in which it became more conscious of itself in the cold light of an externally enforced rationality (Hedetoft, 1999). In this sense, this *remembering* of the Cold War, some thirteen years after it had supposedly concluded, once again gave Americans a space in which "freedom loving people" were opposed to "freedom (and thereby US) haters." The difference was that "terrorists" were all too easily slotted into the space previously reserved for "Communists." Accordingly, a promise was made to defeat the newly defined enemy in the war on terror (Johnson, 2002; see also Morris, 2002; Wang, 2002), the US nation being *re-membered* within our present.

Yet, this Olympic vignette does not stand alone – lest we were to be accused of forcing our contention somewhat. No, the narrative of the 1980 US Olympic Hockey team was about to be further dramatized by Disney resulting in a filmic, Hollywood, version of their efforts in Lake Placid in 1980 titled *Miracle* (2003). Like the Salt Lake City Olympics, following the global symbolic event of the force of 9/11 (Baudrillard, 2001), it is perhaps to be expected that film releases in this post-9/11 period focussed on various issues deemed to be patriotic. Indeed, in November 2001, more than forty top Hollywood executives met for two hours with Karl Rove, George W. Bush's chief political advisor, to discuss ways in which Hollywood could demonstrate its support of the American war drive (cf. Kay, 2002; Klindo and Phillips, 2005). Such discussions are deeply rooted in a history in which studio chiefs have collaborated with Washington (and indeed directly with the military, both in terms of supplying facilities and aircraft and denying such facilities if the script does not "fit" "acceptable" military endeavours) in an array of Second World War (*The Fighting Seabees*, 1944; *The Rear Gunner*, 1943; *Jap Zero*, 1943; *For God and Country*, 1943; and *Target Tokyo*, 1945) and Cold War films (*The Red Menace*, 1949; *I Married a Communist*, 1950; *I Was a Communist for the FBI*, 1951; and *Trial*, 1952). More recently, the Pentagon has "advised," intervened and interfered in productions, rewritten scripts, and placed products in films such as *The Hunt for the Red October*, *Flight of the Intruder*, *Thirteen Days*, *Windtalkers*, and *Stripes*, as well as less expectedly in *Jurassic Park III*, and children's programs such as *Lassie* and *The Mickey Mouse Club* (cf. Kay, 2002; Klindo and Phillips, 2005; Robb, 2005)[4].

Given this history, it is perhaps not surprising that some of the most powerful figures in the motion picture industry (representing Warner Bros., Twentieth Century Fox, Columbia Pictures, Universal Studios, Metro-Goldwyn-Mayer and DreamWorks SKG), corporate figures whose holdings include entertainment companies, such as billionaire Sumner Redstone of Viacom Inc. (which owns Paramount, CBS and UPN), and the major US television networks (ABC, NBC, CBS, Fox, UPN and WB) were gathered to meet with Rove in November 2001 (Klindo and Phillips, 2005). While the multi-billion dollar interests of the movie industry are not identical to those of the Pentagon, there does seem to be a clear recognition that movie industry's profits are bound up with Washington's attempts to seize control of strategic resources in the Middle East and elsewhere (Klindo and Philips, 2005; Robb, 2004). The two-hour meeting at the Peninsula Hotel in Beverly Hills focussed on seven themes: that the US campaign in Afghanistan was a war against terrorism, not Islam; the government's call for "community service" should be publicized; US troops and their families needed to be supported; the 11 September attacks were global attacks requiring a global response; the US campaign was a "war on evil"; the government and the film industry had the responsibility to reassure children of their safety; propaganda should be avoided (Walsh, 2001). This meeting would likely delight activist Jon Alvarez and his loose coalition of Patriotic Americans Boycotting Anti-American Hollywood (PABAAH) groups that have sprung up throughout the United States (and the list of 107 actors and musicians whose films he claims should be boycotted given their anti-war stance). Yet it poses a number of questions about the pedagogical role of film, as a space of translation, in putting particular ideologies and values into public conversation about how a society views itself and the public world of power, events, politics and institutions (Giroux, 2002). Film offers:

> subject positions, mobilize[s] desires, influence[s] us unconsciously, and help[s] construct the landscape of American culture. Deeply imbricated within material and symbolic relations of power, movies produce and incorporate ideologies that represent the outcome of struggles marked by the historical realities of power and the deep anxieties of the times; they also deploy power through the important role they play connecting the production of pleasure and meaning with the mechanisms and practices of powerful teaching machines. Put simply, films both entertain and educate.
>
> (Giroux, 2002, p. 3)

In this context then, the Hollywood version of the Lake Placid Ice Hockey team, *Miracle*, is an important site of critique. In a haunted present – characterized by the realization, if not visualization, of – the deep racial and class-based cleavages so dramatically bought home following Hurricane Katrina in 2005; the inability of the Bush administration to prepare, react or respond; domestic concerns over social (in)security; the nearly 2000 (and rising) number of US soldiers killed in Iraq at the time of writing; the ongoing US presence in Afghanistan; and the human rights injustices in Guantanemo Bay and on home soil enacted as part of the "Patriot Act" and through Homeland Security (see, e.g. Giroux, 2005) – how the past is enacted, how history is represented, becomes a powerful ideological tool in the formation and constant renegotiation of identity. A critical interrogation of *Miracle* then, can aid us in reading sport critically (Birrell and McDonald, 1999), as a key (mediated) space in which particular stories are shaped and circulated; the key question then becomes "how national identities emerge in specific instances and are then translated over time ... how is history, indeed time, represented?" (Bell, 2003, p. 69).

The popularized dinosaur: the extinction of the Cold War

The Cold War agenda, primarily played out, at least initially between the USSR and the United States, was predicated on an exercise of modern sovereignty, deployed foreign and domestic policy that served capital, and, depended upon centralized political power and the military–industrial complex for its smooth operation both at home and abroad (Wang, 2002). Many of the contributors to this volume have discussed the various nation-building narratives that in part created and sustained sovereign states and the imperialist project, sentimental and passionate performances or "... rhetoric, a narrative, a moral drama propelled by the Manichean myth of apocalyptical struggle between forces of good and evil, between capitalism and communism, between democracy and totalitarianism, rationality and barbarism" (Wang, 2002, p. 48). These contributions interrogate the role of sport as *soft-core* questions of culture, as opposed to the *hard-core* issues of the operation of the military industrial complex (Carmichael, 1993; Wang, 2002). In other words, the soft side of the Cold War was ideological; the side of the Cold War that took centre stage in public discourse and imagination.

Given the capacity of sport to be mobilized as a major cultural signifier that can engage national sensibilities, identities, and experiences – de facto cultural shorthand delineating particular national sentiments (Silk and Andrews, 2001; Silk, Andrews and Cole, 2005) – it is understandable that sport should have been deployed as an important weapon in the armories of the United States and the Soviet Union. For example, in the USSR, commitment to the cultural politics and mass theater of festivals and rituals often involved various forms of mass physical culture that condemned elitist and spectator sport. Instead it evoked participation, inclusion and a populism that connected with wider cultural traditions and activities (Roche, 2000). In the United States, the (male) body was also subject to discipline through sporting activity. As Dyreson (1999) points out, utilizing the concept of athletism, industrialists and capitalists employed sport (particularly baseball, although basketball was also integral to social reform) as a way to reconnect the newly urbanized masses to nature, distance the republic from its colonial past, integrate immigrant populations to the "American way," control "unruly" youth, and, mold a productive and functional worker to ensure the growth of the new urban industrial republic. While the

USSR was isolationist for much of the first half of the twentieth century (certainly during the interwar period), sport continued to play an important internal ideological function – in 1920 for example, along with a mass dramatization of the Bolshevik storming of the Winter Palace in 1917, two large sporting events took place. The first was a huge gymnastic display involving 18,000 athletes in the Red Stadium, the second, the inaugural Central Asian Games in Tashkent which involved considerably more participants than the 1920 Olympics in Antwerp (Roche, 2000). These events were followed in 1925 by the first Spartakiade, an Olympic style event that involved Communist athletes from 14 countries and filled the 100,000 seater stadium for the twelve day festival (Roche, 2000). Buoyed by the 1904 St Louis expo and the increasing opportunities for sporting competition overseas (for example at the 1936 Olympic Games in Berlin), the USA was able to utilize sport in the service of particular ideological agendas (no matter how false and exclusionary, especially in terms of class, race and gender these may have been). Yet, it was the entry of the Soviet Union into the Olympics in 1952, sparking a medal table rivalry constantly nourished and analyzed by the media (Miller, Lawrence, McKay and Rowe, 2001), that international sporting events during the Cold War acquired new significance (Bairner, 2001).

The nuances and complexities of many of these encounters are beautifully captured in Kuznetsov and Lukashev's (1977) narrative accounts of USSR–USA sporting encounters. As this text, drawing as it does on first-hand accounts from competitors, coaches, and, journalists, along with the discussions within this book, clearly indicate, the prism of the Cold War formed an important framing device through which both American and Soviet (as well as the plethora of associated national television networks) sport (media) coverage readily reflected and reproduced patterns of inequality, polarization and serve to clearly "mark off" the "other" (De Cillia, Riesgel and Wodak, 1999; Cole and Andrews, 2002; Hogan, 2003; Kinkema and Harris, 1992; Riggs, Eastman and Golobic, 1993; Silk and Falcous, 2005). While sport within the United States has historically been deployed by powerful elites as a tool of social reform, cultural pedagogy and governance, our current post-Cold war climate is one in which Olympic television discourse at least, influenced by American foreign policy, poses the teams of the former Soviet Union as a "fading enemy" (Kinkema and Harris, p.35, 1998).

The now almost pervasive (in terms of its reach and critique) social theory espoused and made famous by Francis Fukyama (1992) suggests that the end of history has been reached following the collapse of Soviet communism, the triumph of Western capitalism and democracy, and, the universalization of Western liberal democracy as the final form of human government. Popular accounts inform us that the Cold War ended in 1989, effectively being replaced with an occupation with globalization. As Wang (2002, p. 45) proposes, "the Cold War, with its confrontation between sovereign nation states of leviathan power, its mutually assured destruction policy, and its ideological conflict, has gone the way of dinosaurs." In place of this supposedly extinct monolith breathes a new age, a global age, one which conjures up a utopian vision of market economy characterized by accelerated economic momentum, free flows of capital without borders, international cooperation, and, global democracy, all policed and supervised by imperial (as opposed to sovereign) rule (Wang, 2002).

Perhaps most explicitly discussed in Hardt and Negri's (2000) *Empire*, this new age is characterized by the displacement of national sovereignty by the global market and global circuits of production – "an array of national and supranational organizations operating under a single logic of rule ... a decentered and deterritoralizing apparatus of rule that progressively incorporates the entire global realm within its open expanding frontiers." (p. xii). For Hardt and Negri, (2000), a new global order has emerged – a new form of sovereignty – made up of formal and informal organizations and institutions (a mixed constitution made up of "monarchic entities" such as the WTO or the Pentagon, "aristocratic entities" such as transnational corporations and "democratic forces" such as national government organizations). These entities and forces, are spread in a global network distribution of biopower – the

> zone characterized by the intersection of these old fields–an economy that is eminently cultural, a cultural field that is equally economic, a politics that comprehends the other two equally, and so forth.
>
> (Hardt and Negri, in Brown and Szeman, 2002, p. 181)

In this formulation, the ideology of economic liberalism no longer needs to serve powers that be; rather, it roams free with the drift of "benign" capital, supported by markets, free trade, transnational organizations, and, supranational juridical structures (Wang, 2002). As opposed then to a world dominated by warring states, as it was in the Cold War, trade wars and trade talks dominate the "free" international market, moral struggle between ideological camps is replaced by (under)development, politics and morality are usurped by economics and management, and nation-states supplanted by supranational entities (Castells, 2000; Wang, 2002).

Yet, the apparent "triumph" of liberal democracy and market capitalism was bought into stark disarray by the events of 11 September 2001 (see, for example, Kellner, 2002a/b; Dallamyr, 2002). Just as the parochial interest of national security and survival was drowned out, as the Cold War tone of strident military and ideological conflict had almost vanished, just as the dinosaur was to become extinct, 11 September provided the catalyst for conjuring up the old spectres (Wang, 2002). The events of, and since, 11 September –a terrible thunderclap (Dallmyr, 2002) – suggest that the rush to proclaim the extinction of the beast may well have been a little premature. Following 11 September 2001, the array of references to Pearl Harbor, the world wars, the Korean conflict, the redefinition of the "enemy," and, nostalgic allusions to a simpler past, all conjure up the spectre of the Cold War (Wang, 2002). Emerging from behind the "mirage of imperial sovereignty," (Wang, 2002, p. 48) the "otherness of the other" (p. 53) was discovered (or perhaps better put, finally acknowledged) and created a rupture (see Cocco and Negri, 2001) in Empire. This discovery meant a re-examination of "we," a realization of one "we" among many others, a recognition and realization that America is part of this finite world (Dallmayr, 2002), and the (re)emergence of a sovereign nation-state that mobilized political will, civic spirit, patriotism, and homeland security that silenced dissent and curtailed civil liberties in a manner reminiscent of the Cold War (Wang, 2002; Sivanandan, 2006). In so doing, in the reassertion of national sovereignty, another Cold War legacy reared its head – the measurement of self against a significant other (Wang, 2002). Yet, who, in our present moment, is the significant other, and, who defines this other?

The mythologizing of the Magic Kingdom

As noted above, Henry Giroux (2002) reminds us that movies are more than a source of shared enjoyment, entertainment, escape; they are also a source of knowledge, their cinematography and narratives fill our conversation, our dreams, we argue over their meanings, their relevance for our lives, they take us out of the worlds which we inhabit, the remote pleasures, burdens and problems that dominate our own social worlds. Films then, deeply imbricated within material and symbolic relations of power, produce and incorporate ideologies, offer up subject positions, mobilize desires, influence us unconsciously, and help construct the landscape of American culture that represent the outcome of struggles marked by the historical realities of power and the deep anxieties of the times (Giroux, 2002). Contextualizing filmic discourse in relation to political economy and transnational capitalism will give us a better understanding of how such forces produce dominant social reading formations that often limit the range of meanings that can be taken up by readers in addressing films and other media texts (Giroux, 2002). In particular, following Silk *et. al.* (2005), we focus on one particularly lustrous example of the interplay between those political forces – which were previously responsible for harnessing and contouring national cultural identity – and commercially driven forces (such as Disney). Together, these forces are increasingly responsible, in at times contradictory ways, for the constitution of the symbolic boundaries of the twenty-first century. In this chapter, we address the place of Disney, existing as it does within a politically sensitive Hollywood film industry, in influencing the manner in which the nation and national identity are represented: how is the "corporate-cultural" nation of the twenty-first century exteriorized through, and internalized within, the operations and machinations of multi-, trans- and supra-national entities (Silk *et. al.*, 2005)?

Disney is everywhere, yet is nowhere; its presence is naturalized, a normalized, banal presence that has slipped relatively unnoticed under the radar of cultural critique[5]. Giroux (1995; 1999; 2002) made an important call to educators and other cultural workers to include the construction of the imagined landscapes of the "culture of children" as an important site of contestation and struggle. He suggested:

> Popular audiences tend to reject any link between ideology and the prolific entertainment world of Disney ... Even more disturbing is the widespread belief that Disney's trademarked innocence renders it unaccountable for the diverse ways in which it shapes the sense of reality it provides for children as they take up specific and often sanitized notions of identity, difference, and history in the seemingly apolitical cultural universe of "the Magic Kingdom."
> (Giroux, 2002, p.105)

However, Disney's corporate and cultural influence – a maze of representations, experiences and products such as box office movies, home videos, theme parks, hotels, sports teams, retail stores, classroom instructional films, CDs, television programs, and family restaurants – powerfully influence, script, and shape childhood (Giroux, 1995; 1999; 2003; 2005). Most assiduously, Giroux (1995; 1999) points towards Disney's legendary self-proclaimed innocence, inflexibility in dealing with social criticism, and paranoid justification for its actions – an institutional ideology that offers all the more reason why it should be both challenged and engaged critically. Thus, through the widespread use of public visual space, Disney inserts itself into a network of power relations that promotes the construction of a closed and total world of enchantment allegedly free from the dynamics of ideology, politics, and power within the imaginary discourse of innocence, civic pride, and entertainment (Giroux, 1995).

Of particular interest in the current chapter is the role of Disney in the construction of the Cold War past. Giroux (1995; 1999) proposed that Disney's role in America's future is to be understood through a particular construction of the past; a politics of innocence as a narrative for shaping public memory and for producing a "general body of identifications" that promote a packaged and sanitized version of American history in the seemingly apolitical, cultural universe of the "Magic Kingdom." Disney's mythologizing then points to the relative capacity of particular organizations, in this sense a $22 billion dollar corporate entity[6], to tell us a story about ourselves; a "partial truth that accentuates particular versions of reality and marginalizes or omits others" (Rowe, McKay, and Miller, 1998, p. 121).

Power play: our present *Miracle*

Disney's *Miracle*, the title of which is drawn from Al Michaels famous television commentary that accompanied the semi-final victory over the USSR, "Do you Believe in Miracles?" focuses on the personal stories, the human drama, of the USA coach Herb Brooks, and the players he chose for the victorious 1980

Olympic team. Gavin O'Connor, the Director of *Miracle*, has suggested that the film would only work if its focus was on the "authenticity" of the hockey action. Indeed, the DVD release of *Miracle* includes a number of "extras" that focus on how the minutiae of the original plays were recreated through the "inventive use of cameras and cameramen on skates," the efforts to "put you smack in the middle of the game" through the recreation of the "intensity" of hockey sounds, and, through the casting of real hockey players, as opposed to actors, who would make the film "smell raw and real." As Soar (2000) has indicated, it appears that cultural workers, in this sense the Disney production crew, may well be less reliant upon some distant punitive audience for their work, relying instead on the closer, internal, community of colleagues as criteria by which the worth of their work is assessed. However, and more pertinent to the current chapter, the DVD offers several "bonus" features, such as the Directors, commentary, the first meeting between Herb Brooks and the filmmakers, and, an ESPN roundtable with winning team members and actor Kurt Russell (who played Brooks) – yet, not one of these features acknowledges, let alone discusses, the *context* of the victory. Without denying the polysemy of reception, it does appear, as Brookey and Westerfelhaus have proposed in discussing the return of auteur theory in such DVD vignettes, that such "direction" can reinforce the preferred meanings encoded at the site of production. Thus, Disney's *Miracle*, at least in terms of production, appears to steer clear of the historical context, preferring instead to focus upon the "raw" authenticity of the sport itself. This contention is supported by a critical reading (Birrell and McDonald, 1999) of *Miracle*. Focussing on the US players as good, white, family "boys" (Aloff, 2004), plucked by Brooks from college hockey, who achieve against the odds, the narrative settles on the myth of meritocracy, individualism, and hard work in subservience to the higher national cause. *Miracle* is male soap opera in every way; masculine melodrama is played out in the aspirations of the college kids picked for the Olympic dream, the trials, tribulations, traumas, fraternal bonding that these boys engage in, and most importantly, in the efforts, willingness, hard work, sweat, guts and blood required to achieve victory.

Yet, this is not to suggest that the film bypasses the socio-historical context of the moment altogether. As McDonald (this text, chapter 12) suggests, in 1980 this event was highly significant to the American populace and provided an important grounding for the similarly regressive discourses eventually deployed by President Ronald Reagan in order to legitimate and intensify the processes of American militarization and global capitalist expansion. While *Miracle's* narrative sweeps through player tryouts, the subsequent warm-up games, and the games that took place during the Lake Placid Olympics, the important climax of the film centres around the Olympic Ice Hockey semi-final victory against the USSR (the final victory against Finland is only addressed through the credits). In this sense, the narrative provides a space in which the hard-work ethic, the willingness to push the male body to almost unimaginable extremes, the individual rivalries and differences (played out in the film through the colleges they attend) are subsumed to the greater national cause: manifest in the inexorable rise from minnow to Reaganite hard body (Kellner, 1995) capable of defeating the all-powerful, all conquering, Soviet Union[7].

Metaphorically, the subsumption of difference was graphically demonstrated in a much lauded scene. Following defeat by Norway in an exhibition game, Brooks (Russell) lined his players up on the ice in an empty arena. On his word, players repeated numerous line drills, pushing their physically exhausted bodies to extreme limits – in some cases beyond limits as a number of the players vomited following each shuttle. Brooks (Russell) would not let up, even as the arena lights were dimmed, asking at the conclusion of each shuttle who his players were and where they were from. Following each answer, in which a player stated his name and his college, they were again made to complete the drill on Brooks's shrill "again" instruction. Finally, and in what is a quite poignant moment in the movie, after another demanding shuttle, Brooks again offered the same question. This time, Mike Eruzione stepped up, offered his name, and instead of the usual name of the college, volunteered: "USA". Upon this Brooks (Russell) terminates the drill. The message is explicit – as Brooks (Russell) barks at his players later in the film "the name on the front of the jersey – USA – is far more important than the one on the back – individual names." Thus, the central tenet of the ideology of nationalism is reinforced – internal diversity and interests be subsumed to the (apparently higher) national cause when facing an external threat. If you will excuse the pun, this power play, is, at least in one sense, like many other sport films, in that it offers a strong element of closure that leaves the audience with a "moral" message and a feeling of uplift (Baker, 2003; Rosenstone, 1995) – defeat of a powerful enemy by depoliticized good boys who endlessly chant (and in our present, *Disney* likely want the audience to join in) "U-S-A, U-S-A".

Indeed, when showing this film in the "*Sporting Hollywood: Contested Identities in the Filmic Popular*" class that one of us teaches at the University of Maryland to undergraduates born well after the Lake Placid games and who, sadly, had no idea of the events, it was stunning to witness the outpouring of emotion, patriotism and pride that was felt by these students. Perhaps this should not have been a surprise, here we were, essentially middle-class college-level kids watching a film about, well, essentially middle-class college kids who achieved above the odds. Yet, it was not so much this narrative, nor the "masculine solidarity and resolve" that impressed these students; rather it was the political moment in which we were watching the film – Spring 2004, a moment of *crisis* in which the US was involved in a relentless, permanent, war on "terror" both domestically (manifest in an internal, domestic war against the poor, youth, women, people of color, and the elderly [Giroux, 2004]) and through its imperialist foreign policy (a continued "presence" in Iraq and Afghanistan [see Harvey, 2003]) – that led to such emotive expression. In this sense, we argue the film is more of a document that represents when it was made – the past being portrayed through the lens of present concerns, a "remembrance [that] is in large measure a reconstruction of the past achieved with data borrowed from the present (Halbachs, 1950, p. 69).

The opening credits of *Miracle* provide, in our view, a particularly powerful public pedagogy. As with our present moment, the film proffers a moment of *crisis*: sweeping through the material and ideological outcomes of a decentred *Pax Americana*. *Miracle* begins by offering a montage of headlines and images that locate the film within a moment of political and economic turmoil and disruption. This is 1980, in Carter's America: Gasoline is scarce, Watergate still casts its shadow over Washington, the Russians invade Afghanistan, and the American embassy in Tehran is seized, US troops are at war in Cambodia, and, there is internal dissent, strife and disunity (Paquin, 2004). This moment of *crisis* is extended throughout the film with the inclusion of selected passages from President Carter's 1980 State of the Union Address in which he attempted to deflect attention from the Iranian hostage crisis together with high unemployment and inflation and in which he blamed the country's dissatisfaction on Vietnam and Watergate. As was Carter's hope, the feats of the 1980 Ice Hockey team fitted the closing epitaph of his State of the Union address: "Together as one people, let us work to build our strength at home, and together as one indivisible union, let us seek peace and security throughout the world. Together let us make of this time of challenge and danger a decade of national resolve and of brave achievement." The film, which cleverly spliced the speech with images of the US team in action, offered a "Washington consensus" – a victorious hockey team would make America feel better about itself (Bowman, 2004; Holleran, 2004). In this sense, the film reiterates what Carter was calling the "crisis of confidence" in America, rather than addressing the real crisis in America at this time: the crisis of confidence in Carter – sport being employed as *soft-power* in what Bowman (2004) terms Cold War revisionism.

Despite these quite powerful moments in *Miracle*, and as suggested above, for the most part, the film does not unduly stress the Cold War narrative. For Holleran (2004), *Miracle*, downplays references to communism, assiduously avoiding any suggestion that the Soviet menace – having seized Hungary, Vietnam, Afghanistan and Eastern Europe – posed a real threat to the United States. We would agree that reference to communism is downplayed, yet, we do feel that the moment of crisis was still present, even if only in the background. Importantly, this allows for a master narrative that emphasizes national unity in the face of threat, yet does not need to go to great lengths to detail the "other" given that the Soviet Union, in our present, is a faded enemy. Thus, and as with other sports films (see Carrington, 1998 for example for a discussion of the downplaying of Alis' political stridency in *When We Were Kings*), the political significance of the moment is lost and there is a misrepresentation of what this moment meant to the populace at this historical juncture (McDonald's discussion of the moment in this volume is almost absent in this representation of the events) – in other words, while there is clearly a threat, the context is in subtle ways avoided, if not, forgotten, and the film offers a little cultural amnesia and a downplaying of Cold War politics. Indeed, there are parallels here with *Ali*, the film version of the life of Muhammad Ali, in which the protagonist's revolutionary black political stance – his symbols of defiance against America, his black consciousness and his Islamic faith – is effectively neutered, in line with present concerns to promote feelgood images of black–white sameness that deny deep conflicts between ethnic groups; Ali's image effectively being hijacked, touted as a triumph over adversity, and appropriated by a political and economic establishment that once attacked him (see Saeed, 2001; Farred, 2003). Indeed, in *Ali*, as with *Miracle*, the political context is never dealt with in detail, rather both films utilize cinematic techniques in which newspaper headlines fly across the screen at remarkable pace as substitute for detail. In *Miracle*, the Cold War context is thus reduced to headlines (and in one case a banner at one of the hockey games) that provides the historically uncertain viewer with all the context – Afghanistan, Watergate, transportation crisis, oil, communism – "required," or, perhaps better put, "*offered*," for us to make sense in our present of these past events. This contention is furthered when one considers the lack of narrative accorded to the Soviets in the film who, in contrast to the detailed construction of the US players, are presented without narrative, as depoliticized, faceless, "opponents."

This stands in stark contrast to the portrayal of Rocky Balboa (played by Sylvester Stallone) in the 1984 film *Rocky IV*[8]. Throughout the genealogy of Rocky movies, Balboa is portrayed as an "ideal" American citizen – a poor son of an Italian immigrant whose rise from rags to riches reminds the movie-goer of all the country has done for its citizens, and, proves that America is the "land of opportunity" (Munfa, 2003). This propaganda is supported in the far from subtle location of the movie – Philadelphia, the "city of brotherly love," the birth of the nation, the home of the Liberty Bell – all of which, during the film's release in 1984 was being challenged by the context of the Cold War and the apparently dangerous communist threat (Munfa, 2003). Following from the official FBI rhetoric, as for example narrated by "former communist" Herbert Philbrick in the official Cold War FBI propaganda film *What is Communism* (1963) that suggested that the Communist party are "lying, dirty, shrewd, godless, murderous, determined … and not an American political party like any other, its an outlaw organization taking its instructions and orders from another government to do everything possible to destroy our government. It's an international, criminal conspiracy," *Rocky IV* utilized a number of common cinematic techniques to demonize Balboa's Soviet enemy, Ivan Drago. Drago is constructed through sensational techniques that emphasize a crude, xenophobic and insensitive belligerence in an unedifying construction of the imaginary line between "us" and "them" (Merskin, 2004; Said, 1997). That is, rephrasing Hall (1997), through drawing upon a few simple, vivid, memorable, easily grasped and widely recognized characteristics, reducing everything to those traits, and exaggerating and simplifying them, Drago becomes abstracted from the film and serves our popular cultural stereotypes of the Soviet male. As Munfa (2003) points out, the lighting of the film serves to enhance the evil aura of Drago – he is shown as imposing with an evil glare, in dark lighting. The narrative offers a telling comparison between Drago's employment of state-of-the-art sport science technology and demonstration of "unearthly" strength, while Rocky's training takes place through utilization of the natural environment; a telling cyborg versus human, technology versus nature, analogy. Further, the use of background music adds to Drago's evil image, as the song "There's No Easy Way Out" by Robert Tepper reminds Rocky of the difficult task ahead of him. Finally, even the make-up and costume of Drago enhance his image as an evil villain; his black mouthpiece and the red circles around his eyes dehumanizing him (Munfa, 2003), while the focus on Drago's training, his reduction to machine, and the inauspicious use of unidentified performance enhancers suggest a cyborgified athlete who destabilizes the boundaries between man, machine and technology; a polluted, non-natural (in relation, ironically, to the corporeal purity of Stallone's character), communist, dehumanized body (see Butryn, 2003; Butryn and Masucci, 2003; Harraway, 1997).

Conversely, in *Miracle*, while brief mention is made of the Soviets' main "weapon" – intimidation – and, while they still appear as emotionless, the Soviet athletes are not demonized; rather, they are very much *in absentia*. As O'Keefe (2004) suggests, while the Soviets are depicted as "utterly humourless" and Soviet coach Viktor Tikhonov's "Brezhnevian eyebrows are comically exaggerated" there is no reference to the "requisite off-ice displays of heartlessness and on-ice dirty tactics that we might have expected." Indeed, with the exception of their star goal-tender (Vladislav Tretiak), one star player who Brooks reduces to looking like Stan Laurel (Boris Mikhailov), and the coach (Viktor Tikhonov), these are nameless individuals. In this sense, as Roger Ebert (2004) suggested on the film's release, *Miracle* "sidesteps" the Soviet athletes,

> it doesn't even bother to demonize the opponents. When the US finally faces the Soviets, they're depicted as – well, simply as the other team. Their coach has a dark, forbidding manner and doesn't smile much, but he's not a Machiavellian schemer, and the Soviets don't play any dirtier than most teams do in hockey.

Thus, with the USSR seen as a "fading enemy" in the present, the film is not faced with needing to reinforce the magnitude or imminence of the "Soviet threat" which had been so pressing twenty years earlier. Additionally, the politics of the coach of the US team, Herb Brooks, played by Kurt Russell, was played down. The emphasis was on Brooks as a caring, if somewhat detached, family man (indeed, playing on the masculine melodrama, he spent Christmas with his new hockey family), whose "abrasiveness and unabashed anti-communism … [was] toned down, almost to vanishing point" (Bowman, 2004).[9]

While the wider political context is somewhat toned down, it is not however, totally absent. Brooks is, for example, shown in a dimly lit office listening on the phone as the Olympic chairman of selectors informs him that, following the spectre of a boycott, Brezhnev had told Carter to "screw himself" and that the Soviet team would be traveling to play in the Olympic hockey tournament. Further, during the semi-final game with the United States, the Director assures the ascendancy of capitalism through splicing in a Coca-Cola commercial that aired during the 1980 Winter Olympics and has the tag-line "Have a Coke and Smile" after yet another shot of an emotionless Soviet bench. Yet, we suggest these superficial references – as opposed to detailed contextual understanding of the moment – were historically unsure allusions to the "defeat" of communism and the Cold War context and that they relate more to the moment, also a moment of *crisis*, in which the film was released. That is, the brief, marginal allusions to the Cold War suggestively point to a cultural politics of the present – somewhat emblematically embedded within the film given that the semi-final scene described above was preceded by a shot of a sparkling scene of the New York City skyline, lingering on the glistening twin towers, prior to cutting to the Soviet bench during the game at Madison Square Garden – that centres on the defeat of a newly defined "enemy" in a less certain, permanent, war on terror.

Asymmetry: Cold War spectres in a ruptured present

Miracle was released at what we have called a time of ontological disruption in the United States, a post 9/11 context in which there was a re-examination of "we", a realization of one "we" among many others, and the (re)emergence of a sovereign nation-state within the confines of a new sovereignty, a new Empire predicated on a decentered and deterritoralizing apparatus of market rule. As Wang (2002) proposed, to this point, it was "as if America and the civilized world had lived in a soothing dream, only to be rudely awakened and thrown back to the rugged terrain of Cold War conflict, to paranoiac security needs, the bloody conflict of giant powers, the tightening of boundaries, and the hysterical assertion of national identity" (Wang, 2002, 46). Perhaps not surprisingly, following Rowe *et al.* (1998) at this time of rupture, "the nation is conjured up at those moments when an affective unity can be posited against the grain of divisions" (p. 120) and as that national–political, economic, and military sovereignty becomes even more undermined, "the greater the need for states to construct a semiotically potent cultural nation" (p. 133). As Johnson (2002) revealed in his analysis of political rhetoric, this was a moment in which President Bush, in his 20 September 2001, address to the US Congress, rolled out a national "we." This new "we" was fundamental in Bush's internal (re)constitution of America:

> they hate what they see right here in this chamber – a democratically elected government. Their leaders are self-appointed. They hate our freedoms – our

freedom of religion, our freedom of speech, our freedom to vote and assemble and disagree with each other.

(President Bush, 20 September 2001 cited in Johnson, 2002, p. 216)

Of course, juxtaposed with "we" – which was evidently expanded to an "us," an "unprecedented global consensus" (Tony Blair, 12 October 2001, in Johnson, 2002, p.217) – was the concept of "they," a definition of *the* enemy, a paradoxically diminishing "other" – the terrorists (Johnson, 2002). Yet, unlike the Cold War in which there existed a bounded, tangible and clearly defined enemy, the enemy of today – the "terrorist" – is, in Baudrillard's (2001) terms, a boundary-less, decentred, opponent. Unlike the Cold War then, the present "war on terror" is far from symmetrical (Hardt and Negri, 2004); rather, as Baudrillard (2001) proposes:

> In a traditional universe, there was still a balance between good and evil, according to a dialectical relation, which maintained at all costs the tension and balance of the moral universe – a little like the face-off the two powers maintained during the Cold War, assuring a balance of terror. So there is no supremacy of one over the other. This balance is broken when there is a complete extrapolation of the good (hegemony of the positive over all forms of negativity, exclusion of death and of any other adverse power – the triumph of the values of good all the way). From there, the balance is broken, and it is as if evil would recover an invisible autonomy and develop exponentially.

In our present then, a supposedly "post-historical" world (Fukuyama, 1993) devoid of communism and in which capitalism reigns supreme, the geopolitics of the old world has been cartographically and epistemologically reordered, the balance has been broken, and the "enemy" has been recast. For Baudrillard (2001, p.137), the disappearance of communism and the global triumph of liberal power, meant for the appearance of a ghostly enemy that insinuates itself like a virus and that reappears in all the cracks of power: Islam. Such asymmetry for Baudrillard (2001, p.137) leaves the "global superpower completely disarmed"; as such this war takes on a fundamentally different character to the Cold War, and others that have preceded it:

> The first two world wars were traditional. The first one put an end to European supremacy and colonialism; the second ended Nazism; and the third, which really took place in the form of a Cold War and détente, ended communism. Gradually, each moved the world closer to a univocal world order. Today, through all its current convulsions, the latter is virtually achieved, and faces antagonistic forces everywhere … the fourth war is elsewhere. It haunts every global order, all hegemonic domination.
>
> (Baudrillard 2001, p.136)

Similarly, Hardt and Negri (2004) suggest that the leaders of the United States and its allied nation-states seemed to learn reluctantly after September 11 2001 that the enemy they face is not a unitary sovereign nation-state but rather a network – a ubiquitous, nebulous enemy, characteristic of a new era of asymmetrical conflicts (Hardt and Negri, 2004). While it could be argued that a network enemy was present in the Cold War–communism, as the enemy, may have taken the form of a sovereign state (Soviet Union and then China, Cuba, North Korea, North Vietnam and others), but it was also a fleeting and ephemeral network in that insurrectionary armies, revolutionary parties, political organizations, trade unions and any number of other organizations could potentially be communist – for the most part, in the Cold War, the network enemy was partially hidden to the extent that it was constantly over-coded in terms of the socialist states and thus thought to be merely so many dependent agents of the primary sovereign enemy, the Soviet Union (Hardt and Negri, 2004).

Thus, following Hardt and Negri (2004) and Baudrillard (2001), at the conclusion of the Cold War, nation-states no longer cloud our view and "we" are faced with a ghostly enemy, which, like a virus, haunts "us" and "infiltrates" the global capitalist order. As Morris (2002) suggests, while this present war – perhaps more infinite in scope and endless in duration than previous evocations of war – does constitute something of a break with Cold War policy, it relies on the rhetoric and ideology of the Cold War. That is, for Bush, and indeed for Blair, the populace must be convinced that the enemy is out there, a tangible collective (in Afghanistan, Iraq or wherever), that can be identified as the "other," not "us." In this sense, as Wang (2002, p. 46) argues, there has been a return to the rugged terrain of Cold War conflict, to paranoia, to phobia, to security, to the bloody conflict of giant powers, the tightening of boundaries, and the hysterical assertion of national identity. Herein lays the miracle of *Miracle*. Not only does it reassert a sense of self – a remembrance of what it means to be "we" – it takes "us" back to time when things were a lot simpler. Clearly, for Americans, as even CNN were able to point out, the world felt like a more hostile place after 9/11 – *Miracle*'s appeal is that it takes us back to a time when things were more black and white – "us" against "them" (CNN, 2004).

Indeed, as Hogan (2003) proposed in respect to the 2003 Salt Lake City Opening Ceremony narrative, this was a time of innocence in which evocations of the US "war on terror" were dominated by images of White American masculinity – an appeal to a whiteness not troubled by the threats to the mores, practices, and social relations on which American families, traditional values, and the nation are said to have been founded (Kusz, 2001) and that sustains the more long-standing subordination of women and ethnic minorities in the United States. Disney's *Miracle* thus offers a narrative, that as the film itself suggests, frees the "fire within" (Aloff, 2004) through Brooks' ability to form a collective coming together against the odds to achieve a notorious national victory. The same narrative, "The Fire Within," was later rolled out as the theme of the 2002 Salt Lake City Winter Olympics to "embody the spirit of hope, competition and teamwork" (NBC Olympic Coverage, 2002) providing a continuity between the past and / in the present. Miracle, similar to the cinema release of Seabiscuit, "offered [Americans] solace in films and perhaps even presidents that seduce us through promises of easy victories and performances of innocence (past, present, and future) through ignorance" (Cole and Cates, 2003). It does so through a historical amnesia that forgets who "they" were – the Russians were not explicitly demonized or dehumanized in Miracle – allowing for a reassertion of the spectres of the Cold War without "Communists." In other words, through forgetting, through representation of the Lake Placid Olympic games as being almost devoid of real, menacing, realised Cold War rhetoric, the film provides Americans a space in which a relatively bland and not especially threatening enemy (Soviets as represented in Miracle) were juxtaposed with "freedom loving people" making it all the easier, as Hogan (2003) argued with regard to the Salt Lake City games, to slot "terrorists" into the space previously reserved for "communists" – a symbolic assertion of American power, a promise to once again defeat its enemies in the "war on terror" (p. 108). Of course, this says nothing of the racisms, degraded images of Arabs, Muslims, and those who "look Arab or Muslim," official immigration policies, the directives of the Department of Homeland (In)Security, racial profiling on highways and at airports, or the physical and psychological abuse on the bodies and minds of abject US citizens (see for example, Ahmed, 2002; Giroux, 2005; Harvey, 2003; McLaren and Martin, 2004; Merskin, 2004; Sivanandan, 2006). In this sense, and somewhat rearticulating Morris (2002), Miracle can be seen as a powerful pedagogical device which in a moment in which the barbarism of a war is imagined to be out there, on foreign soil, was bought home, yet was quickly rendered "foreign" again. Thus, Miracle offers a perverse form of public pedagogy, that conditions, if not trains, consumers in the doctrines of Bush's fanatical, "proto-fascist," neo-conservative, visions of geo-political-militaristic domination, a vision that explicitly and implicitly views the United States as culturally, morally, and politically superior to all other nation-states, that sets the parameter of capital accumulation as the only way to achieve success, is based on regime change, pre-emptive strikes, full spectrum dominance, domestic surveillance, and, serves as the beacon of Republican virtue in this world promoting "democracy," "human rights" and the "international rule of law" (Giroux; 2004; 2005; Hardt and Negri, 2005; Harvey, 2003 Sivanandan, 2006). Disney's Miracle then, serves as a powerful (sporting) economy of affect through which power, privilege, politics and position are (re)produced (see Andrews, 1995; Clarke, 1991; Giroux, 1994; Grossberg, 1992; Silk and Falcous, 2005).

Concluding comments: re-membering the nation in a permanent state of exception

Following Giroux (1995; 1999), within this chapter, we critically interrogated how Disney films work to construct meanings, induce pleasures, and reproduce ideologically loaded fantasies. *Miracle* can be framed within the classic work of Ernest Renan (1990, in Billig, 1995, p. 36) who proposed that juxtaposed with the processes of remembering, forgetting was a "crucial element in the creation of nations." In this sense, *the* national collective memory (that is legitimated within the dominant mode of social regulation and reproduction of the time) is a representation of history that, as Billig (1995, p.37), points out, is simultaneously an exercise in remembering and collective forgetting: "the nation, which celebrates its antiquity, celebrates its historical recency" (p. 37). Thus, in our present, versions of past-ness, no matter how invented, acquired, embellished – what is forgotten and what is remembered – can act as a powerful cohesive force, binding disparate members of nations together, demarcating the boundaries between us and them, self and foreign, alien and other, and can become embedded within the very fabric of the nation (Bell, 2003).

Collective amnesia, the selective remembering and forgetting, is not a result of absent-mindedness, it is a result of the carefully contoured reconstitution of the past by powerful groups at particular points in time that can *train*, or entertain, us in our historicity, our being-in-history (Healy, 1997, p.5). The "presence of the past within the present" (Nora, 1989, p. 20) then points to important questions regarding which "national histories" are told, by whom, and in regard to what, and how, they recollect (De Cillia *et. al.*, 1999)? Most importantly, this raises questions over why particular histories are told, forgotten, remembered; in whose interests are particular versions of the past that emphasize a "preferred" sense of national identity, told (Grossberg, 1996)? Disney's *Miracle* then, is not a literal construction, a retrieval, of the Cold War context (indeed, much of the context was de-emphasized); rather, the construction points to a powerful, despite self-proclaimed *Disney* innocence, as opposed to arbitrary, exploitation and colonization of the past in the interests of the present (Hutton, 1988; Schwartz, 1989). Thus, Disney's national mythologizing, is a far from innocent narrative that "simplifies, dramatizes and selectively narrates the story of a nation's past and its place in the world, its historical eschatology: a story that elucidates its contemporary meaning through (re)constructing its past" (Bell, 2003. p.75). Indeed, *Miracle*, is part of a wider moment in which the Bush administration and its media apologists have repeatedly compared the foreign and domestic measures that are being carried out under the mantle of a "war against terrorism" to the Cold War against the Soviet Union. Located in a revival of the Cold War methods of military coup, assassination and mass slaughter that were utilized by American imperialism, particularly in the former colonial and oppressed countries, throughout the latter half of the twentieth century, a return to McCarthyism, and the utilization of the FBI as a political policing apparatus to suppress those who oppose the foreign and domestic policy of the ruling elite, the specters of the Cold War are revised in the efforts to pursue US economic and geopolitical aims (Vann, 2001). In line with Giroux (1995; 2002) then Disney's miraculous mythology of the Cold War offers a sanitized, simpler, innocent Cold War politics, one in which, through (male) sacrifice to the "national good" a vacuous enemy can be defeated in a traditional war.

Disney's *Miracle* is thus fully inserted into a network of power relations (allegedly free from the dynamics of ideology, politics, and power) that shapes the public sphere (Giroux, 2002) in the recent shifts in the conditions and nature of war and political violence (Hardt and Negri, 2004). If traditionally war has been conceived as the armed conflict between sovereign political entities; in the imperialist project of the United States (see Harvey, 2003), it is becoming a general phenomenon, global and interminable. In this way, rather than war being the state of exception (that is, in normal circumstances, society is free from war), Hardt and Negri (2004) propose that the state of exception has become permanent and general, the exception has become the rule, pervading both foreign relations and the homeland. As indicated in this chapter, and drawing upon the specters of the Cold War, the US, and indeed, British governments, have made concerted efforts to continue to define an "other" against a moral, ethical, sovereign "us." This "other," no longer bounded by indeterminate spatial and indeed temporal boundaries, however, can no longer be conceived as being "outside"; the "other" and the "dangerous classes" inside are thus "increasingly indistinguishable from one another and serve together as the object of the war effort" (Hardt and Negri, 2004 p. 14). Mobilized within this context, the release of films like *Miracle* provide solace in the easy defeat of a spatially bounded enemy – the defeat of a "traditional" enemy in a new kind of war – no matter how false such an assertion may be. Rolled out as part of Karl Rove's Hollywood propagandist juggernaut, *Miracle*, provides us with an innocent past, a past that focuses on white, middle-class college boys, who through hard work, the subsumption of individual interests and diverse loyalties and identities, perseverance, and, a little sweat, can overcome any enemy, no matter who, no matter how powerful or mighty. *Miracle* presents us with a commercially packaged, sanitized and filtered history, a national mythology – a *popcorn patriotism* if you like – that, like other Disney productions before it, offers a politics of innocence that erases complex issues, cultural differences, and social struggles in the shaping of public memory (Giroux, 1995). Indeed, we should not forget, in 2004, Disney refused to release Michael Moore's *Farenheit 9/11* due to its political content. *Miracle*, bound within the political-economy of film production, thus reworks the sporting past within the appropriation, and mobilization of US corporo-political-militaristic need, offering an insidious space for Cold War revisionism in the name of President Bush's present geo-political realities. As Giroux (2002) indicates, such representations must both be challenged and engaged; not only does such public pedagogy proffer support for a neo-conservative "proto"-fascism in the US (Harvey, 2003; Giroux, 2005), as this example reveals, it also points to a disturbing deployment of the vaults of history in the present, permanent, war on terror.

References

Ahmed, M. (2002). "Homeland Insecurities: Racial Violence the Day After September 11." *Social Text, 72*, 20, 3, pp. 101–115.

Aloff, M. (2004). "Letter from New York." *Dance View Times.* 2, 9. Available at: http://www.danceviewtimes.com/dvny/aloff/winter04/030104.htm (accessed 12/4/05)

Andrews, D.L. (1995). "Excavating Michael Jordan: Notes on a Critical Pedagogy of Sporting Representation." In G. Rail and J. Harvey (Eds.) *Sport and postmodern times: Culture, gender, sexuality, the body and sport.* Albany, NY: State University of New York Press.

Andrews, D.L. (1998). "Feminizing Olympic reality: Preliminary dispatches from Baudrillard's Atlanta." *International Review for the Sociology of Sport*, 33(1), pp. 5–18.

Baker, A. (2003). *Contesting Identities: Sports in American Film.* Champaign/Urbana: University of Illinois Press.

Bairner, A. (2001). *Sport, Nationalism and Globalization: European and North American Perspectives.* Albany: State University of New York Press.

Baudrillard, J. (2001). "The Spirit of Terrorism." *Le Monde* (2 November 2001). Available at: http://www.egs.edu/faculty/baudrillard/baudrillard-the-spirit-of-terrorism.html (accessed 1/18/04).

Bell, D.S. (2003). "Mythscapes: Memory, Mythology, and National Identity." *British Journal of Sociology*, 54, 1, pp. 63–81.

Billlig, M. (1995). *Banal Nationalism.* London: Sage.

Bowman, J. (2004). "Post-Cold War Propaganda." *The American Spectator* (31 March 2004). Available at: http://www.jamesbowman.net (accessed 3/23/05)

Bromley, R. (1988). *Lost Narratives: Popular Fictions, Politics and Recent History.* London: Routledge.

Brookey, R. and Westerfelhaus, R. (2002). "Hiding Homoeroticism in Plain View." *Critical Studies in Media Communication*, 19, 1, pp. 21–43.

Brow, J. (1990). "Tendentious Revisions of the Past in the Construction of Community." *Anthropology Quarterly*, 64, 1, pp. 7–17.

Brown, M. and Szeman, I. (2002). "The Global Coliseum: On Empire." *Cultural Studies*, 16, 2, pp. 177–192.

Bryman, A. (1995). *Disney and His Worlds.* London: Routledge.

Butryn, T. (2003). "Posthuman Podiums: Cyborg Narratives of Elite Track and Field Athletes." *Sociology of Sport Journal*, 20, pp. 17–39.

Butryn. T. and Masucci, M. (2003). "Its Not About the Book: A Cyborg Counternarrative of Lance Armstrong." *Journal of Sport and Social Issues*, Volume 27, No. 2, pp. 124–144.

Carmichael, V. (1993). Framing History: The Rosenberg Story and the Cold War. Minneapolis: University of Minnesota Press.

Carter, J. (1980). State of the Union Address (23 January 1980). Available at: http://www.jimmycarterlibrary.org/documents/speeches/su80jec.phtml (accessed 12/5/05).

Carrington, B. (1998). "Audio Visual Review: When We Were Kings." *International Review for the Sociology of Sport*. 33, 1, pp. 75–77.

Castells. M. (2000). *The Rise of the Network Society* (2nd Edition). Oxford: Blackwell Publishers.

Clarke, J. (1991). *New Times and Old Enemies: Essays on Cultural Studies in America*. London: Harper Collins.

Clinton, P. (2004). "Olympic hockey film "Miracle" a winner." Available at: http://www.cnn.com/2004/SHOWBIZ/Movies/02/05/review.miracle/ (accessed, 12/4/05).

Cole, C.L. and Andrews, D.L. (2002). "The Nation Reconsidered." *Journal of Sport and Social Issues*, 26, 2, pp. 123–124.

Cole, C.L. and Cates, C. (2003). "The People's Horse." *Journal of Sport and Social Issues*, 27, 4, pp. 327–329

Cocco, G. and Lazzarato, M. (2002). "Ruptures within Empire, the Power of Exodus: Interview with Toni Negri." *Theory, Culture and Society*, 19, 4, pp. 187–194.

Dallmayr, F. (2002). "Lessons of September 11." *Theory, Culture and Society*, 19, 4, pp. 137–145.

De Cillia, R., Reisgel, M., and Wodak, R. (1999). "The Discursive Construction of National Identities." *Discourse and Society*, 10, 2, pp. 19–173.

Dyreson, M. (1999). "Nature by Design: Modern American Ideas about Sport, Energy, Evolution, and Republics, 1865–1920." *Journal of Sport History*, 26, 3, pp. 447–469

Ebert, R. (2004). *Miracle*. Available at: http://rogerebert.suntimes.com/apps/pbcs.dll/article?AID=/20040206/REVIEWS/402060304/1023 (accessed 2/6/04).

Farred, G. (2003). *What's My Name? Black Vernacular Intellectuals*. Minneapolis: University of Minnesota Press.

Fukuyama, F. (1993). *The End of History and the Last Man*. Perennial/HarperCollins Publishers: New York.

Giardina, M. (2005). *Sporting Pedagogies: Performing Culture and Identity in the Global Age*. New York: Peter Lang.

Giroux, H. (1994). *Disturbing Pleasures: Learning Popular Culture*. New York: Routledge.

Giroux, H. (1995a). "Animating Youth: The Disnification of Children's Culture," *Socialist Review*, 24, 3, pp. 23–55.

Giroux, H. (1999). *The Mouse that Roared: Disney and the End of Innocence*, Lanham, MD: Rowman & Littlefield.

Giroux, H. (2001). "Cultural Studies as Performative Politics." *Cultural Studies <=> Critical Methodologies*, 1, 1, pp. 5–23.

Giroux, H. (2002). *Breaking into the Movies: Film and the Culture of Politics*. Oxford: Blackwell.

Giroux, H. (2002). *Terrorism* and the Fate of Democracy After September 11th. *Cultural Studies <=> Critical Methodologies*, 2, 1, pp. 9–14.

Giroux, H. (2003) *The abandoned generation: Democracy beyond the culture of fear*. New York: Palgrave Macmillan.

Giroux, H. (2004). "War Talk, the Death of the Social, and the Disappearing Children: Remembering the Other War." *Cultural Studies <=> Critical Methodologies*, 4, 2, pp. 206–211.

Giroux, H. (2005). *The Terror of Neoliberalism*. New York: Palgrave.

Grossberg, L. (1992). *We gotta get out of this place: Popular Conservatism and Postmodern Culture*. London: Routledge.

Grossberg, L. (1996). "History, politics and postmodernism: Stuart Hall and cultural studies." In S. Hall, D. Morley and Chen, K. (eds). *Stuart Hall: Critical Dialogues in Cultural Studies* (151–173). London: Routledge.

Grossberg, L. (1997). *Bringing it all Back Home: Essays on Cultural Studies*. Durham, NC: Duke University Press.

Gruneau, R. (1989). *Making spectacle: A case study in television sports production*. In L. A. Wenner (Eds.), *Media, Sports, and Society*. Newbury Park, CA: Sage, pp. 134–156.

Halbwachs, M. (1950). *The Collective Memory*, trans. Francis J. Ditter, Jr. and Vida Yazdi Ditter. New York: Harper Collins.

Hall, S. (1997). "The Spectacle of the Other." In Hall, S. (Ed). *Representation: Cultural Representations and Signifying Practices*. London: Sage, pp. 223–279.

Haraway, D. (1997). *Modest Witness@second millennium.femaleman meets oncomouse*. New York: Routledge.

Hardt, M. and Negri, A. (2000). *Empire*. Cambridge: MA: Harvard University Press.

Harvey, D. (2003). *The New Imperialism*. Oxford: Oxford University Press.

Hedetoft, U. (1999). "The Nation-State Meets the World: National Identities in the Context of Transnationality and Cultural Globalization." *European Journal of Social Theory*, 2, 1, pp. 71–94.

Hiassen, C. (1998). *Team Rodent: How Disney Devours the World*. New York: Ballantyne Books.

Hogan, J. (2003). "Staging the Nation: Gendered and Ethnicized Discourses of National Identity in Olympic Opening Ceremonies." *Journal of Sport and Social Issues*, 27, 2, pp. 100–123.

Holleran, S. (2004). "Miracle on Ice Offered an Escape From 1979." Available at: http://www.capmag.com/article.asp?ID=3533 (accessed 12/05/05).

Hutton, P. (1988). "Collective Memory and Collective Mentalitites: Halbwachs-Ariès Connection," *Historical Reflections*, 15, pp. 311-322.

Johnson, R. (2002). "Defending Ways of Life: The (Anti-)Terrorist Rhetorics of Bush and Blair." *Theory, Culture and Society*, 19, 4, pp. 211–231.

Kay, J. (2002). "Hollywood's Ideological War." Available at: http://www.wsws.org/articles/2002/mar2002/war-m23.shtml. (accessed 11/12/2005).

Kellner, D. (2002a). "Theorizing Globalization." *Sociological Theory*, 20, 3, pp. 285–305.

Kellner, D. (2002b). "September 11, Social Theory and Democratic Politics." *Theory, Culture and Society*, 19, 4, pp. 147–159.

King, S. (2004). *War Games: The Culture of Sport and Militarization of Everyday Life*. Spotlight paper presented at the 5th Biannual International Crossroads in Cultural Studies Conference. Urbana, IL: University of Illinois, Urbana-Champaign.

Kinkema K. and Harris, J. (1998). "MediaSport Studies: Key Research and Emerging Issues." In Wenner (ed.) *MediaSport*. Routledge: New York, pp. 27–56.

Klindo, M. and Phillips, R. (2004). "Military Interference in American Film production." Available at: http://www.wsws.org/articles/2005/mar2005/holl-m14.shtml (accessed 11/12/2005).

Kusz, K. W. (2001). "'I want to be the minority': The politics of youthful white masculinities in sport and popular culture in 1990s America." *Journal of Sport and Social Issues*, 25(4), pp. 390–416.

Kuznetsov, V. and Lukashev, M. (1977). *USSR–USA Sports Encounters*. Moscow: Progress Publications.

McDonald, M. (2005). "Imagining Benevolence, Masculinity and Nation: Tragedy, Sport and the Transnational Marketplace." In Silk, M., Andrews, D.L. and Cole, C. (eds) (2005). *Sport and Corporate Nationalisms*. Oxford: Berg, pp. 127–142.

McDonald, M. and Birrell, S. (1999). "Reading Sport Critically: A Method for Interrogating Power." *Sociology of Sport Journal*, 16, pp. 283–300.

McClaren, P. (2002). "George Bush, Apocalypse Sometime Soon, and the American Imperium." *Cultural Studies <=> Critical Methodologies*, 3, 2, pp. 327–333.

McLaren, P. and Martin, M. (2004). "The Legend of the Bush Gang: Imperialism, War and Propaganda." *Cultural Studies <=> Critical Methodologies*, 4, 2, pp. 281–303.

Merskin, D. (2004). "The Construction of Arabs as Enemies: Post September 11 Discourse of George W. Bush." *Mass Communication and Society*, 7, 2, pp. 157–175.

Miller, T., Lawrence, G., McKay, J. and Rowe, D. (2001). *Globalization and Sport: Playing the World*. London: Sage.

Morris, R. (2002). "Theses on the Questions of War: History, Media, Terror." *Social Text*, 72, 20, 3, pp. 150–175.

Munfa, M. (2003). "Yo America, let's beat those commies: Pro-American propaganda in Rocky IV. Living in the Digital World," 2(2). Available at:http://www.duke.edu/~mepetit/DigitalWorld/spring2003/munfapaper.html (accessed 12/4/05)

O'Keefe, D. (2004). "Evil empire(s) on ice." Available at: http://www.sevenoaksmag.com/culture/01_evil_empires.html (accessed, 12/4/05)

O'Keefe, D. (2005). Review: "*Jarhead* misses target, badly." Available at: http://www.sevenoaksmag.com/commentary/86_comm6.html (accessed 12/4/05).

Paquin, A. (2004). Review: "Miracle." Available at: http://efilmcritic.com/review.php?movie=8662&reviewer=287 (accessed 12/4/05).

Riggs, K., Eastman, S. and Golobi, T. (1993). "Manufactured Conflict in the 1992 Olympics: The Discourse of Television and Politics." *Critical Studies in Mass Communication*, 19, pp. 253–272.

Robb, D. (2004). *Operation Hollywood: How the Pentagon shapes and censors the movies*. Amherst, NY: Prometheus.

Roche, M. (2000). *Mega-Events and Modernity: Olympics and Expos in the Growth of Global Culture*. London and New York: Routledge.

Rosenstone , R. (1995). *Visions of the Past*. Cambridge, Mass.: Harvard University Press.

Rowe, D., McKay, J., and Miller, T. (1998). "Come Together: Sport, Nationalism and the Media Image." In L. Wenner (ed.), *MediaSport* London and New York: Routledge, pp. 119–33.

Saeed, A. (2003). "Whats in a Name? Muhammad Ali and the Politics of Cultural Identity." In A. Bernstein and N. Blain (eds) *Sport, Media and Society: Global and Local Dimensions*, London: Frank Cass.

Said, E. (1997). *Covering Islam: How the Media and the Experts Determine how we see the rest of the World*. New York: Vintage.

Schwartz, B. (1982). "The Social Context of Commemoration: A Study of Collective Memory," *Social Forces* 61, pp. 396–402.

Silk, M. and Andrews, D.L. (2001). "Beyond a Boundary: Sport, Transnational Advertising, and the Reiminaging of National Culture," *Journal of Sport and Social Issues*, 25, 2, pp. 180–202.

Silk, M., Andrews, D.L. and Cole, C. (eds) (2005). *Sport and Corporate Nationalisms*. Oxford: Berg.

Silk, M. and Falcous, M. (2005). "One Day in September / One Week in February: Mobilizing American (Sporting) Nationalisms." *Sociology of Sport Journal*, 22, 4, pp. 447–441.

Sivanandan, A. (2006). "Race, Terror and Civil Society." *Race and Class*, 47, 3, pp. 1–8.

Soar, M. (2000). "Encoding advertisements: Ideology and meaning in advertising production." *Mass Communications and Society*, 3(4), pp. 415–437.

Vann. M. (2001). "US propagandists invoke the Cold War." Available at: http://www.wsws.org/articles/2001/oct2001/cold-o30.shtml (accessed 12/4/05).

Walsh, D. (2001). "Hollywood enlists in Bush's war drive." Available at: http://www.wsws.org/articles/2001/nov2001/holl-n19.shtml (accessed 12/4/05).

Wang, B. (2002). "The Cold War, Imperial Aesthetics, an Area Studies." *Social Text*, 72, 20, 3, pp. 46–65.

Notes

1   For a more detailed discussion of the role of sport in the response to the events of 11 September, 2001, see Giardina, 2005; King, 2004; McDonald, 2005; Silk and Falcous, 2005)

2   While this is a significant date, as Ladson-Billings (2003) proposes, it takes history to determine whether it will become a teleological fault line. For Ladson-Billings (2003), there are an infinite number of chronological combinations – pre-4 April 1968 (assassination of Martin Luther King) and post-4 April 1968; pre-summer of 1963 and post-summer of 1963 (bombing of the little girls in the Birmingham, Alabama church); pre-summer of 1955 and post-summer of 1955 (murder of Emmett Till). Following Ladson-Billings, we feel it important to problematize the appropriation of this day in September as simply "9/11" – absent of any year denotation.

3   What else would we expect from the interplay – what Gruneau (1989) terms the elective affinity – between media, sponsors and broadcasters, yet one that is particularly pronounced between the NBC and Olympic "partners" (see Andrews, 1998).

4   At the time of writing, we "eagerly" await the cinematic release of *Jarhead*, a film that apparently offers a stripped down and sanitized account of the present war in/on Iraq. The film, released as George W. Bush's approval ratings reached all-time lows, is "jarringly off point to anyone thinking about the implications of a war fought for oil and Empire" and "relegates to a few irrelevant lines the serious critique of US motivations in the Middle East" (O'Keefe, 2005) that are addressed in Anthony Swofford's book of the same title. Again, while only conjecture, *Jarhead* appears as another example of a powerful public pedagogy rolled out as a supposedly depoliticized popular cultural form.

5   In addition to the work by Giroux, Alan Bryman's Disney and his Worlds (1995) and Carl Hiassen's Team Rodent (1998) are notable exceptions and, in their different ways, provide accounts of the cultural significance of the Disney corporation.

6   In 1995, The Walt Disney Company bought Capital Cities/ABC acquiring the large ABC News franchise for $19 billion, expanding its holdings to include the ABC Publishing Group, ESPN Magazine, ten owned and operated television stations, thirty radio stations, eleven cable channels, interests in television and film production and distribution, internet sites, and various music and theatre investments. Disney is one of the top five companies that owns the majority of American media and has influence at the global scale as well. Announced 5 August 1995, this buyout move catapulted this already dominant global content producer to a fully integrated media giant. Source: http://www.idleaudience.com/conglomerationnation/conglomerates/disney/index.html (accessed 6/12/05).

7   Perhaps not surprisingly, this Disneyized version of USA patriotism does not offer any notion of class struggle or class difference in 1980s USA. Indeed, difference is only ever presented among the team through college hockey rivalries easily overcome through cohering to the greater cause (USA). While perhaps an analytical stretch, this speaks to the emergent 1980s Reaganism in which class struggle was displaced from the political agenda, difference individualized, and overcome through individual effort.

8   *Rocky IV* was not the only sports film to use the East–West conflict as a central narrative line at this time. For example, *American Flyers* (1985) (starring Kevin Costner) centred around cycle road racing and featured plucky American riders facing nameless, machine-like automatons representing the USSR.

9   This is somewhat ironic, given that Brooks' tactical focus for Olympic victory has been read by some as being similar to an ideology of totalitarian socialism. For example, Aloff (2004) suggests Brooks was not interested in the virtuosity of individual players, rather he encouraged a collectivity that could join their hearts and minds, at least for a period of time, to work for a goal larger than personal ambition.

Chapter 17

Beyond the stadium, and into the street

Sport and anti-Americanism in South Korea

Eunha Koh, David L. Andrews and Ryan White

South Korea has had longstanding ties with the USA, Japan, North Korea, the former USSR and China that spanned the colonial, Cold War and post-Cold War eras. These interconnections have helped make clear the fluid and fractured nature of political and cultural relationships between and within nation states. South Korea's role as an allied nation, as a post-colonial country, and presently as half of the now divided Korean peninsula has helped produce the contemporary social and geographical landscape of the country and indeed that of north-east Asia more generally. As the chapters in this book have shown, socio-political relationships between countries are often manifest within and magnified through sport. Using this notion as a critical lens, we focus on how recent anti-American sentiment that has broken the conventional US–South Korea geo-political alliance is related to international sporting events. In particular, this chapter deals with recent anti-American thoughts, feelings, and actions in (South) Korea, centering on two international events held in 2002 – the Winter Olympics and World Cup soccer finals. Through the following discussion we aim to explicate how anti-Americanism arose, developed, and changed through a series of national/international events in post-Cold War Korea.

Anti-American sentiment and anti-Americanism in South Korea

Anti-Americanism, admittedly a problematic term in the first instance in that its meaning "floats" (Hall, 1990) depending on the context in which it is evoked, usually refers to adversarial feelings, opinions, or activities that oppose American policies, cultures, values, and/or ideologies (Lee, K.R., 2004). As anti-Americanism is the refusal of American values, cultures, customs and policies, it is difficult to dislodge once it is established. Though related, anti-American sentiment, in the strict sense, is "criticism of certain American policies," whereas anti-Americanism is the "refusal of America as a whole" (Shim, 2005). Anti-American sentiment is not necessarily hostile to America, and could be weakened or even disappear if US–Korea relations improve, or (potentially) disruptive issues become resolved. In regard to the Korean–American alliance then, anti-American sentiment requires improvement of institutions and procedures between Korea and the US, while anti-Americanism refuses the legitimacy of the relationship in the first instance (Shim, 2005). While we recognize the nuanced difference between the two terms and how they relate to the Korean–American alliance, as a point clarification for this project, we use the terms anti-Americanism and anti-American sentiment interchangeably. Further, though their meanings often overlap (Lee, K.R., 2004, Lim, H.S., 1994) anti-Americanism more closely defines our theoretical direction (Lee, J.B., 2004; Rubinstein, 1985).

To explain the origins of anti-Americanism worldwide, Shim (2005, pp. 21–25) has identified three separate theories. First, *power balance theory* states that America became the world's leader and broke the previous balance of power after the Cold War, thus revealing its unilateralism. Second, *anti-globalization theory* argues that anti-Americanism appeared as the resistance to neo-liberal globalization led by the US. Third, *identity conflict theory* claims that the manifestation of fear that power and influence of America might invade conventional culture and tradition caused anti-Americanism. We believe that in the South Korean case, *power balance theory* most accurately describes the rise in anti-Americanism.

Using *power balance theory*, there are two different methods for analyzing the cause(s) of anti-Americanism in Korea (Shim, pp. 26–31). The first perspective understands anti-Americanism in Korea as a natural consequence of economic development and democratization. The second sees it as a highly ideological phenomenon led by pro-communists who follow the North Korean line. In this instance, we are more compelled to align ourselves with the first explanation *power balance theory* offers for the rise of anti-Americanism in South Korea. Initially, we are drawn to this notion by *the fact* that, as the Cold War concluded and reconciliation and cooperation was discussed between South and North Korea, Korean people started to distance themselves from anti-communist ideologies. This is compounded by the fact that Korea was experiencing a shift in dominant governmental and generational direction – one that moved away from celebrating Korea–US relations and toward anti-Americanism. This shift can be described through three main points.

First, since Dae-Jung Kim took office as president of South Korea (in 1998), the government has worked on improving their relationship with North Korea, while leaving its connection with the US unattended. Second, younger generations of South Koreans who cared little for their alliance with the United States during the Korean War are becoming the dominant center of Korean society. Third, Korean citizens are experiencing an upsurge of pride due, in large part, to economic development, a more powerful democracy, and escalating international recognition. Through these forms of national pride, Korean citizens believe that America's attitude toward their country should change since Korea's national power has been enhanced through democracy, and not necessarily, overt exclusionary nationalism. However, this is unlikely to occur during a cultural moment in America where its introversion and self-affirming "greatness" becomes manifest in its maintenance of various forms of control and influence over Korea.

As a result of American pretentiousness, throughout the general public and intellectual community in Korea, anti-Americanism has reached new heights. Moreover, the mass media and internet have become viable pipelines for Anti-US voices, while books criticizing America are so pervasive that their existence is no longer considered a new political issue (Chung, 2005; Lee, K.R., 2004; Shim, 2005). The recent onset of what has been described as "alliance fatigue" or "alliance drift" (Shim, 2005, p.11) has been marked by a breakdown of the "blood alliance" between Korea and the United States.

This breakdown has taken some time to manifest itself in South Korea, and the term "anti-Americanism" has only recently become popular in common Korean vernacular. As mentioned above, through the Korean War and its aftermath, South Korea and the US formed a blood alliance. America was Korea's greatest support system for economic and cultural development, as well as a powerful force in Korean politics. Given this apparently mutually beneficial relationship, historically, it has been difficult to express anti-Americanism in Korea. However, through a series of social uprisings and, important to this chapter, sporting events, this relationship, marked by fifty years of seemingly benign international connectivity, now finds itself at a divisive impasse.

Politically, and ideologically perhaps, the first overt expression of anti-Americanism started in 1980 with Gwangju resistance. After this incident, college students and public intellectuals began taking up the "anti-American" causes in Korea (Lee, K.R., 2004). Further, as the Cold War came to a close, a few specific incidents provided an opportunity to express dissatisfaction with, and criticism of, the US. Given the generational and governmental shifts in Korea, these anti-American sentiments began to define public opinion, based in large part on the shifting of the contemporary socio-political terrain.

With the background mentioned above, such as weakened anti-communism and the Korean-American alliance, the enhanced pride of Korean people due to improvements in the Korean economy, democracy and international recognition, there were a few incidents that stirred Korean nationalistic fervor and ignited anti-American sentiment. In sport, long regarded as a site to celebrate and confirm a "love of nation" (Appadurai, 2000, p. 130), two key moments where Korean nationalism slipped into exclusionary anti-Americanism were the 2002 Salt Lake City Olympics and the 2002 FIFA Soccer World Cup. To best contextualize the Korea/US (sporting) relationship within the contemporary conjecture (Grossberg, 2006), we will situate it by discussing the relationship between America, Korea and some neighboring Asian countries through the colonial and Cold War eras.

The invader and the ally: the post-colonial context

Since the early twentieth century, Japan and America have been defined by South Koreans as the invader and the ally respectively. In 1910, Japan began a thirty six-year relationship as colonizer of South Korea. Though the period of occupation was similar to that by Western countries in Asia, antagonism of Korean people against Japan is much stronger than any other post-colonial countries toward their former colonizers. For example, countries formerly under British rule use English as their official language and have established similar laws, public administrations, and educational systems. Interestingly these countries also use pictures of the Queen of England on local currencies and a form of the UK national flag on their own national flag. In the sporting context, Silk (2002) has outlined how the Commonwealth Games are an example of how the UK and its former colonies create an image of uninhibited cooperation.

On the contrary, in Korea, there exists no pretense of friendship between themselves and their former rulers, as Koreans hold very antagonistic attitudes and feelings toward Japan. For example, they have tried to remove any remnants of Japanese colonization in the government and school systems. Culturally, Korea refused to adopt Japanese as their primary language, through the voluntary efforts of Koreans following their liberation from Japan in 1945. Moreover, the Korean government banned all Japanese popular culture from their country until 1998 when it was allowed in limited forms. In 2004, the Korean government began to allow Japanese movies, music and games to infiltrate consumption centers. Further, though cable television was given some flexibility (though no "entertainment" programs are allowed), programs on public media are limited to sports, documentaries, and news reports, while jointly produced dramas and domestically premiered movies were also permitted.

Importantly, anti-Japanese sentiment is also clearly shown in and through sports. During any event between Japan and Korea, television ratings skyrocket, hyper-nationalist cheers are heard from the stands, and, such is the intensity of these occasions, some spectators even suffer from heart attacks. This type of nationalist fervor proved beneficial to Korean national teams who, bolstered by the hatred of Japan, often won these matches. It was commonly supposed during the Cold War era that sports acted as a substitute for war between countries. Now, with the Cold War over, post-colonial sporting events between Japan and Korea certainly lent credence to this argument. Even during Japanese rule, sport was used to inspire anti-Japanese feelings, as clandestine forms of resistance were acted out although superficial Korean obedience to their inhibitors. In fact, at this time sport was the only method by which a Korean could dominate Japan and express patriotism (Koh and Lee, 2004). Thus through these sporting events, symbolic battles for the restoration of national rights were fought between Korean and Japanese athletes (Koh, 2003).

Unlike Japan, America has long been a (South) Korean ally. The United States dispatched and lost troops during the Korean War and when the Korean peninsula was divided between South and North, the US chose to support South Korea to combat USSR's support of North Korea. For more than fifty years after an armistice between the two countries was declared in 1953, America kept its own troops in Korea in an effort to prevent further uprisings. Moreover, throughout the Cold War era, America remained a faithful ally by providing military and economic support to help South Korea recover in the aftermath of the war. Through this relationship, the United States was able to exact a large amount of influence over South Korea, and provided a socio-political model of government and governmentality (Grossberg, 2006, p. x) which Korea was, in some ways, forced to follow.

A direct result of this occupation could be seen through the influx of American culture into Korea. American popular culture such as rock-and-roll, movies, and television dramas became important components in the lifestyle of the young generation, while written English became more popular on billboards and merchandise logos. Furthermore, America-friendly attitudes were also expressed in and through sporting events. Korea aligned itself with American political ideologies by boycotting the 1980 Moscow Olympics, while Korean professional sports were established using Major League Baseball (MLB), National Basketball Association (NBA), and the Professional Golfers' Association (PGA) as models. Though broadcasting of American professional sports games on TV or cable started only recently, American players have enjoyed popularity in Korea for decades. In fact, Koreans regarded America not only as a political ally but also as a sporting ally.

The brother and the neighbor: two Koreas and the US during and after the Cold War

While the United States and USSR were the ideological driving forces of the Cold War era, South Korea and North Korea were actually located at the war's front line. For South Korea, their ally and enemy were strictly demarcated: America as the friend and North Korea the foe. Antagonism toward North Korea was due in large part to the fear of war, since South Korea was inferior to North Korea economically and militarily well into early 1970s. Since South Korea did not have enough resources to defend itself against North Korea and its economy was not healthy enough to prepare for possible war the economic and military occupation of South Korea by the United States was welcomed. Simultaneously, South Korea provided an important strategic military region where the United States could confront the USSR via North Korea. Given the considerable influence the US had over South Korea, America was able to cultivate a culture of fear of the communist menace, which served to quell criticism of the South Korean government. Until President Dae-Jung Kim was inaugurated in 1998, the conservative right-wing party took control of the government. During this time the conservative party firmly maintained a pro-American policy, while schools were forced to teach anti-communist curricula.

However, from the 1980s, the South Korean economy began to show significant growth, while North Korean economic strategies failed causing most of the country's citizens to suffer economic hardship. Through the socio-political weakening of North Korea, the fear of war lessened significantly and South Koreans sympathized with their North Korean brothers suffering under dictatorship. In the late 1990s, after the "Sunshine policy" of Dae-Jung Kim's government as well as a summit conference between the South and North, many Koreans refused to believe that North Korea was a threat.

As the United States has fallen out of favor with popular political opinion in South Korea, support for North Korea has risen inversely. During the 1980s, this anti-American sentiment came from a small group of leftists and college campuses. They claimed that Americans used South Korea as pawn for their own military benefits. Further, these groups charged that the responsibility for Korean North/South division lay not only with the former USSR but also the United States. In other words, the popular notion that the United States was the savior of South Korea came under fire and began to be replaced by the idea that America was to blame for Korean strife. At that time, however, the South Korean government used military force to quell demonstrations and maintained a pro-America policy. Moreover, while most Koreans had diverse perspectives towards North Korea and America, most still agreed that America was an important ally that needed to be appeased.

Since that time, South Korea's economy has exploded to the point that it is ranked as the eleventh strongest in the world. Now tiring from being on what they considered the wrong end of a unilateral relationship with the United States, South Korea demanded to be treated as an economic equal. However, now that North Korea poses little threat either to South Korea or the United States, the façade of a mutually beneficent relationship has been revealed, and neither country perceives their alliance as desirable (Hwang, B. Y., 2002; Shim, 2005, p. 14).

Consequently, through the change, or the demand for change, in the Korea-America alliance, relationships between six countries in north-east Asia and the Pacific (South Korea, North Korea, the USA, Japan, China, and Russia) have become more complicated. The downfall of the former USSR following the Cold War created a reduced need for American military support in South Korea. At the same time, North Korea lost its main supporter and was forced to become one of the few countries that were closed to the world, China accelerated its "Open Door policy," and South Korea actively pursued a policy of support for and cooperation with North Korea. The implementation and execution of the "Sunshine Policy" in 1998, was a key component of the change in Asian social, economic, and political policies. Though America remained South Korea's strongest ally, a redefinition in their relationship was demanded by younger generations of South Koreans.

Anti-Americanism in a new generation: Salt Lake Olympics and cultural anti-Americanism

The 2002 Salt Lake City Winter Olympic Games provided special meaning to Americans who had experienced the terror of 9/11 just a few months previously. According to Silk and Falcous (2005), the Bush administration tried to use this event as an opportunity to demonstrate that the United States was still a dominant force in contemporary society. However, the strategy backfired as, internationally, the Games were criticized for overt American nationalism. Pennington (2002) reported that the Salt Lake City Olympics actually evoked anti-American fervor and revived Cold War era antagonisms. Initially, for Koreans, the 2002 Olympic Games did not draw much attention since South Korea was busy hosting the 2002 FIFA World Cup. Additionally, in Korea the Winter Olympics have historically not been as popular as the Summer Olympics (Vander Velden, Ryu and Koh, 2002) since Korea has been in around tenth place in the Summer Olympics for the last two decades – ranking tenth in the LA Olympics, fourth in Seoul Olympics, seventh in the Barcelona Olympics, eighth in the Atlanta Olympics, and twelfth in the Sydney Olympics – and the only medals that could be expected in the Winter Olympics were through short-track speed skating.

Given their fellow countrymen and women's position as relative favorites at the 2002 Winter Olympics, Koreans viewed the event in droves. Their allegiance was rewarded when the women came through for South Korea by capturing two gold and two silver medals, but the men disappointed by failing to achieve medals. Korean disappointment was compounded by the disqualification of Dong-Sung Kim who was the apparent winner of the Men's 1500m final. Unfortunately, the judges of the race claimed that Kim blocked American short-track skater Apolo Anton Ohno on the last lap, and awarded Ohno the gold. In a survey conducted in the US right after the Salt Lake City Olympics, sixty-eight percent of experts on Korean issues answered that they were concerned about the potential rise of anti-Americanism in South Korea. The anti-American response to the 2002 Winter Olympics short-track controversy could have been made relatively meaningless had there not existed other prevalent issues that popularized these sentiments such as: the Bush Administration's "hard line" stance toward North Korea, US trade pressure and protectionist measures, the location of US military bases, and incidents involving the US military or individual US soldiers. Further raising the ire of Koreans were President Bush's claims that North Korea was part of the world's "Axis of Evil" (Falcous and Silk 2005; Silk and Falcous, 2005). In effect, through sporting controversy, South Korea was able to act out its feelings against the United States.

Though it might be thought too simplistic to pinpoint a single incident evoking anti-Americanism in Korea, nationalism as experienced through sport can evoke "full attachment" (Appadurai, 2000, p. 132), and provide a space for hatred of "others." Following Appadurai (2000), it is important to consider the power of sports in evoking patriotism, as he explains:

> Legitimation is in fact tied up with issues of consent, compliance and the procedural recognition of the modern state by its citizens. Full attachment (or patriotism or loyalty, in more common terms) involves something more than the imputation of legitimacy to a sovereign state by its citizen. Its surplus of affect (which is also justification for using the concept of 'full attachment' rather than the easily available ideas of patriotism, loyalty, or, simply, nationalism) is more libidinal than procedural.
>
> (p. 131)

As such, we argue that the short-track incident helped trigger anti-American sentiment to those who, for various reasons, had not concerned themselves with international politics. A Korean newspaper captured this sentiment with the statement that (Park, 2002a):

> Sports influence mostly the younger generations. Bush's 'Axis of Evil' triggered anti-Americanism among intellectuals and the older generations, but the Salt Lake City incident can be understood as extending anti-Americanism to the youth.

Interestingly it was the younger generation of Koreans who expressed the strongest anti-American sentiment. This generation of young adults had not experienced the Korean War, the poverty or the reconstruction that their elders had endured. Since their lives have always been experienced in relative material abundance this is a "new generation with no debt" (Lee, G.H., 2002), and has become a "generation with pride in their own culture" (Lee, K.R., 2004). Moreover, the anti-Americanism of this younger generation is markedly different from the political anti-Americanism of the past. In a very real sense, then, these individuals ironically enjoy the relative peace and prosperity represented by the United States, yet are highly anti-American. Complicating matters is the fact that they do not speak out against America in a political sense, or espouse pro-North Korean beliefs like anti-American activists in the 1980s. So on the one hand "they express Anti-Americanism so strongly that they make older generation worried, but still enjoy the sit-com 'Friends'" (Song, 2003).

As such, this new generation's anti-Americanism is necessarily different from "political anti-Americanism" experienced in the past. More specifically and following Hong (2003) there have been three stages of anti-Americanism in Korea: (a) political anti-Americanism that asserts anti-Americanism and anti-autocracy at the same time, (b) "right to live" anti-Americanism that tried to protect people from the unequal relationship between South Korea and America such as crimes by US army personnel, harm caused by US army training, environmental pollution, and pressure to open up national markets, and (c) cultural anti-Americanism started by the disqualification of Dong-Sung Kim in 2002 Olympics (Lee, K.R.,

2004; Shim, 2005). In other words, whereas the anti-Americanism movement flourished around college towns in the 1980s and centered on structural political issues, recent anti-Americanism provides space for subversion through the refusal to purchase "American" products. This systematic boycott of American products has been popularized through the internet and McDonalds, Burger King, KFC, Dunkin' Donuts, Starbucks coffee, Coca Cola, Hershey's, Polo, Nike, Levis and Guess all experienced profit shortfalls as a result of these boycotts. Furthermore, hatred of American patriotism in Hollywood movies minimized attendances at these films in South Korea. For instance, *Collateral Damage* and *Black Hawk Down* made $37.6 million and $146.7 million profits respectively in America, but only drew audiences of 200,000 and 300,000 in Korea. Donga Ilbo, a prominent Korean daily newspaper commented that, "the new generation's anti-Americanism is not refusing America but it seems to be refusing the arrogance of America" (Hur, Lee and Cho, 2002).

Despite the seemingly superficial level of anti-Americanism present within younger generations, it is also important to understand the importance of the internet as a tool to proliferate these ideologies. For Korean youth, the internet is not merely a method of collecting information, but a pipeline of multi-discursive communication. On the internet, younger Korean generations have been offered a place for individual expression (though often through commodities) where they can meet, talk, shop, enjoy various cultural products and discuss off-line incidents. Since the internet provides no time or space limits, their feelings have a space to be heard and can spread quickly. For example, when Dong-Sung Kim was disqualified, Korean dissatisfaction was felt through anti-American sentiments as stories of who "stole the gold medal" were disseminated almost instantaneously. Quickly following the event, over 100 pro-Korea/anti-America web sites were created (Hwang, H.T., 2002). On these sites were pictures, movies, and anti-American songs depicting Bush and Ohno in negative ways.

The swiftness and power of anti-American ideologies in Korea resulting from the race soon became an international incident. Following the event on 21 February, NBC conducted an online survey that 11,000 people voted on – ninety-six percent of whom answered that the disqualification was not fair. The negative reaction was so strong that NBC had to close down the survey site after having had it online for only an hour (Kang, 2002; Chang, 2002). Moreover, the IOC homepage was paralyzed with complaints about the disqualification, and they announced that 16,000 emails were received within twelve hours from Korea, which resulted in the breakdown of IOC's web server (Yunhap News, 2002).

Though anti-Americanism within Korea grew as a result of the 2002 Salt Lake City Olympics, other countries that were related to the speed-skating incident were absolved. For example, the umpire who disqualified Dong-Sung Kim was Australian, and given the anti-American response to the controversy, it would have made sense if Koreans had also expressed anti-Australian sentiments.

However, Korean dissatisfaction over the event was directed solely at America. Even Korean hatred for Japan was overlooked in their reaction to Apolo Ohno who figured prominently in the media following his gold medal victory. Ohno has a Japanese father and American mother, and though he identifies himself as American, through his last name and phenotypical appearance he could easily be mistaken for Japanese. Despite his outward Japanese appearance, and long-held antagonisms by Korea toward Japan, the Korean media solely identified him as American – evidenced by the numerous media stories that claimed the gold medal he won was "stolen by America." The hostility directed toward the US suggests a weakened hatred toward Japan and a new emphasis on anti-Americanism in Korea.

Widespread anti-America sentiment has become an important issue in the South Korea–America alliance. These feelings were largely influenced by the disqualification of Dong-Sung Kim in the Salt Lake City Olympics, and its effect on Korean society was felt in three separate ways: it spread anti-Americanism to younger generations of Koreans who were indifferent to American ideologies and politics; the use of technology, particularly the internet, demonstrated the relative power of Korean youth to shift dominant sentiment in their country; and it marked a shift in the characteristics of the anti-American movement away from "political anti-Americanism" and toward "cultural anti-Americanism."

It is a paradox that Bush's comment about the "Axis of Evil" reinvigorated the weakened "Sunshine policy [of peaceful coexistence between South and North Korea]." Further, as a result of the rise of anti-American sentiments, one Korean newspaper even argued that these feelings come at an economic cost to the United States. Anti-Americanism induced by Bush's announcement and the Salt Lake City incidents will affect the negotiation of F-15K (fighter plane) sales. While public opinion is anti-American, it would be hard for the government to purchase F-15K (Park, 2002a).

Red Devils and candles: World Cup, the US Army and the people's anti-American movement

Later in 2002, the World Cup Soccer Finals were jointly held in South Korea and Japan marking the first time the World Cup was hosted in Asia. The World Cup was the biggest sporting event held in Korea since the 1988 Seoul Olympics, and it captured the attention of their population accordingly. However, despite garnering similar amounts of public fervor, there was a key difference in the way the population experienced the 1988 Olympics and the 2002 World Cup. The 1988 Olympics were used as a form of economic and political development, whereas the World Cup was an opportunity for Korean people to celebrate the nation.

Important to our argument are the South Korean team's fervent supporters, nicknamed the Red Devils. The Red Devils, whose nickname originated with the 1983 Korean National Youth Football Team, experienced tremendous growth as a cultural and economic need arose for a systematic fan culture for the National Team. In 1997, the Red Devils, this name now attaching to supporters of the Korean National team, started as a small group of fans but grew to encompass nearly all of the Korean population during the 2002 World Cup. Stadiums and streets were filled with Koreans wearing red shirts that proclaimed "Be the Reds." Given that the color red had long represented "Palgangyi," or in other words, communists in Korea, the use of that color to identify collectively with Korea marked a sea change in popular ideology. This phenomenon of "post-ideology" led by the "World Cup learning effect" (Lee, G.H., 2002) further implied a weakening of anti-communist and anti-North Korean principles in the South.

Though support from the Red Devils for the Korean national team was strong, their most passionate and popular following could be found in Kwang-Hwa-Mun square. Kwang-Hwa-Mun is the south gate of Kyung-Bok-Gung, a palace of the Chosun dynasty located in Seoul, South Korea. One of the government buildings located nearby was the US embassy, and considering the anti-Americanism present in South Korea at the time, law enforcement was on high alert. For example, during the Korea versus Poland match eighteen police companies surrounded the American embassy to provide security against the 100,000 Red Devil fans.

During the Korea versus USA match, even more security was used to prevent any Red Devil uprisings. One daily magazine quoted Jung-Sik Shin, head of the Government Information Agency, as stating that:

> The Korea vs. America game is a very important game for the Korean team to proceed to the final 16. In order to prevent a disgraceful incident, our government is making protection plans. To prevent anti-Americanism oriented comments on the internet, the police dispatched 600 cyber cops. Government requested newspapers and other media not to publish any reports or articles stimulating anti-Americanism.
>
> (Park, T.G., 2002b)

During the match held on 10 June, in spite of torrential downpours, about one million people gathered together in the streets at eighty-one different places to cheer for Korea. About 300,000 gathered in Kwang-Hwa-Mun Square near the US embassy. The police dispatched 6,000 officers to the scene but there were no anti-Americanist demonstrations as the Red Devils maintained their peaceful reputation (Lee, J.G., Lee, T.H. and Lee, W.B., 2002).

This does not suggest that the people of Korea had moved on from what they considered past indiscretions committed against them by the United States. For example, one of the most famous incidents during the World Cup was the goal ceremony performed by a Korean player named Jung-Hwan Ahn. With the South Korean team trailing by a goal late in the second half, Ahn equalized with a brilliant effort. Following the play Ahn, parodying the disqualification of Dong-Sung Kim at Salt Lake City, pretended to speed-skate while his team-mate,

Chun-Soo Lee acted as Ohno beside him. The idea for the celebration was proposed anonymously on the internet, and the players agreed to take part in the performance. The response in Korea was resoundingly positive, and though it was a form of peaceful protest, the Korean reaction was an open expression of anti-Americanism broadcast throughout the world.

Anti-Americanism in Korea welled up again three days later when two middle-school girls were hit by a US armored car. On 13 June 2002, Mi-Sun Shim and Hyo-Soon Shin were hit by an AVLM and died on site. The United States immediately acted under the Status of Armed Forces Agreement (SOFA), a treaty between the Republic of Korea and the United States, and put their soldiers on trial. The courts not guilty verdict on 20 November, which resulted in sending the soldiers involved back to America, was met with Korean skepticism. Anti-Americanism rose, as Koreans felt that the incident demonstrated that the United States did not respect post-war Korea. The anger Koreans felt about the incident and the conduct of the US Army was displayed through a nationwide candle demonstration. On 30 November, the "Candle Memorial Ceremony" was held in Kwang-Hwa-Mun Square. Ten thousand people from various backgrounds as well as 130 non-governmental organizations participated. During the demonstration some called for the withdrawal of the US army, prompting President Bush to respond. On 13 December, Bush telephoned President Kim to express his condolences and agreed to order a detailed investigation into the incident, but this did not prevent the candle demonstrations from continuing every Saturday. In fact, a day later, on 14 December, 100,000 people gathered at Kwang-Hwa-mun Square and anti-American demonstrations spread to fifty-five cities nationwide and fifteen other countries.

Though the death of the schoolgirls seemed unintentional, the Korean reaction is important because there have been intentional criminal acts by the US Army on the people of Korea in the past. The people's anti-American movement (Lee, K.R., 2004) further suggests that due, in part, to economic development and generational shift, dominant Korean feelings toward the United States are becoming more negative. Chosun Ilbo, a leading daily newspaper argued that older Korean generations also did not accept the verdict and wanted to join anti-American groups (Cho, 2002). Further, according to the result of a survey conducted by Kang Ro Lee (2004), sixty-seven percent of Koreans answered that their perception of America had "became worse" during the last couple of years which is a marked shift from a 1981 study by Jin Woo Kim who reported that sixty-one percent of the Korean population named the United States as their favorite country (p. 19).

This change in attitude toward America in Korea, has been met with some change in US policy. Thomas Hubbard, the then American ambassador in South Korea said at a Korea Society seminar in September 2002 (Han, 2002): "In the past, we needed to deal with a few important people. But now we have to consider public opinions of Korean people. We will focus on public diplomacy." Further, though the candle demonstration took place in December, not in June when the accident happened, some argue that anti-American expression was due to the residual nationalistic fervor created in and through the Olympic and World Cup events (Kim, J.H., 2002) in addition to the verdict that was brought in November. In other words, the candle demonstration was not only a space to grieve for the girls, but also an expression of anger toward America. Interestingly, the peaceful candle demonstrations took place at Kwang-Hwa-Mun Square, the same gathering point for the Red Devils during the World Cup.

Not only were the demonstrations and World Cup street cheering conducted in the same place, but anti-American sentiments were expressed similarly through both events. For example, the gatherings were organized, evaluated, and stories were published largely through the use of the internet. This suggests that the power of young people in Korea is growing in opposition to traditional political leaders, since they are the primary users of the internet, and were able to organize these anti-American protests. Further, as the candle demonstrations were attended by many different generations of Koreans (in comparison to the youthful following at the World Cup), we argue that young people's power is spreading to the point that they are able to reach more people than just themselves.

Traditional forms of media also helped inspire overt, anti-American nationalism. While the internet was an organizational hub for street cheering and the candle demonstration, these expressions were also promoted and supported by the traditional forms of mass media. Positive stories about the anti-Americanism present through the Red Devil cheering, and in the response to the two girls' deaths, were printed *en masse*. According to Kim and Kim (2003), these positive stories of anti-Americanism in the Korean media are a relatively new occurrence, as they pointed out that the manner in which the media framed the demonstrations had changed from past incidences of anti-Americanism. This change is marked by a move from security and national profit-first mentality (decidedly pro-American) to one of speaking out against its current neo-colonizer.

Generally when the Korean media depicts demonstration incidents they typically stress violent or abnormal aspects of the demonstration and play up radical aspects of the event for dramatic effect. They tend to focus on individual demonstrators and compare them negatively with the police to help formulate criticism of demonstrators, and/or downplay the violence of the police (Kim and Kim, 2003; McLeod, 1995; McLeod and Hertog, 1992; Salmon and Moh, 1994; Tarrow, 1994). However, the mass media responded differently in regard to the candle demonstrations. The reports on the event stated that the demonstrators were regular people, peaceful events were emphasized, and there were repeated allusions to the humanity of the two dead girls. Unlike past pro-government reporting, the media also focussed on the "inequality of SOFA [the Status of Forces Agreement governing the presence of US troops in Korea]" (Kim and Kim, 2003). Using Callaghan and Schnell (2001), we argue that the "framing effect operated so media-constructed version of reality induced anti-American sentiment of viewers". As such, we further posit that the mass media's reporting style helped forge social change in Korean "perceptions of America." Thus the framing style of the media largely explains why the US Army incident led to the candle demonstrations, to the amplification of anti-American sentiments and to calls for a reconstruction of the relationship between South Korea and the United States.

Conclusion

Hosting the World Cup Soccer Finals provided Koreans with an opportunity to confirm their pride in and express their love of their country. Simultaneously, it became an outlet for anti-American sentiments that became public in the aftermath of the Salt Lake City Olympic speed-skating controversy. Thus the short-track incident in the Salt Lake City Olympics and the Soccer World Cup finals, coupled with other social issues such as US policies and attitudes toward South and North Korea, and the "not guilty" verdict for the US Army soldiers, helped proliferate anti-Americanism in Korean society. Additionally these incidents reinforced Koreans' "full attachment" to their nation. This was experienced through the Korean soccer players performing a peaceful protest during their post-goal celebration against "gold medal stealing" America and by those that participated in the candle demonstration. These non-violent protests, have provided a space for South Korea to express their dissatisfaction with their relationship with the United States.

The anti-Americanism present during the two international sporting events speaks to the changing face of the Korean/American relationship. First, younger generations who were previously indifferent to international relations or national politics actively participated in the movement. Second, the internet played an important role in evoking, disseminating and confirming anti-American sentiment while conventional media helped reaffirm its presence. Third, unlike anti-American movements in the past, which were organized and performed by small groups of anti-American activists, ordinary Korean citizens began to participate in the anti-American movement, which came to be dubbed the "people's anti-American movement." Through this movement "political anti-Americanism" was replaced by "cultural anti-Americanism" that is less radical in terms of social justice, but has been more successful in reaching more people.

Many argue that sport is a mere diversion, but in the case of Korean--American international relations sport played an important role in evoking and expressing anti-American ideologies. Through sport, Koreans demonstrated their belief that their relationship with the United States needed to become more bilateral. Ironically however, there are paradoxes in the South Korean–American relationship. Although there exist negative feelings toward Americans by Koreans, they also buy American cultural products, including the broadcasting rights to American professional sport. In other words, on the one hand the Korean people argue that they dislike America, but spend their time and money learning English and studying in the United States. As such, the United States is unlikely to be persuaded to enact any "real" change in their relationship with South Korea, particularly since the anti-American sentiment surrounding the 2002 Olympics and World Cup is waning.

References

Appadurai, A. (2000). "The grounds of nation-state: Identity, violence and territory." In K. Goldmann, U. Hannerz, & C. Westin(Eds.), *Nationalism and internationalism in the post-cold war era*, London: Routledge. pp. 129–142.

Callaghan, K. and Schnell, F. (2001). "Assessing the democratic debate: How the news media frame elite policy discourse." *Political Communication, 18*(2), pp. 183–214.

Chang, H.S. (2002). "Let's give Kim Dong-Sung a gold medal made of national fund-raising." *Donga Ilbo*, 2002. 2. 21. 17:36.

Cho, S.G. (2002). "Lee Hoi-Chang faces an emergency : With anti-American fever, Roh before the wind, Lee against the wind." *Weekly Chosun*, 1732.

Chung, I.J. (2005). "R.O.K.-US relationships and Korean nationalism in global era: Toward reflexive nationalism." *History Education*, 94, pp. 241–270.

Falcous, M, and Silk, M., (2005), "Manufacturing consent: Mediated sporting spectacle and the cultural politics of the 'War on Terror'." *International Journal of Media and Cultural Politics, 1* (1), pp. 59–65.

Grossberg, L. (2006). "Does cultural studies have futures? Should it? (or what's the matter with New York?): Cultural studies, contexts and conjunctures." *Cultural Studies, 20*(1), pp. 1–32.

Hall, S. (1990). "Cultural identity and diaspora." In J. Rutherford (Ed.), *Identity: Community, culture, difference*. London: Lawrence and Wishart, pp. 222–237.

Han, J.H. (2002). "The US pays attention to anti-American sentiment in Korea." *Munhwa Ilbo*, 2002. 11. 21. 11:48.

Hong, S.T. (2003). *Anti-American textbook for thoughtful Koreans*. Seoul: Dang Dae.

Hur, M.M., Lee, S.H., and Cho, I.Y. (2002). "From 'political anti-Americanism' to 'cultural anti-Americanism'." *Donga Ilbo*, 2002. 3. 7. 14:55.

Hwang, B.Y. (2002). "Korean problem or world problem?: Elimination of the different perspectives on North Korean nuclear will resolve South Korea–America conflict." *Weekly Chosun*, 1823.

Hwang, H.T. (2002). "Sentimental anti-Americanism." *Donga Ilbo*, 2002. 3. 25. 18:38.

Kang, H.S. (2002). "Ohno's homepage 'down'." *Yonhap News*, 2002.2. 21. 17:23.

Kim, J.H. (2003). "A year after 'the death of two middle school girls': The influence of candle demonstration on Korean society." *Weekly Chosun*, 1756.

Kim, Y.H. and Kim, H.J. (2003). "Anti-Americanism and the media in South Korea." *The Korean Journal of International Relations, 43*(2), pp. 123–149.

Koh, E. and Lee, W.Y. (2004). "The condition of a Korean sport celebrity: Se Ri Pak and corporate nationalism." *Korean Journal of Sport Sociology, 17*(1), pp. 121–137.

Koh, E. (2003). "Chains, challenges and changes: The making of women's football in Korea." *Soccer and Society, 4*(2–3), pp. 67–79.

Lee, J.B. (2004). *Korean civil society and anti-American movement: Autonomy or alliance*. Seoul: Orum.

Lee, J.G., Lee, T.H. and Lee, W.B. (2002). "Korea! Forever!: 'Victory Korea' in heavy rain at Gwanghwamun." *Donga Ilbo*, 2002. 6. 10. 18:00.

Lee, K.H. (2002). "How to see 'the death of two middle school girls' and the US issue." *Labour Society Bulletin*, 71, pp. 34–39.

Lee, K.R. (2004). "The analysis of the developmental process of anti-Americanism in South Korea). *The Korean Journal of International Relations*, 44(4), pp. 239–261.

Lim, H.S. (1994). "Perception of the United States after the liberation. Yoo *et al.*(Eds.)," *Korean perception of the United States: A history of its formation.* Seoul: Min Eum Sa, pp. 253–275.

McLeod, D.M. (1995). "Communicating deviance: The effects of television news coverage of social protest." *Journal of Broadcasting and Electronic Media*, 39(1).

McLeod, D.M. and Hertog, J.K. (1992). "The manufacture of public opinion by reporters: Informal cues for public perceptions of protest groups." *Discourse and Society*, 3(3), pp. 259–279.

Nye, J.S. Jr. (1991). *Bound to lead: The changing nature of American power.* New York: Basic Books.

Park, T.G. (2002a). "Bush urges a fire and Salt Lake adds oil: Anti-American sentiment reached the climax." *Pressian.* 2002. 2. 22. 10:06.

Park, T.G. (2002b). "'The government should grandly trust the people!': Over-protection of the US embassy is to impair people's dignity." *Pressian.* 2002. 6. 7. 14:40.

Pennington, B. (2002). "2002 games: Riveting sport and an angry backlash." *New York Times,* 2002. 2. 24.

Rubinstein, A.Z. (1985). *Anti-Americanism in the third world: Implications for US foreign policy.* New York: Praeger.

Salmon, C.T. and Moh, C.Y. (1994). "The spiral of silence: Linking individual and society through communication." In J.D. Kennamer (Ed.), *Public opinion, the press, and public policy.* Westport: Praeger, pp. 144–161.

Shim, Y.S. (2005). *Anti-Americanism in Korea: Is there an alternative?* Seoul: Samsung Economics Research Institute.

Silk, M.L. (2002). "'Bangsa Malaysia': Global sport, the city and the media refurbishment of local identities." *Media, Culture and Society*, 24(6), pp. 775–794.

Silk, M. and Falcous, M. (2005). "One day in September/A week in February: Mobilizing American (Sporting) nationalisms." *Sociology of Sport Journal*, 22(4), pp. 447–471.

Song, H.G. (2003). *What is happening in Korea?* Seoul: Samsung Economics Research Institute.

Tarrow, S. (1994). *Power in movement: Social movement, collective action and politics.* Cambridge: Cambridge University Press.

Vander Velden, L., Ryu, H.J. Koh, E.H. (2002). "Motives for Following the Olympic Games: A Comparison of American and Korean Interests in 2000 and 2002." Paper presented at the *15th World Congress of Sociology*, Brisbane, Australia, July 7–13, 2002.

Yonhap News (2002). IOC homepage paralyzed. *Yonhap News*, 2002. 2. 22. 08:36.

Index